W9-DHK-559

# Effective Sales Catalog Design

## An International Catalog and Brochure Collection

P·I·E BOOKS

# copyright

## Effective Sales Catalog Design



P·I·E BOOKS

Villa Phoenix Suite 301, 4-14-6, Komagome, Toshima-ku, Tokyo 170-0003 Japan
Tel: 03-3940-8302 Fax: 03-3576-7361 e-mail: piebooks@bekkoame.ne.jp
ISBN 4-89444-098-9 C3070 Printed in Hong Kong

The Designs Used On The Front Cover Were Provided by

Acrobat / Carina Orschulko / Club Med K.K. / Conran Studio
Fiorucci Srl / K-O Creation / Pinkhaus / Planet Design Company
Studio Seireeni / Syuna & Bani

This book is Volume 2 of our "Catalog Graphics" series, the first of which focused exclusively on Japanese catalogs. For this international edition, we have assembled sales catalogs from countries all over the world. Outstanding in design and practical in approach, nearly 200 examples are presented, categorized by business for easy reference.

Visual attractiveness is a key element in drawing consumers' interest and arousing their buying impulses, but turning these interests and impulses into actual purchases requires information: price, size, features, descriptions. Without a doubt, the biggest challenge faced when designing a sales-provoking catalog is creating a beautiful layout that contains all of the information that the consumer really needs, while at the same time preserving the integrity of the product's image.

Looking at the works included in this book, one can see that each catalog has been calculatedly created, taking careful aim at a specific target. It may be a toy catalog, intended for a market consisting mainly of children, in which fun-to-look-at, cute designs contain easy-to-read prices and product information. Or a fashion or jewelry catalog, where product images explode across full pages, where a delicate balance must be maintained in the layout allowing prices and other text information to share those pages without detracting from the atmosphere. A truly effective catalog can only be created if one understands the mind of the reader, the consumer.

Recently, as in mail order sales, the trend has been to make purchases directly from a catalog without having seen or touched the item itself. This trend is increasing, making catalogs an even more important and influential sales medium. We hope that this book will stimulate your sensitivities, and prove useful in the creation of even more effective catalog.

Finally, we would like to express our appreciation to all of our contributors, for sending us so many examples of exceptional catalog design.

P·I·E BOOKS

Dies ist der zweite Band unserer "Catalog Graphics" Buchserie, wobei der erste ausschließlich auf Kataloge aus Japan konzentrierte. Für diese internationale Ausgabe haben wir Kataloge aus aller Welt zusammengetragen. Die etwa 200 hier präsentierten Beispiele, alle herausragend in Design und praktischem Gebrauchswert, sind kategorisiert nach Branchen.

Visuelle Attraktivität ist das Schlüsselelement, um das Interesse des Kunden anzuziehen und Kaufimpulse zu vermitteln. Aber um dieses Interesse auch in einen aktuellen Kauf umzusetzen, braucht es Informationen: Preis, Größe, Eigenschaften, nähere Beschreibungen. Ohne Zweifel ist die größte Herausforderung bei der Gestaltung eines verkaufsaktiven Kataloges das besondere Layout. Darin sollen alle, den Kunden interessierenden Informationen untergebracht werden können und gleichzeitig soll auch die Integrität des Produkt-Images bewahrt werden.

Betrachtet man die Arbeiten in diesem Buch, so kann man erkennen, daß jeder Katalog mit Kalkül kreiert wurde. Immer wurde sorgfältig auf das spezifische Ziel geachtet. So kann ein Spielzeug-Katalog, der auf einen größtenteils aus Kindern bestehenden Markt gerichtet ist, durch sein anheimelndes Design mit Spaß zu betrachten sein und besonders leicht zu erfassende Preis- und Produktinformationen enthalten. Bei einem Mode- oder Schmuck-Katalog hingegen, bei dem Produkt-Abbildungen über die Seiten hinweg schier explodieren, muß, um nicht die Atmosphäre zu stören, im Layout eine delikate Balance bewahrt werden zwischen den Bildern und den Preis- und anderen Text-Informationen. Ein wirklich effektiver Katalog kann nur gestaltet werden, wenn man den Leser, den Kunden versteht.

Wie im Versandhandel wird heute bei vielen Firmen nach Katalogen gekauft, ohne die Ware im Original gesehen oder angefaßt zu haben. Dieser Trend verstärkt sich und macht Kataloge ein noch wichtigeres und einflußreicheres Verkaufsmedium. Wir hoffen, daß dieses Buch Ihre Sensitivität stimulieren und Ihnen bei der Kreation noch effektiverer Kataloge nützlich sein wird. Zum Schluß möchten wir allen danken, die uns so viele außergewöhnlich gut gestaltete Kataloge gesandt haben.

P·I·E BOOKS

# contents

Découverte

# editorial notes

## credit format

Main Products
Credit heading
CL:Client
Creative staff
*CD: Creative director
*AD: Art director
*D: Designer
*P: Photographer
*I: Illustrator
*CW: Copywriter
*ST: Stylist
*DF: Design Firm
Country of submittor
Year of completion
Size: height×width(mm)

※ Please note that some credit data has been omitted at the request of the submittor.

# home

homes & construction

interiors & exteriors

lifestyle

electrical goods

The Power of Change
moveable walls
the economics of
power
change
leaders in moveability

flexible work environments worldwide
CLESTRA HAUSERMAN
our
imagine the possibilities
w r

savings
By creating a mobile landscape of offices for teaming and "weekend re-organizations," we have seen measurable savings in real estate needs and have optimized our clients' growth potential. Clestra Hauserman's ability to marry creative solutions, twenty-first century technology and a well crafted product works for me and my clients.

enhance your workspace

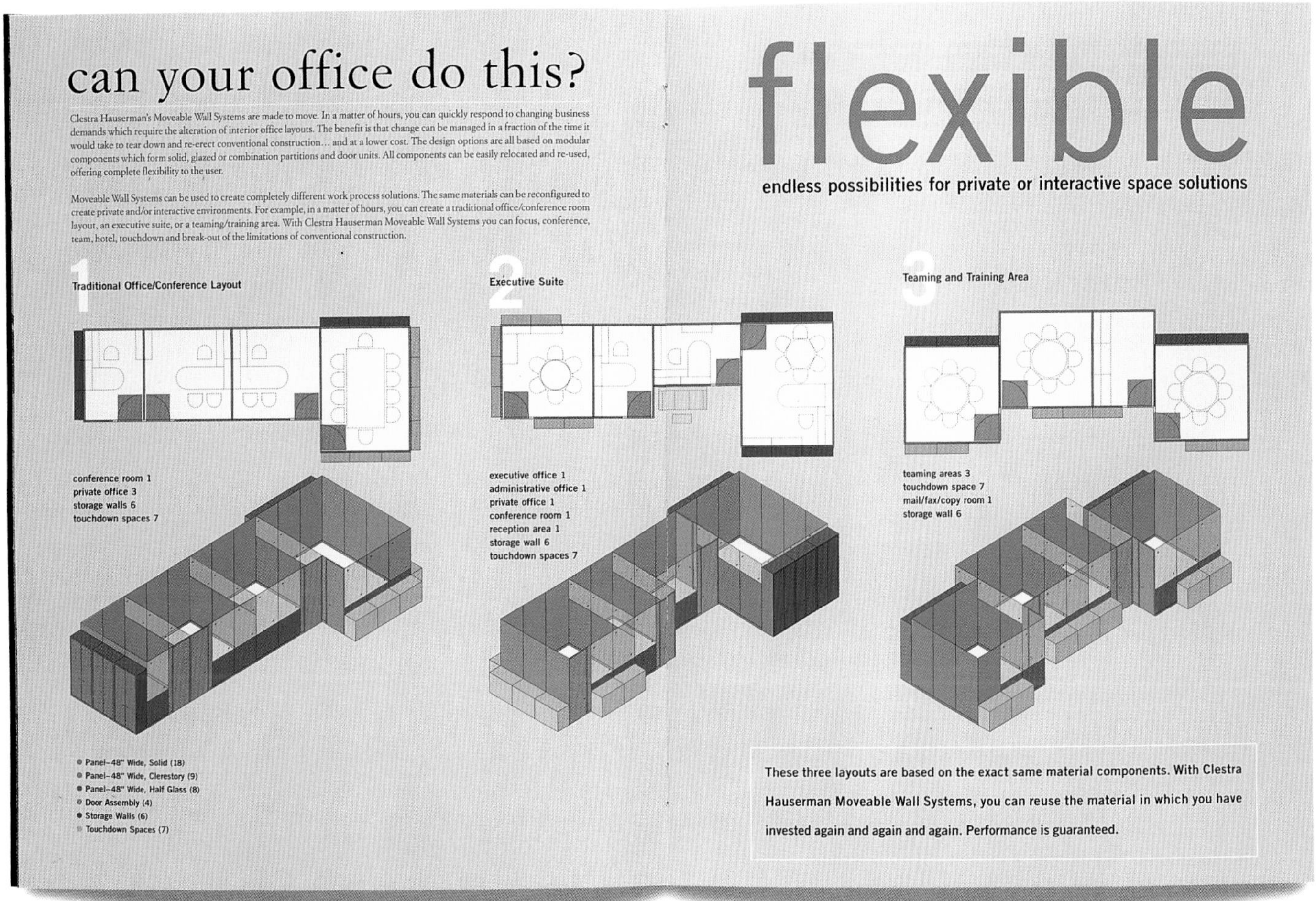

# can your office do this?

Clestra Hauserman's Moveable Wall Systems are made to move. In a matter of hours, you can quickly respond to changing business demands which require the alteration of interior office layouts. The benefit is that change can be managed in a fraction of the time it would take to tear down and re-erect conventional construction… and at a lower cost. The design options are all based on modular components which form solid, glazed or combination partitions and door units. All components can be easily relocated and re-used, offering complete flexibility to the user.

Moveable Wall Systems can be used to create completely different work process solutions. The same materials can be reconfigured to create private and/or interactive environments. For example, in a matter of hours, you can create a traditional office/conference room layout, an executive suite, or a teaming/training area. With Clestra Hauserman Moveable Wall Systems you can focus, conference, team, hotel, touchdown and break-out of the limitations of conventional construction.

# flexible

**endless possibilities for private or interactive space solutions**

1 Traditional Office/Conference Layout

conference room 1
private office 3
storage walls 6
touchdown spaces 7

2 Executive Suite

executive office 1
administrative office 1
private office 1
conference room 1
reception area 1
storage wall 6
touchdown spaces 7

3 Teaming and Training Area

teaming areas 3
touchdown space 7
mail/fax/copy room 1
storage wall 6

- Panel–48" Wide, Solid (18)
- Panel–48" Wide, Clerestory (9)
- Panel–48" Wide, Half Glass (8)
- Door Assembly (4)
- Storage Walls (6)
- Touchdown Spaces (7)

These three layouts are based on the exact same material components. With Clestra Hauserman Moveable Wall Systems, you can reuse the material in which you have invested again and again and again. Performance is guaranteed.

**Office Partisions**

CLESTRA HAUSERMAN CL, I: Clestra Hauserman CD, AD, D: Joyce Nesnadny / Timothy Lachina CD, AD: Mark Schwartz D: Gregory Oznowich / Michelle Moehler P: Design Photography, Inc. CW: Pat Turnbull DF: Nesnadny + Schwartz USA 1996 *SIZE: 294×298*

Convis beeindruckt im Detail

Ausstattung

Haus Drei - der Glaspalast. Weitblick statt Enge, Ausblick statt Grenzen. Die Großzügigkeit der Räume erhebt Sie über das Einerlei beschränkter Möglichkeiten. Tagsüber durchflutet das Licht Ihre Stätte der Produktivität, nachts sind Sie leuchtendes Beispiel für andere.

Fassade – Glaswürfel

Fassade – Glaswürfel

Glaswürfel – Innenansicht

Glaswürfel – Innenansicht

Glaswürfel – Innenansicht

## Haus Drei

| Vermietbare Flächen Haus 3 in Quadratmeter | | | | |
|---|---|---|---|---|
| | Ost | West | Glaswürfel | Gesamt |
| 2 UG | | 79.43 | | 79.43 |
| 1 UG | | 79.43 | | 79.43 |
| EG | 425.06 | 238.47 | 226.02 | 889.55 |
| 1 OG | 393.17 | 253.13 | 350.62 | 996.92 |
| 2 OG | 442.89 | 271.68 | 339.04 | 1 053.61 |
| 3 OG | 442.89 | 271.65 | 341.72 | 1 056.26 |
| 4 OG | 442.89 | 271.65 | 341.72 | 1 056.26 |
| 5 OG | | 568.19 | 345.18 | 913.37 |
| Gesamt | 2 146.90 | 2 033.63 | 1 944.30 | 6 124.83 |

Fassade – Glaswürfel

## Office Building

CONVIS CL: Blumenauer CD: Karl W Henschel AD, D: Andrea Gugau P: René Spalek
CW: Daniel Henschel DF: Sign Kommunikation Germany 1997 *SIZE: 320×220*

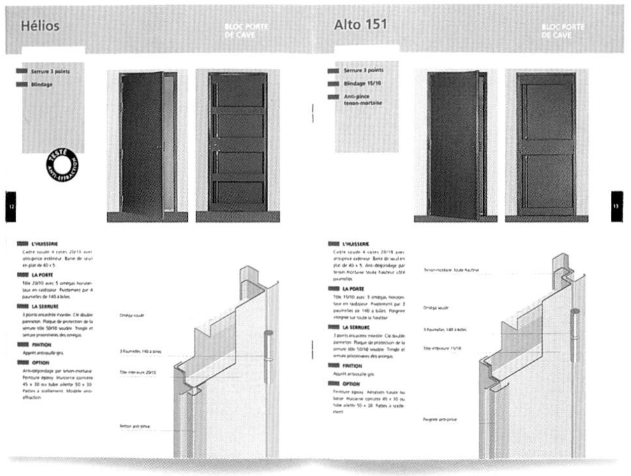


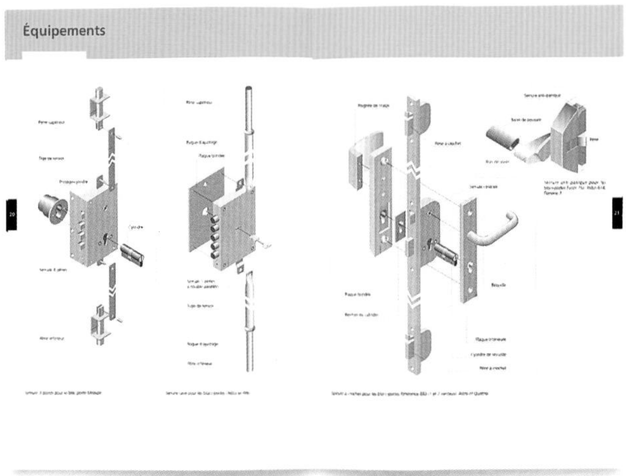


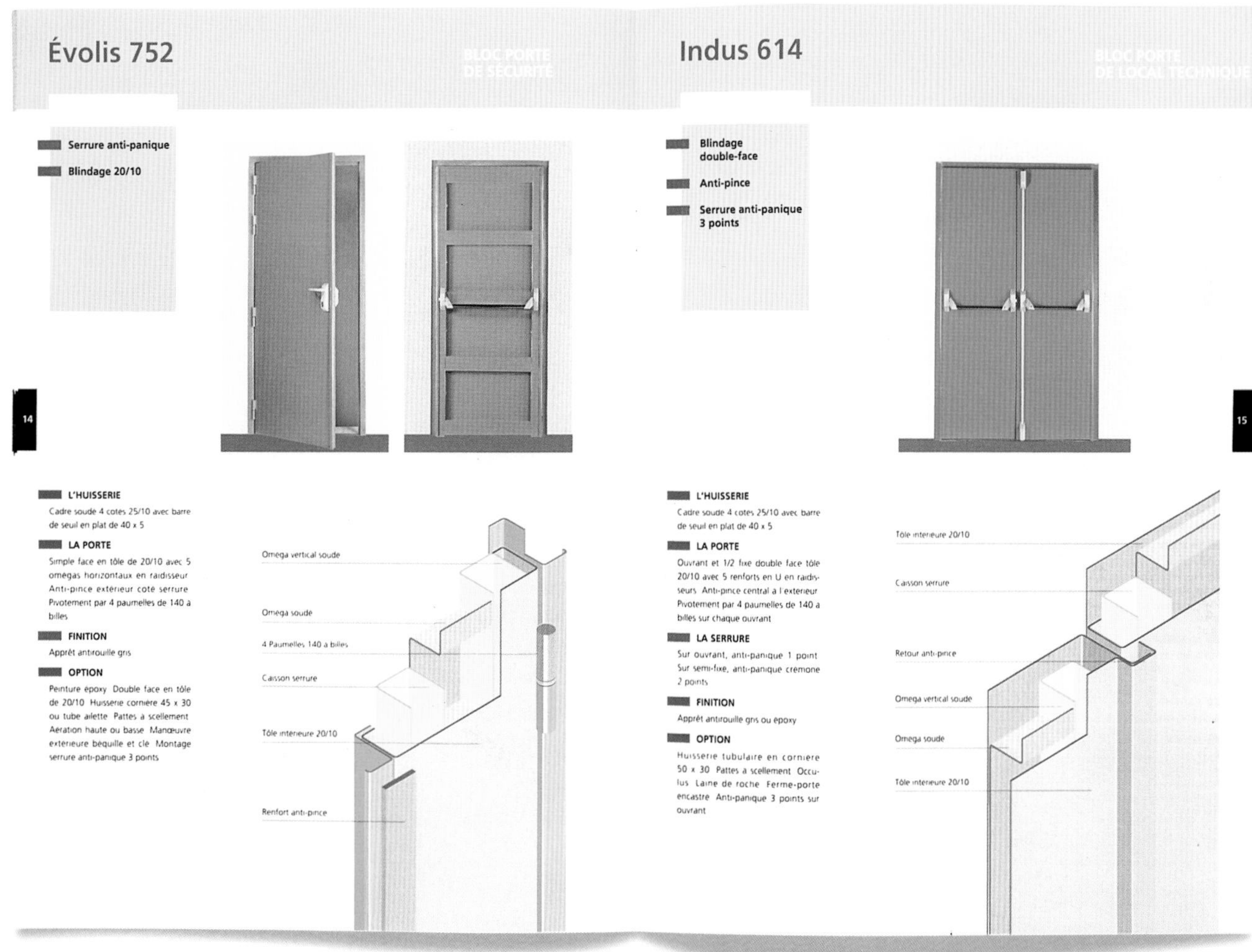


## Doors

BLINDAGES DE FRANCE CL: BDF AD: Michel Raby D: Noëlle Prinz P: Bernard Rossi I: Antoine Raby DF: ICI Design France 1997 *SIZE: 296×210*

Schon die Römer wußten die Vorteile eines offenen Hauptraumes zu schätzen: Unser Erdgeschoßatrium kombiniert Ästhetik mit Funktion.
Das Atrium ist eine prominente Anlaufstelle für Gäste und ein interessanter Meeting-Point für alle Besucher. Zugleich dient es der Orientierung im Hause selbst.
Offenheit und Transparenz - wesentliche Charakteristika des gesamten Hauskonzeptes. Man spürt ein fantastisches, beinahe „luftiges" Raumklima.
bregenz tourismus
Tourismushaus Bregenz
Statik
DI Ernst Mader
Belruptstraße 44
A-6900 Bregenz
T (05574) 44 129
F (05574) 44 129 - 33
Haustechnik
GMI Ingenieure
Gasser und Messner
Schulgasse 22
A-6850 Dornbirn
T (05572) 33 777
F (05572) 33 777 - 7
Bauaufsicht
I+R Schertler GesmbH
Hofsteigstraße 4
A-6923 Lauterach
T (05574) 68 88
F (05574) 79 108
Bauherr
Tourismushaus Bregenz Errichtergemeinschaft GesmbH
Hypo-Passage 1
A-6900 Bregenz
T (05574) 414-0
F (05574) 414-437
Elektrotechnik
Elmar Graf GesmbH
In Steinen 5
A-6850 Dornbirn
T (05572) 23 074
F (05572) 22 861
Bodenmechanik
DI Anton Plankel
Baumweg 3
A-6923 Lauterach
T (05574) 79 811
F (05574) 71 520
Architektur
Rudolf Prohazka
Architekt DI
Vorlaufstraße 5
A-1010 Wien
T (01) 535 05 55
F (01) 532 85 32
Bauphysik
Arch. DI Dr. Lothar Künz
Marktstraße 3
A-6971 Hard
T (05574) 77 851
F (05574) 61 689
Vermessung
DI Reinhard Klocker
Gerberstraße 6/2
A-6900 Bregenz
T (05574) 42 080
F (05574) 45 755 - 21
Von der Infrastruktur profitieren alle Mieter. Prominente Plazierung, Frequenz und funktionelle Räumlichkeiten bringen ein optimales Umfeld.
Tourismushaus Bregenz | 10 - 11
KUB und Landestheater
Pendeln zwischen Tradition und Moderne. Bewegung hin zu Kunst und Unterhaltung.
Knotenpunkt Bregenz
Per Bahn ankommen oder abfahren heißt Reisen auf die sanfte Art. Und mit dem PKW gibt's schnelle Verbindungen in die Schweiz und nach Deutschland.
Bregenzer Festspiele
6.000 Sitzplätze, internationale Produktionen und der See ist Regisseur.
Die Vorarlberger Landesbibliothek
Im revitalisierten Gebäude gibt's Bücher, Bücher und nochmals Bücher. Von

## Office Building

TOURISMUSHAUS BREGENZ CL: Hypo Bank CD, AD, D: Kurt Dornig P: Harald Peter CW: Hermann Braendle DF: Dornig Grafik Design Austria 1997 *SIZE: 297×210*

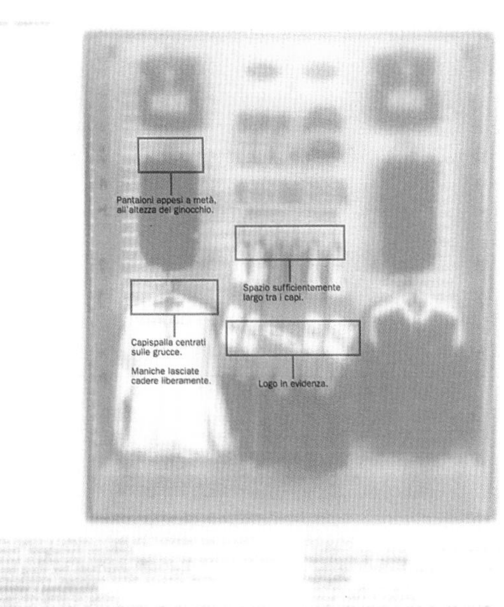
Pantaloni appesi a metà,
all'altezza del ginocchio.
Spazio sufficientemente
largo tra i capi.
Capispalla centrati
sulle grucce.
Maniche lasciate
cadere liberamente.
Logo in evidenza.

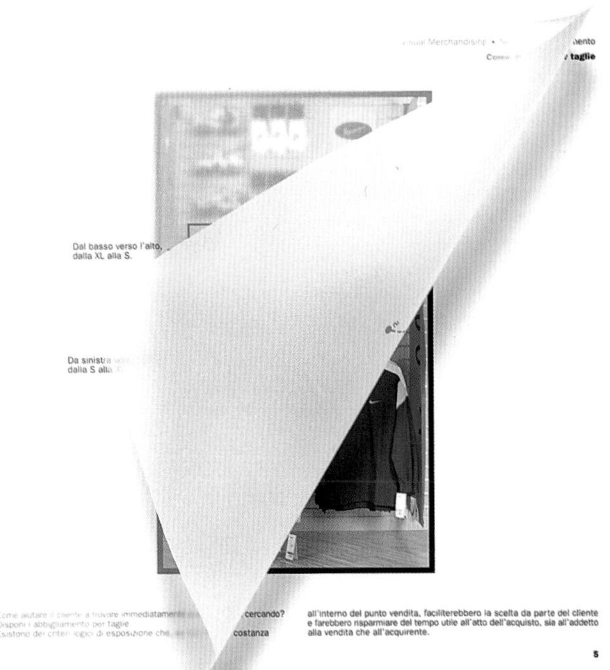
Dal basso verso l'alto,
dalla XL alla S.
all'interno del punto vendita, faciliterebbero la scelta da parte del cliente
e farebbero risparmiare del tempo utile all'atto dell'acquisto, sia all'addetto
alla vendita che all'acquirente.
5

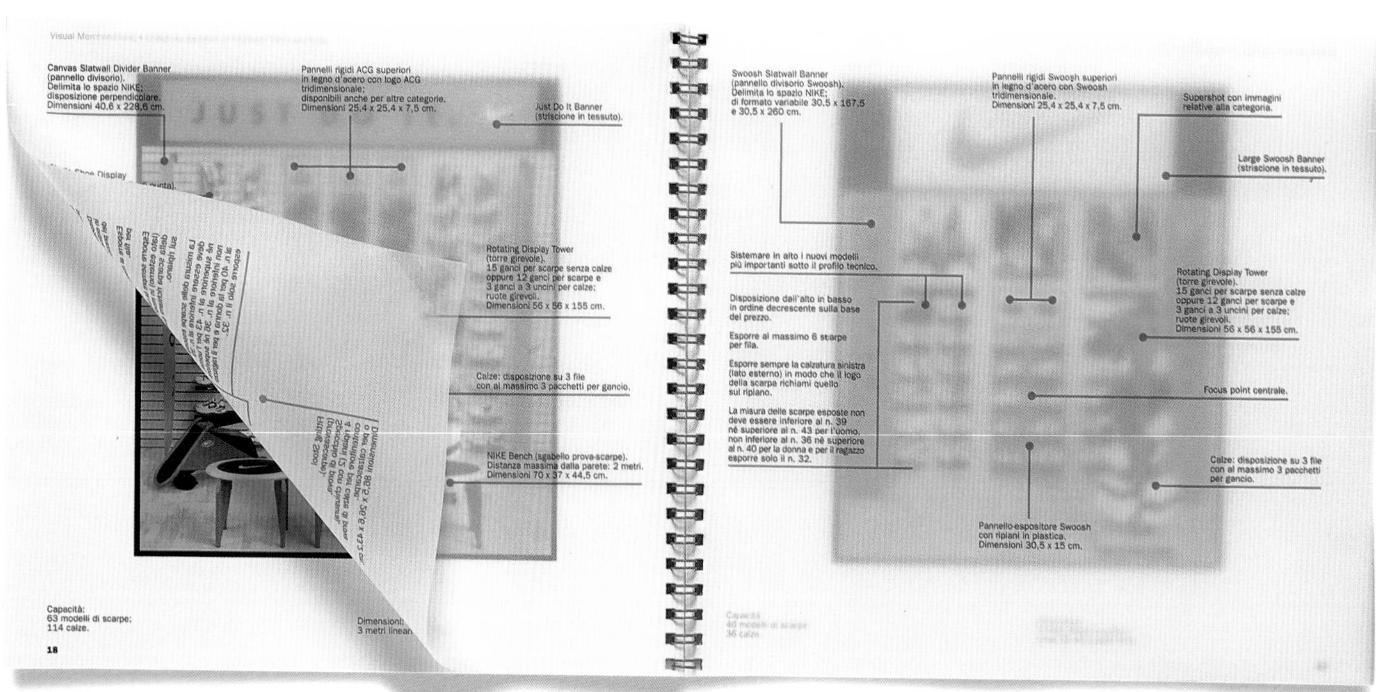
Canvas Slatwall Divider Banner
(pannello divisorio).
Delimita lo spazio NIKE;
disposizione perpendicolare.
Dimensioni 40,6 x 228,6 cm.
Pannelli rigidi ACG superiori
in legno d'acero con logo ACG
tridimensionale;
disponibili anche per altre categorie.
Dimensioni 25,4 x 25,4 x 7,5 cm.
Just Do It Banner
(striscione in tessuto).
Rotating Display Tower
(torre girevole).
15 ganci per scarpe senza calze
oppure 12 ganci per scarpe e
3 ganci a 3 uncini per calze;
ruote girevoli.
Dimensioni 56 x 56 x 155 cm.
Calze: disposizione su 3 file
con al massimo 3 pacchetti per gancio.
NIKE Bench (sgabello prova-scarpe).
Distanza massima dalla parete: 2 metri.
Dimensioni 70 x 37 x 44,5 cm.
Capacità:
63 modelli di scarpe;
114 calze.
18
Swoosh Slatwall Banner
(pannello divisorio Swoosh).
Delimita lo spazio NIKE;
di formato variabile 30,5 x 167,5
e 30,5 x 260 cm.
Pannelli rigidi Swoosh superiori
in legno d'acero con Swoosh
tridimensionale.
Dimensioni 25,4 x 25,4 x 7,5 cm.
Supershot con immagini
relative alla categoria.
Large Swoosh Banner
(striscione in tessuto).
Sistemare in alto i nuovi modelli
più importanti sotto il profilo tecnico.
Disposizione dall'alto in basso
in ordine decrescente sulla base
del prezzo.
Esporre al massimo 6 scarpe
per fila.
Esporre sempre la calzatura sinistra
(lato esterno) in modo che il logo
della scarpa richiami quello
sul ripiano.
La misura delle scarpe esposte non
deve essere inferiore al n. 39
nè superiore al n. 43 per l'uomo,
non inferiore al n. 36 nè superiore
al n. 40 per la donna e per il ragazzo
esporre solo il n. 32.
Rotating Display Tower
(torre girevole).
15 ganci per scarpe senza calze
oppure 12 ganci per scarpe e
3 ganci a 3 uncini per calze;
ruote girevoli.
Dimensioni 56 x 56 x 155 cm.
Focus point centrale.
Calze: disposizione su 3 file
con al massimo 3 pacchetti
per gancio.
Pannello-espositore Swoosh
con ripiani in plastica.
Dimensioni 30,5 x 15 cm.

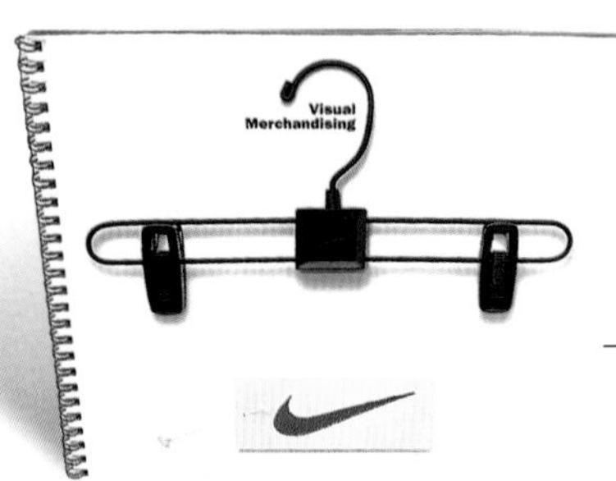
Visual
Merchandising

## Sport Shoes and Apparel Shop Plan

NIKE CL: Nike Italy AD: Giovanni Pizigati P: Fabio Romani CW: Antonella Bandoli DF: Matite Giovanotte Italy 1997 *SIZE: 219×240*

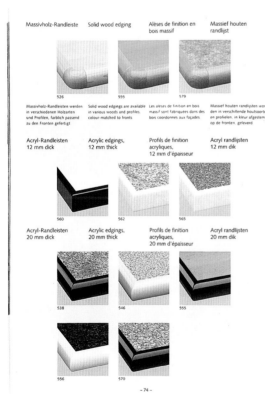

Poggenpohl form 2000 CX 102 lichtgelb

Front lichtgelb Kunststoff matt. Alle Kanten gerundet. Umfeld in Kombinationsfarbe Maple Dekor. Alternativen: Umfeld blütenweiß, lichtgrau, lichtgelb. Bügel-Griff verchromt.

Front in matt, light yellow laminate. All edges rounded. Accessories in combination colour: sycamore decor. As alternatives: accessories in blossom-white, light grey, light yellow. Chrome-plated bow handle.

Façade en mélaminé mat jaune clair. Tous chants arrondis. Environnement dans le coloris de combinaison décor érable. Alternatives possibles: environnement blanc marguerite, gris clair, jaune clair. Poignée étrier chromée.

Front in lichtgeel kunststof mat. Alle kanten afgerond. Accessoires in kombinatiekleur maple dekor. Alternatieven: accessoires bloesemwit, lichtgrijs, lichtgeel. Beugelgreep verchroomd.

– 16 –

form 2000 CX
Preisgruppe 0

CX 100 · CX 102 · CX 103 · CX 134

– 17 –

Massivholz-Randleiste | Solid wood edging | Alèses de finition en bois massif | Massief houten randlijst

526 · 555 · 579

Massivholz-Randleisten werden in verschiedenen Holzarten und Profilen, farblich passend zu den Fronten gefertigt.

Solid wood edgings are available in various woods and profiles, colour-matched to fronts.

Les alèses de finition en bois massif sont fabriquées dans des bois coordonnés aux façades.

Massief houten randlijsten worden in verschillende houtsoorten en profielen, in kleur afgestemd op de fronten, geleverd.

Acryl-Randleisten 12 mm dick | Acrylic edgings, 12 mm thick | Profils de finition acryliques, 12 mm d'épaisseur | Acryl randlijsten 12 mm dik

560 · 562 · 565

Acryl-Randleisten 20 mm dick | Acrylic edgings, 20 mm thick | Profils de finition acryliques, 20 mm d'épaisseur | Acryl randlijsten 20 mm dik

538 · 546 · 555

556 · 570

– 74 –

Arbeitsplatten aus Massivholz-Sandwichaufbau 20/20 | Solid wood worktops Sandwich construction 20/20 | Plans de travail en bois massif / Construction composite 20/20 | Massief houten werkbladen Sandwich opbouw 20/20

712 Ahorn · 713 Teak · 714 Nußbaum · 715 Buche massiv

Arbeitsplatten aus Granit | Granite worktops | Plans de travail en granit | Werkbladen van graniet

801 Bianco sardo (Sardinien) · 804 Labrador hell (Norwegen) · 806 Nero Belfast (Südafrika)

807 Rosa Sardo (Sardinien) · 808 Multicolor rot (Indien) · 809 Paradiso (Indien)

810 Kaschmir white (Indien) · 811 Giallo Veneziano (Brasilien) · 812 Verde Maritaka (Brasilien)

813 Baltic braun (Finnland) · 814 Impala (Südafrika) · 815 Rosso Balmoral (Norwegen)

– 75 –

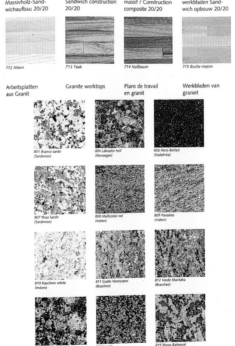

form 2000
MODERN CLASSICS
Küchen · Kitchens · Cuisines · Keukens
poggen pohl

**System Kitchens**

POGGEN POHL CL: Poggen Pohl CD, D: Bildstein P: Riphins DF: Agentor Bildstein Germany 1998 *SIZE: 296×210*

401 HUDSON
402 LUGALORE
407 ANNA
408 ADORNO
403 BABEL
404 PORTOBELLO
409 ZIP
405 NORMANDIE
406 LE COQ
411 MANILLA
THE CONRAN SHOP
CHAIRS + BARSTOOLS

201 KINTBURY
202 ESPRESSO
203 CUBA
204 DETROIT
205 PONT
206 FLINT
207 ISOKON
208 TRURO
OCCASIONAL + DINING TABLES

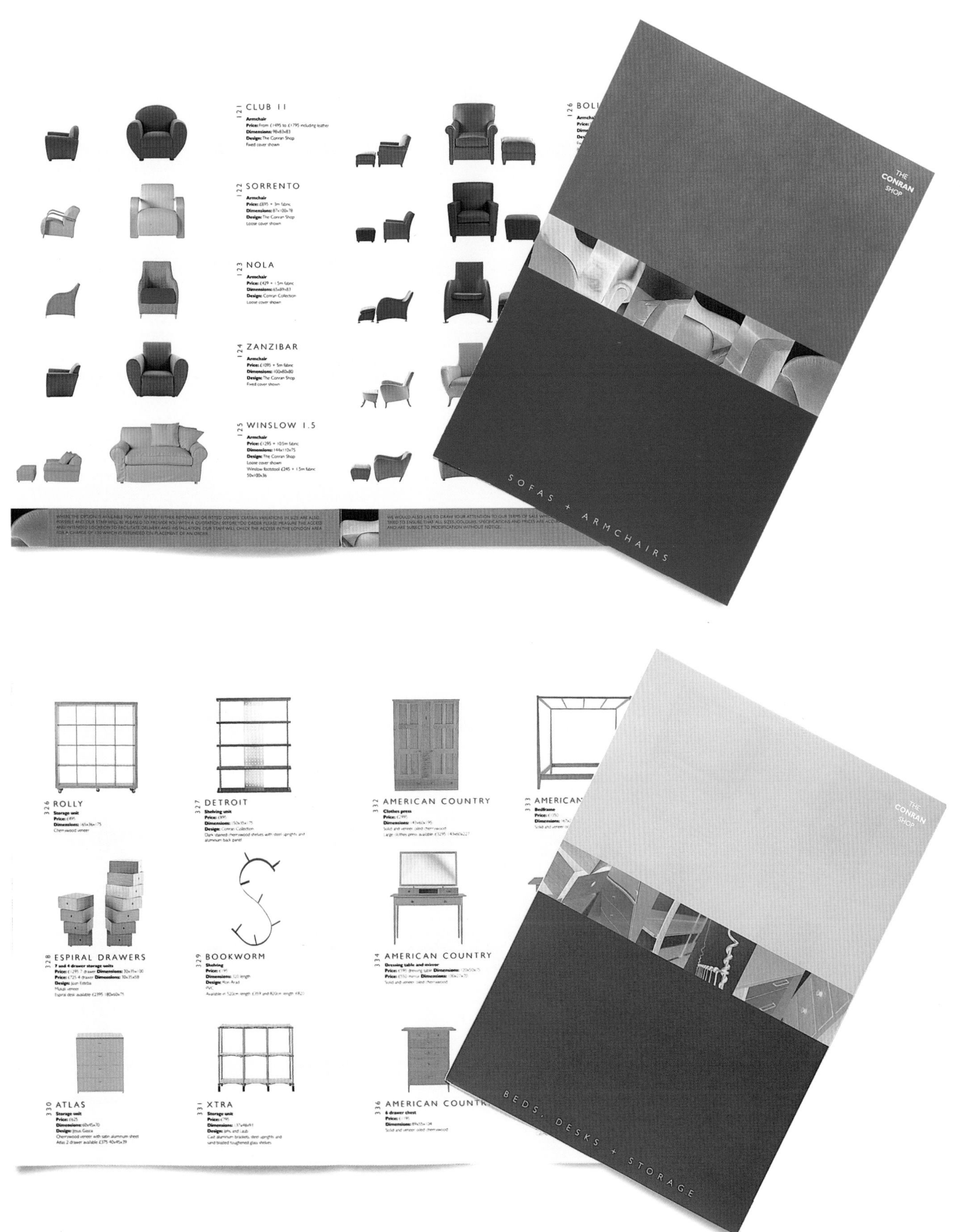


## Interior Goods & Furniture

THE CONRAN SHOP CL: Conran Shop CD: Alex Willcock AD: Robin Rout D: Phil Hobday P: James Merrill CW: Simon Willis DF: Conran Studio UK 1998 *SIZE: 297×210*

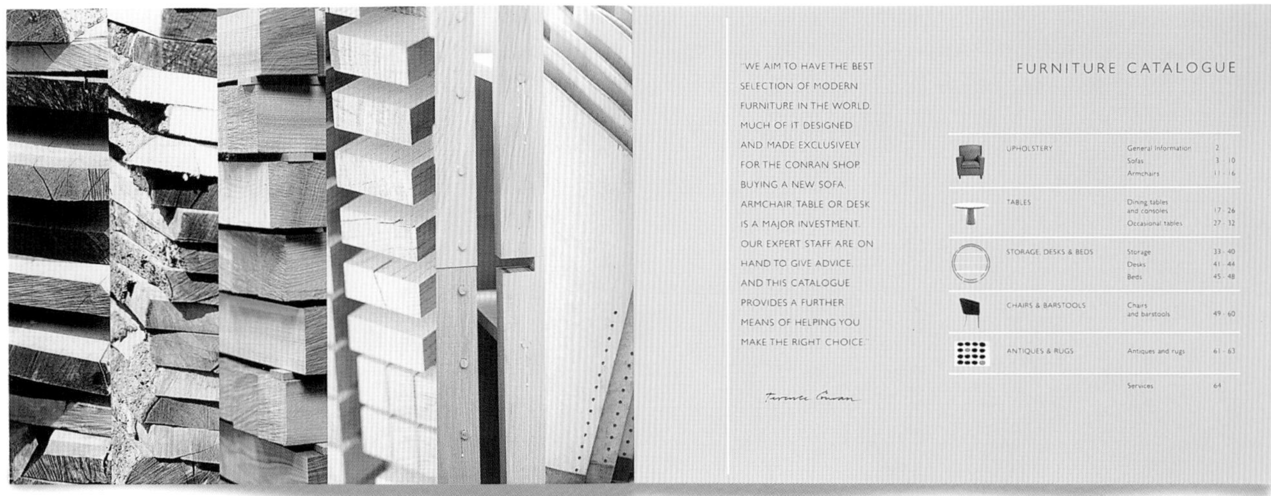
"WE AIM TO HAVE THE BEST SELECTION OF MODERN FURNITURE IN THE WORLD. MUCH OF IT DESIGNED AND MADE EXCLUSIVELY FOR THE CONRAN SHOP. BUYING A NEW SOFA, ARMCHAIR, TABLE OR DESK IS A MAJOR INVESTMENT. OUR EXPERT STAFF ARE ON HAND TO GIVE ADVICE, AND THIS CATALOGUE PROVIDES A FURTHER MEANS OF HELPING YOU MAKE THE RIGHT CHOICE."
FURNITURE CATALOGUE
UPHOLSTERY
TABLES
STORAGE, DESKS & BEDS
CHAIRS & BARSTOOLS
ANTIQUES & RUGS
Services

CONRAN COLLECTION
UPHOLSTERY
SOFAS

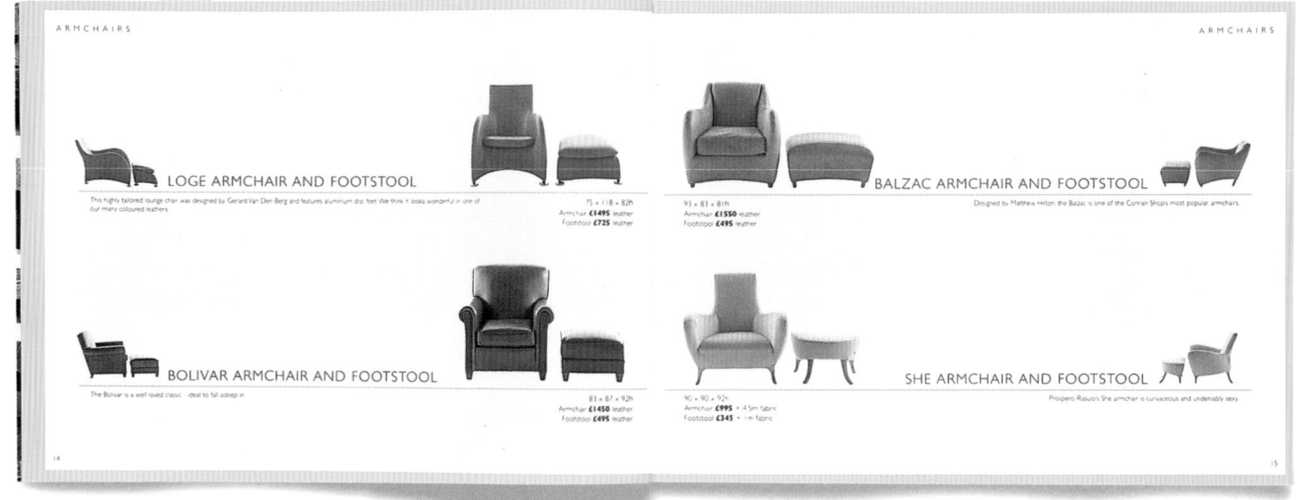
ARMCHAIRS
ARMCHAIRS
LOGE ARMCHAIR AND FOOTSTOOL
BALZAC ARMCHAIR AND FOOTSTOOL
BOLIVAR ARMCHAIR AND FOOTSTOOL
SHE ARMCHAIR AND FOOTSTOOL

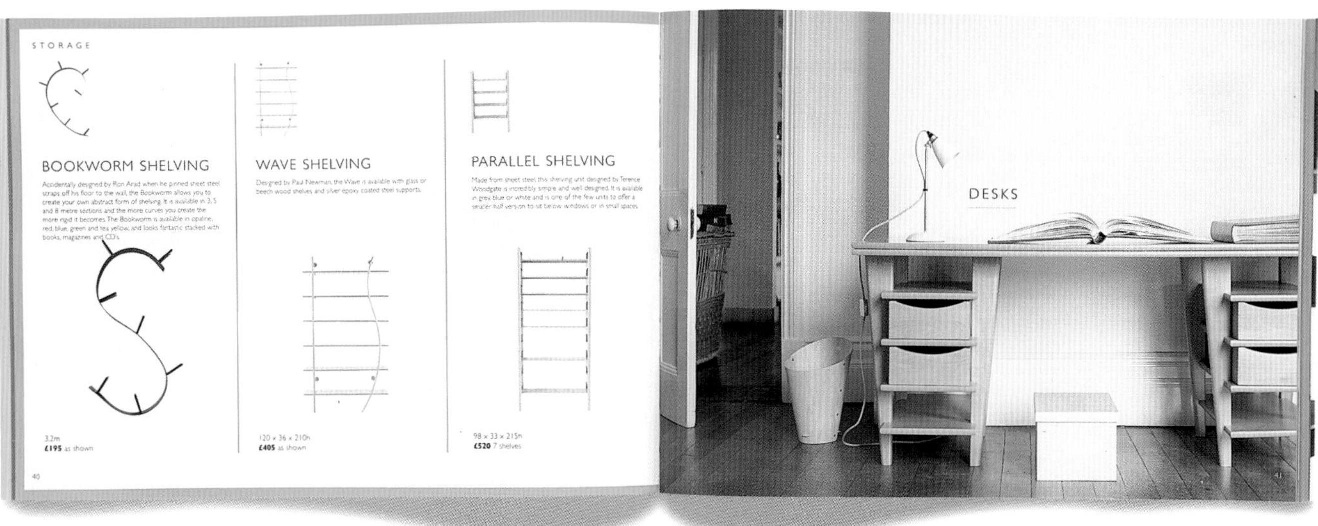

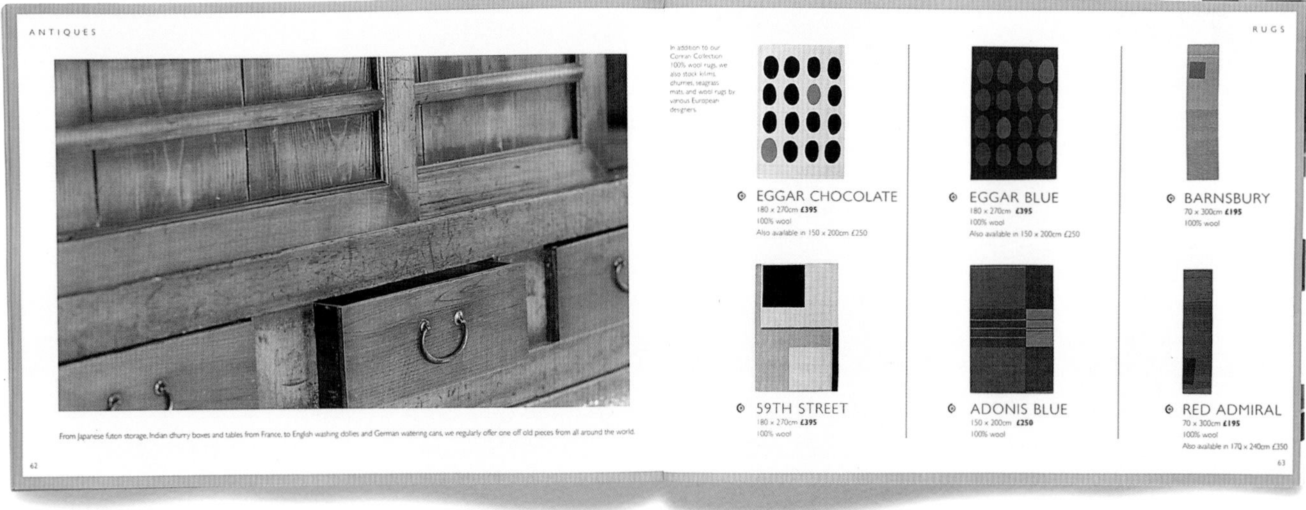


THE CONRAN SHOP

## Interior Goods & Furniture

THE CONRAN SHOP CL: Conran Shop CD: Alex Willcock AD: Robin Rout D: Phil Hobday P: James Merrill CW: Simon Willis DF: Conran Studio UK 1998 *SIZE: 210×296*

sheets is one of life's great pleasures. Conran Collection be
79
Apollo cotton 65x65cm pillowcase £29 duvet covers from £99 Paradou green linen/cotton 50x75cm pillowcase £25 duvet cover
Paradou blue linen/cotton 50x75cm pillowcase £25 duvet covers from £99 Brunelys linen/cotton 50x75cm pillowcase £25 du
Ocean cotton knit 65x65cm pillowcase £17.50 duvet covers from £49
78
Quite simply, we wanted to develop the best cups and saucers, plates, bowls, cutlery and glasses that money can buy. Each product has been through a meticulous development process over the last two years before finally going on sale. Whether it is our everyday white porcelain or our fine bone china, Conran Collection combines excellence and affordability, beauty and function.
24
onran Collection furniture draws on years of experience. The range represents for us the culmination
ss that has seen working sketches tweaked, prototypes refined and samples perfected so that the finished
comfortable, is durably made and looks terrific. Simple, elegant solutions for modern living.

Winkfield leather black travel clock £75
Facing page:
leather tan travel clock £75
leather black desk clock £85
leather tan desk clock £85
Ghost white wall clock £59
Grand central 1 metre wall clock £325
Turbine pewter alarm clock £55
Ghost aluminium wall clock £59
200 years. Our 'Bath' range combines traditional skills with a Modernist aesthetic: past and present in perfect harmony.
30
£2.50
CONRAN
COLLECTION

## Interior Goods & Furniture

CONRAN COLLECTION CL: Conran Collection CD, AD: Alex Willcock D: Rachel Marshall / Phil Hobday / Manuela Columbo P: Earl Carter CW: Simon Willis DF: Conran Studio UK 1998 *SIZE:210×210*

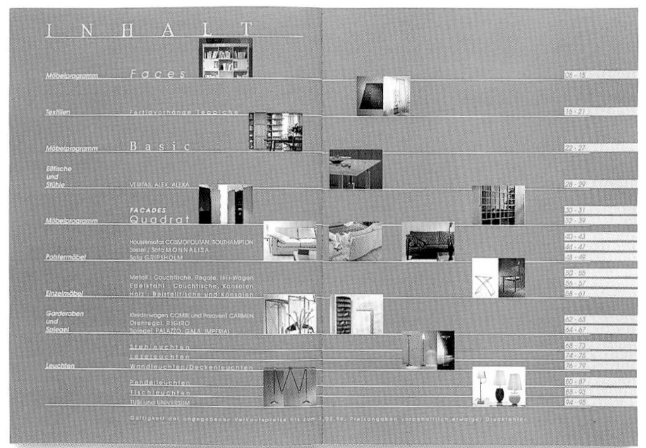

Das Lichtüber dem Tisch

Pendelleuchten

Andreas Weber Design

1. Zeus

Pendelleuchte mit oder ohne Höhenverstellung. Opalglas weiß, Metallelemente Nickel matt, Chrom poliert, Messing matt oder poliert, Zahnstange Chrom matt, E 27 max. 100 W, ab 1.350,- Durch die bewegliche Stufenlinse ist die Große des Lichtkegels auf dem Tisch einstellbar.
Varianten: **Zeus Uno**, **Zeus Duo**, mit und ohne Deckenschienen wie bei den Modellen **Diana** und **Neptun**.

80 Pendelleuchten

2. Diana-Duo

Pendelleuchte, höhenverstellbar (ca. 50 cm), Kabel-Standardlänge für 300 cm Deckenhöhe (kürzen möglich, auch länger lieferbar), Verstellbereich seitlich je 60 cm links und rechts, Deckenschiene 140 cm, Durchmesser Leuchtenkörper 24,5 cm, Nickel matt, Chrom poliert, Messing matt oder poliert, 2 x Leuchtmittel R7s Halogen, 100 W/220 V, 2.790,-
Varianten: **Diana Uno**, mit und ohne Deckenschiene, mit und ohne Höhenverstellung, **Diana Duo** ohne Deckenschiene, ab 1.350,-

3. Neptun-Uno

Pendelleuchte, höhenverstellbar (ca. 50 cm), Kabel-Standardlänge für 300 cm Deckenhöhe (kürzen möglich, auch länger lieferbar), Abstand Baldachin-Umlenkrolle, max. ca. 100 cm, Durchmesser Glaskörper 16 cm, Nickel matt, Chrom poliert, Messing matt oder poliert, E 27 max.100 W, 1.190,-
Varianten: **Neptun Uno** ohne Deckenschiene, mit und ohne Höhenverstellung, **Neptun Duo** mit und ohne Deckenschiene, ab 990,-

Pendelleuchten 81

## Furniture & Lighting

CHRISTINE KRÖNCKE INTERIOR DESIGN CL: Christine Kröncke Interior Design CD: Christine Kröncke
AD, D, DF: Andreas Weber P: Ralph C. Stradtmann / Wolfgang Pulfer Germany 1998 *SIZE: 277×209*

## Floor Mat

SBEMCO INTERNATIONAL CL: Sbemco International CD, AD, D, I: John Sayles D: Jennifer Elliott P: Bill Nellans CW: Wendy Lyons DF: Sayles Graphic Design USA 1996 *SIZE: 279×216*

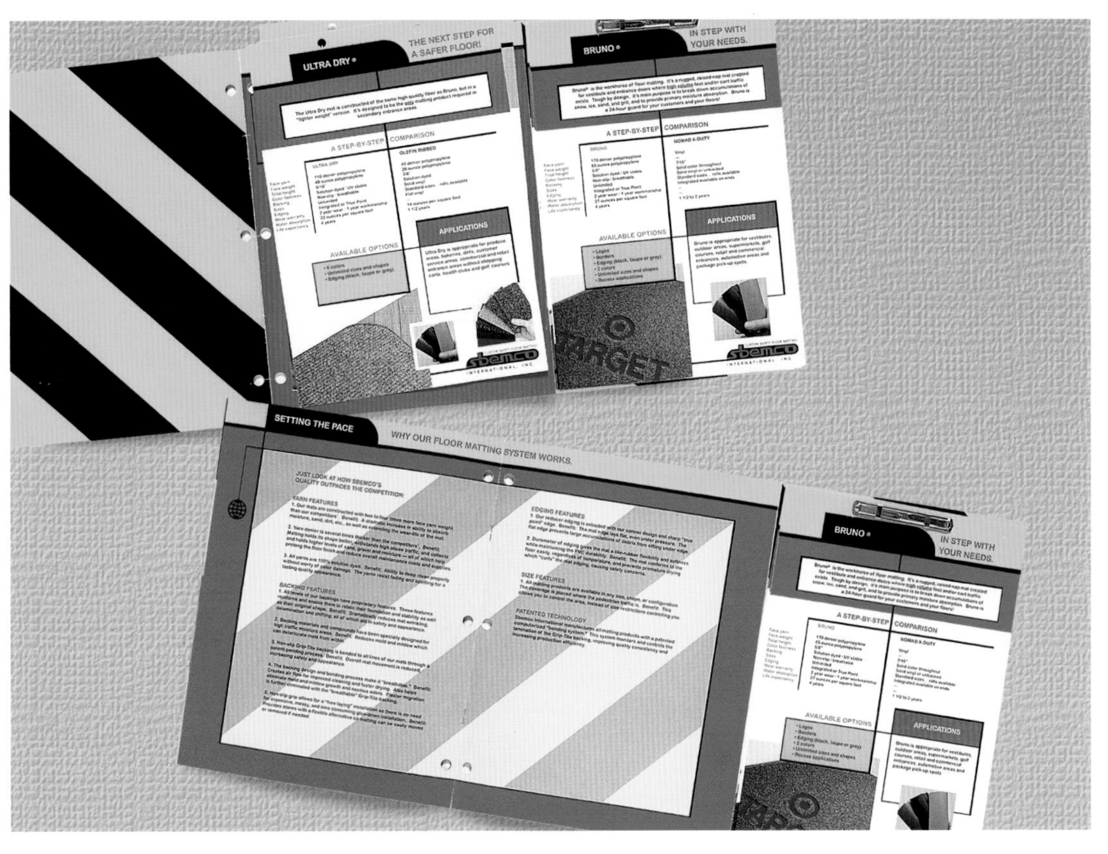

## Housewares & Furniture

CRATE AND BARREL CL, DF: Crate and Barrel CD: Alessandro Franchini D: Paula Bodnar P: Alan Shortall ST: Betty Barquin USA 1998 *SIZE: 216×259*

white on white.
form in form
11-A-a Emanuel Babled Flower Vase
¥ 98,000
11-A-b Emanuel Babled Flower Vase
¥ 98,000
11-A-c Emanuel Babled Flower Vase
¥ 98,000
IDÉE page › 10
15 Legs
A
B
C
D
E
F
G
H
I
J
K
L
M
N
O
IDÉE page › 21

**Interior Goods & Furniture**

IDÉE  CL: IDÉE Co., Ltd.  AD, D: Osamu Misawa  P: Masayuki Hayashi/ Shoji Miyamoto/ Yutaka Sakano/ Mamoru Minamiura
ST: Masayo Motegi  Japan  1998  *SIZE: 296×230*

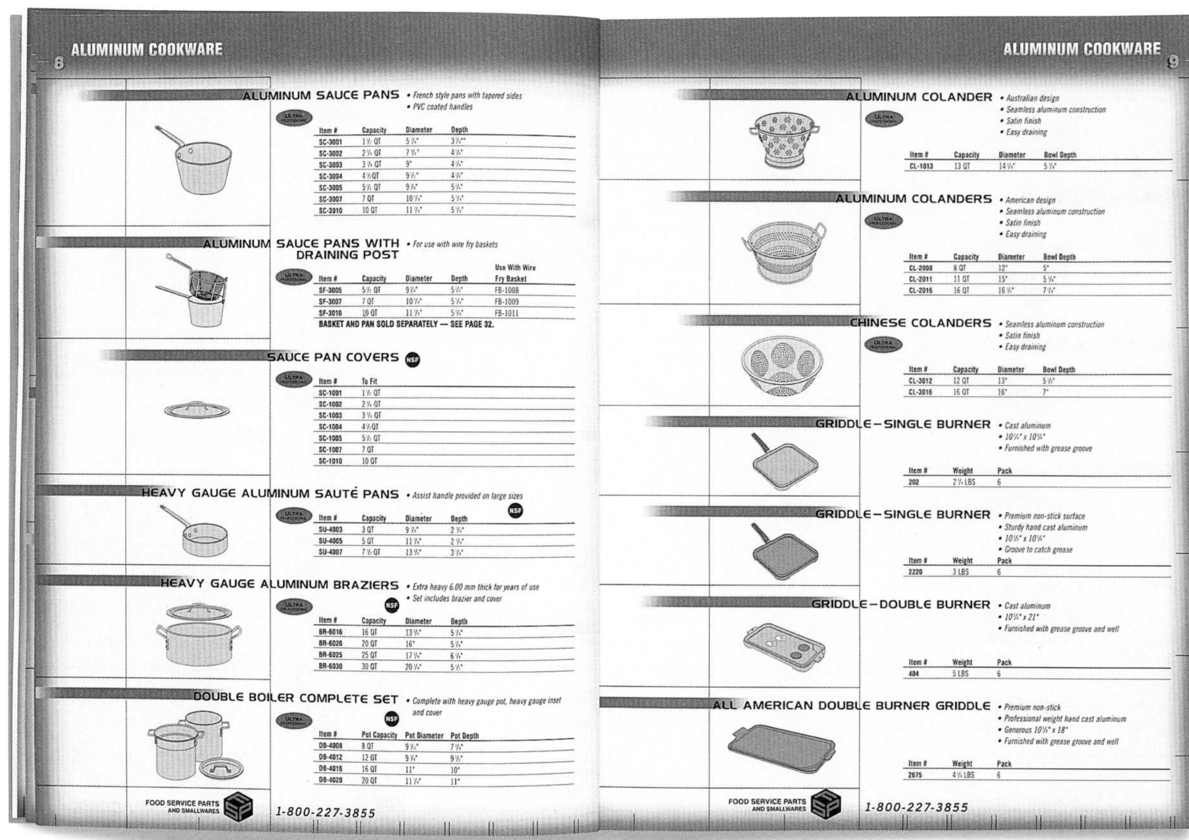

ALUMINUM COOKWARE 8

**ALUMINUM SAUCE PANS**
- French style pans with tapered sides
- PVC coated handles

| Item # | Capacity | Diameter | Depth |
|---|---|---|---|
| SC-3001 | 1 1/2 QT | 5 7/8" | 3 7/8" |
| SC-3002 | 2 3/4 QT | 7 3/4" | 4 1/4" |
| SC-3003 | 3 3/4 QT | 9" | 4 1/4" |
| SC-3004 | 4 1/2 QT | 9 1/2" | 4 1/2" |
| SC-3005 | 5 1/2 QT | 9 3/4" | 5 1/4" |
| SC-3007 | 7 QT | 10 1/4" | 5 1/4" |
| SC-3010 | 10 QT | 11 7/8" | 5 1/8" |

**ALUMINUM SAUCE PANS WITH DRAINING POST**
- For use with wire fry baskets

| Item # | Capacity | Diameter | Depth | Use With Wire Fry Basket |
|---|---|---|---|---|
| SF-3005 | 5 1/2 QT | 9 3/4" | 5 1/4" | FB-1008 |
| SF-3007 | 7 QT | 10 1/2" | 5 1/4" | FB-1009 |
| SF-3010 | 10 QT | 11 7/8" | 5 3/4" | FB-1011 |

BASKET AND PAN SOLD SEPARATELY — SEE PAGE 32.

**SAUCE PAN COVERS** NSF

| Item # | To Fit |
|---|---|
| SC-1001 | 1 1/2 QT |
| SC-1002 | 2 3/4 QT |
| SC-1003 | 3 3/4 QT |
| SC-1004 | 4 1/2 QT |
| SC-1005 | 5 1/2 QT |
| SC-1007 | 7 QT |
| SC-1010 | 10 QT |

**HEAVY GAUGE ALUMINUM SAUTÉ PANS**
- Assist handle provided on large sizes

NSF

| Item # | Capacity | Diameter | Depth |
|---|---|---|---|
| SU-4003 | 3 QT | 9 7/8" | 2 3/8" |
| SU-4005 | 5 QT | 11 7/8" | 2 3/4" |
| SU-4007 | 7 1/2 QT | 13 3/4" | 3 1/4" |

**HEAVY GAUGE ALUMINUM BRAZIERS**
- Extra heavy 6.00 mm thick for years of use
- Set includes brazier and cover

NSF

| Item # | Capacity | Diameter | Depth |
|---|---|---|---|
| BR-6016 | 16 QT | 13 3/4" | 5 7/8" |
| BR-6020 | 20 QT | 16" | 5 7/8" |
| BR-6025 | 25 QT | 17 3/4" | 6 1/4" |
| BR-6030 | 30 QT | 20 1/4" | 5 1/2" |

**DOUBLE BOILER COMPLETE SET**
- Complete with heavy gauge pot, heavy gauge inset and cover

NSF

| Item # | Pot Capacity | Pot Diameter | Pot Depth |
|---|---|---|---|
| DB-4008 | 8 QT | 9 7/16" | 7 7/8" |
| DB-4012 | 12 QT | 9 3/4" | 9 1/2" |
| DB-4016 | 16 QT | 11" | 10" |
| DB-4020 | 20 QT | 11 7/8" | 11" |

FOOD SERVICE PARTS AND SMALLWARES 1-800-227-3855

ALUMINUM COOKWARE 9

**ALUMINUM COLANDER**
- Australian design
- Seamless aluminum construction
- Satin finish
- Easy draining

| Item # | Capacity | Diameter | Bowl Depth |
|---|---|---|---|
| CL-1013 | 13 QT | 14 3/4" | 5 7/8" |

**ALUMINUM COLANDERS**
- American design
- Seamless aluminum construction
- Satin finish
- Easy draining

| Item # | Capacity | Diameter | Bowl Depth |
|---|---|---|---|
| CL-2008 | 8 QT | 12" | 5" |
| CL-2011 | 11 QT | 15" | 5 3/4" |
| CL-2016 | 16 QT | 16 1/2" | 7 1/4" |

**CHINESE COLANDERS**
- Seamless aluminum construction
- Satin finish
- Easy draining

| Item # | Capacity | Diameter | Bowl Depth |
|---|---|---|---|
| CL-3012 | 12 QT | 13" | 5 1/2" |
| CL-3016 | 16 QT | 16" | 7" |

**GRIDDLE—SINGLE BURNER**
- Cast aluminum
- 10 1/4" x 10 1/4"
- Furnished with grease groove

| Item # | Weight | Pack |
|---|---|---|
| 202 | 2 3/4 LBS | 6 |

**GRIDDLE—SINGLE BURNER**
- Premium non-stick surface
- Sturdy hand cast aluminum
- 10 1/4" x 10 1/4"
- Groove to catch grease

| Item # | Weight | Pack |
|---|---|---|
| 2220 | 3 LBS | 6 |

**GRIDDLE—DOUBLE BURNER**
- Cast aluminum
- 10 1/4" x 21"
- Furnished with grease groove and well

| Item # | Weight | Pack |
|---|---|---|
| 404 | 5 LBS | 6 |

**ALL AMERICAN DOUBLE BURNER GRIDDLE**
- Premium non-stick
- Professional weight hand cast aluminum
- Generous 10 1/4" x 18"
- Furnished with grease groove and well

| Item # | Weight | Pack |
|---|---|---|
| 2675 | 4 3/4 LBS | 6 |

FOOD SERVICE PARTS AND SMALLWARES 1-800-227-3855

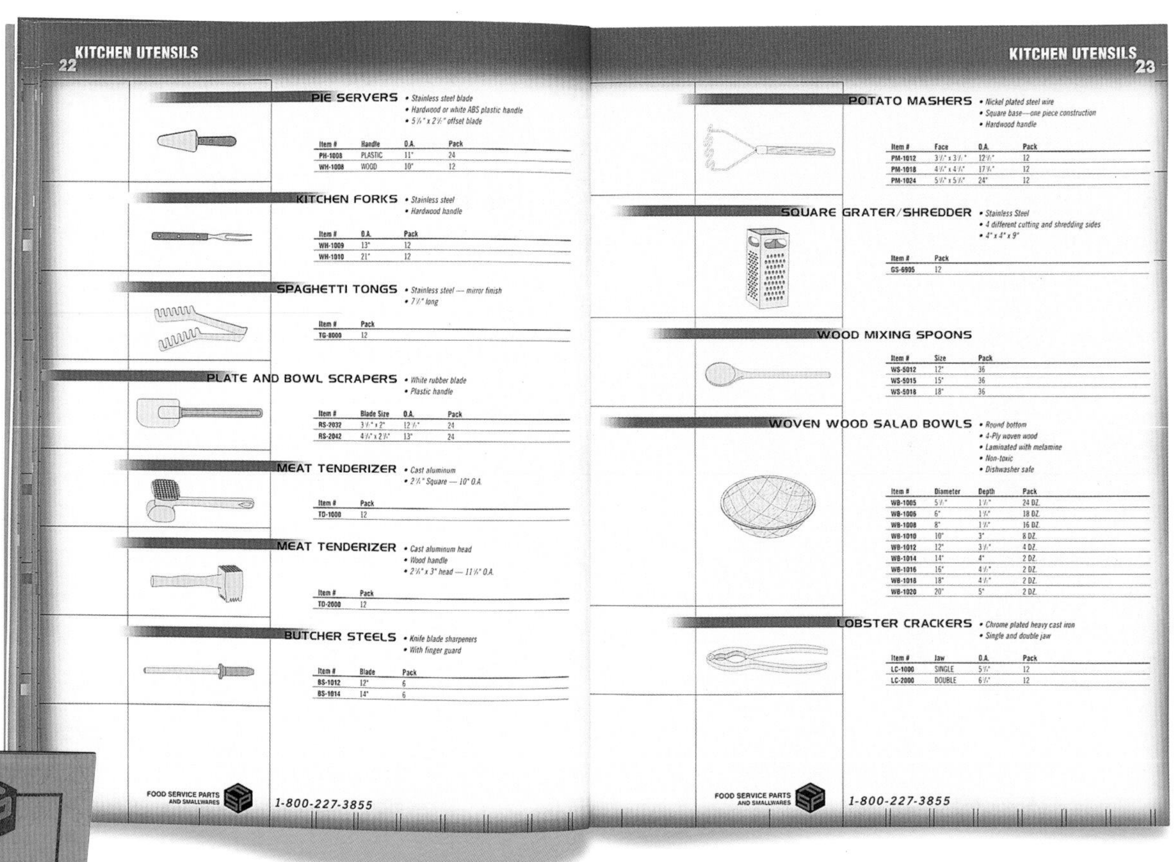

KITCHEN UTENSILS 22

**PIE SERVERS**
- Stainless steel blade
- Hardwood or white ABS plastic handle
- 5 1/4" x 2 1/2" offset blade

| Item # | Handle | O.A. | Pack |
|---|---|---|---|
| PH-1008 | PLASTIC | 11" | 24 |
| WH-1008 | WOOD | 10" | 12 |

**KITCHEN FORKS**
- Stainless steel
- Hardwood handle

| Item # | O.A. | Pack |
|---|---|---|
| WH-1009 | 13" | 12 |
| WH-1010 | 21" | 12 |

**SPAGHETTI TONGS**
- Stainless steel — mirror finish
- 7 1/2" long

| Item # | Pack |
|---|---|
| TG-8000 | 12 |

**PLATE AND BOWL SCRAPERS**
- White rubber blade
- Plastic handle

| Item # | Blade Size | O.A. | Pack |
|---|---|---|---|
| RS-2032 | 3 1/2" x 2" | 12 1/2" | 24 |
| RS-2042 | 4 1/2" x 2 3/4" | 13" | 24 |

**MEAT TENDERIZER**
- Cast aluminum
- 2 1/4" Square — 10" O.A.

| Item # | Pack |
|---|---|
| TD-1000 | 12 |

**MEAT TENDERIZER**
- Cast aluminum head
- Wood handle
- 2 1/4" x 3" head — 11 1/4" O.A.

| Item # | Pack |
|---|---|
| TD-2000 | 12 |

**BUTCHER STEELS**
- Knife blade sharpeners
- With finger guard

| Item # | Blade | Pack |
|---|---|---|
| BS-1012 | 12" | 6 |
| BS-1014 | 14" | 6 |

FOOD SERVICE PARTS AND SMALLWARES 1-800-227-3855

KITCHEN UTENSILS 23

**POTATO MASHERS**
- Nickel plated steel wire
- Square base—one piece construction
- Hardwood handle

| Item # | Face | O.A. | Pack |
|---|---|---|---|
| PM-1012 | 3 1/2" x 3 1/2" | 12 1/2" | 12 |
| PM-1018 | 4 1/4" x 4 1/4" | 17 3/4" | 12 |
| PM-1024 | 5 1/4" x 5 1/4" | 24" | 12 |

**SQUARE GRATER/SHREDDER**
- Stainless Steel
- 4 different cutting and shredding sides
- 4" x 4" x 9"

| Item # | Pack |
|---|---|
| GS-6905 | 12 |

**WOOD MIXING SPOONS**

| Item # | Size | Pack |
|---|---|---|
| WS-5012 | 12" | 36 |
| WS-5015 | 15" | 36 |
| WS-5018 | 18" | 36 |

**WOVEN WOOD SALAD BOWLS**
- Round bottom
- 4-Ply woven wood
- Laminated with melamine
- Non-toxic
- Dishwasher safe

| Item # | Diameter | Depth | Pack |
|---|---|---|---|
| WB-1005 | 5 1/2" | 1 1/2" | 24 DZ. |
| WB-1006 | 6" | 1 3/4" | 18 DZ. |
| WB-1008 | 8" | 1 3/4" | 16 DZ. |
| WB-1010 | 10" | 3" | 8 DZ. |
| WB-1012 | 12" | 3 1/2" | 4 DZ. |
| WB-1014 | 14" | 4" | 2 DZ. |
| WB-1016 | 16" | 4 1/2" | 2 DZ. |
| WB-1018 | 18" | 4 1/2" | 2 DZ. |
| WB-1020 | 20" | 5" | 2 DZ. |

**LOBSTER CRACKERS**
- Chrome plated heavy cast iron
- Single and double jaw

| Item # | Jaw | O.A. | Pack |
|---|---|---|---|
| LC-1000 | SINGLE | 5 3/4" | 12 |
| LC-2000 | DOUBLE | 6 1/4" | 12 |

FOOD SERVICE PARTS AND SMALLWARES 1-800-227-3855

FOOD SERVICE PARTS AND SMALLWARES

JOHN S. DULL & ASSOCIATES, INC. 1997

## Restaurant Supplies

JOHN S DULL & ASSOCIATES CL: John S Dull & Associates D: Beth Elliott / James W Moore I: Outside Enterprises DF: Elliott Design USA 1997 *SIZE: 280×216*

AIRPORT 2744
18/10 Chromnickel-Stahl,
poliert und mattiert
Klinge Edelstahl, geschmiedet
AZUR 2720
18/10 Chromnickel-Stahl, mattiert
Klinge Edelstahl, geschmiedet
HANSEATIC 2733
18/10 Chromnickel-Stahl,
poliert und mattiert
Klinge Edelstahl, geschmiedet
TREND 2790
18/10 Chromnickel-Stahl, poliert
Klinge Edelstahl

In praktischer Vielfalt präsentiert sich das Besteck JESSICA. Die Serie aus hochwertigem Edelstahl umfaßt auch Salat-, Fisch-, und Dessertbestecke, sowie ein komplettes Vorlegeset.
Für jedes ZWILLING Besteck gibt es ein spezielles Zubehör-Programm.
JESSICA 2757
18/10 Chromnickel-Stahl, poliert
Klinge Edelstahl, geschmiedet

ZWILLING®-Kinderbestecke
ZWILLING® Grill- und Steakmesser-Sätze
ZWILLING
BESTECKE

**Kitchen Utensils**

ZWILLING J. A. HENCKELS CL: Zwilling J. A. Henckels Japan Ltd. Japan 1998 *SIZE: 270×135*

Simple
Like all great designs, EarthShell® containers are ingenious in their simplicity. The ingredients are baked in a mold to produce an airy honeycombed structure that is lightweight and insulating. The equipment used is similar to machines that make cookie wafers and ice cream cones.
Already, three major U.S. packaging companies have been licensed to manufacture EarthShell® products ... with more to follow.
It is a production process with many environmental advantages. EarthShell® packages are formed by simply evaporating water in a common baking process. The production and distribution of a paper or polystyrene sandwich container consumes significantly more energy than an equivalent EarthShell® package. A paper container also creates more overall air and water pollution.

EarthShell

EarthShell costs about the same as conventional packaging. (But far, far less, is the price we pay environmentally...) Perhaps the most important thing an EarthShell® package contains is ... opportunity. For better, more responsible disposable packaging in the twenty-first century and beyond.

Introducing
EarthShell
Nature's
own
Container

## Disposal Fast-Food Containers

EARTHSHELL CL: EarthShell Corporation AD, D: John Hornall D: Jana Nishi / Bruce Branson-Meyer / Virginia Le P: Tom Collicott I: Julia LaPine CW: Pamela Mason Davey DF: Hornall Anderson Design Works, Inc. USA 1996 *SIZE: 286×286*

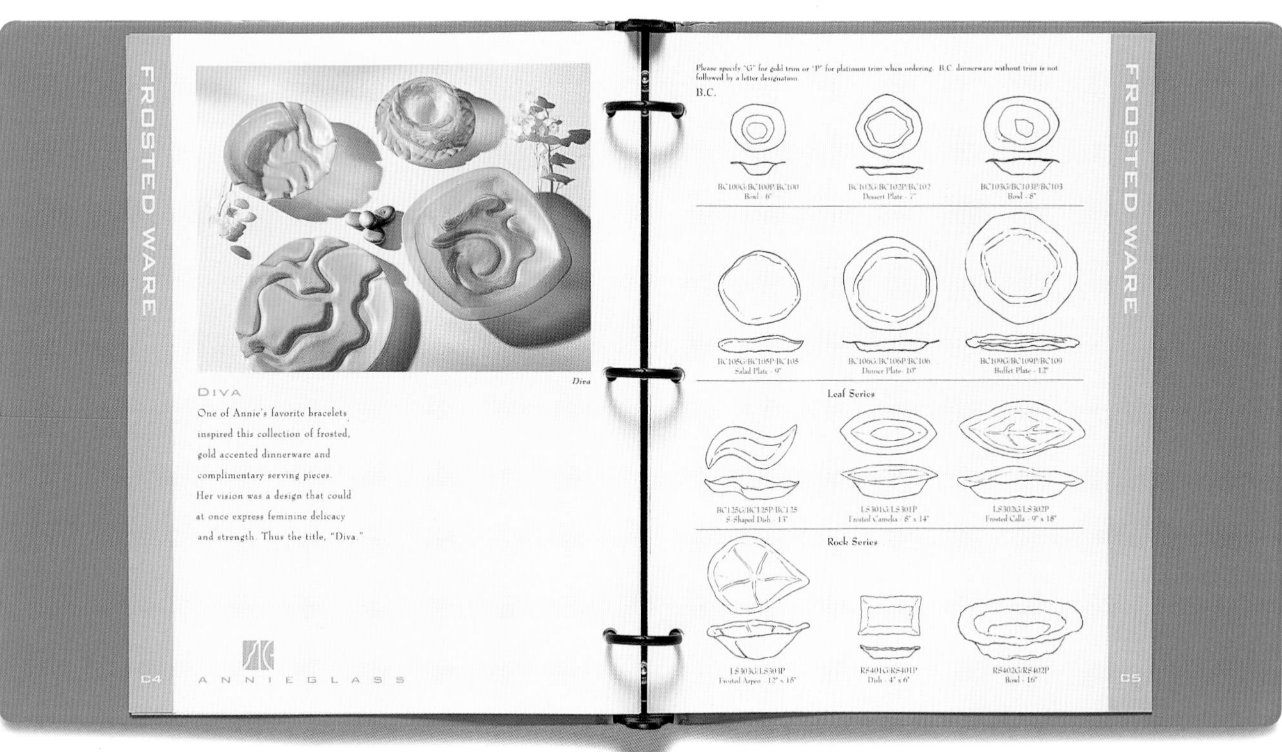
FROSTED WARE
DIVA
One of Annie's favorite bracelets inspired this collection of frosted, gold accented dinnerware and complimentary serving pieces. Her vision was a design that could at once express feminine delicacy and strength. Thus the title, "Diva."
ANNIEGLASS
B.C.
Leaf Series
Rock Series

COLOR SERIES
THE COLORS OF ANNIEGLASS
RIPPLE
(previous page)
Rhythmic contours and a vibrant palette imbue the Ripple pattern with a strong, graphic quality, echoing the undulating tides of the Pacific Ocean.
Amethyst
Iris
Emerald
Lilac
Sky Blue
Mango
Kiwi
Aquamarine
Teal
TRIANGLES AND BOATS
Hawaii's lush flora and fauna inspired the colors of our boats and triangles. We like to fill the boats – modeled after native vessels which populate the waters between the islands – with fruit, flowers or floating candles. Bold shapes and sun-drenched colors make our triangle plates the perfect backdrop for appetizers, salads and other choice delicacies.
Triangles and Boats
MIX AND MATCH
When you layer elements from the Color series, each cluster of luminous, lead-free tones adds a delightfully seductive quality to your table.
ANNIEGLASS

## Glassware

ANNIEGLASS CL: Annieglass, Inc. CD: John Muller AD, D: Scott Chapman P: RJ Muna I: Kelly Burke CW: Pat Piper DF: Muller + Company USA 1997 *SIZE: 291×261*

1 En smuk hyldest til naturen i form, farve og udtryk at Ole Kortzau Natura kunstserie i hvid, gul, grøn eller blå. Vase. 20 cm **265,-.** Vase, 12 cm **195.** Fad, 18 cm **125,-.**

2 Ole Jensen har for Royal Copenhagen designet en serie køkkenredskaber der harmonerer med den ny tids tendenser og behov - det vil sige køkkenredskaber med flere funktioner og alt overflødigt skåret væk. Plus et streif af humor! "Ole" the kande i gul fajance. 1,20 l **595,-.**

3 Karafler designet af Ole Jensen. Hvid porcelæn. 1,45 l **275,-.** Glas. 1,45 l **250,-.**

4 Ole Jensen har et godt greb om både form og funktion. Råkostjern i lyseblå fajance og rustfrit stål. H: 26 cm **498,-.**

5 Nemmere kan det ikke være: En enkelt vippebevægelse og Ole Jensens dørslag i gul fajance bliver til en praktisk serveringsskål. 80 cl **475,-.**

6 Kombineret juicekande og appelsinpresser i gul fajance. 73 cl **395,-.**

7 Ole Jensen går nye veje med denne utraditionelle serie i hvidt porcelæn. Skål, 40 cl **145,-.** Tallerken, 31,5 cm **175,-.** Kop, 20 cl **125,-.**

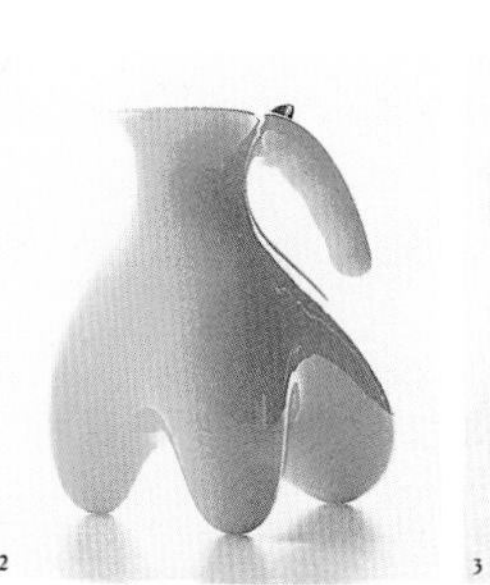

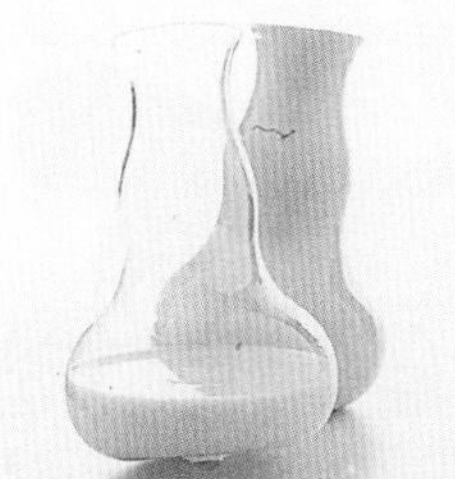

107

## Household Goods

ROYAL SCANDINAVIA CL: Royal Scandinavia A/S CD, D: Cecilie Grut AD: Janne Ferslew P: Graae & Bangsbo
CW: Barbara Berger DF: Ferslew Advertising Denmark 1998 *SIZE: 275×225*

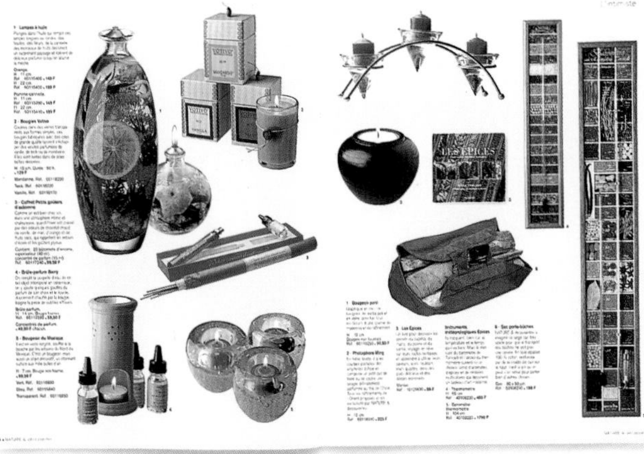

GAMME «MÉMOIRE D'UN INSTANT»

*C'est à Forcalquier, dans la Provence de Giono, que Patrick Lions a créé ces produits pour NATURE & découvertes ; chaque parfum est le fruit d'un assemblage subtil d'huiles essentielles réalisé par les parfumeurs de Grasse ; leur présentation (flacon de verre dépoli pour les bougies, papier de soie de couleur pour les encens et les concentrés) participe à la poésie de ces odeurs qui évoquent l'enfance, la nature, une certaine douceur de vivre.*

*Chaque senteur se décline en 3 formes :*
*Bougie : H : 8 cm - durée : environ 30 h.* **• 79,50 F**
*Concentré de parfum : flacon de 45 ml* **• 49,50 F**
*Bâtonnets d'encens : boîte de 20* **• 25 F**

CAFÉ SOUS LA TONNELLE
Les arômes réconfortants du café torréfié et de la noisette grillée, mêlés à l'harmonie de la vanille.
***Bougie • Réf.: 60116110***
***Concentré • Réf.: 60115900***
***Bâtonnets • Réf.: 60115980***

PETIT GOÛTER D'AUTOMNE
Chocolat chaud, vanille et miel, confitures et fruits secs... Le souvenir des goûters au retour de l'école, quand les feuilles craquent sous les pas.
***Bougie • Réf.: 60116140***
***Concentré • Réf.: 60115930***
***Bâtonnets • Réf.: 60116000***

UN DIMANCHE AU CABANON
L'odeur fraîche, verte et tentante du potager où l'on cueille ses provisions pour déjeuner sous les canisses : tomates, cassis, basilic, céleri.
***Bougie • Réf.: 60116160***
***Concentré • Réf.: 60115950***
***Bâtonnets • Réf.: 60116030***

SOIR D'ÉTÉ EN PROVENCE
Le charme retrouvé des beaux jours à la campagne et la senteur douce et pointue des herbes sèches.
***Bougie • Réf.: 60116120***
***Concentré • Réf.: 60115910***
***Bâtonnets • Réf.: 60115990***

SIESTE SOUS LE FIGUIER
La tiédeur d'un après-midi d'été aux effluves exquises de bois vert légèrement amer qui vient arrondir une note suave de pêche sauvage et de figue.
***Bougie • Réf.: 60116090***
***Concentré • Réf.: 60115880***
***batônnets • Réf.: 60115960***

SECRETS D'ENFANCE
Le charme retrouvé de la maison de grand-mère, sur des notes d'amande amère, de cire, de vanille et d'herbe.
***Bougie • Réf.: 60116130***
***Concentré • Réf.: 60115920***
***Bâtonnets • Réf.: 60116010***

NATURE APRÈS LA PLUIE
L'odeur authentique et fraîche de l'eau du ciel, avec, en fond, celle rassurante de la terre forestière.
***Bougie • Réf.: 60116100***
***Concentré • Réf.: 60115890***
***Bâtonnets • Réf.: 60115970***

VEILLÉES ET CONTES D'HIVERS
Le parfum chaud, puissant et épicé du bois de cannelle, des tonalités fruitées d'écorces d'orange... comme un Noël d'antan.
***Bougie • Réf.: 60116150***
***Concentré • Réf.: 60115940***
***Bâtonnets • Réf.: 60116020***

NATURE *& art de vivre* 9

## Nature-inspired Goods

NATURE & DÉCOUVERTES CL: Nature & Découvertes CD, AD, D, P, I, DF: The En'Print Team
France 1998 *SIZE: 300×231*

## Kitchen Utensils

BODUM CL: Bodum Japan 1998 *SIZE: 519×335*

**Kitchen Utensils & Tableware**

BODUM CL: Bodum Japan 1998 *SIZE: 297×210*

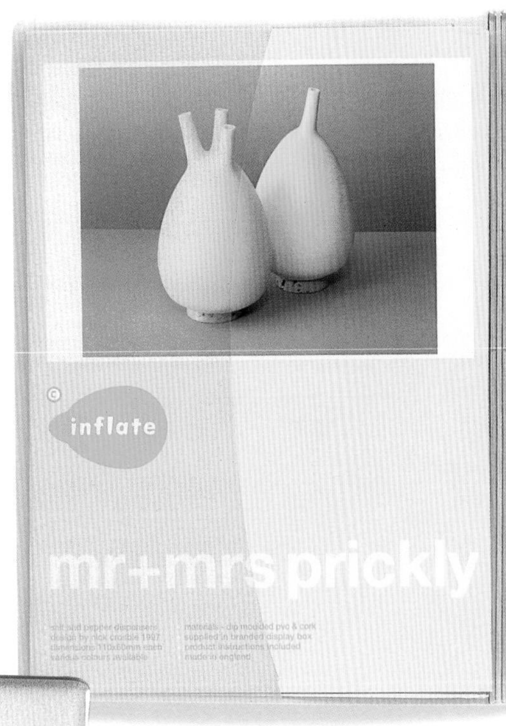


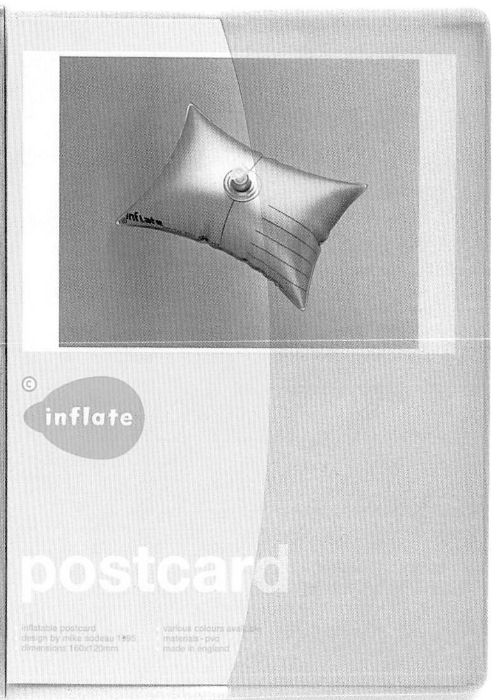

## Household Goods

INFLATE CL, DF: Inflate Ltd. UK 1998 *SIZE: 224×165*

ARZBERG
NEWS
1997
CULT GHIRLANDA
CULT SUNSET
KOALA KLUB X-MAS
TRIC:
DER MESSEHIT
12 SEITEN SPECIAL
SPRING FAIR
12-PAGE TRIC SPECIAL

**Household Goods**

ARZBERG CL: Arzberg Germany 1996 *SIZE: 297×210*

WOOP!
CUTTING BOARD
Designed by GEAR ATELIER
GA-F-05 GRAFITE
GA-F-04 FOREST
PRAIA SEM VIGILÂNCIA
GA-F-03 OCE
GA-F-01 ROSSO
Product size (mm): 255L X 220W X 7.5H
Material: Birch wood (Polypropylene handle)
Color choice: 4
LONGFORD INDUSTRIAL LTD SUITE 16A TRUST TOWER 68 JOHNSTON ROAD HONG KONG TEL (852)
MOBY
BUTTER DISH
Designed by GEAR ATELIER
GA-C-04 CITRUS (Translucent)
GA-C-05 FROST (Translucent)
GA-C-06 DAWN
GA-C-01 LEMON (Translucent)
GA-C-08 LIBE
GA-C-07 PUDDING
GA-C-02 AQUA (Translucent)
GA-C-03 LAGOON (Translucent)
Product size (mm): 208L x 148W x 98H
Cacti
orange juicer
Product size (mm): 130L X 120W X 185H
Material: Polypropylene (Food-grade)
Color choice: 8
Piscis [tray]
Product size (mm): 483L X 440W X 65H (Round tray)
Material: Stainless steel tray (Polyamide handles)
Steel tray - Black (Polyamide handles)
Color choice of handles: 5
Sirena [hanger]
Product size (mm): 104W X 73H X 52D
Material: Polypropylene
Color choice: 3
Gift box size (set of 3): 140 X 54 X 293mm³

HAPPY FISH
BOTTLE COOLER
Designed by GEAR ATELIER
LIVING GEAR
GA-B-02 AQUA
GA-B-04 CITRUS
GA-B-03 LAGOON
GA-B-01 LEMON
Product size (mm): 148D X 225H
Material: Polypropylene
Color choice: 4
LONGFORD INDUSTRIAL LTD SUITE 16A TRUST TOWER 68 JOHNSTON ROAD HONG KONG TEL (852) 2866 2298 FAX (852) 2861 0041
Woop!
cutting board
Product size (mm): 255L X 220W X 75H
Material: Birch wood (Polypropylene handle)
Color choice of handle: 4
Octopus egg cup
Product size (mm): 68L X 68W X 63H
Material: Polyethylene cup (Food-grade)
Polypropylene stand (Food-grade)
Color choice: 4
Gift box size (set of 4): 176 X 176 X 73mm
Moby butter dish
CACTI
ORANGE JUICER
Designed by GEAR ATELIER
GA-A-07 LEMONADE
NEW
GA-A-03 CREAMERY
GA-A-06 JELLY FISH
GA-A-05 JELLY BEAN
GA-A-08 AQUA
NEW
GA-A-01 CACTUS
Product size (mm): 130L X 120W X 185H
Material: Polypropylene (Food-grade)
Color choice: 8


## Household Goods

LIVING GEAR CL, DF: Longford Industrial Limited / Gear Atelier Limited CD, AD: Dennis Chan / May Wong D: Kit Cheung / Tracy Lee P: Andy Lam Hong Kong 1995-1997 *SIZE: 280×204/369×559*

## Dog Goods

SYUNA & BANI CL: Syuna & Bani AD, D, P: Mitsuhiro Miyazaki P: Yasuko Aridome / Tomoko Hyomori Japan 1998 *SIZE: 149×102*

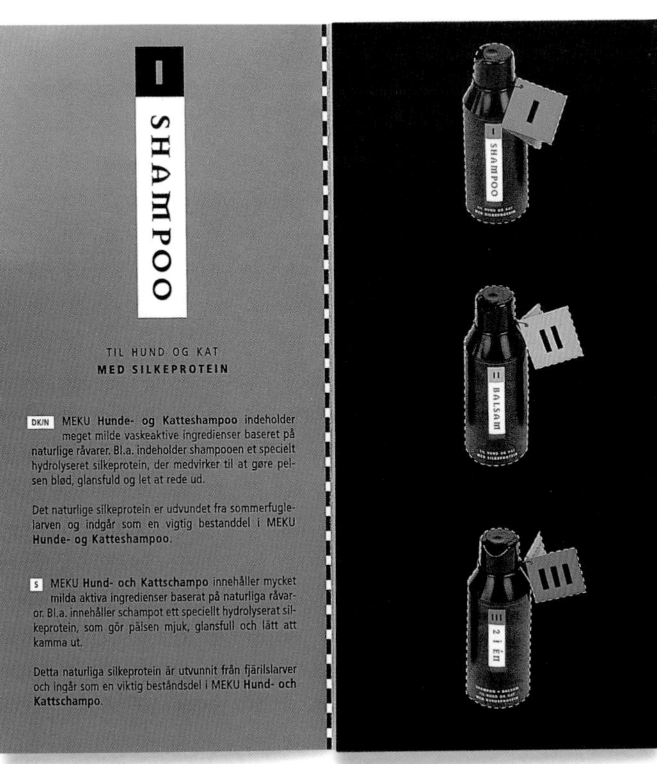
I
SHAMPOO
TIL HUND OG KAT
MED SILKEPROTEIN
DK/N MEKU Hunde- og Katteshampoo indeholder meget milde vaskeaktive ingredienser baseret på naturlige råvarer. Bl.a. indeholder shampooen et specielt hydrolyseret siikeprotein, der medvirker til at gøre pelsen blød, glansfuld og let at rede ud.
Det naturlige silkeprotein er udvundet fra sommerfuglelarven og indgår som en vigtig bestanddel i MEKU Hunde- og Katteshampoo.
S MEKU Hund- och Kattschampo innehåller mycket milda aktiva ingredienser baserat på naturliga råvaror. Bl.a. innehåller schampot ett speciellt hydrolyserat silkeprotein, som gör pälsen mjuk, glansfull och lätt att kamma ut.
Detta naturliga silkeprotein är utvunnit från fjärilslarver och ingår som en viktig beståndsdel i MEKU Hund- och Kattschampo.
I
II
III

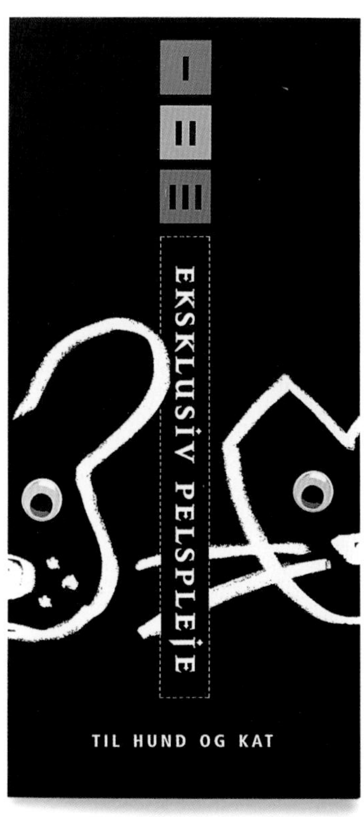
I
II
III
EKSKLUSIV PELSPLEJE
TIL HUND OG KAT

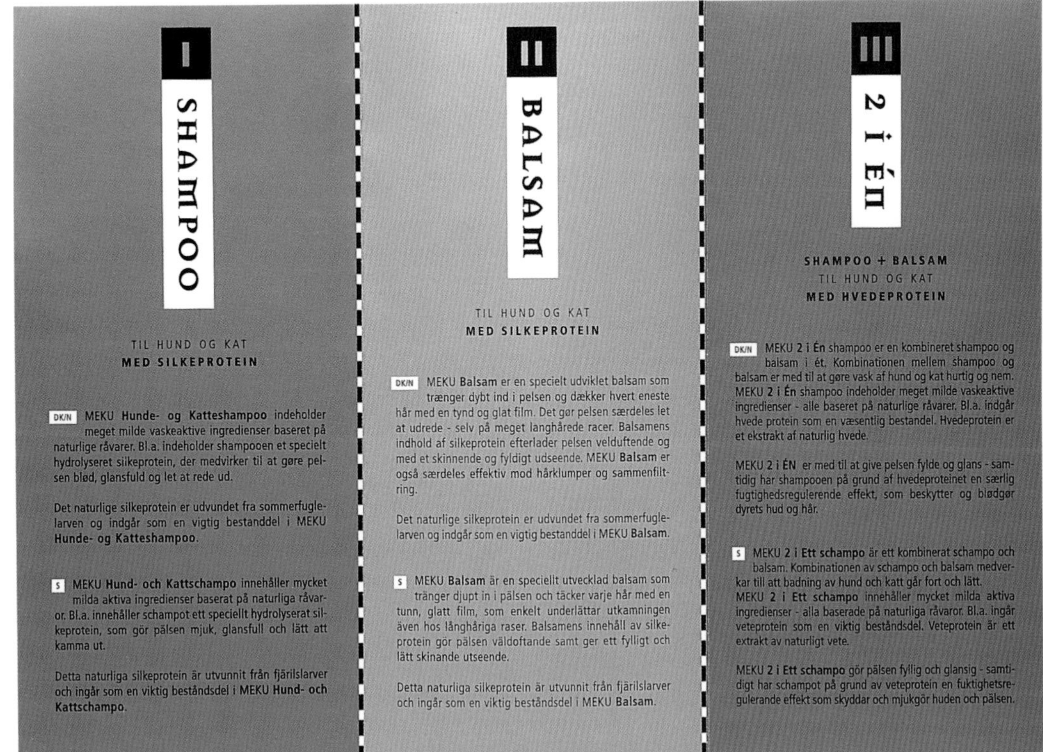
I
SHAMPOO
TIL HUND OG KAT
MED SILKEPROTEIN
DK/N MEKU Hunde- og Katteshampoo indeholder meget milde vaskeaktive ingredienser baseret på naturlige råvarer. Bl.a. indeholder shampooen et specielt hydrolyseret siikeprotein, der medvirker til at gøre pelsen blød, glansfuld og let at rede ud.
Det naturlige silkeprotein er udvundet fra sommerfuglelarven og indgår som en vigtig bestanddel i MEKU Hunde- og Katteshampoo.
S MEKU Hund- och Kattschampo innehåller mycket milda aktiva ingredienser baserat på naturliga råvaror. Bl.a. innehåller schampot ett speciellt hydrolyserat silkeprotein, som gör pälsen mjuk, glansfull och lätt att kamma ut.
Detta naturliga silkeprotein är utvunnit från fjärilslarver och ingår som en viktig beståndsdel i MEKU Hund- och Kattschampo.
II
BALSAM
TIL HUND OG KAT
MED SILKEPROTEIN
DK/N MEKU Balsam er en specielt udviklet balsam som trænger dybt ind i pelsen og dækker hvert eneste hår med en tynd og glat film. Det gør pelsen særdeles let at udrede - selv på meget langhårede racer. Balsamens indhold af silkeprotein efterlader pelsen velduftende og med et skinnende og fyldigt udseende. MEKU Balsam er også særdeles effektiv mod hårklumper og sammenfiltring.
Det naturlige silkeprotein er udvundet fra sommerfuglelarven og indgår som en vigtig bestanddel i MEKU Balsam.
S MEKU Balsam är en speciellt utvecklad balsam som tränger djupt in i pälsen och täcker varje hår med en tunn, glatt film, som enkelt underlättar utkamningen även hos långhåriga raser. Balsamens innehåll av silkeprotein gör pälsen väldoftande samt ger ett fylligt och lätt skinande utseende.
Detta naturliga silkeprotein är utvunnit från fjärilslarver och ingår som en viktig beståndsdel i MEKU Balsam.
III
2 i Én
SHAMPOO + BALSAM
TIL HUND OG KAT
MED HVEDEPROTEIN
DK/N MEKU 2 i Én shampoo er en kombineret shampoo og balsam i ét. Kombinationen mellem shampoo og balsam er med til at gøre vask af hund og kat hurtig og nem. MEKU 2 i Én shampoo indeholder meget milde vaskeaktive ingredienser - alle baseret på naturlige råvarer. Bl.a. indgår hvede protein som en væsentlig bestandel. Hvedeprotein er et ekstrakt af naturlig hvede.
MEKU 2 i ÉN er med til at give pelsen fylde og glans - samtidig har shampooen på grund af hvedeproteinet en særlig fugtighedsregulerende effekt, som beskytter og blødgør dyrets hud og hår.
S MEKU 2 i Ett schampo är ett kombinerat schampo och balsam. Kombinationen av schampo och balsam medverkar till att badning av hund och katt går fort och lätt.
MEKU 2 i Ett schampo innehåller mycket milda aktiva ingredienser - alla baserade på naturliga råvaror. Bl.a. ingår veteprotein som en viktig beståndsdel. Veteprotein är ett extrakt av naturligt vete.
MEKU 2 i Ett schampo gör pälsen fyllig och glansig - samtidigt har schampot på grund av veteprotein en fuktighetsreglerande effekt som skyddar och mjukgör huden och pälsen.

## Petcare Products

MEKU PETCARE CL: Meku A/S CD, AD, D, I, P: Vibeke Nodskov CW: Soren Sonne DF: Leo Pharmaceutical Products Denmark 1997 *SIZE: 210×99*

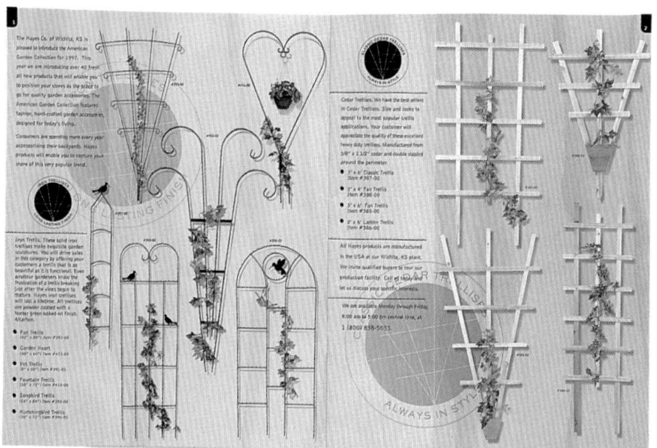

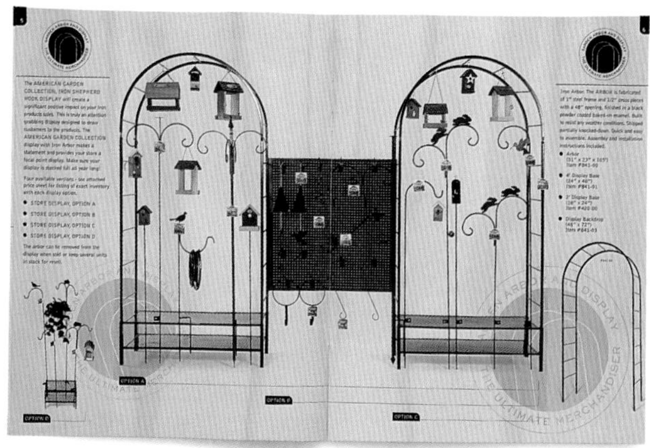

17

FASHIONABLE FEEDERS AND HOUSES FOR THE BIRDS

Your store will have a substantial increase in bird feeder and house sales when you offer Hayes feeders and houses. All Hayes feeders and houses are hand-crafted of all natural weather resistant cedar. Hayes feeders have easy fill lids, long lasting nylon rope and quality plexiglas. Hayes houses come with sturdy wire loops for hanging. Houses feature eye catching miniatures.

Hayes feeders and houses are not only great quality functional items... Hayes feeders and houses are beautiful garden ornaments and make great gift items. Their unique style will give your customers that already have a feeder a reason to buy another one.

- Americana Inn (5″ x 5″ x 8″) Item #509-05
- Americana Cafe 1 1/2 lbs of seed (8″ x 5″ x 12″) Item #525-01
- Cedar Lake Combo 2 1/2 lbs of seed (19″ x 8″ x 11″) Item #505-01
- Daisy Inn (5″ x 5″ x 10″) Item #518-06
- Daisy Deli 1 1/2 lbs of seed (8″ x 5″ x 12″) Item #525-00
- Cedar Creek Combo 1 1/2 lbs of seed (14″ x 7″ x 9″) Item #508-10
- Bless This Nest (5″ x 5″ x 7″) Item #508-22
- Backyard Cafe (8″ x 7″ x 8″) Item #728-14

18

FASHIONABLE FEEDERS AND HOUSES FOR THE BIRDS

- Countryside Chapel Combo 2 lbs of seed (12″ x 8″ x 14″) Item #513-01
- Countryside Chapel (7″ x 8″ x 14″) Item #513-00
- Village Chapel (5″ x 6″ x 10″) Item #510-01
- Sunflower House (5″ x5″ x 7″) Item #508-21
- Sunflower Cafe 1 1/2 lbs of seed (8″ x 7″ x 8″) Item #728-13

## Garden Products

THE HAYES COMPANY CL: The Hayes Co. CD, AD, D, I: Sherrie & Tracy Holdeman P: ETS Graphics Inc. CW: Clark Jackson
DF: Insight Design Communications USA 1996 *SIZE: 279×215*

## Statuary

SCHNECKEN STATUARY CL: Schnecken Statuary D: Daniel R. Smith P: Michael Willet I, CW: Kathleen Stone DF: Command Z USA 1997 *SIZE: 198×141*

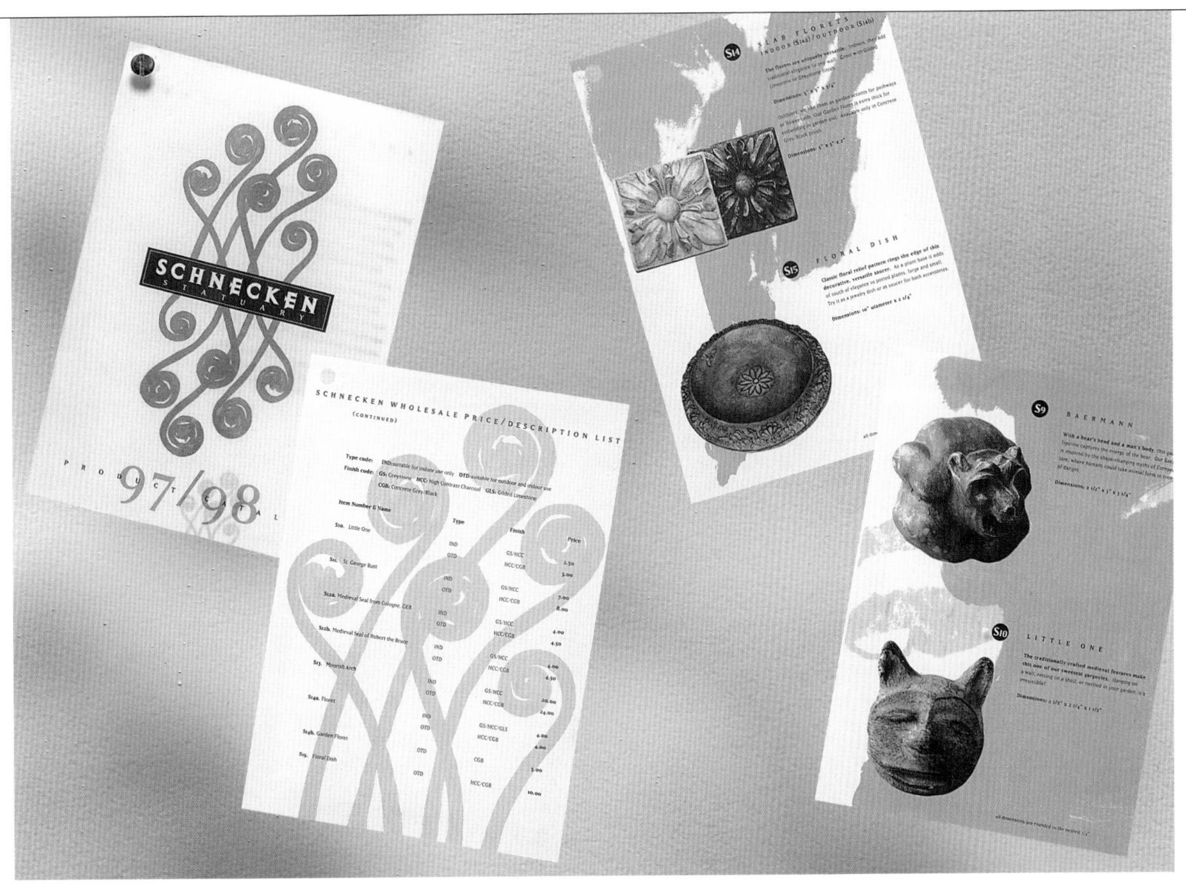

## Vintage Clocks

TIMEWORKS CL: Timeworks, Inc. D: Krysten Bonzelet P: David Belda CW: Steve Kowalski / John Kowalski DF: Kowalski Designworks, Inc. USA 1998 *SIZE: 280×215*

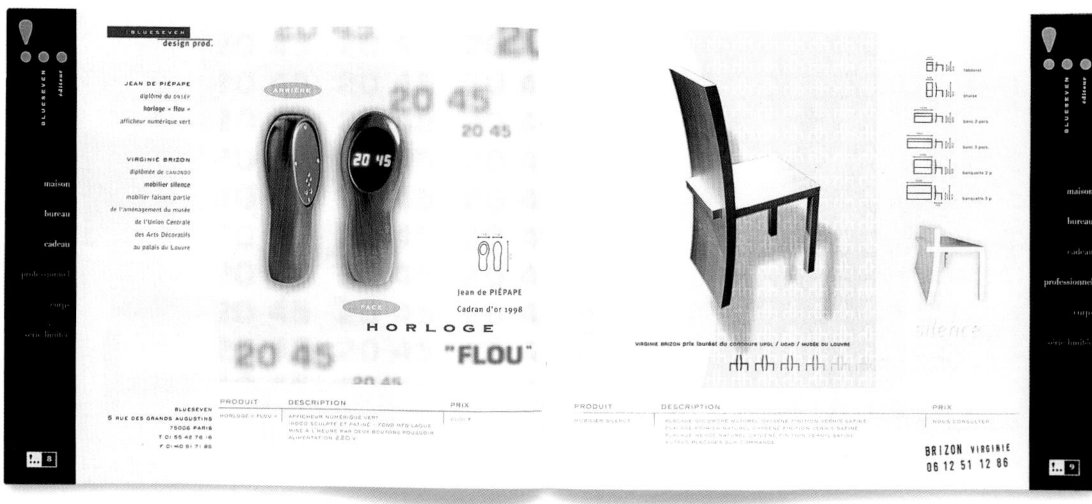

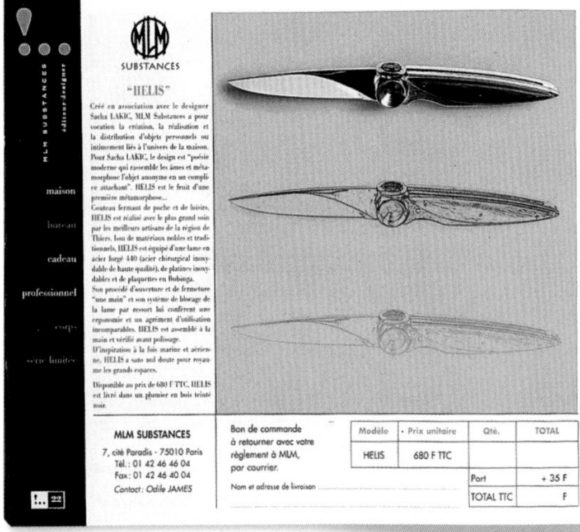

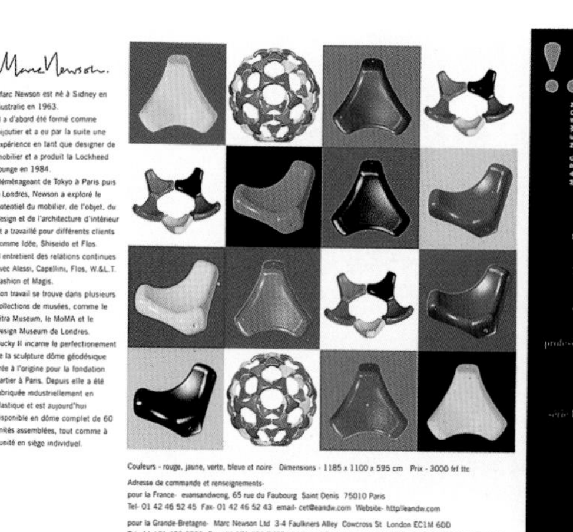

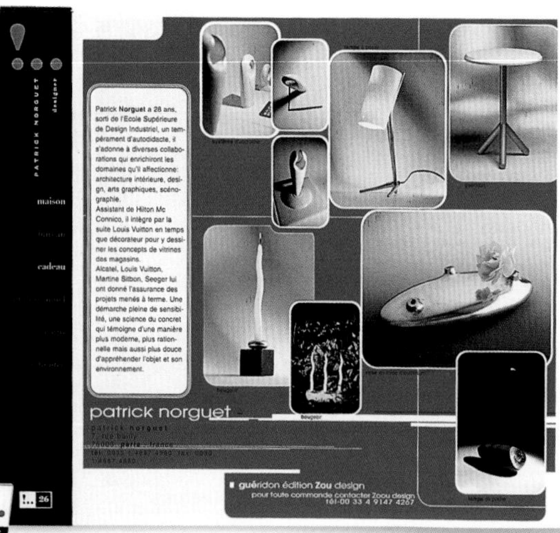

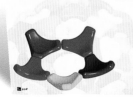

## Interior Goods

CATA! CL: Lesmon Design DF: evansandwong France 1998 *SIZE: 199×241*

## Furniture

MICHAEL SODEAU PARTNERSHIP CL: Michael Sodeau Partnership CD, AD, D:Fabian Monheim / Sophia Wood P: David Simmonds I: Michael Sodeau CW, DF: Fly UK 1998 *SIZE: 99×209*

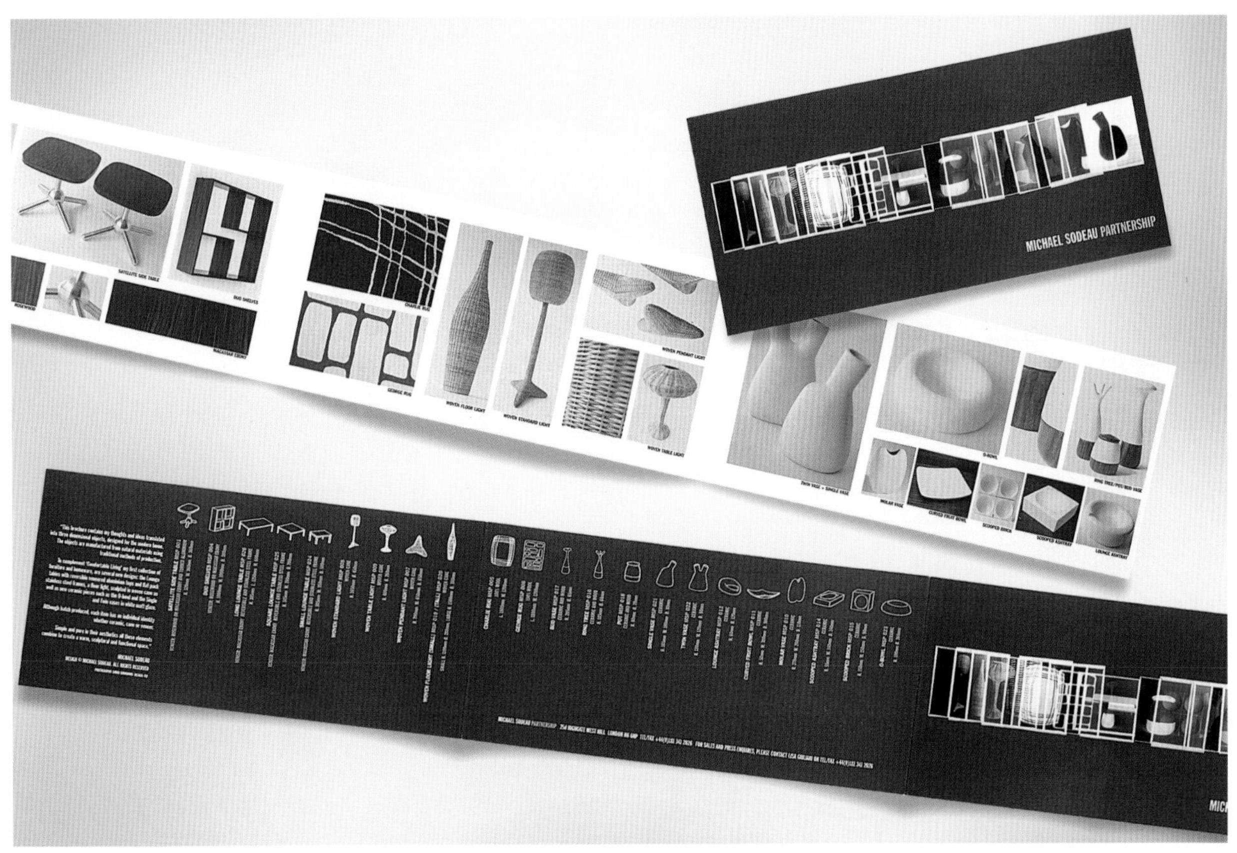

## Household Goods

SONY PLAZA CL: Sony Plaza Japan 1998 *SIZE: 347×260*

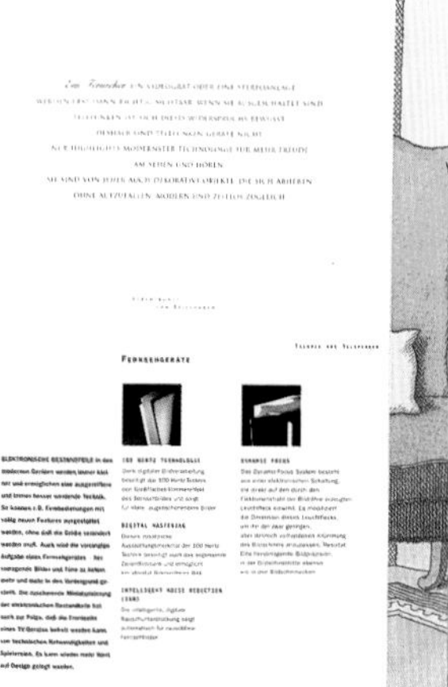

Telefunken ist die Geschichte von *technologischen Fortschritten*, die durch das 20. Jahrhundert hindurch Fernseh- und Videotechnik gefördert haben. Das *Wesentliche* dieses Know-How's konzentriert Telefunken in seinen Fernseh- und Videogeräten: solche Geräte werden denjenigen angeboten, die dieselben *Qualitätsansprüche* stellen.

GROßBILD-FERNSEHGERÄTE

MIT BLACK D.I.V.A.-BILDRÖHRE

**PALcolor S 4400**

Mit seiner Synthese aus traditioneller Telefunken-Eleganz und hohem Bedienungskomfort bietet dieses formschöne TV-Gerät die Bildqualität der Black D.I.V.A.-Bildröhre mit allen Bedienungsfunktionen, die den technischen Stand unserer Produkte widerspiegeln.

**Standard**
PAL/SECAM/NTSC (AV).

**Empfang**
- Kabeltuner mit Hyperband.

**Bild**
- 63 cm Bilddiagonale, 59 cm sichtbar
- Black D.I.V.A.-Bildröhre mit Telefunken-Spitzentechnik: superflacher Bildschirm mit verbesserter Kontrast- und Bildqualität, perfekten und beständigen Farben.
- Kontrast-Automatik (ICE): automatische Kontrastregelung je nach Raumhelligkeit für verbesserten Sehkomfort.

**Ton**
- 2 x 20 W Stereo-Musikleistung.
- 4 Lautsprecher.
- Raumklang für noch mehr Klangerlebnis.

**Bedienungskomfort**
- 59 Programmspeicherplätze.
- Autoprogrammierung: Sendersuchlauf und Speicherautomatik.
- Elektronische Kindersicherung.
- Videotext und Top-Text.
- Bild-Regie-System für Dialog-Menüsteuerung.
- Zoom-Funktion: zur Bildvergrößerung und zur Unterdrückung der schwarzen Streifen bei Filmen im Breitwandformat.
- Abruftaste für die gespeicherten Einstellungen (Lautstärke, Helligkeit, Farbe und Kontrast).
- Automatische Abschaltung (einige Minuten nach Sendeschluß und Erscheinen des Testbildes).
- Möglichkeit des Zapping zwischen den gespeicherten Programmen.
- Ein- und Ausschaltzeit programmierbar.

**Beleuchtete Fernbedienung**

**Anschlüsse an der Geräte-Vorderseite**
- Kopfhörer-Anschluß.
- 2 Audioeingänge.
- Videoeingang.
- S-Videoeingang.

**Anschlüsse an der Geräte-Rückseite**
- 2 Euro-AV-Anschlüsse.
- 2 Audioausgänge.
- Antennenanschluß.
- 2 Lautsprecher-Anschlüsse für Zusatz- bzw. Surround-Lautsprecher.

**Dieses Modell ist auch in Nußbaumdekor lieferbar.**

**PALcolor S 5400**

Die gleichen Merkmale wie beim PALcolor S 4400, jedoch mit größerer Bildröhre:

**Bild**
- 72 cm Bilddiagonale, 68 cm sichtbar.
- Intelligent Scanning Control: die Technik für mehr Kontrastschärfe des Bildes.

**Dieses Modell ist auch in Nußbaumdekor lieferbar.**

19
TELEFUNKEN
1996 1997

## TVs & Videotape Decks

TELEFUNKEN CL: Telefunken CD, AD: Alain Lachartre P: Nicolas Profit / Thierry Laroche I: Pierre Le-Tan / Loustal / Floc'h / Benoit CW: Philippe Blanchard DF: Vue Sur La Ville France 1996 *SIZE: 296×210*

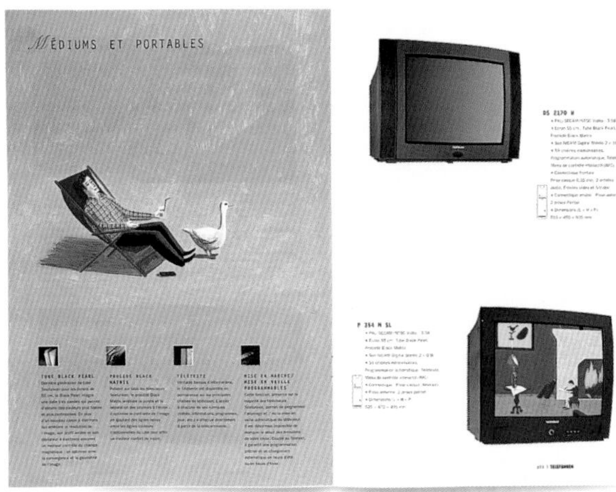


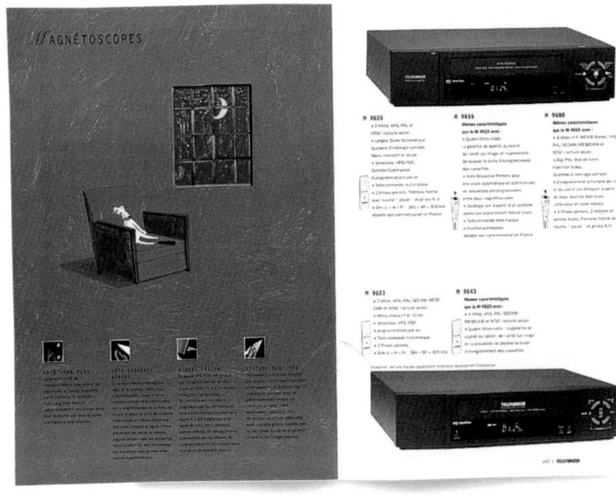


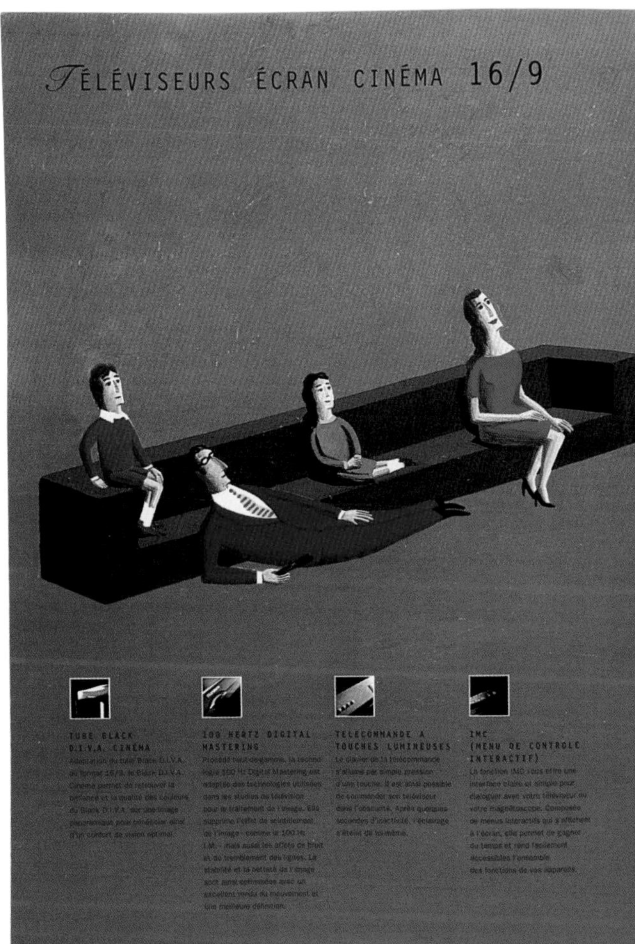

**Cinévision 28 M-N**
• PAL/SECAM/NTSC Vidéo : 3.58 / 4.43.
• Ecran 70 cm, Tube Black D.I.V.A. Cinéma
• Son NICAM Digital Stéréo 2 × 20 W
• Fonction Zoom, Télétexte, Menu de contrôle interactif (IMC)
• Télécommande à touches lumineuses
• Connectique : Prise casque (frontale), Prise antenne, 2 Prises péritel, 2 sorties audio, Prises haut-parleurs ou prises surround supplémentaires.
• Dimensions (L × H × P) : 715 × 509 × 514 mm

**Cinévision 32 M-N**
**Mêmes caractéristiques que le Cinévision 28 M-N avec :**
• Ecran 82 cm, Intelligent Scanning Control (ISC).
• 2 haut-parleurs + boomer arrière
• Connectique frontale : 2 entrées audio, Entrée vidéo, Entrée S-Vidéo.

**Cinévision 24 M SL**
• PAL/SECAM/NTSC Vidéo : 3.58 / 4.43
• Ecran 61 cm, Tube Black D.I.V.A. Cinéma.
• Son NICAM Digital Stéréo 2 × 20 W, 3 haut parleurs.
• Fonction Zoom, Télétexte, Menu de contrôle interactif (IMC)
• Télécommande à touches lumineuses
• Connectique : Prise casque (frontale) 2 Prises péritel, Prise antenne, Prises haut parleurs ou prises surround supplémentaires
• Dimensions (L × H × P) 618 × 433 × 473 mm

p3 ) TELEFUNKEN

## TVs & Videotape Decks

TELEFUNKEN CL: Telefunken CD: Alain Lachartre AD: Remi Joutet P: Nicolas Profit / Thierry Laroche I: Benoit CW: Philippe Blanchard DF: Vue Sur La Ville France 1997 *SIZE: 296×210*

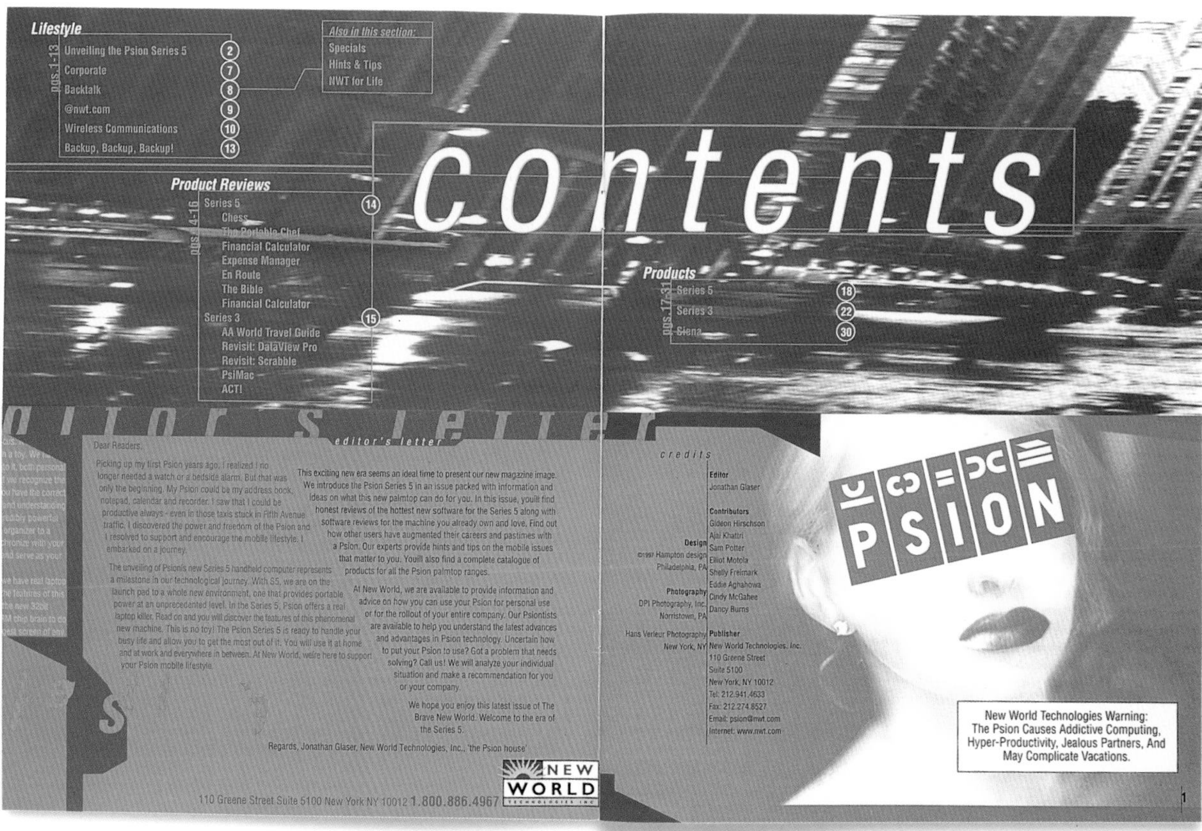
Lifestyle
pgs. 1-13
Unveiling the Psion Series 5 2
Corporate 7
Backtalk 8
@nwt.com 9
Wireless Communications 10
Backup, Backup, Backup! 13
Also in this section:
Specials
Hints & Tips
NWT for Life
contents
Product Reviews
pgs. 14-16
Series 5 14
Chess
The Portable Chef
Financial Calculator
Expense Manager
En Route
The Bible
Financial Calculator
Series 3 15
AA World Travel Guide
Revisit: DataView Pro
Revisit: Scrabble
PsiMac
ACT!
Products
pgs. 17-31
Series 5 18
Series 3 22
Siena 30
editor's letter
Dear Readers,
Picking up my first Psion years ago, I realized I no longer needed a watch or a bedside alarm. But that was only the beginning. My Psion could be my address book, notepad, calendar and recorder. I saw that I could be productive always - even in those taxis stuck in Fifth Avenue traffic. I discovered the power and freedom of the Psion and I resolved to support and encourage the mobile lifestyle. I embarked on a journey.
The unveiling of Psion's new Series 5 handheld computer represents a milestone in our technological journey. With S5, we are on the launch pad to a whole new environment, one that provides portable power at an unprecedented level. In the Series 5, Psion offers a real laptop killer. Read on and you will discover the features of this phenomenal new machine. This is no toy! The Psion Series 5 is ready to handle your busy life and allow you to get the most out of it. You will use it at home and at work and everywhere in between. At New World, we're here to support your Psion mobile lifestyle.
This exciting new era seems an ideal time to present our new magazine image. We introduce the Psion Series 5 in an issue packed with information and ideas on what this new palmtop can do for you. In this issue, you'll find honest reviews of the hottest new software for the Series 5 along with software reviews for the machine you already own and love. Find out how other users have augmented their careers and pastimes with a Psion. Our experts provide hints and tips on the mobile issues that matter to you. You'll also find a complete catalogue of products for all the Psion palmtop ranges.
At New World, we are available to provide information and advice on how you can use your Psion for personal use or for the rollout of your entire company. Our Psiontists are available to help you understand the latest advances and advantages in Psion technology. Uncertain how to put your Psion to use? Got a problem that needs solving? Call us! We will analyze your individual situation and make a recommendation for you or your company.
We hope you enjoy this latest issue of The Brave New World. Welcome to the era of the Series 5.
Regards, Jonathan Glaser, New World Technologies, Inc., 'the Psion house'
NEW WORLD
110 Greene Street Suite 5100 New York NY 10012 1.800.886.4967
credits
Editor
Jonathan Glaser
Contributors
Gideon Hirschson
Ajai Khattri
Sam Potter
Elliot Motola
Shelly Freimark
Eddie Aghahowa
Cindy McGahee
Dancy Burns
Design
©1997 Hampton design
Philadelphia, PA
Photography
DPI Photography, Inc.
Norristown, PA
Hans Verleur Photography
New York, NY
Publisher
New World Technologies, Inc.
110 Greene Street
Suite 5100
New York, NY 10012
Tel: 212.941.4633
Fax: 212.274.8527
Email: psion@nwt.com
Internet: www.nwt.com
PSION
New World Technologies Warning:
The Psion Causes Addictive Computing,
Hyper-Productivity, Jealous Partners, And
May Complicate Vacations.
1

UNVEILING
THE NEW PSION SERIES 5
(handheld computer)
Imagine going from airplane flight to commercial space travel. We all know it will happen, but when? The breakthrough made by the new Psion Series 5 handheld computer is as dramatic. The S5 has literally soared through the technological barrier offering a handheld computer that will change the way we manage our lives. Everyone from the daytime user to the most powerful executive user will find it usable and indispensable.
Flip open S5 and you will realize the brilliance of its design. A "real" laptop-style keyboard glides out. We challenge you to find anything in comparison - fast and easy typing on a pocket computer is now reality. Remarkably, Psion has kept the S5 similar in weight and size to its predecessor, the Series 3. That's where the similarity ends! The huge backlit LCD screen blinks to life and reacts to the tap of a finger or a stylus pen to activate functions, navigate menus, zoom-in, and yes, you can sign your name with "digital ink." That's just the beginning. This thing is outrageous! It is a benchmark in mobile technology. From entering an address to browsing the Internet or synchronizing with a PC, the Psion S5 is everything to everyone – a simple organizer or your mobile office. At New World Technologies, we have dubbed S5 "the laptop-killer."
So how does it work?
S5's pen stylus is stored in a nifty, spring-loaded slot. Eject it with a simple flick. And don't overlook the raised base that cleverly prevents S5 from toppling over when you tap the screen. Tap, type, tap and off you go! A powerful feature is "object embedding." Another foreign concept? Simply put, you can display a sketch, graph, spreadsheet or even sound recording in any application. So why not put a picture of your employees alongside their phone numbers, or a voice recording of directions with your scheduled appointment, or a full graph in the presentation you are writing. In fact, dictaphone buttons on the outside let you record voice memos without even opening the Psion and then transfer them to another Psion via wireless infrared "point and shoot."
2
COOL
DYNAMIC
BOLD
SMOOTH
SLEEK
HI-TECH
1.800.886.4967
NEW WORLD
CompactFlash – Psion Memory disks for S5
CompactFlash Cards are a new standard of computer storage. They are inserted into your Psion Series 5 for storing add-on programs, your data, or simply to back-up data. They can read and write data at nearly instantaneous speeds, and use very little power ensuring extra-long battery life for your Psion. CompactFlash differs slightly from the Psion SSD (for Series 3). They are smaller and capable of storing more data – 2MB, 4MB & 8MB available now – 16Mb coming soon.
3

# Special Offers
from New World Technologies, Inc.

**Manufacturer's Rebate**

$50 Manufacturer's Rebate on Series 3c 1MB or 2MB
Until September 30, 1997

NWT Value
Series 3c 2MB $449 - $50 rebate = $399
Series 3c 1MB $349 - $50 rebate = $299

The correct pronunciation for "Psion" is Sigh-On.

**Internet Bundle Rebate** (only at New World Technologies, Inc.)

Series 3c 1MB – handheld computer
Travel Modem – 14.4 modem
PsiMail – Internet and Email software
PsiFax – Faxing software
(Regular Price $649)
Bundle Price $599 - $50 Rebate = $549
Save $100

(See Ordering information on page 17)

## Hints & Tips

1 Organize your Series 5 documents — save your files in subject folders.
2 Create a quick note jotter for your Series 5 — create a database with fields for notes and the date and ensure it is sorted by date.
3 Use CTRL T to switch the right-hand toolbar on your Series 5 on and off.
4 Sorting Series 3c database — remember it takes longer to search a sorted database unless it has been saved.
5 Attach notes to your S3c appointments — use Psion + to add/view small notes to your AGENDA entries.
6 Set a one-letter system password — this allows owner information to come up but prevents others playing with your Psion, and it's not too cumbersome to enter.
7 Never replace main batteries first if both main and backup are low — the backup is there to save data while you replace your main AA batteries. If the backup is low or weak, it will not do its job and you could lose your data.
8 Switching on the Status window on Series 3c — in the built-in applications and many others you can use the Ctrl Menu keystroke to switch between a large, small or no status window on the right side of your screen.
9 Switching between tasks on Series 3c — you can use Shift System to switch between all the running tasks.
Everything emboldened on your Series 3c (or underlined on your Series 5) System screen is an open file in a running application.

12

# Backup

Psion fell out skydiving into the Algarve? No problem! Your data's safe on your CompactFlash backup disk.

## NWT For Life

Every serious Psion user could figuratively say they "put out a fire or two" by having their Psion at hand. Just two months away from retirement and 20 years of service as a NYC Emergency Rescue Fire Fighter, Charles Emory and his Psion literally brave the heat!

Being a firefighter is aggressive work and Charlie's Psion has not only survived the HIGH heat of a burning building, but a lot of knocking around, and "a lot of sweat! I get drenched head to toe while in there. It's very physical, but my Psion always comes out all right." This is certainly no exaggeration as Charlie spent most of his career assigned to the busiest firehouse in the world—Ladder 33.

"This thing keeps my every move," Charlie's schedule is irregular to say the least, "which would really mess me up without my Psion. The guys who man the firehouse will come to me to see what happened on a particular day even before they check the daily journals." Beyond the usual database and agenda programs, Charlie depends on his Psion for all the fire fighting codes needed when a fire breaks in addition to various paramedic procedures and nutritional facts.

Charlie is a decorated Vietnam Veteran and has been honored with many citations of valor and heroism in his life-saving fire fighting career. When not on the fire fighting scene, you might catch him pursuing his second career as an actor!

Charles Emory—Decorated Firefighter, Actor, Psion User

### Why Do You Need to Backup?

Don't get me wrong - the Psion is rugged! I have never needed to restore my data from a backup. It is designed to roll with the blows of mobile use. However, things can go wrong. You could lose your Psion, it could be stolen, dropped in the swimming pool, chewed up by your Rotweiller. The Psion is a computer and just like all computers it needs to be backed up regularly. Let's face it, your most important information is stored on your Psion.

### Death in Dataville

I will simply not sell Psions to my friends if they don't get a backup. Why? Let me paint the picture. My friend Jack got a new Psion. He said he was in a rush and he wanted to "play" with the machine for a week or two before he invested in any extras. A few weeks turned into a few months. Then one day I got a call from Jack. He was in a state. His five-year-old took out all the batteries and he couldn't find his schedule for the week. "What are you going to do?!" he demanded. "There is nothing I can do," I responded. "You'll have to put all your data back in, Jack." "Back in?" he moaned, "From where?"

### There Are Two Ways to Backup Your Psion

1. You can backup to a PC using PsiWin, or PsiMac if you have a Macintosh. Luckily, new Series 5 owners will find the PC link and software included.
2. You can get a Flash memory card for your Psion. These cards simply slot into your Psion. Remember, don't keep the memory card in your Psion. If you lose your Psion, you've lost your backup, too.

NEW WORLD
1.800.886.4967 Check in at our web site for the latest Psion information

13

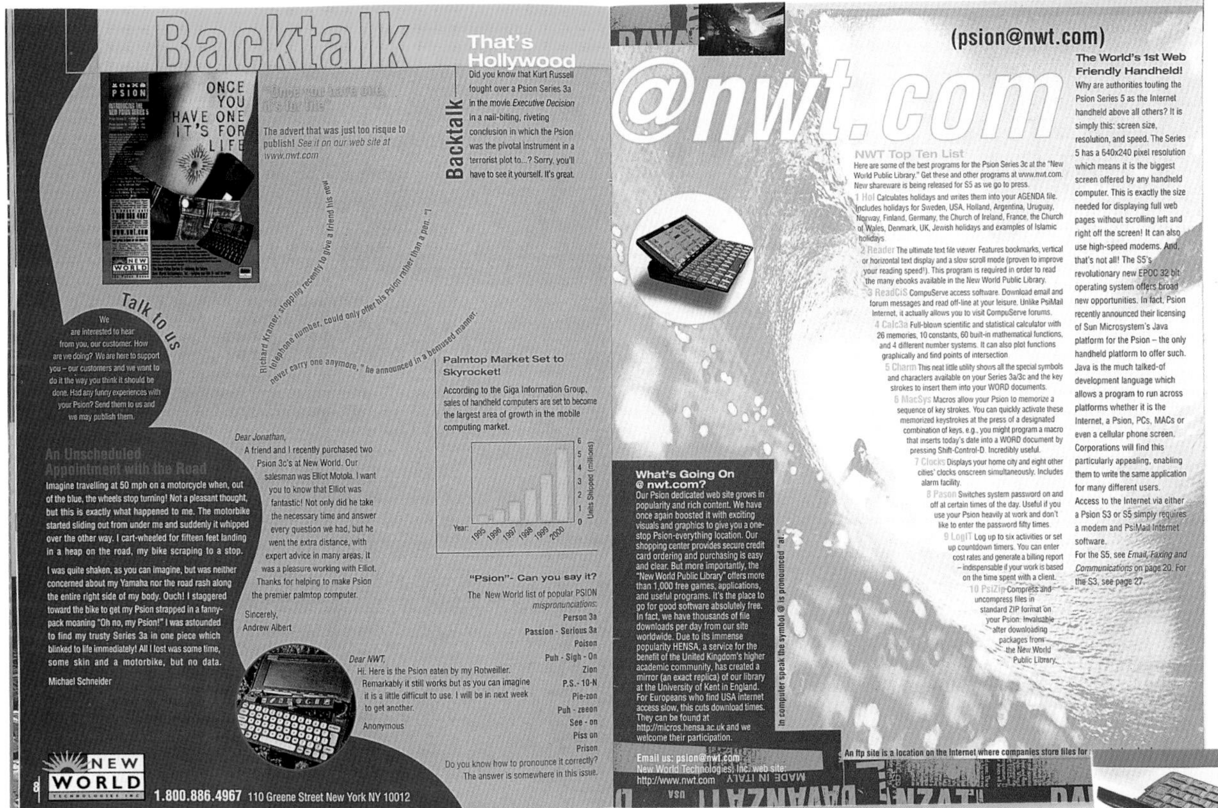

# Backtalk

ONCE YOU HAVE ONE IT'S FOR LIFE

"Once you have one, it's for life"
The advert that was just too risque to publish! See it on our web site at www.nwt.com

### That's Hollywood

Did you know that Kurt Russell fought over a Psion Series 3a in the movie *Executive Decision* in a nail-biting, riveting conclusion in which the Psion was the pivotal instrument in a terrorist plot to...? Sorry, you'll have to see it yourself. It's great.

Richard Kramer, slopping recently to give a friend his new telephone number, could only offer his Psion rather than a pen. "I never carry one anymore," he announced in a bemused manner.

### Talk to us

We are interested to hear from you, our customer. How are we doing? We are here to support you – our customers and we want to do it the way you think it should be done. Had any funny experiences with your Psion? Send them to us and we may publish them.

### An Unscheduled Appointment with the Road

Imagine travelling at 50 mph on a motorcycle when, out of the blue, the wheels stop turning! Not a pleasant thought, but this is exactly what happened to me. The motorbike started sliding out from under me and suddenly it whipped over the other way. I cart-wheeled for fifteen feet landing in a heap on the road, my bike scraping to a stop.

I was quite shaken, as you can imagine, but was neither concerned about my Yamaha nor the road rash along the entire right side of my body. Ouch! I staggered toward the bike to get my Psion strapped in a fanny-pack moaning "Oh no, my Psion!" I was astounded to find my trusty Series 3a in one piece which blinked to life immediately! All I lost was some time, some skin and a motorbike, but no data.

Michael Schneider

Dear Jonathan,
A friend and I recently purchased two Psion 3c's at New World. Our salesman was Elliot Motola. I want you to know that Elliot was fantastic! Not only did he take the necessary time and answer every question we had, but he went the extra distance, with expert advice in many areas. It was a pleasure working with Elliot. Thanks for helping to make Psion the premier palmtop computer.
Sincerely,
Andrew Albert

Dear NWT,
Hi. Here is the Psion eaten by my Rotweiller. Remarkably it still works but as you can imagine it is a little difficult to use. I will be in next week to get another.
Anonymous

### Palmtop Market Set to Skyrocket!

According to the Giga Information Group, sales of handheld computers are set to become the largest area of growth in the mobile computing market.



### "Psion" - Can you say it?

The New World list of popular PSION mispronunciations:
Person 3a
Passion - Serious 3a
Poison
Puh - Sigh - On
Zion
P.S. - 10-N
Pie-zon
Puh - zeeon
See - on
Piss on
Prison

Do you know how to pronounce it correctly? The answer is somewhere in this issue.

NEW WORLD
8 1.800.886.4967 110 Greene Street New York NY 10012

# @nwt.com

(psion@nwt.com)

### NWT Top Ten List

Here are some of the best programs for the Psion Series 3c at the "New World Public Library." Get these and other programs at www.nwt.com. New shareware is being released for S5 as we go to press.

1 Hol Calculates holidays and writes them into your AGENDA file. Includes holidays for Sweden, USA, Holland, Argentina, Uruguay, Norway, Finland, Germany, the Church of Ireland, France, the Church of Wales, Denmark, UK, Jewish holidays and examples of Islamic holidays.
2 Reader The ultimate text file viewer. Features bookmarks, vertical or horizontal text display and a slow scroll mode (proven to improve your reading speed!). This program is required in order to read the many ebooks available in the New World Public Library.
3 ReadCiS CompuServe access software. Download email and forum messages and read off-line at your leisure. Unlike PsiMail Internet, it actually allows you to visit CompuServe forums.
4 Calc3a Full-blown scientific and statistical calculator with 26 memories, 10 constants, 60 built-in mathematical functions, and 4 different number systems. It can also plot functions graphically and find points of intersection.
5 Charm This neat little utility shows all the special symbols and characters available on your Series 3a/3c and the key strokes to insert them into your WORD documents.
6 MacSys Macros allow your Psion to memorize a sequence of key strokes. You can quickly activate these memorized keystrokes at the press of a designated combination of keys, e.g., you might program a macro that inserts today's date into a WORD document by pressing Shift-Control-D. Incredibly useful.
7 Clocks Displays your home city and eight other cities' clocks onscreen simultaneously. Includes alarm facility.
8 Psion Switches system password on and off at certain times of the day. Useful if you use your Psion heavily at work and don't like to enter the password fifty times.
9 LogIt Log up to six activities or set up countdown timers. You can enter cost rates and generate a billing report – indispensable if your work is based on the time spent with a client.
10 PsiZip Compress and uncompress files in standard ZIP format on your Psion. Invaluable after downloading packages from the New World Public Library.

### The World's 1st Web Friendly Handheld!

Why are authorities touting the Psion Series 5 as the Internet handheld above all others? It is simply this: screen size, resolution, and speed. The Series 5 has a 640x240 pixel resolution which means it is the biggest screen offered by any handheld computer. This is exactly the size needed for displaying full web pages without scrolling left and right off the screen! It can also use high-speed modems. And, that's not all! The S5's revolutionary new EPOC 32 bit operating system offers broad new opportunities. In fact, Psion recently announced their licensing of Sun Microsystem's Java platform for the Psion – the only handheld platform to offer such. Java is the much talked-of development language which allows a program to run across platforms whether it is the Internet, a Psion, PCs, MACs or even a cellular phone screen. Corporations will find this particularly appealing, enabling them to write the same application for many different users.

Access to the Internet via either a Psion S3 or S5 simply requires a modem and PsiMail Internet software.

For the S5, see *Email, Faxing and Communications* on page 20. For the S3, see page 27.

### What's Going On @ nwt.com?

Our Psion dedicated web site grows in popularity and rich content. We have once again boosted it with exciting visuals and graphics to give you a one-stop Psion-everything location. Our shopping center provides secure credit card ordering and purchasing is easy and clear. But more importantly, the "New World Public Library" offers more than 1,000 free games, applications, and useful programs. It's the place to go for good software absolutely free. In fact, we have thousands of file downloads per day from our site worldwide. Due to its immense popularity HENSA, a service for the benefit of the United Kingdom's higher academic community, has created a mirror (an exact replica) of our library at the University of Kent in England. For Europeans who find USA internet access slow, this cuts download times. They can be found at http://micros.hensa.ac.uk and we welcome their participation.

Email us: psion@nwt.com
New World Technologies, Inc. web site: http://www.nwt.com

In computer speak the symbol @ is pronounced "at"

An ftp site is a location on the Internet where companies store files for ...

The Brave New world
NEW WORLD
no.9

**Palmtop Computers**

NEW WORLD CL: New World Technologies D: Stacie Hampton P: Dpi Photography / Hans Verleur Photography
CW: New World Technologies DF: Naked Sheep USA 1997 *SIZE: 280×217*

## Electronics & Home Products

ADRAY'S CL: Adray's AD, D: Steve Trapero DF: Steve Trapero Design USA 1992 *SIZE: 280×215*

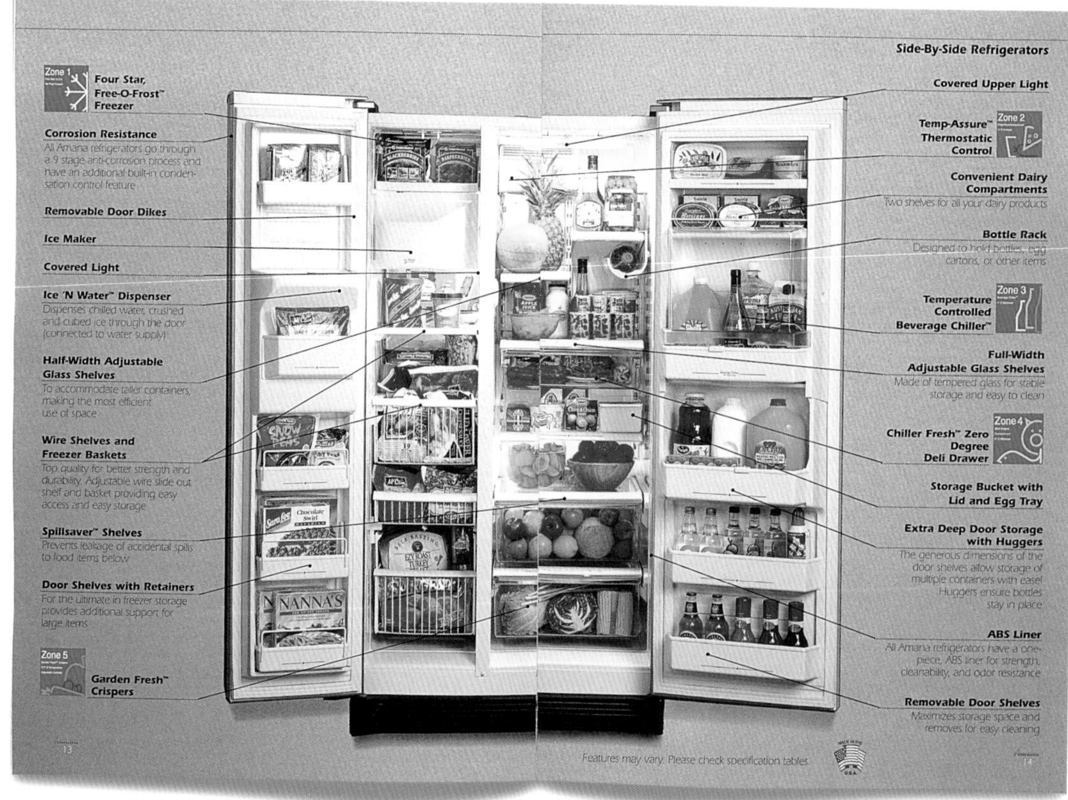

## Refrigerators

AMANA CL: Amana Appliances AD, D: Jake Vande Weerd P: French Studios
CW: Muna Matthews DF: JW Morton & Associates USA 1997 *SIZE: 295×210*

# food

food & beverage

Tobacco

## Refreshment FOR HOT SUMMER DAYS

Quick: put up a hammock (or find another good retreat), kick off your sandals, and settle back with a satisfying mug of Starbucks *Gazebo Blend*™. @ Now *this* is summer. @ The natural sweetness of sun-ripened fruit is here. And a floral aroma, fresh as a garden in bloom. @ From no fewer than six East African nations we search year-round for the right combination of sparkling brightness, sweet flavors, and just a touch of wildness. @ And this year, thanks to superb crops and our growing friendships in the coffee world, *Gazebo Blend*™ is better than ever. @ Enjoy it hot. Or chill it down in any number of iced beverages (we've included a few favorite recipes in the catalog's center...) @ But do make sure to enjoy it today. @ Because *Gazebo Blend*™ is available only through Labor Day. And then, like summer itself, it's gone.

*Gazebo Blend™ has arrived! And what could be more convenient than ordering our coffee by phone?*

*Also in this issue: our collection of baked goods (page 5); great new gift ideas for weddings, graduations, Father's Day, and more (on the inside back cover); and easy iced beverage recipes to save (in the catalog's center).*

## EXCLUSIVE DELIGHTFUL

**A. NEW GAZEBO BLEND™ DAY AND NIGHT SET**
Presenting *Gazebo Blend*™ ... the essence of summer. Out of Africa come the tangy, wild flavors that make this coffee equally refreshing hot or over ice. For summer nights, *Decaf Gazebo Blend*™ ... medium-bodied ... intensely aromatic ... complex and fruity. And for enjoying both, the 15 oz. hand-painted Italian Bellini Solar and Bellini Moon mugs that are ours exclusively. Two 1/2 lbs.

$27.95 587X *Gazebo Blend*™ Day and Night Set

**B. HAND-PAINTED ITALIAN STORAGE JAR**
A sunny work of art for your counter, and a great way to keep coffee fresh. Each is individually made and hand-painted. Unique ... artful ... one-of-a-kind.

$29.95 108332 Bellini Solar Storage Jar, holds 1/2 lb.

**C. EXPLORE THE WORLD**
Twice the adventure of our other samplers. Featuring elegant *Guatemala Antigua*, traditional *Arabian Mocha Java*, exotic *Sumatra*, full-bodied *Estate Java*, bright, rich *Kenya*, hearty *Yukon Blend*®, *House Blend*, our most popular coffee; and for summer, *Gazebo Blend*™, with its crisp, sweet taste. Also available: our exclusive Blends of Summer Sampler, with *Gazebo Blend*™, *House Blend*, *Yukon Blend*®, and *Arabian Mocha Java*.

$32.95 DSSX Deluxe World Sampler, eight 1/2 lb. bags
$16.95 BLSX Blends of Summer Sampler (not shown), four 1/2 lb. bags

1

## STOCK UP ON SUMMER'S BRIGHTEST MUGS

**A. DECAF COLOMBIA**
Smooth and mellow. Very light-bodied. (Swiss Water Process)

$8.95/lb. DCO

**B. FRESH, COLORFUL, HAND-PAINTED IN ITALY.**
New from Italy, these whimsical mugs are made of sturdy stoneware and painted by hand. On them, the freshest fruits and vegetables in the garden!

*Sberna Garden Mugs, 16 oz. each*
$9.95 108583 Carrot
$9.95 108580 Tomato
$9.95 108579 Strawberry
$9.95 108581 Eggplant
$34.95 840712 Sberna Garden Mugs, Set of 4 (save $1.20 per mug!)

**C. COLOMBIA NARIÑO SUPREMO**
Unusually full-bodied. A unique walnut-like flavor. And so full of the flavor that made Colombian coffee famous, we negotiated the rights to the entire supply.

$7.95/lb. COL

**D. THE INDISPENSABLE COMMUTER MUG**
Just the thing for your morning drive. With a low center-of-gravity for stability. A non-skid base. And a drink-thru lid that twists securely into place. 16 oz.

$12.95 107151 Blue/Silver Logo Commuter Chub Mug
223587 White Logo Commuter Chub Mug (not shown)
$15.95 100469 World Stamp Commuter Mug

4

## OUR COFFEE MENU

**TO ASSIST YOU** with your coffee selections, we've grouped our coffees from mild to more complex to assertive. In each category, our exclusive blends are listed before our high-grown *arabica* varietals. Save this handy guide to refer to when selecting all your Starbucks coffee.

**STARBUCKS FRESH-ROASTED COFFEES**

| Coffee Variety | Description | Price/Code |
|---|---|---|
| **LIVELY IMPRESSIONS** *Bright, Mild, and Welcoming* | | |
| House Blend | Our most popular coffee...lively and well-balanced | $7.65/lb. HOU |
| Viennese Blend | Great with dessert...lively, with a smoky finish | $7.95/lb. VIE |
| Kona* | Smooth and gentle, as mild as a trade wind | $13.95/lb. KON |
| Mexico Altura | Livelier than Kona, with a slightly nutty flavor | $6.75/lb. MEX |
| Costa Rica Tres Rios | Lively, fragrant, and tangy, with a morning brightness | $7.55/lb. COS |
| Panama La Florentina* | Smooth and bright, with caramelly richness | $7.85/lb. PAN |
| Ethiopia Sidamo* | From coffee's birthplace...sweet and floral | $7.75/lb. SID |
| Ethiopia Yergacheffe* | Medium-bodied and sweet, with a delicate floral aroma | $7.75/lb. YRG |
| **RICH TRADITIONS** *Deep, Complex, and Satisfying* | | |
| Yukon Blend® | Deep, earthy, and smooth...Latin America meets Indonesia | $7.75/lb. YUK |
| Caffè Verona® (80/20 Blend) | Rich and creamy, accented by a subtle sweetness | $7.85/lb. VER |
| Espresso Roast | A Starbucks classic...caramelly sweet and spicy | $7.75/lb. ESP |
| Italian Roast | Slightly darker than Espresso...sturdy and sweet | $7.75/lb. ITA |
| Guatemala Antigua | Complex, elegant, and refined...hints of cocoa and spice | $7.85/lb. GUA |
| Colombia Nariño Supremo | Unusually full bodied, with a unique walnutty flavor | $7.95/lb. COL |
| New Guinea Peaberry | Supremely well-balanced...an under appreciated treasure | $6.95/lb. NGA |
| Kenya | Bright, rich and sweet...a hint of black currant | $7.85/lb. KEN |
| **BOLD EXPRESSIONS** *Diverse, Distinctive, and Intriguing* | | |
| Gold Coast Blend® | The ultimate blend...complex, sweet and intriguing | $8.95/lb. GCO |
| Arabian Mocha Java | Coffee's first blend...powerful Java and exotic Mocha | $9.95/lb. AMJ |
| French Roast | Our darkest roast...smoky and intense | $7.75/lb. FRE |
| Arabian Mocha Sanani | Wild and untamed...exotically spicy, mysteriously sweet | $13.95/lb. SAN |
| Ethiopia Harrar* | Very wild and exotic, with berry like flavor and aroma | $8.95/lb. HAR |
| Estate Java | Full bodied, powerful, and peppery | $7.75/lb. JAV |
| Sumatra | Our most popular varietal...syrupy, deep and earthy | $7.95/lb. SUM |
| Sulawesi | A rare treasure...smooth, buttery, woodsy and very satisfying | $10.25/lb. SUL |
| **DECAFFEINATED CLASSICS** *Rich Flavors, Rewarding Character* | | |
| Decaf House Blend | Light and lively, with well-rounded flavors | $7.95/lb. DHB |
| Decaf Viennese Blend | Hearty, sweet, and slightly smoky...great with dessert | $7.95/lb. DVB |
| Decaf Espresso Roast | Smooth and spicy, with caramelly sweetness | $7.95/lb. DRO |
| Decaf Mocca Java (SWP) | A delicate blend of Java and mild, sweet Ethiopia | $9.35/lb. DMJ |
| Decaf Colombia (SWP) | Smooth and mellow, very light bodied | $8.95/lb. DCO |
| Decaf Guatemala* | Elegant and sophisticated, with hints of cocoa and spice | $8.35/lb. DGU |
| Decaf Sumatra | Our most flavorful decaf...thick, smooth, and earthy | $8.35/lb. DSU |

**Please call about availability when ordering*

To order these coffees individually or in groups, call:
**1-800-782-7282 (1-800-STARBUC)**
For more detailed descriptions of each of our coffees, please call and we'll be happy to send you our "The World of Coffee" brochure at no charge.

*Starbucks Summer Catalog 1994*

# Coffee Bean Roaster & Specialty Foods

STARBUCKS COFFEE CL: Starbucks Coffee Company AD, D: Jack Anderson D: Julie Lock / Leslie MacInnes / Julie Keenan P: Darrell Peterson I: Julia LaPine CW: Pamela Mason-Davey DF: Hornall Anderson Design Works USA 1993 *SIZE: 267×228*

## Coffee Bean Roaster & Specialty Foods

STARBUCKS COFFEE CL: Starbucks Coffee Company AD, D: Jack Anderson D: Julie Lock / Leslie MacInnes / Julie Keenan P: Darrell Peterson I: Julia LaPine CW: Pamela Mason-Davey DF: Hornall Anderson Design Works USA 1992 *SIZE: 267×156*

A PASSION FOR CHOCOLATE

**✱ A. MOUTH-WATERING MELTAWAYS**
Lovingly made by hand, for Starbucks. Lusciously, concocted of dark and milk chocolates – from fine *chocolatiers*, of course. And so superbly blended, their smooth, creamy, truffle-like centers seem to just... melt away.

*Each individually wrapped. Each package 6 oz.*

| | | |
|---|---|---|
| **$22.95** | 840580 | Set of all four mouth-watering flavors, 24 oz. total |
| **$5.95** | 106904 | Mint Espresso Meltaways made with zesty peppermint oil |
| | 102814 | Raspberry Meltaways with the true taste of ripe berries |
| | 106906 | Toffee Meltaways with chunks of buttery toffee |
| | 100324 | Espresso Meltaways featuring our own roasty espresso |

**B. CHOCOLATE-COVERED CONFECTIONS**
On the outside, the finest of chocolate. On the inside, your choice of delicious surprises. Sweet Bing cherries drizzled with milk chocolate... Richly roasted *Sumatra* beans coated with fine white chocolate... Smoky, dark *French Roast* beans enrobed in dark chocolate... A dusting of confectioner's sugar over buttery toffee and golden almonds.

| | | |
|---|---|---|
| **$19.95** | 104191 | All Four Confection Rounds, 31.5 oz. total |
| **$5.50** | 103139 | Milk Chocolate/Toffee Almonds, 8 oz. |
| | 103140 | Milk Chocolate/Bing Cherries, 8.5 oz. |
| | ✱ 103144 | White Chocolate/*Sumatra* Beans, 7.5 oz. |
| | ✱ 103145 | Dark Chocolate/*French Roast* Beans, 7.5 oz. |

THE RICHEST REWARDS

**✱ C. STARBUCKS CHOCOLATE BARS**
Blended with a little of the unexpected:
– orange peel, almond, and bittersweet chocolate
– chewy cherries and pecans with milk chocolate
– white chocolate studded with chocolate-covered raisins
– luscious milk chocolate and sweet toffee chunks

**$7.75** 106975 Starbucks Chocolate Bars, Set of four, 10 oz.

**✱ D. THE HEART'S DELIGHT GIFT SET**
A passionate pairing of coffee and chocolate. One pound of creamy, rich *Caffè Verona® (80/20 Blend)* together with espresso and toffee meltaways, orange and toffee chocolate bars, and chocolate-covered cherries and almonds.

| | | |
|---|---|---|
| **$32.95** | 574X | The Heart's Delight Gift Set |
| **$7.85**/lb. | VER | Rich, buttery *Caffè Verona® (80/20 Blend)* |



4 CLOSED MEMORIAL DAY

1-800-STARBUC 5

The Art of Brewing Great Coffee: Measuring

*Grind... fresh cold water brought to the boil... immediate enjoyment – all are important in brewing the best possible cup. But first and most essential is using enough coffee.*

*To determine the ideal proportion, first measure the water capacity of your brewer with a measuring cup. Then divide the total number of ounces you've figured by six. This will establish the "magic number" of Starbucks scoops you'll need to brew a fantastically flavorful pot.*

*The simple rule is 2 tablespoons of ground coffee – or one Starbucks scoop – per 6 oz. cup.*

TO ORDER CALL 1-800-STARBUC
(1-800-782-7282)
Special Holiday Hours 11/15 - 12/22
Mon. - Fri. 5am - 10pm
Sat. & Sun. 6am - 8pm (Pac. Time)

FOR THE HOLIDAYS AND EVERY MORNING

**✱ STORAGE FROM STARBUCKS**
Even though Starbucks coffee is rushed from our roasters to special flavor-locked bags within two hours, freshness begins fading the moment the vacuum seal is broken. Oxygen, light, heat and moisture are coffee's enemies. These special storage jars are your best defense. They're made of high-quality stoneware. With sturdy stainless steel clasps that lock down the lid airtight.

*Small jar for 1/2 lb.*
**$24.95** 330980 Green
**$19.95** 421766 White

*Large jar for 1 lb.*
**$29.95** 330981 Green
**$24.95** 427470 White

**THE CLASSIC FRENCH PRESS**
Of all the ways to brew coffee at home, we prefer the plunger method. The coffee is more flavorful... no papery-filter taste in the way. Just a full-bodied, fragrant cup to enjoy. The Bodum Chambord of course, is the Ferrari of French Presses. Stylish. Chrome-plated. Elegant and authentic. Grind – Coarse.

**$49.00** 330508 3-cup (12 oz.)
**$59.00** 330509 8-cup (32 oz.)
**$69.00** 330510 12-cup (48 oz.)

**SIMPLE. RELIABLE. THE BODUM BISTRO.**
Don't let its affordability fool you: the Bistro possesses all the coffee brewing prowess of any French Press. Simply pour in coarse grounds, add hot water, wait four minutes (no more, no less), and push. The plunger's fine mesh screen filters downward, leaving the grounds at the bottom and you with a perfectly brewed cup of coffee. Grind – Coarse.

**$17.50** 447358 3-cup (12 oz.)
**$19.95** 447366 8-cup (32 oz.)
**$29.95** 447374 12-cup (48 oz.)

**✱ BLADE GRINDING, RE-DEFINED**
One of those neat, efficient tools that solves, once and for all, the consistency problem (where some beans get ground to powder, while others are barely chipped...) The grind chamber actually slopes here, so all the beans get whizzed through the blades evenly. And your grind – be it anything from coarse to fine – ends up uniform throughout. All this for only $19.95.

**$19.95** Starbucks Blade Grinder
224205 White
224208 Black

**BRISK BREW**
A wonderful little workhorse that packs into a briefcase, sets up easily, and brews an 8 oz. cup of delicious drip coffee in a matter of minutes. The basket holds the right proportions. The water gets hot enough, fast. And at 6 1/4" x 4 1/2," it's the perfect travel companion. Grind – Fine.

**$32.95** 106450
Brisk Brew Coffeemaker

*The Brisk Brew, all packed up and ready to go.*

11

## Coffee Bean Roaster & Specialty Foods

STARBUCKS COFFEE CL: Starbucks Coffee Company AD, D: Jack Anderson D: Julie Lock / Leslie MacInnes / Julie Keenan P: Darrell Peterson I: Julia LaPine CW: Pamela Mason-Davey DF: Hornall Anderson Design Works USA 1993 *SIZE: 267×156*

**Tea & Coffee**

WHITTARD OF CHELSEA CL: Whittard Of Chelsea CD, AD: Nigel Warren D: Carole Pilling
P: Oliver Stothert DF: Acrobat UK 1998 *SIZE: 297×210*

## Chocolates

GODIVA CL: Cambell Japan, Inc. AD: Yukiko Mase D: Franklin Labbé P: Naoko Hiroishi CW: Seiko Nagamatsu
DF: Desgrippes Gobe & Associates Japan 1998 *SIZE: 210×100*

DESIGN YOUR OWN

*Our hand-crafted chocolate pieces are always special. Even more special, is an Ethel M Chocolate assortment hand-selected by you. Choose from our array of fresh, mouthwatering chocolates. Whether to keep or to give, a Design-Your-Own assortment always has just the right pieces. Along with, of course, your own special touch.*

In each pound, you can choose up to four varieties of chocolate. Milk Chocolate and Dark Chocolate versions each count as one variety. For example, you could get a one pound box containing Almond Butter Krisp (one variety), Lemon Creams (one variety), Macadamia Nut Clusters in Milk Chocolate (one variety) and Macadamia Nut Clusters in Dark Chocolate (one variety).

** If your selections include Liqueur Creams, please see the important note on page 6 for regulations regarding the shipping of Liqueur Creams.*

**Design Your Own Assortment**
**1 lb. 69001* $14.50**
**2 lbs. 69021* $26.50**

16 *To Order, Call Toll Free: 1-800-638-4356*

## Chocolates

ETHEL M CHOCOLATE CL: Ethel M Chocolate CD, AD, D: Jose' A. Serrano P: Carl Vanderschuit
CW: John Kuraoka DF: Mires Design Inc. USA 1995 *SIZE: 238×178*

Even though it's possible to "declare" a vintage almost any year from Grade A/B vineyards, Martinez' winemaker is exacting. Martinez Vintage Porto must not only measure up, in a series of blind tastings, to official approval, "it has to be the best the vineyard can produce."
VINTAGE PORTO IS what happens when EVERYTHING – SUN, grapes, rain, and the winemakers' skill – come together just right. Less than two percent of all Porto produced becomes this "best of the best." And given that their Vintage Portos are the standards by which great houses are judged, Martinez is proud to present:
Martinez "Master's Reserve" takes its name from the honor held by Charles Gassiot, the second Gassiot to work at Martinez. In 1894, he was named "Master" of the Vintners' Livery Company in London, in charge of tasting and rating the fine wines of the day. Master's Reserve, with its deep ruby color, full body, and hint of dried plums, is a Porto of which we are sure he'd approve.
MARTINEZ VINTAGE PORTO 1985
Wine Spectator 92 point rating, Decanter Magazine ★★★★
Deep black-red in color; rich, concentrated, and fruity.
MARTINEZ VINTAGE PORTO 1991
Wine Spectator 91 point rating, Decanter Magazine ★★★★
A deep perfume of cedar, cassis, and plum; rich, balanced, supple.
Fourth Place, International Wine Challenge
MARTINEZ VINTAGE PORTO 1994
Wine Spectator 95 point rating
"A classy young port, full-bodied and brimming with fruit flavor and silky, fine tannins that kick in on the finish…A subtle young wine that takes you by surprise." – James Suckling, Wine Spectator
Wine Spectator, Top 100 wines of 1997
MARTINEZ
MASTER'S RESERVE
PORT

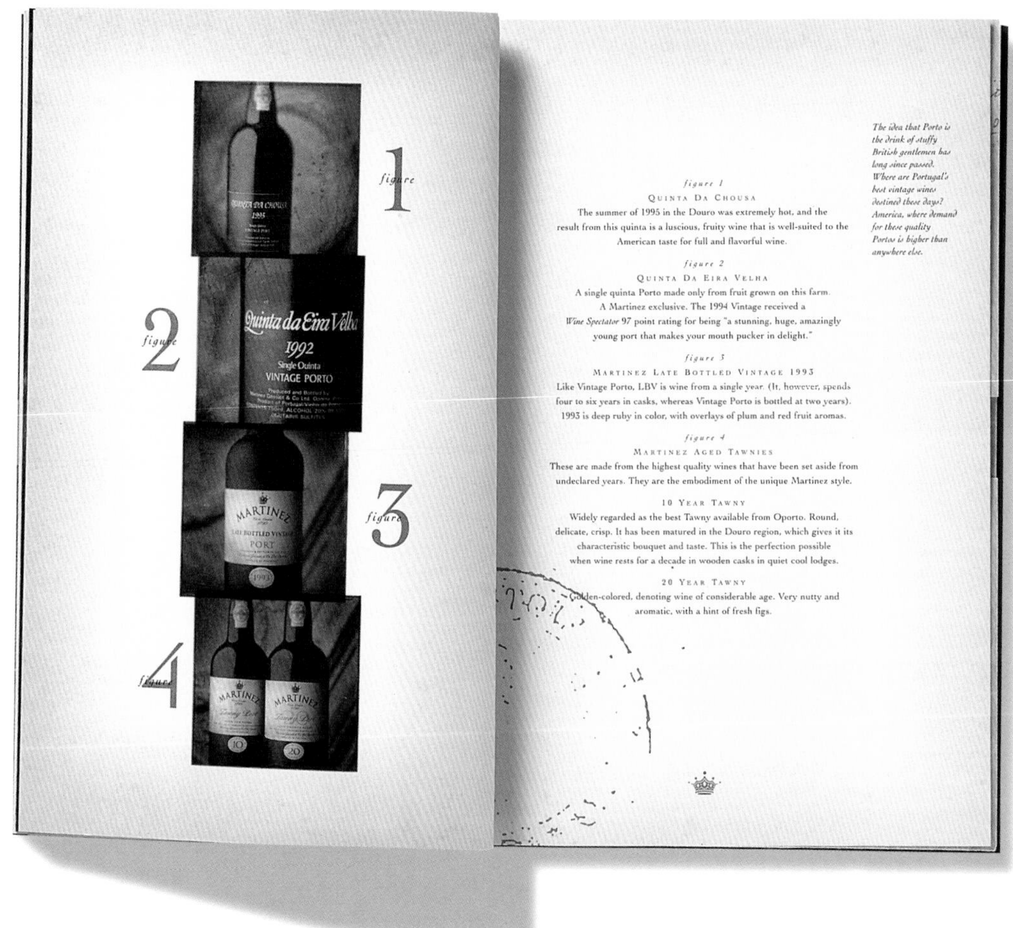

figure 1
figure 2
figure 3
figure 4
Quinta da Eira Velha
1992
Single Quinta
VINTAGE PORTO
figure 1
QUINTA DA CHOUSA
The summer of 1995 in the Douro was extremely hot, and the result from this quinta is a luscious, fruity wine that is well-suited to the American taste for full and flavorful wine.
figure 2
QUINTA DA EIRA VELHA
A single quinta Porto made only from fruit grown on this farm. A Martinez exclusive. The 1994 Vintage received a Wine Spectator 97 point rating for being "a stunning, huge, amazingly young port that makes your mouth pucker in delight."
figure 3
MARTINEZ LATE BOTTLED VINTAGE 1993
Like Vintage Porto, LBV is wine from a single year. (It, however, spends four to six years in casks, whereas Vintage Porto is bottled at two years). 1993 is deep ruby in color, with overlays of plum and red fruit aromas.
figure 4
MARTINEZ AGED TAWNIES
These are made from the highest quality wines that have been set aside from undeclared years. They are the embodiment of the unique Martinez style.
10 YEAR TAWNY
Widely regarded as the best Tawny available from Oporto. Round, delicate, crisp. It has been matured in the Douro region, which gives it its characteristic bouquet and taste. This is the perfection possible when wine rests for a decade in wooden casks in quiet cool lodges.
20 YEAR TAWNY
Golden-colored, denoting wine of considerable age. Very nutty and aromatic, with a hint of fresh figs.
The idea that Porto is the drink of stuffy British gentlemen has long since passed. Where are Portugal's best vintage wines destined these days? America, where demand for these quality Portos is higher than anywhere else.

## Wines & Ports

MARTINEZ CL: Stimson Lane AD, D: Jack Anderson / Lisa Cerveny D: Heidi Favour / Mary Chin Hutchison
P: Tom Collicott Map Illustrator: John Fretz Calligrapher: Nancy Stentz CW: Pamela Mason Davey
DF: Hornall Anderson Design Works, Inc. USA 1998 *SIZE: 242×181*

MARTINEZ
Est. 1790
PORTO
MASTERS
478329
CHOUSA
ONE HUNDRED years before the Bordeaux REGION WAS DEMARCATED in France, a decree in
Portugal went out: the land sixty miles inland from Oporto, measuring sixty-seven miles long and at most 15.6 miles wide, would mark the exact boundaries of the Douro region, and strict measures to insure its wines' authenticity were set. Quality was to be intensely protected; only wines produced in the valley's three districts could be called Porto. And of those three growing districts, the Upper Douro, east of Tua, was considered finest of all. It's here, in sunny south-facing vineyards on steep rocky slopes, that the Port house of Martinez Gassiot was established in 1790.
YOU NEVER KNOW, one year to the next, WHEN THE DAY WILL come: when the grapes
are exploding with flavor; when a summer's noon carries a hint of autumn in the air. Each grower judges his vines and the weather, then decides the precise moment to pick. Grapes are gathered by hand in baskets, then gently crushed and fermented. In 1820, a particularly rich, concentrated harvest made for a difficult vinification and unusually sweet wines. The British response was extraordinary! And so what began as an anomaly is now the norm. Throughout the Douro, wineries arrest fermentation early by adding grape brandy, and it's this that gives Porto such sweetness, color, and backbone.

## Wines

VICHON CL: Vichon Napa Valley AD: Bill Cahan D: Sharrie Brooks P: Tony Stromberg / John Casado / David Peterson / Daniel Arsenault
CW: Rich Hinkle DF: Cahan & Associates USA 1996 *SIZE: 236×101*

## Home-made Agricultural Products

FILAK CL: Janez Filak AD, D: Žare Kerin P: Janez Pukšič CW: Janez Filak DF: Kompas Design D. D. Slovenia 1997 *SIZE: 130×94*

## Catering Service

ARTI-SJOK CL: Arti-Sjok D: Marty Schoutsen P: Carine Bex / Studio Reinout vd Bergh DF: Opera Ontwerpers Netherlands 1997 *SIZE: 120×109*

## Delicatessen Foods

CAL BLE CL: Tetraktys CD, D, I: Ramon Enrich AD, D: Lluis Jubert P: Ramon Pallarés CW: Tetraktis DF: Espai Grafic
Spain 1996 *SIZE: 299×221*

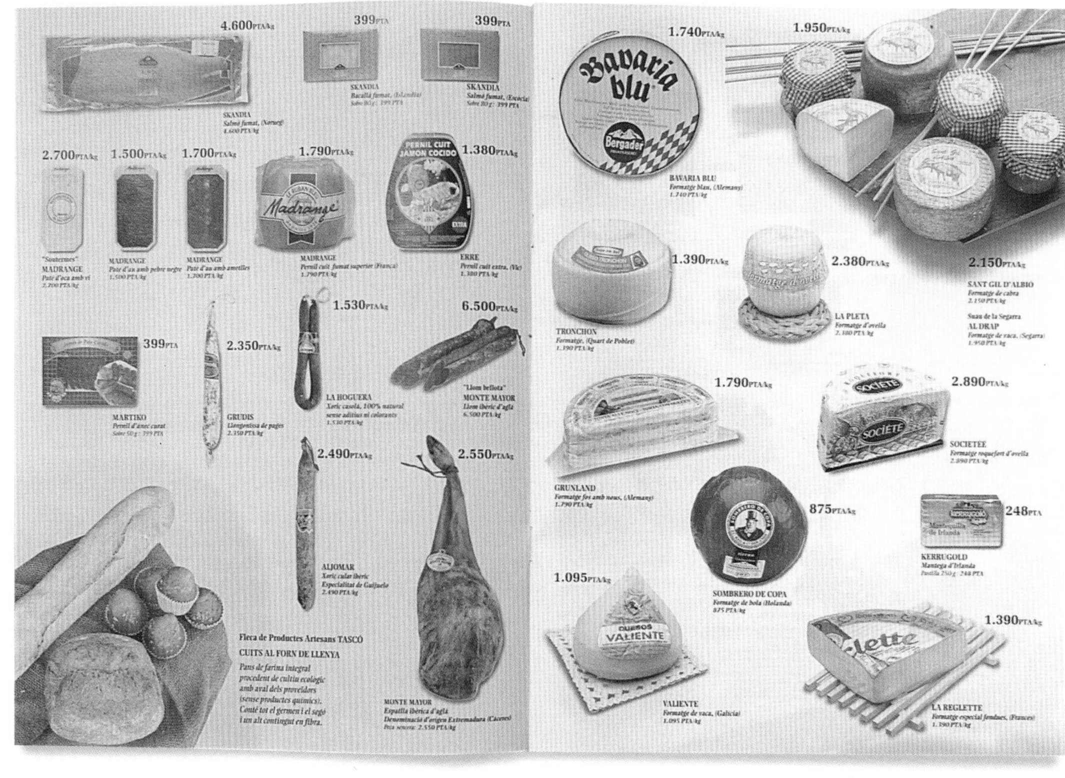

## Fruits & Foods

TAKANO CL: Takano Co. Ltd. CD: Masaaki Miula, Plus1 D: Youichi Matsushita, Plus1 P: Osamu Sakou, Jam Studio
CW: Misako Morimoto Japan 1998 *SIZE: 297×220*

## Natural Organic Food Products

ORGANIC GARDENS CL: Organic Gardens CD, AD, D, I: James Wai Mo Leung AD, D: Teddy Lam P: Keith Bradley CW: Alice Wong / Astor Kwong DF: Genesis Advertising Co. Hong Kong 1996 *SIZE: 210×149*

## Pizza Home Delivery

PIZZA-LA CL: Four Seeds Corporation AD, D: Yasushi Abe P: Takashi Oyama CW: Kensei Mitsuoka Japan 1998 *SIZE: 209×153*

TOBACCO
THE SPIRIT OF QUALITY
COLLECTION
PREMIER CRU
KENTUCKY BIRD
CUBA CIGA
STYRKE & K
TOBAKSNYDELSE
– LIVSKVALITET I HVERDAGEN
MY OWN BLEND
HISTORIEN BAG MY OWN BLEND
STANDARDBLANDINGER

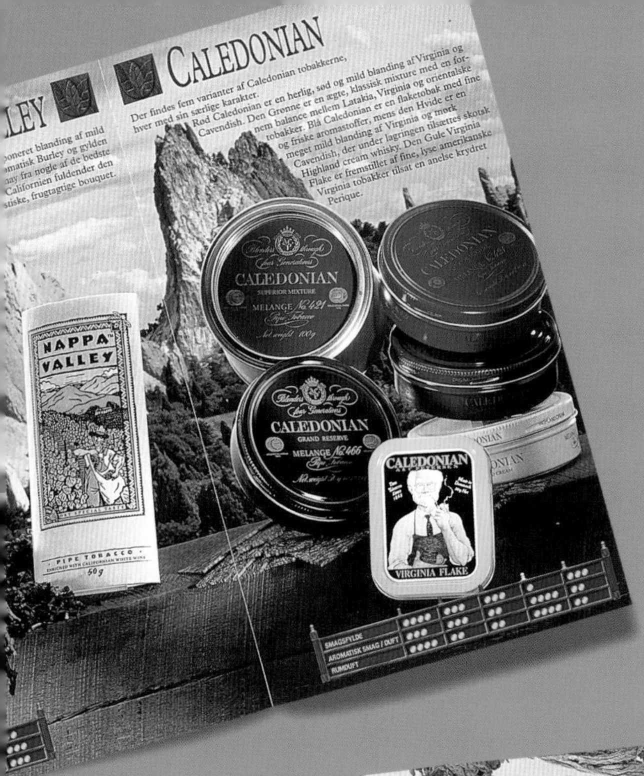

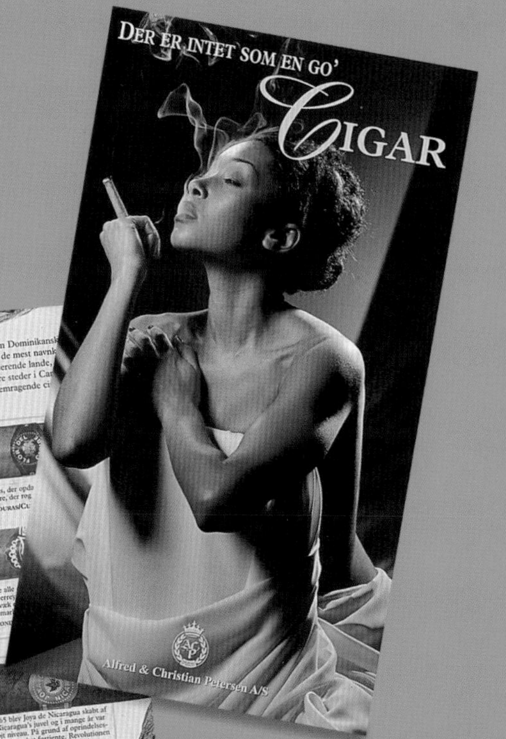

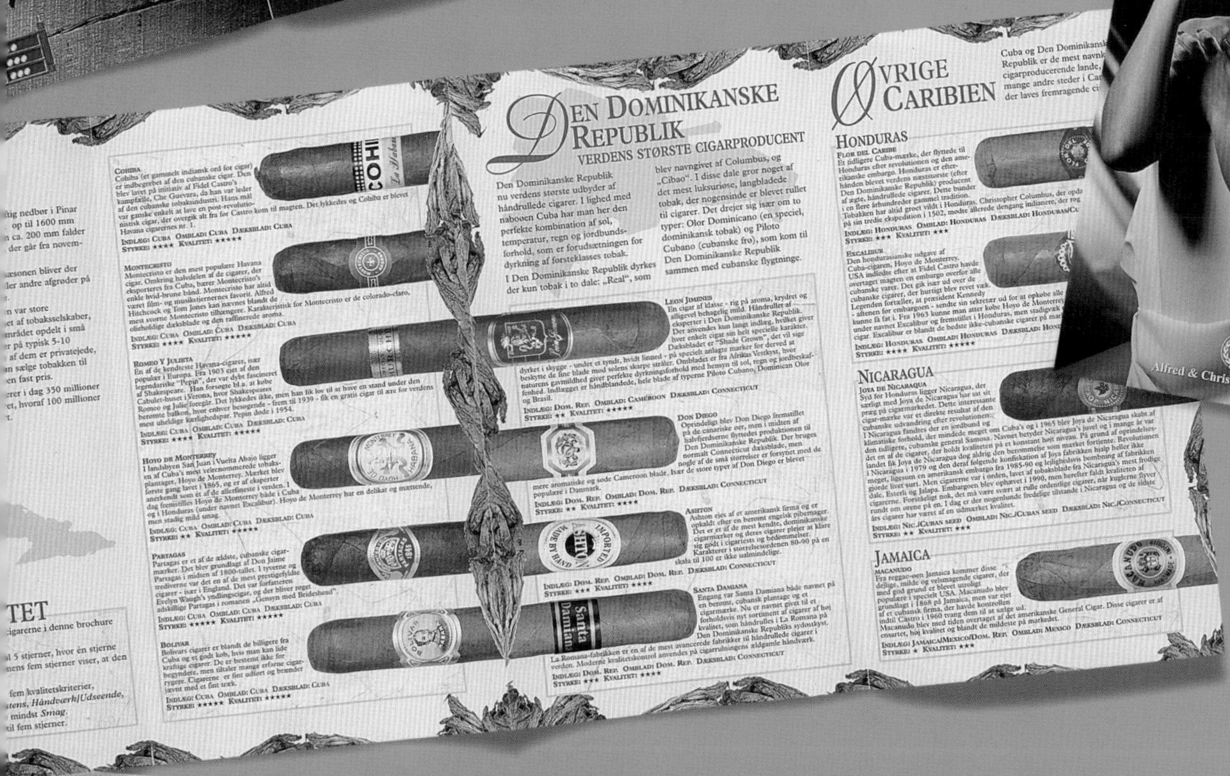

CALEDONIAN

DEN DOMINIKANSKE REPUBLIK
VERDENS STØRSTE CIGARPRODUCENT

ØVRIGE CARIBIEN

HONDURAS

NICARAGUA

JAMAICA

DER ER INTET SOM EN GO' CIGAR

Alfred & Christian Petersen A/S

**Tobacco**

TOBACCO COLLECTION CL: Alfred & Christian Petersen A/S CD, CW: Karsten Jeppesen AD: Torben Nielsen P: Svend Pedersen DF: Dybdahl Reklame Denmark 1998 *SIZE: 245×140*

**Tobacco**

CIGAR CL: Alfred & Christian Petersen A/S CD, CW: Karsten Jeppesen AD: Torben Nielsen P: Svend Pedersen DF: Dybdahl Reklame Denmark 1997 *SIZE: 245×140*

**Tobacco**

MY OWN BLEND CL: Alfred & Christian Petersen A/S CD, CW: Karsten Jeppesen AD: Torben Nielsen P: Svend Pedersen DF: Dybdahl Reklame Denmark 1997 *SIZE: 245×141*

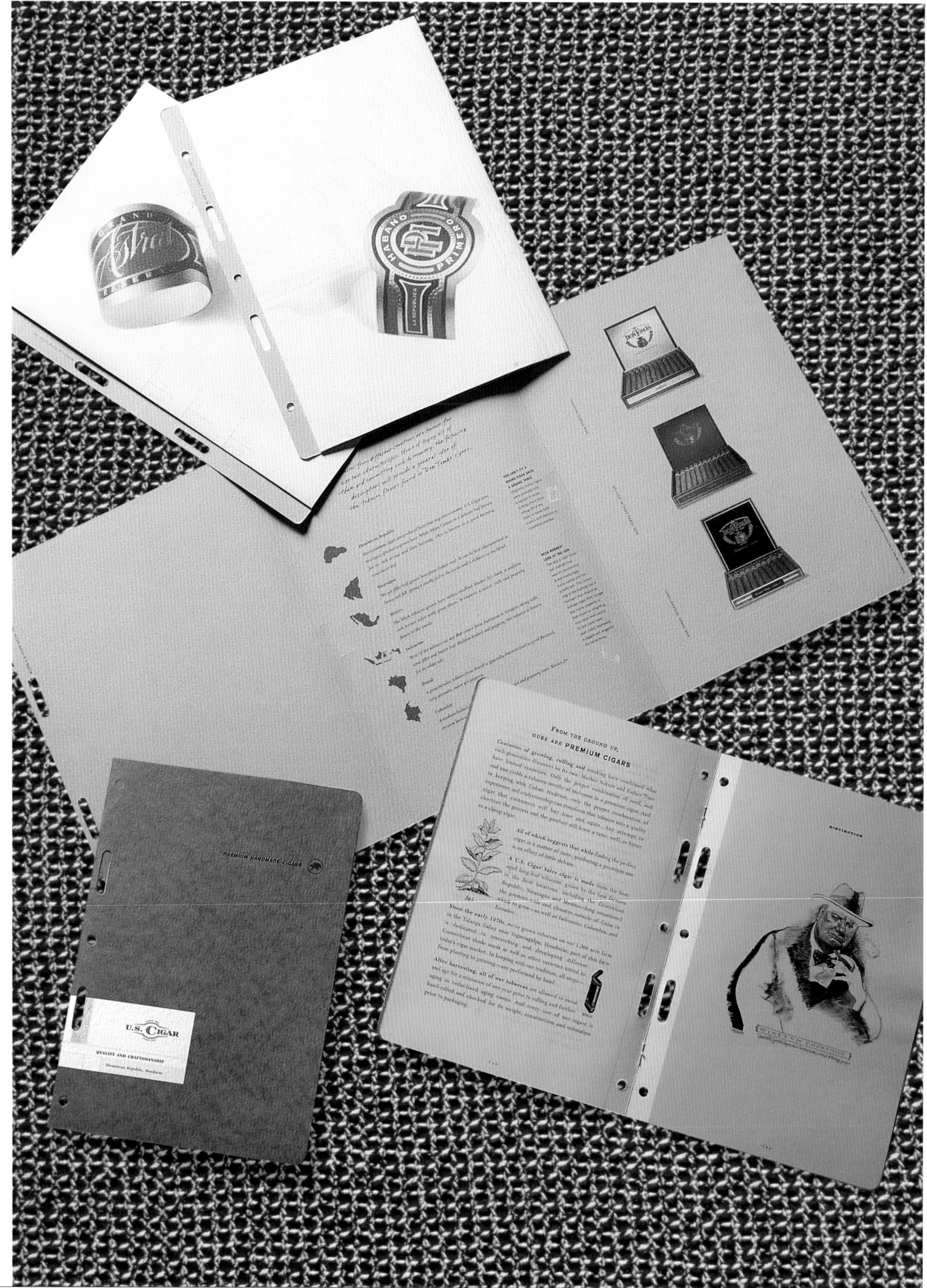


## Cigars and Tobacco Products

US CIGAR CL: US Cigar AD: Jack Anderson AD, D: Larry Anderson D: Mary Hermes / Mike Calkins / Michael Brugman P: David Emmite I: John Fretz / Jack Unruh / Bill Halinann CW: John Frazier DF: Hornall Anderson Design Works, Inc. USA 1998 *SIZE: 254×179, 297×216*

# fashion

cosmetics & body care

accessories

apparel

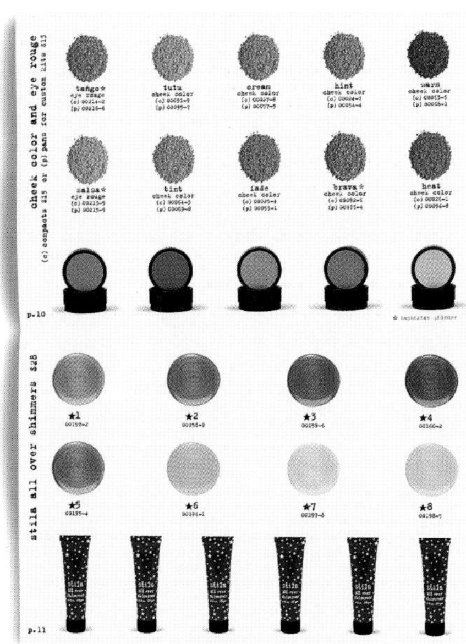

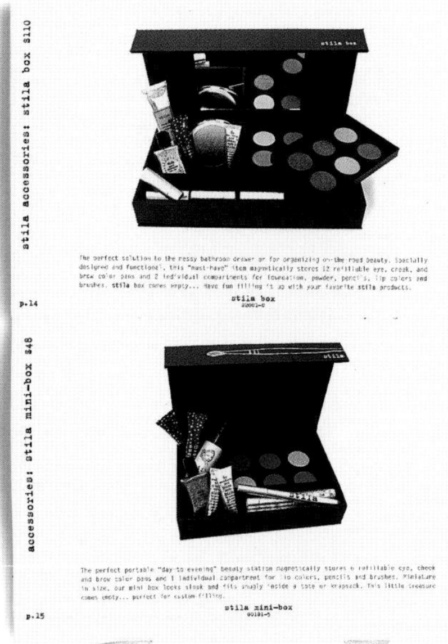

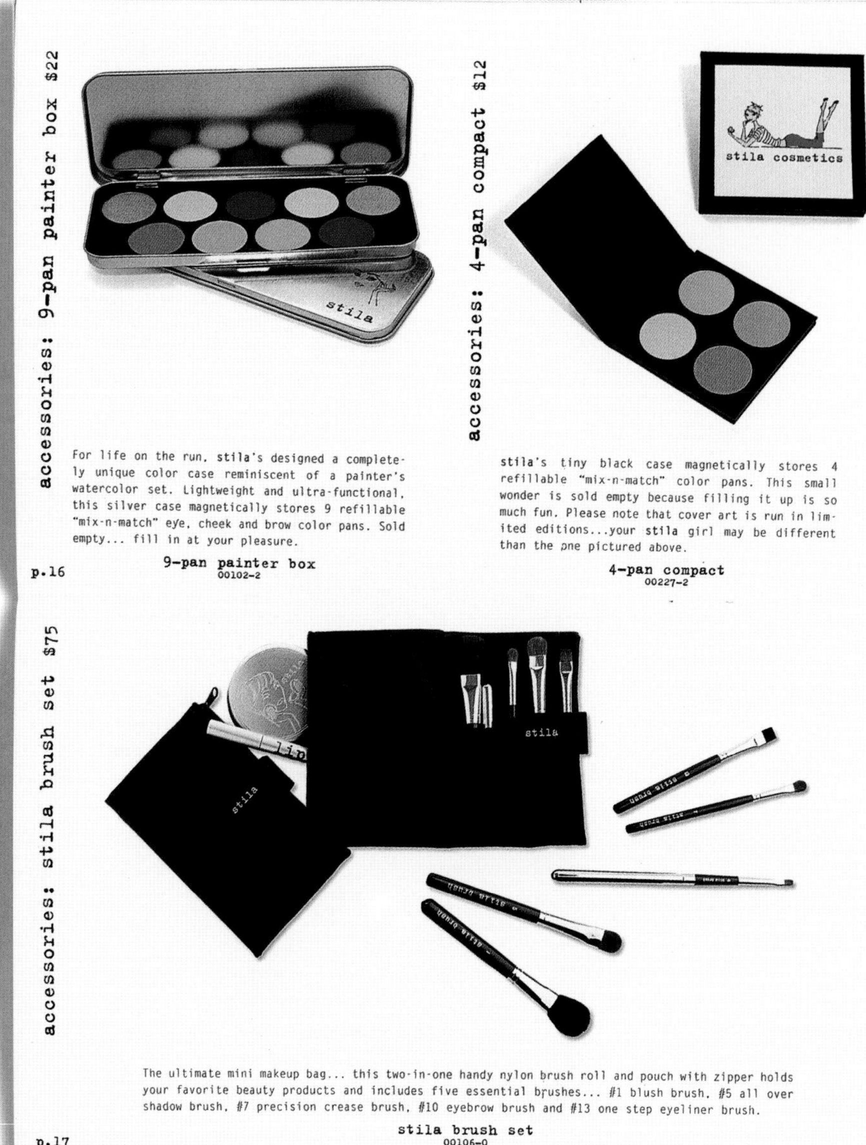
accessories: 9-pan painter box $22
For life on the run, stila's designed a completely unique color case reminiscent of a painter's watercolor set. Lightweight and ultra-functional, this silver case magnetically stores 9 refillable "mix-n-match" eye, cheek and brow color pans. Sold empty... fill in at your pleasure.
p.16
9-pan painter box
00102-2
accessories: 4-pan compact $12
stila cosmetics
stila's tiny black case magnetically stores 4 refillable "mix-n-match" color pans. This small wonder is sold empty because filling it up is so much fun. Please note that cover art is run in limited editions...your stila girl may be different than the one pictured above.
4-pan compact
00227-2
accessories: stila brush set $75
The ultimate mini makeup bag... this two-in-one handy nylon brush roll and pouch with zipper holds your favorite beauty products and includes five essential brushes... #1 blush brush, #5 all over shadow brush, #7 precision crease brush, #10 eyebrow brush and #13 one step eyeliner brush.
p.17
stila brush set
00106-0

stila by mail

## Cosmetics

STILA BY MAIL CL, DF: Stila By Mail CD, AD: Kierna Terrisse D: Anne Burdick P: Challenge Roddie I: Caitlin Dinkins CW: Rozanna Leo-Fields USA 1998 *SIZE: 190×127*

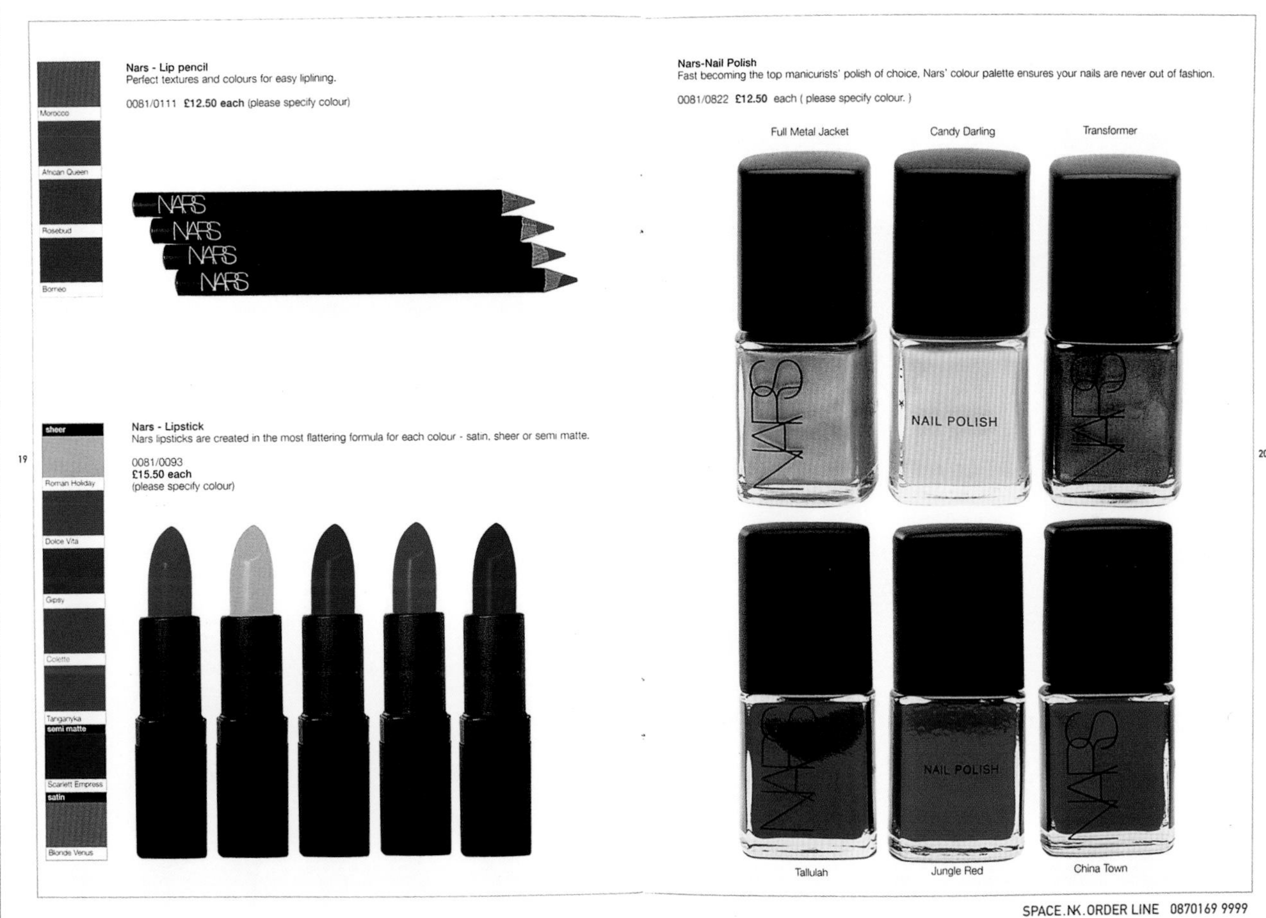

**Cosmetics**

SPACE NK CL, CD, AD, D, P, I, DF: Space NK Ltd CW: Nicky Kinnaird UK 1998 *SIZE: 210×149*

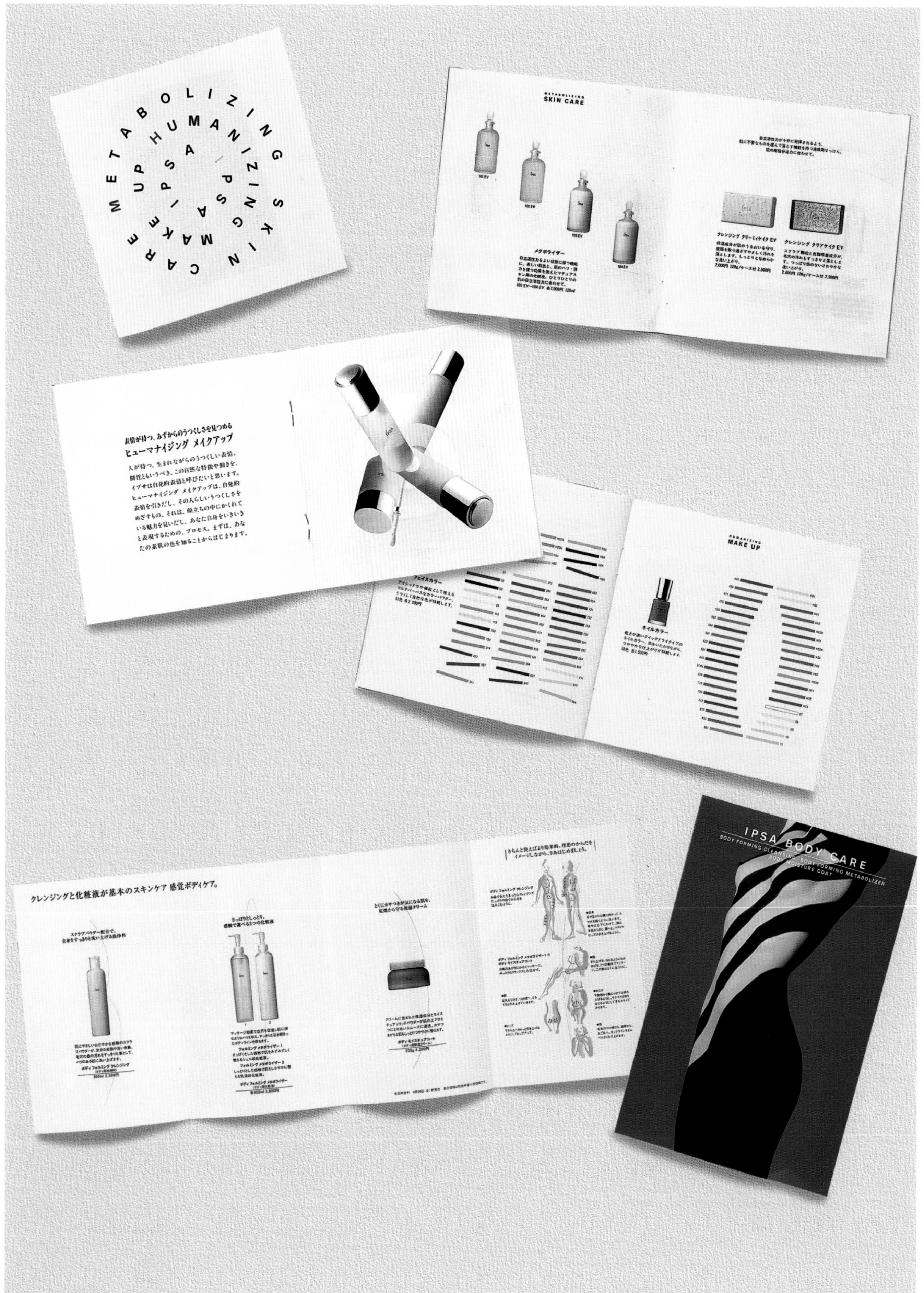


## Cosmetics

IPSA CL: IPSA Co., Ltd. CD, AD: Kenji Ohishi D: Takashi Itoh DF: CSF Wood Japan 1998 *SIZE: 120×120*
CD, AD: Kenji Ohishi D: Takashi Itoh P: Francis Giacobetti I: Noriko Otobe CW: Fumiko Shiraishi DF: CSF Wood Japan 1998 *SIZE: 180×119*

## Cosmetics

AYURA CL: Ayura Laboratories Inc. Japan 1995 *SIZE: 110×110*

# Creating your own indoor garden

It is among the flowers, fruits and herbs that we find our inspiration and the ingredients for our distinguished line of toiletries, fragrances and fine foods. A dedication to quality, tradition and the environment is the foundation on which our garden has grown.

Take time to create your own private garden, an oasis in the midst of your life. Give yourself some time and space. The products within these pages are for the 90's, easy to use yet effective, time saving yet luxurious, modern yet natural. So pamper yourself and look to the energy of nature.

Crabtree & Evelyn

CRABTREE & EVELYN

Aromathology™

This unique range draws upon our extensive knowledge of herbals and the principles of aromatherapy – a complex, natural science which uses aromatic, pure essential plant oils to help promote overall health and a sense of emotional well-being. For clarity and ease of use, we have created four special essential oil blends.

Relaxation

Oils to calm and comfort, banishing anxiety and stress.

Concentration

Help to focus and ease mental fatigue.

Romance

Create a relaxed warm mood, open and affectionate to inspire romance.

Restoration

Renew energy and zest with oils that revive and sharpen your mind.

ESSENTIAL OIL BLENDS
When certain complementary essential oils are combined, they create 'synergy' which enhances the effect of the key benefits of each oil.

SHOWER GEL
Choose a shower gel infused with lavender, clary sage and tangerine essential oils for Relaxation, or our Restoration gel with cedarwood, orange and grapefruit oils to help revive and restore energy.

BODY LOTION
Our aromatic body lotions are infused with pure essential oils to inspire Relaxation or Romance.

CANDLES
Enhance your personal space. Use our Aromathology™ Pillar and Votive Candles to create an atmosphere that is Relaxing, Romantic or Energizing.

MASSAGE OIL
Enjoy the benefits of an enhanced massage with our specially blended Relaxation or Romance Massage Oil.

SMELLING SALTS
Infused with a special blend of essential oils, to help revive your spirits and to restore physical and emotional balance.

PULSE POINT BALM
Our convenient balm is available in four categories: Relaxation (includes Deep Rest/Sleep), Restoration (includes Headache Aide), Romance and Concentration.

## Toiletries

CRABTREE & EVELYN CL, DF: Crabtree & Evelyn Ltd. Project Director: Frederic Puech Hong Kong 1998 *SIZE: 191×192*

Avocado
CRABTREE & EVELYN
Avocado Oil
Body Lotion
250 ml e 8.5 FL OZ
CRABTREE & EVELYN
Song De Chine
CRABTREE & EVELYN
SONG
DE CHINE
Vanilla
CRABTREE & EVELYN
Vanilla
BATH GEL
250 ml e 8.5 FL OZ
CRABTREE & EVELYN
Vanilla
BODY LOTION

**WHAT TO DO EVERY DAY... ORIGINS MUST HAVES.**

A. **NIGHT-A-MINS™** Mineral-enriched moisture lotion. To build strong skin while you sleep. Discover the dramatic work that's done in the dark when the hypnotic aromas of Valerian, Orange, Neroli and Vanilla post a do-not-disturb sign on stress and tension, while skin-invigorating minerals and vitamins pump up skin's resistance to daily assaults. Rest assured, once wimpy, weary, worn-thin skin awakens with a surge of inner strength.
1.7 fl. oz./50 ml - **£25.00**

B. **EYE DOCTOR™** Moisture care for skin around eyes. Nature's recommended caretakers, including cooling Cucumber, soothing Rosemary and energizing Ginseng, help counter eye-aging crow's feet, de-pouf puffs and fade dark shadows from sight to make fragile skin around eyes look and feel better. And Green Tea Extract helps fight off free radical damage.
.5 fl. oz./15 ml - **£22.50**

C. **STARTING OVER®** To see new skin each day. When skin shows lines, flaky patches, sun damage or an uneven complexion, worn out cells may have settled on skin's surface. Watch and feel how Origins special blend of alpha hydroxy fruit acids gently lifts old layers and speeds them on their way, while Vitamin A signals new skin to rise up and take their place. Lines seem to retreat, damage fades and skin shows a smoother, more radiant surface each day. 1 fl. oz./30 ml - **£20.00**

D. **NEVER A DULL MOMENT®** Skin's youthful glow depends on how light bounces off its surface. When top layers of cells are aligned, skin reflects light. But over time, cells become ragged. Light scatters in a bazillion directions. The result is strictly dullsville. There is a bright side. Nature's potent enzyme, Papain from crushed Papaya, dissolves lackluster cells and gobbles them up with no irritating friction while finely ground Apricot and Mango Seeds polish skin to perfection. Skin beams with youthful exuberance. Looks radiant, untarnished by time. net wt. 4.4 oz./125 g - **£20.00**
**(from September 1, 1998)**

**SPECIALISTS**

**COLOUR**

**BATH • BODY • HAIR**

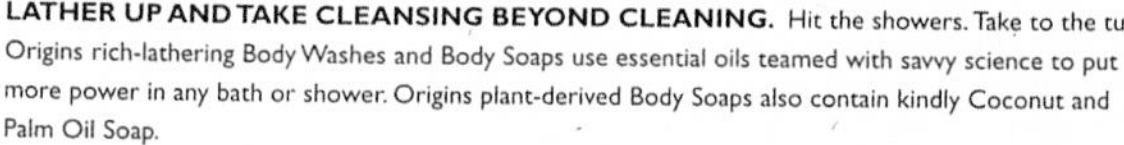

**LATHER UP AND TAKE CLEANSING BEYOND CLEANING.** Hit the showers. Take to the tub. Origins rich-lathering Body Washes and Body Soaps use essential oils teamed with savvy science to put more power in any bath or shower. Origins plant-derived Body Soaps also contain kindly Coconut and Palm Oil Soap.

A. **TRUE GRIT®** Fruit-Sloughing Body Gel and Body Soap. Nature's cloud-chasers create loofah-like action to break through debris and slough clinging flakes away. Included are Jojoba Beads and Apricot Seeds to slough, soften and smooth rough skin, plus French Peppermint Pays to refresh and recharge skin.
**Soap** net. wt. 4 oz./125 g - **£7.50**
**Body Gel** 5 fl. oz./150 ml - **£14.50**

B. **CLEAN COMFORT®** Soothing Body Wash and Body Soap. If run-of-the-milled body cleansers are so bothersome that skin crawls at mere contact, let nature's caretakers, including Licorice, Lavandin, Sage and Indian Palmarosa, coddle sensitive bodies.
**Soap** net. wt. 4 oz./125 g - **£7.50** **Body Wash** 6.7 fl. oz./200 ml - **£14.50** 13.4 fl. oz./400 ml - **£22.50**

C. **SKIN DIVER®** Active Charcoal Body Wash and Body Soap. When the day's debris gets under your skin, Activated Charcoal draws out deep dwelling pore-cloggers and environmental toxins before they breed blemishes, while nature's purifiers dissolve impurities and absorb environmental toxins.
**Soap** net. wt. 4 oz./125 g - **£7.50** **Body Wash** 6.7 fl. oz./200 ml - **£14.50** 13.4 fl. oz./400 ml - **£22.50**

D. **JUMP START™** Stimulating Body Wash and Body Soap. If you get run down easily, let nature's spark plugs help charge your batteries and get your system pumping up to speed to restore a rosy glow.
**Soap** net. wt. 4 oz./125 g - **£7.50** **Body Wash** 6.7 fl. oz./200 ml - **£14.50** 13.4 fl. oz./400 ml - **£22.50**

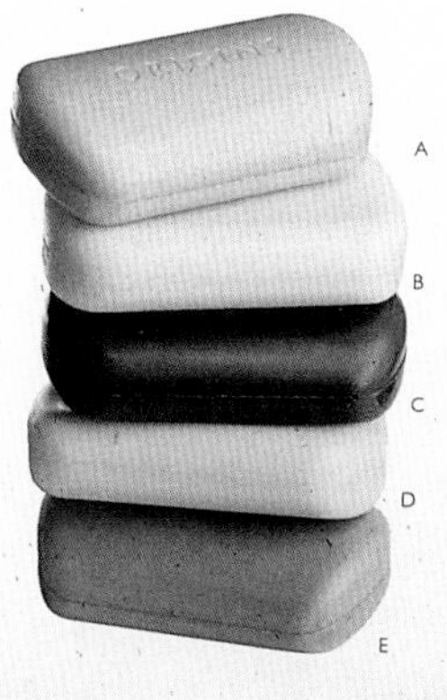

E. **MINT CONDITION™** Skin-Cooling Body Wash and Body Soap. If you hate to get up in the morning, let nature's eye-openers, including Spearmint, Wintergreen and Eucalyptus give sleepy body skin a tingly wake-up call.
**Soap** net. wt. 4 oz./125 g - **£7.50** **Body Wash** 6.7 fl. oz./200 ml - **£14.50** 13.4 fl. oz./400 ml - **£22.50**

All prices are suggested retail.

**BATH • BODY • HAIR**

## Cosmetics

ORIGINS CL: Origins CD: Anelle Miller AD: Paul Boucher P: David Dimicco USA 1998 *SIZE: 155×152*

## Wristwatches

GRAND MILLI CL: Seiko Corporation DF: Hiro Creative Co., Ltd. Agency: Office L & G Japan 1998 *SIZE: 250×60*

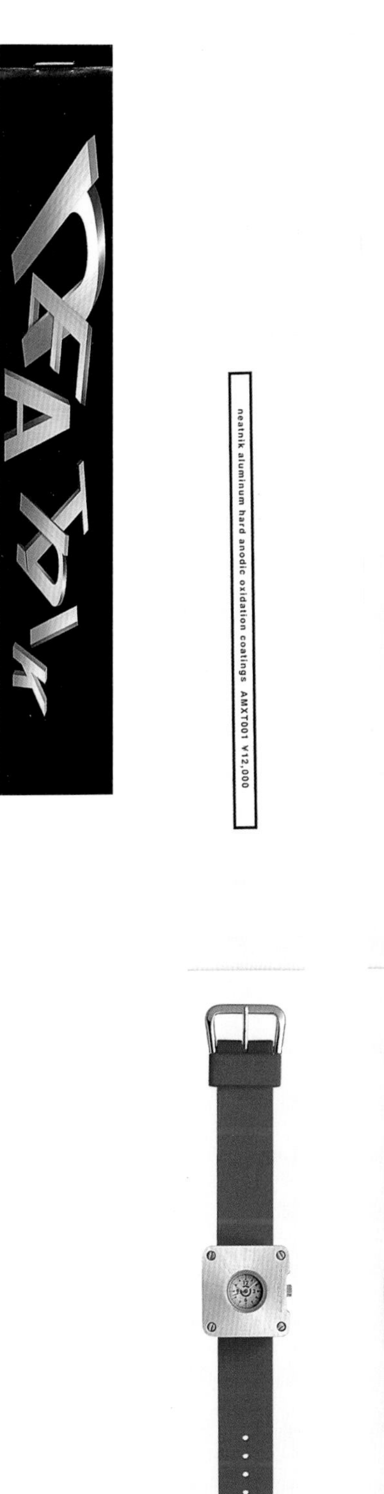


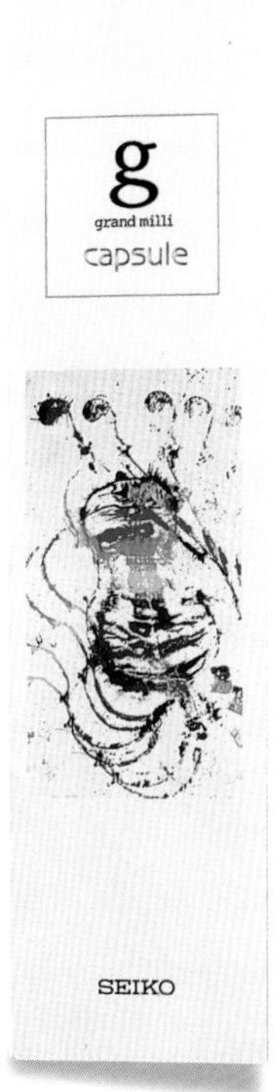


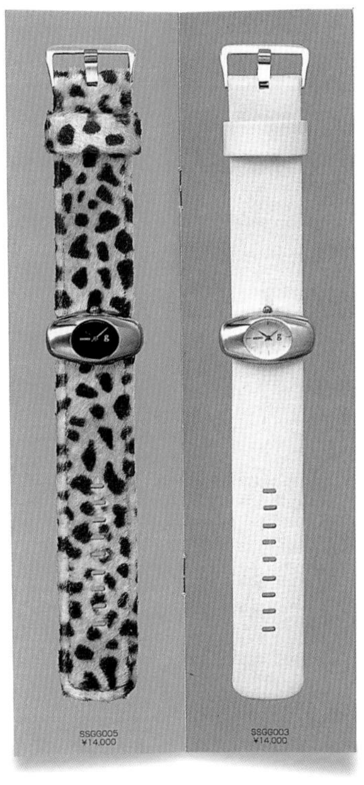

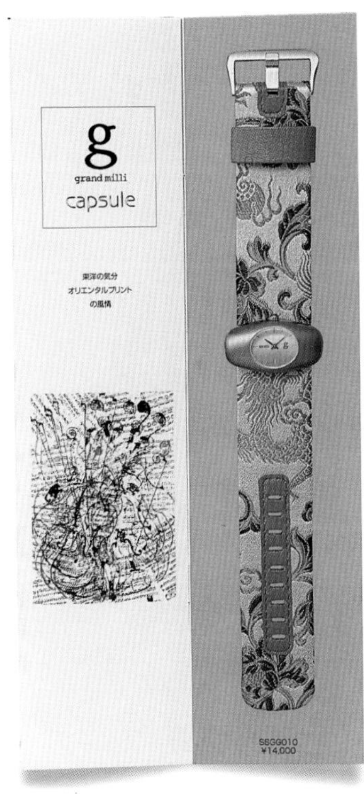

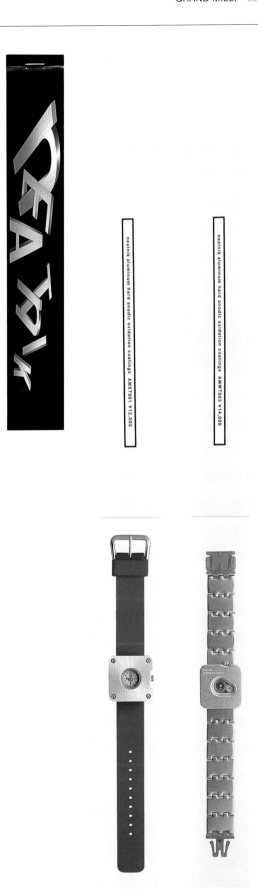

## Wristwatches

ALBA NEATNIK CL: Seiko Corporation CD, CW: Shigeki Yamakado AD, D: Hideki Nakajima
P: Tatsuya Kawai Japan 1998 *SIZE: 40×249*

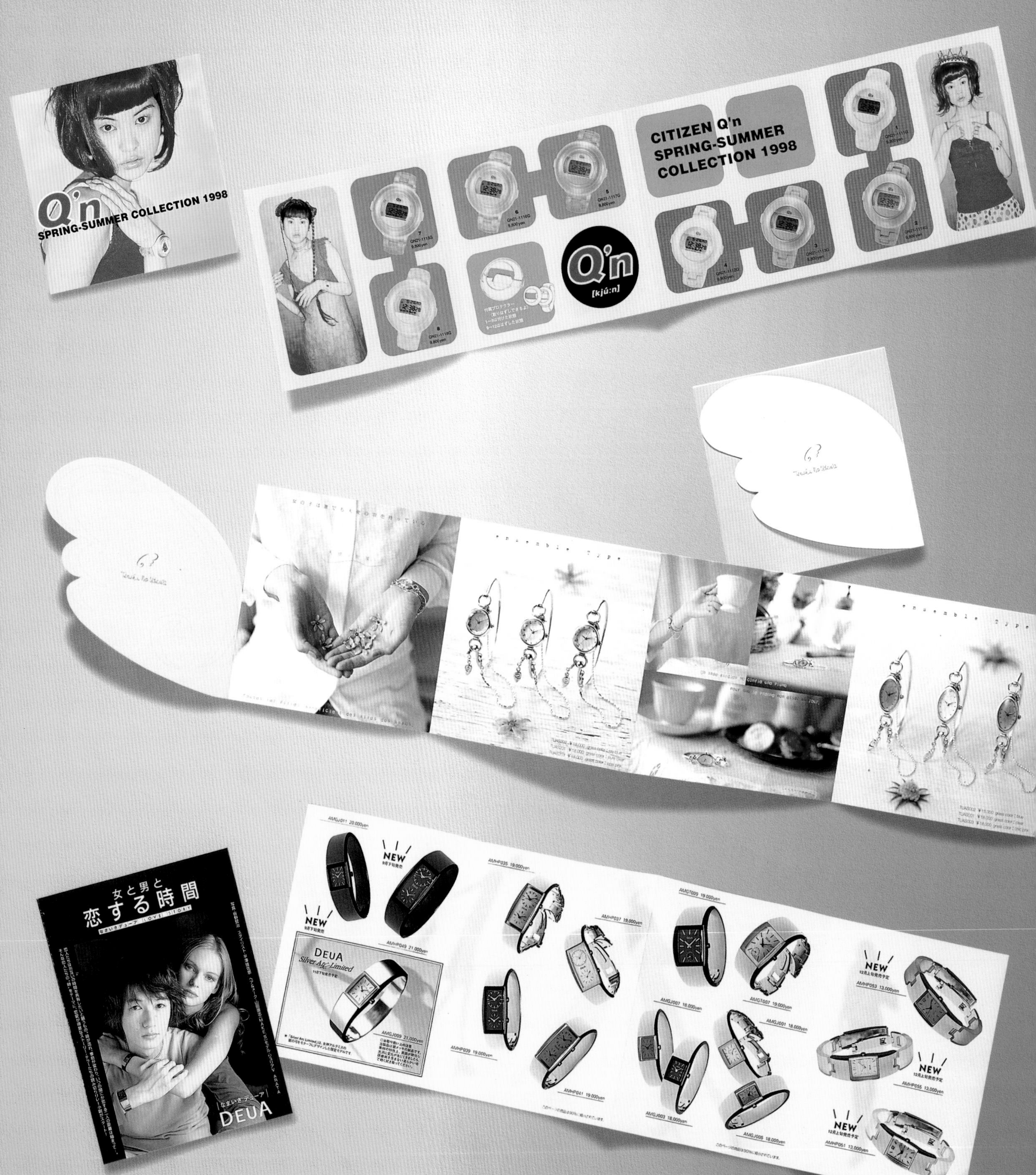


**Wristwatches**

Q'N CL: Citizen Trading Co., Ltd. Japan 1998 *SIZE: 105×105*

**Wristwatches**

TIC-TAC CL: Across, Co., Ltd. CD, AD, CW: Yoko Shimizu D, P: Akihiro Shimizu P: Shoichi Kondoh
DF: Gulliver Keikaku Co., Ltd. Japan 1998 *SIZE: 105×105*

**Wristwatches**

ALBA DEUA CL: Seiko Corporation CD: Yoshiei Okutsu AD: Tatsuo Sumii D: Hiroyuki Nomura
P: Kenji Itano CW: Kyoko Yukishima Japan 1998 *SIZE: 160×121*

## Wristwatches

RENOMA CL: Citizen Trading Co., Ltd. Japan 1998 *SIZE: 209×149*

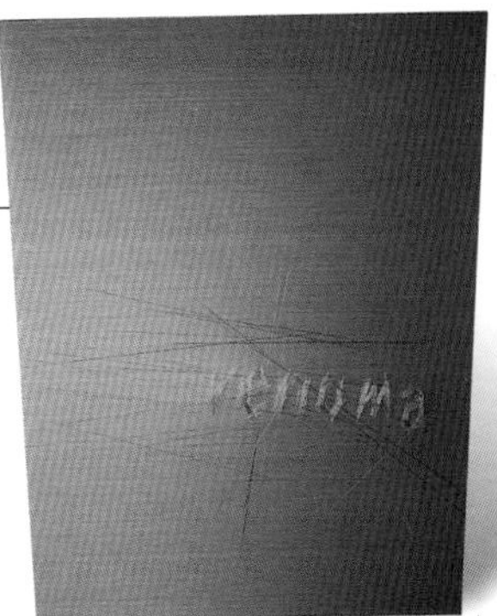
renoma

REA49-1421 SS ¥26,000
クリスタルガラス 日常生活用防水
REA48-1421 SS ¥26,000
クリスタルガラス 日常生活用防水
REA48-1422 SS ¥26,000
クリスタルガラス 日常生活用防水
REA49-1422 SS ¥26,000
クリスタルガラス 日常生活用防水
REA48-1423 SS ¥26,000
クリスタルガラス 日常生活用防水
REA49-1423 SS ¥26,000
クリスタルガラス 日常生活用防水

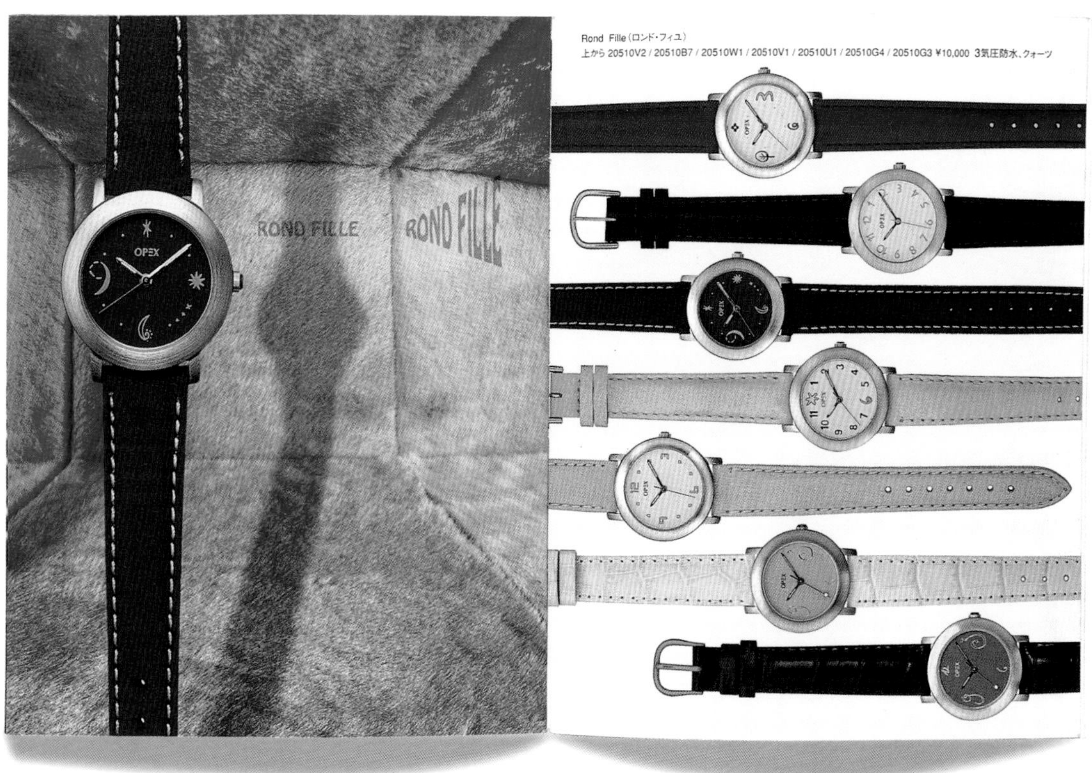
Rond Fille（ロンド・フィユ）
上から 20510V2 / 20510B7 / 20510W1 / 20510V1 / 20510U1 / 20510G4 / 20510G3 ¥10,000 3気圧防水、クォーツ
OPEX
ROND FILLE
ROND FILLE

OPEX
tic-tac

## Wristwatches

OPEX CL: Across Co., Ltd. CD: Yoko Shimizu AD, D: Akihiro Shimizu P: Shoichi Kondoh DF: Gulliver Keikaku Co., Ltd. Japan 1998 *SIZE: 133×105*

Have a

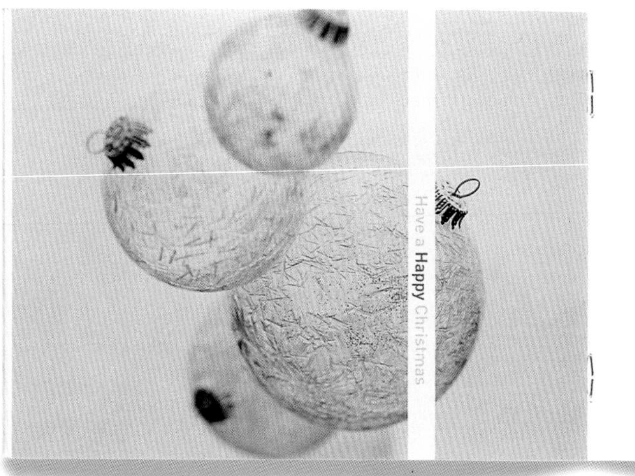
Have a Happy Christmas

## Jewelry

4°C CL: F. D. C. Products Inc. AD: Masahiko Araki D: Keiko Ikeda P: Tamotsu Ikeda
DF: Windows Corporation Japan 1998 *SIZE: 150×110*

**Jewelry**

4°C CL: F. D. C. Products Inc. AD, DF: Stoïque + Co P: Yoshihiro Kawaguchi Japan 1998 *SIZE: 151×110*

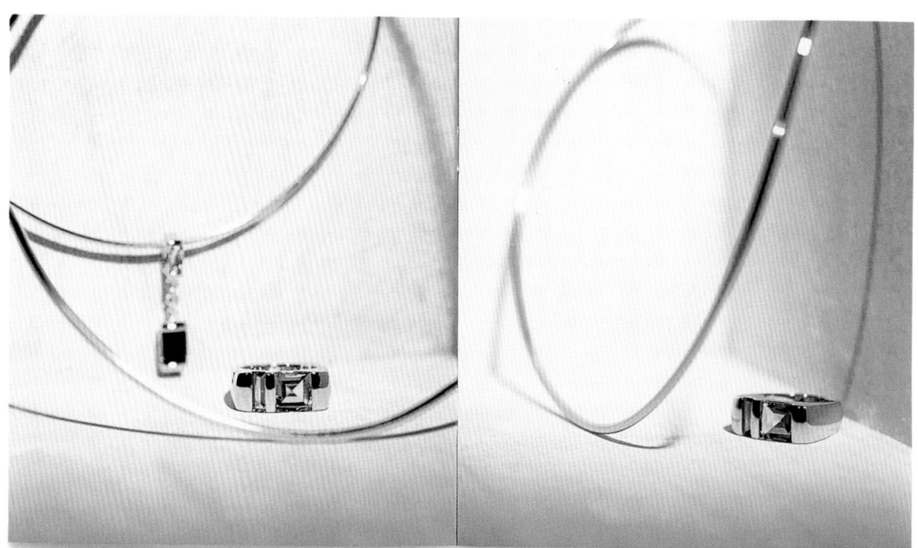

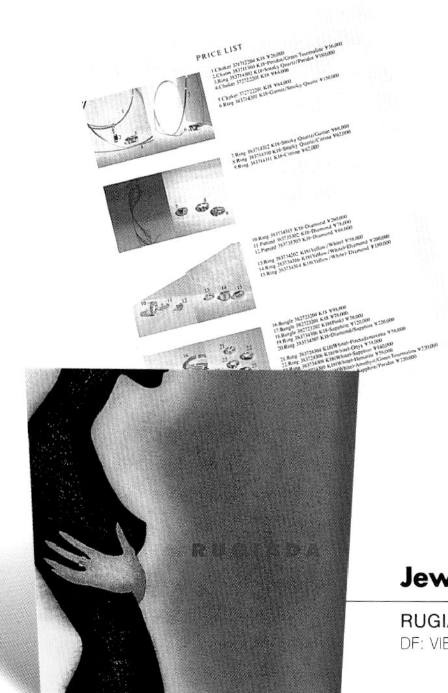


## Jewelry

RUGIADA CL: F. D. C. Products Inc. CD: Yumiko Hisanaga P: Toshitaka Niwa I: Kareem Iliya
DF: VIE Inc. Japan 1998 *SIZE: 170×150*

Main droite (de droite a gauche): Sautoir : 280 F - Sautoir : 200 F - Sautoir : 250 F
Sautoir : 200 F - Bracelet 5 rangs : 280 F - Collier : 280 F
Collier : 150 F (existe en argenté) - Collier : 150 F
Collier : 280 F (existe en gris) - Ceinture : 200 F

10

Dormeuses : 200 F (existent en noir, rouge et gris) Sautoir : 200 F (existe en rouge, gris, noir et perle)

Main gauche: Montre : 850 F - Bracelet : 300 F (existe en bleu) - Bracelet : 160 F
Jonc vermeil : 360 F (existe en argent)

11

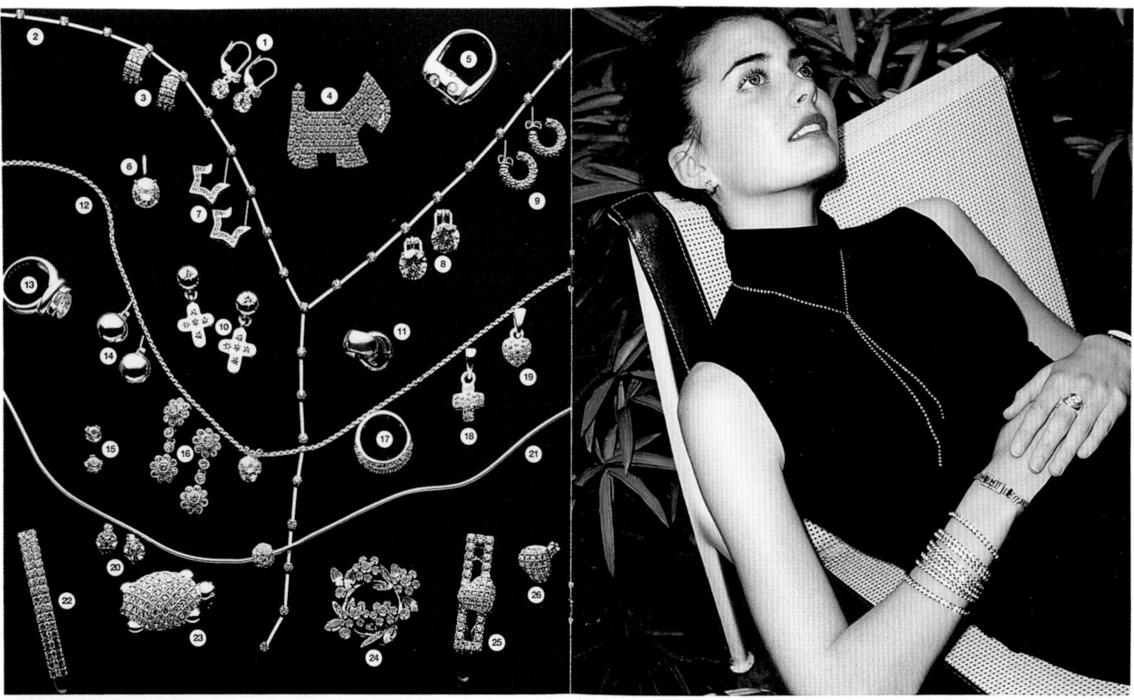

1 Dormeuses argent et oxyde de zirconium : 320 F 2 Collier : 220 F (existe en doré)
3 Boucles d'oreilles percées : 160 F (existent en violet, noir, rouge et topaze) 4 Broche : 250 F
5 Bague argent et oxyde de zirconium : 850 F (existe en vermeil) 6 Pendentif argent et oxyde de zirconium : 140 F (existe en vermeil)
7 Boucles d'oreilles percées : 250 F 8 Boucles d'oreilles clip argent et oxyde de zirconium : 280 F (existe en vermeil)
9 Créoles percées : 180 F 10 Boucles d'oreilles percées : 160 F (existe en bleu, gris, topaze et rouge) 11 Créoles argent : 200 F
12 Collier argent et oxyde de zirconium : 200 F (existe en vermeil) 13 Bague argent et oxyde de zirconium : 650 F (existe en vermeil)
14 Boucles d'oreilles percées argent : 200 F 15 Boucles d'oreilles percées strass : 100 F 16 boucles d'oreilles percées : 160 F
17 Bague argent et oxyde de zirconium : 180 F (existe en vermeil) 18 Pendentif : 100 F 19 Pendentif : 100 F (existe en doré)
20 Boucles d'oreilles percées : 120 F (existent en violet, noir, rouge, topaze et bleu) 21 Collier : 150 F (existe en doré) 22 Barrette : 80 F
23 Broche : 240 F 24 Broche : 400 F 25 Barrette : 90 F (existe en mauve, rouge et bleu) 26 Boucles d'oreilles clip : 200 F

12

Créoles oreilles percées : 160 F (existent en violet, noir, rouge et topaze)
Collier : 280 F (existe en noir)

Main gauche: Bague argent : 650 F (existe en vermeil)

Main droite: Bracelet : 350 F (existe en doré)
Bracelet : 200 F l'un (existe en rouge, violet et topaze)

## Jewelry

AGATHA CL: Agatha Japan 1998 *SIZE: 298×210*

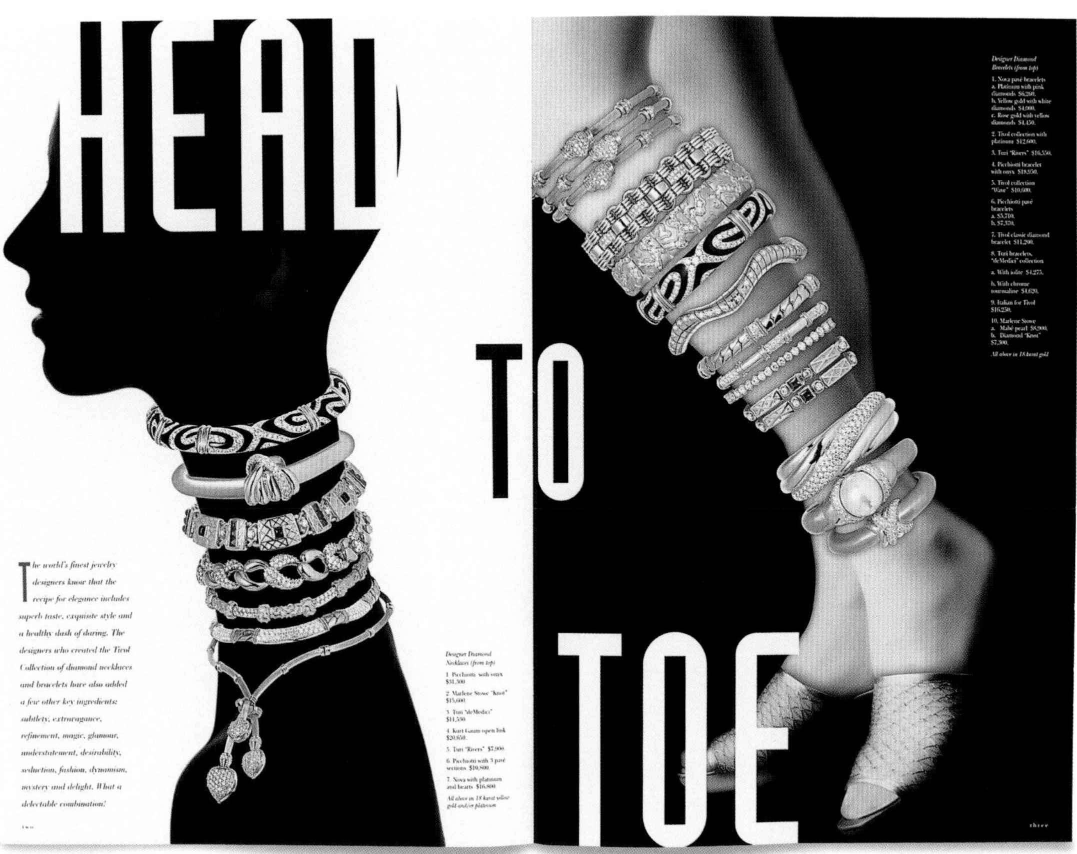

## Jewelry

TIVOL CL: Tivol CD, AD, D: John Muller AD, D: Scott Chapman P: Michael Regnier I: Andrea Pospisilova CW: David Marks DF: Muller + Company USA 1996 *SIZE: 408×280*

## Jewelry

RONALD ABRAM JEWELLERS CL: Ronald Abram Jewellers CD, AD, D: Steve Lau D: Alex Leung CW: Lee Wolter Co. Ltd. DF: Twice Graphics Hong Kong 1995 *SIZE: 210×145*

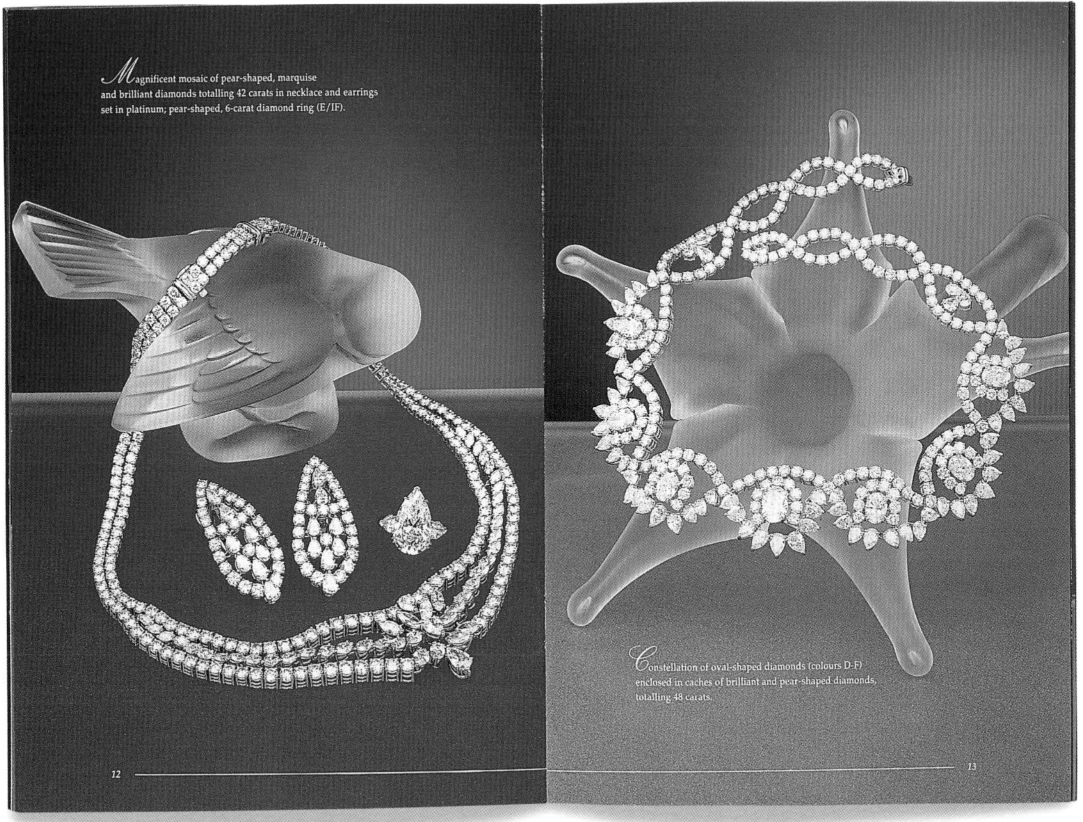

Magnificent mosaic of pear-shaped, marquise and brilliant diamonds totalling 42 carats in necklace and earrings set in platinum; pear-shaped, 6-carat diamond ring (E/IF).
Constellation of oval-shaped diamonds (colours D-F) enclosed in caches of brilliant and pear-shaped diamonds, totalling 48 carats.
12
13


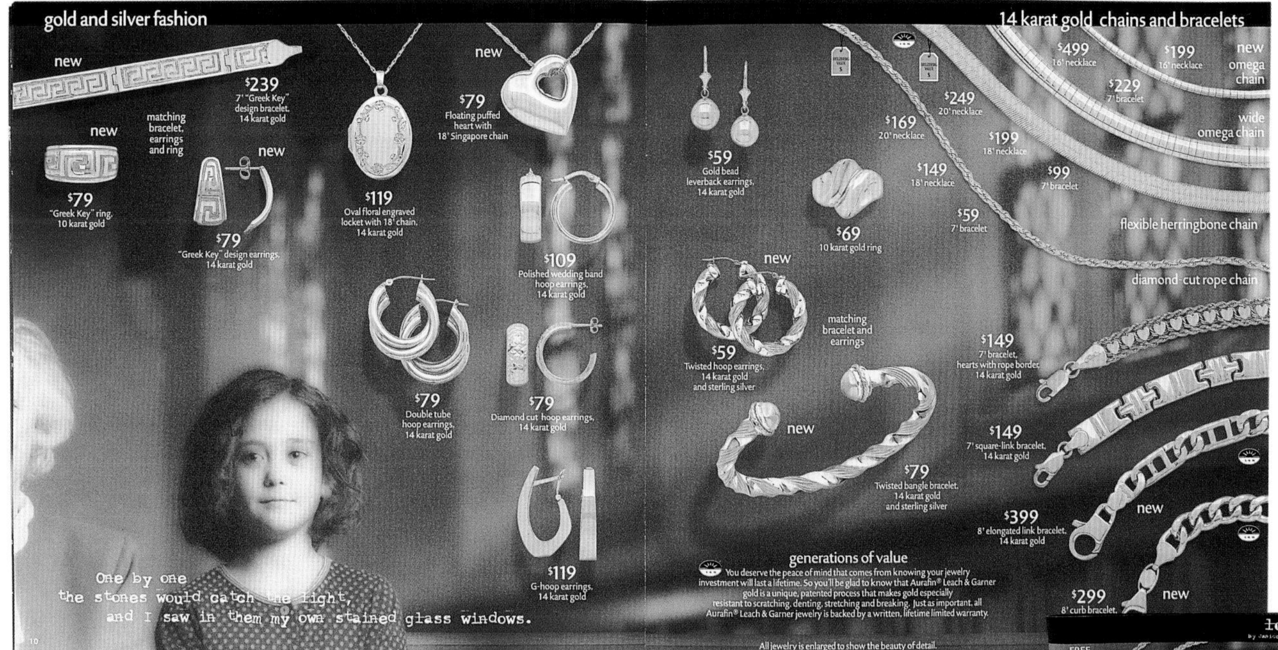


## Jewelry

HELZBERG DIAMONDS CL: Helzberg Diamonds CD: John Muller AD, D: Joann Otto P: Michael Regnier / Steve Wiberg CW: Janice Henson DF: Muller + Company USA 1997 *SIZE: 273×274*

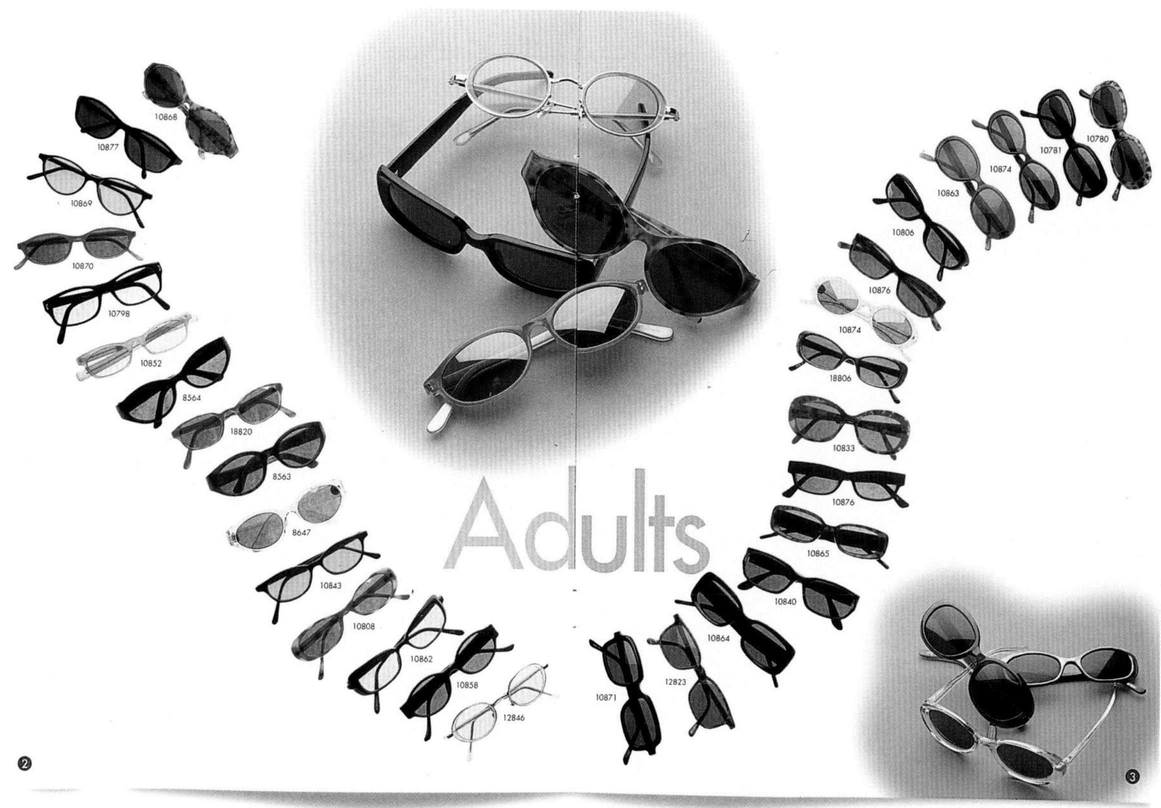


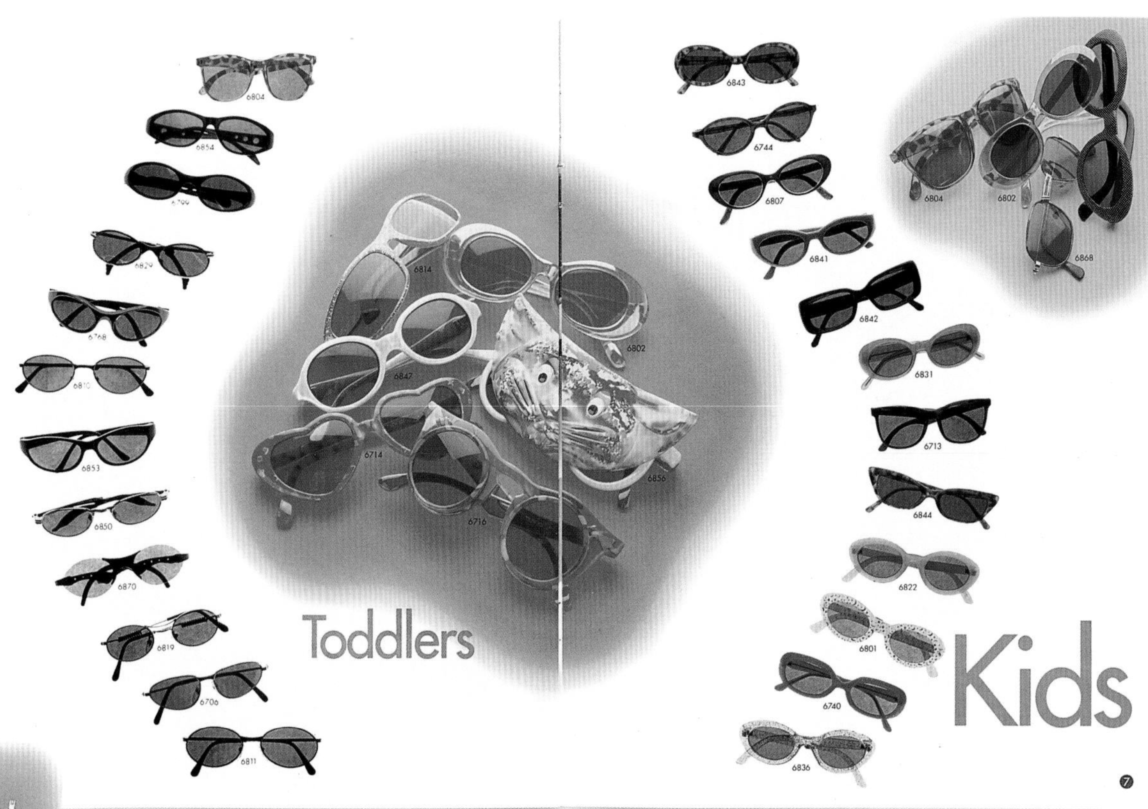


PAN OCEANIC
Eyewear

**Sunglasses**

PAN OCEANIC EYEWEAR CL: Pan Oceanic Eyewear, Ltd. CD, CW: Howard Levy AD: Ed Hamway
P: Steve Young DF: Howard Levy Design USA 1998 *SIZE: 279×215*

This
is
[x]oor. Introducing a new line of polarizing sunglasses so advanced it could only come from Polaroid. We've got polarizing technology nailed. We should—we invented it. Now we're bringing it to you in sleek, lightweight frames, designed to feel as great as they look.
[x]oor is Polaroid's ultimate sunglass lens—the result of more than 60 years of optical research and over 100 patents in the polarization field. (That's a lot.) [x]oor sunglasses filter out 99.9% of the glare and block 100% of those nasty UV rays. And they look great too, so no one ever has to know about all that time spent in the lab.
The [x]oor vision system is so unique that it's patented and only available in [x]oor sunglasses from Polaroid. You can buy this technology from us now—or wait until our patents run out and buy it from everyone else. You decide.


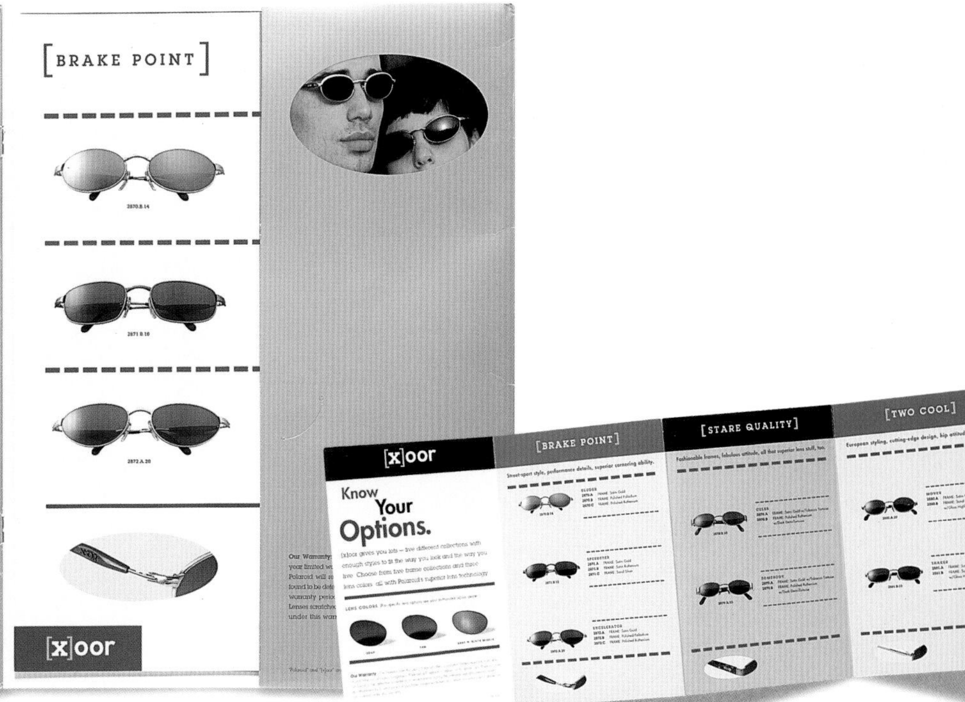

[URBANE RENEWAL]

The Urbane Renewal collection—classic styling, urban attitude, intelligent design details, so money.

Stop

*[x]oor sunglass lenses contain a patented polarizing filter that enhances clarity, improves contrast, and kills glare dead.

[x]oor

What do you want to see? All the angles. Every possible advantage. Who's on first. The shortest distance between two points. The fast lane. The green. The goal. The net. Your chip shot's splash. Beautiful people. Daydreams. Your own reflection. Family ties. [x]oor The cop with the radar gun. Different perspectives. The big picture. The point of it all. The competition fading. Your lawn growing. Mirages. Someone hailing your cab. A view from the corner office. Sunsets on every continent. The quality of life without glare.

**Sunglasses**

[X]OOR CL: Polaroid Corporation CD: Alexander Isley D: Jessica Simmons CW: Cameron Tuttle
DF: Alexander Isley Inc. USA 1997 *SIZE: 293×229*

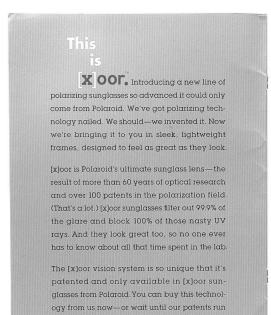

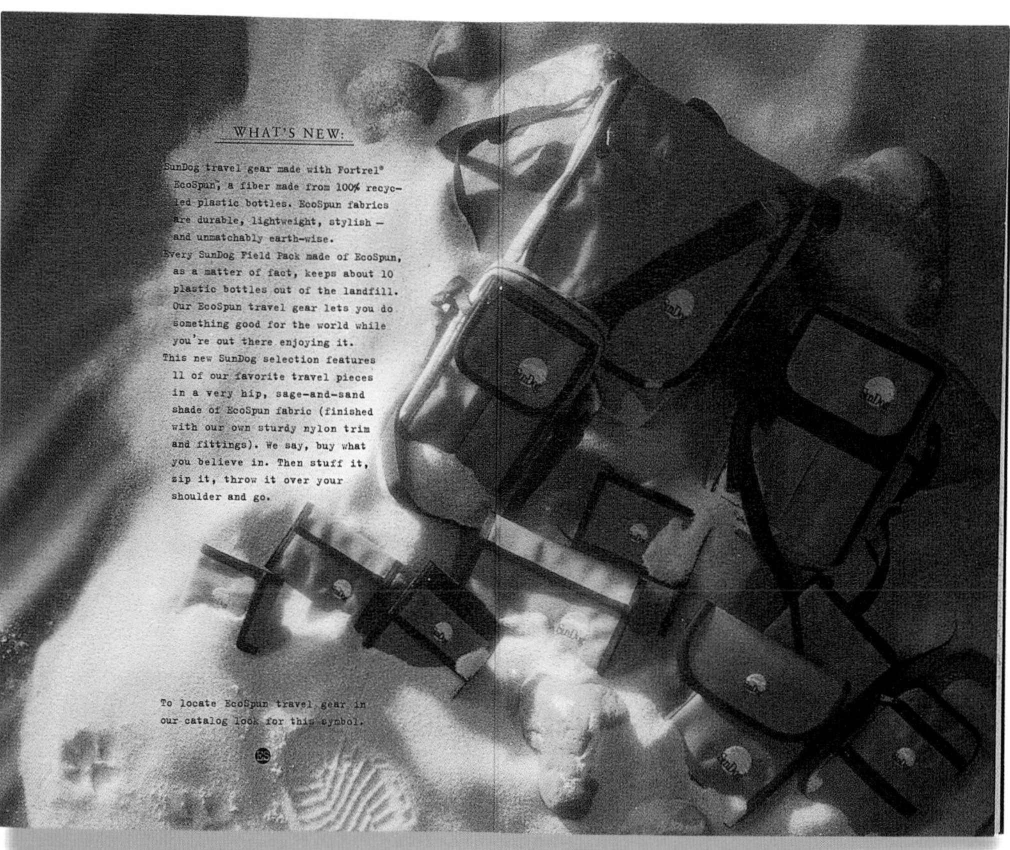


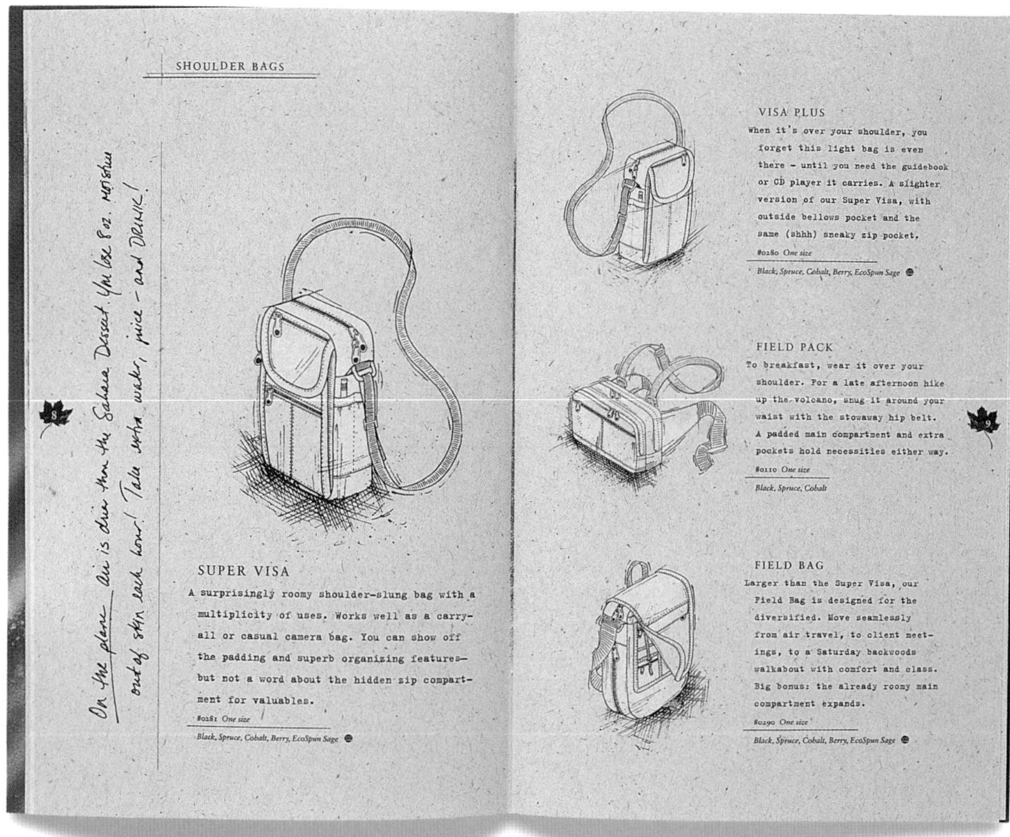

## Outdoor Accessories

SUNDOG CL: SunDog, Inc AD, D: Jack Anderson D: David Bates P: Darrell Peterson I: Todd Connor
CW: Julie Huffaker DF: Hornall Anderson Design Works USA 1995 *SIZE: 216×140*

DOONEY & BOURKE
NEW COLLECTION CABRIOLET
CANVAS WITH NATURAL VEGETABLE TANNED LEATHER TRIM,
BRASS ZIPPER.
SMALL BUCKET BAG
SHOWN IN TAN. $195, STYLE C307.
ALSO AVAILABLE IN RED, NAVY, BROWN, OR BLACK.
MINI BUCKET BAG
SHOWN IN BLACK. $175, STYLE C318.
ALSO AVAILABLE IN TAN, RED, OR NAVY.
TRAVEL BAG, SHOWN IN NAVY
$265, STYLE C317.
ALSO AVAILABLE IN TAN OR BLACK.
CARPET BAG, SHOWN IN RED
AND TAN. $210, STYLE C322.
ALSO AVAILABLE IN NAVY, BROWN,
AND BLACK.
SMALL DOMED SATCHEL
SHOWN IN TAN. $210, STYLE C301.
MINI ZIP, SHOWN IN RED
$150, STYLE C319.
BOTH AVAILABLE IN TAN, RED, NAVY,
BROWN, OR BLACK.
6
Lodis
LOS ANGELES
EXPANDABLE OFFICE ON THE GO
$425, STYLE 602NX.
AVAILABLE IN BLACK ONLY.
BRIEFCASE LADIES, $295, STYLE 578RW-NX.
BRIEFCASE CLASSIC, $315, STYLE 579RW-NX.
AVAILABLE IN BLACK WITH ROSEWOOD HANDLE ONLY.
BLACK 6-RING PLANNER WITH ROSEWOOD ACCENT
$105, STYLE 750RW-NX.
EL PORTAL
ORDER BY PHONE 1 800 723-7568
7

EL PORTAL COLLECTIONS
Refined style richly enhanced by color and texture.
EL PORTAL
NORTH-SOUTH TOTE
SHOWN IN BLUE / GREEN / COPPER.
9" x 10-3/4" x 3-1/2,"
$165, STYLE 186-816.
ALSO AVAILABLE IN BLACK / SILVER & BROWN COMBO.

EL PORTAL COLLECTIONS
Elegant, graceful artistry
MOSAIC RECTANGULAR CLUTCH
WITH REMOVABLE METALLIC STRAP.
SHOWN IN BLUE / GREEN / COPPER.
9-1/2" x 6-1/2" x 3," $196, STYLE 186-722.
ALSO AVAILABLE IN BLACK / SILVER & BROWN COMBO.

EL PORTAL LUGGAGE

## Bags

EL PORTAL LUGGAGE CL: El Portal Luggage CD, AD, D: Andrew Janson D: Aporn Khananusit
P: Ron Derhacopian Agency: Benenson Janson USA 1998 *SIZE: 275×212*

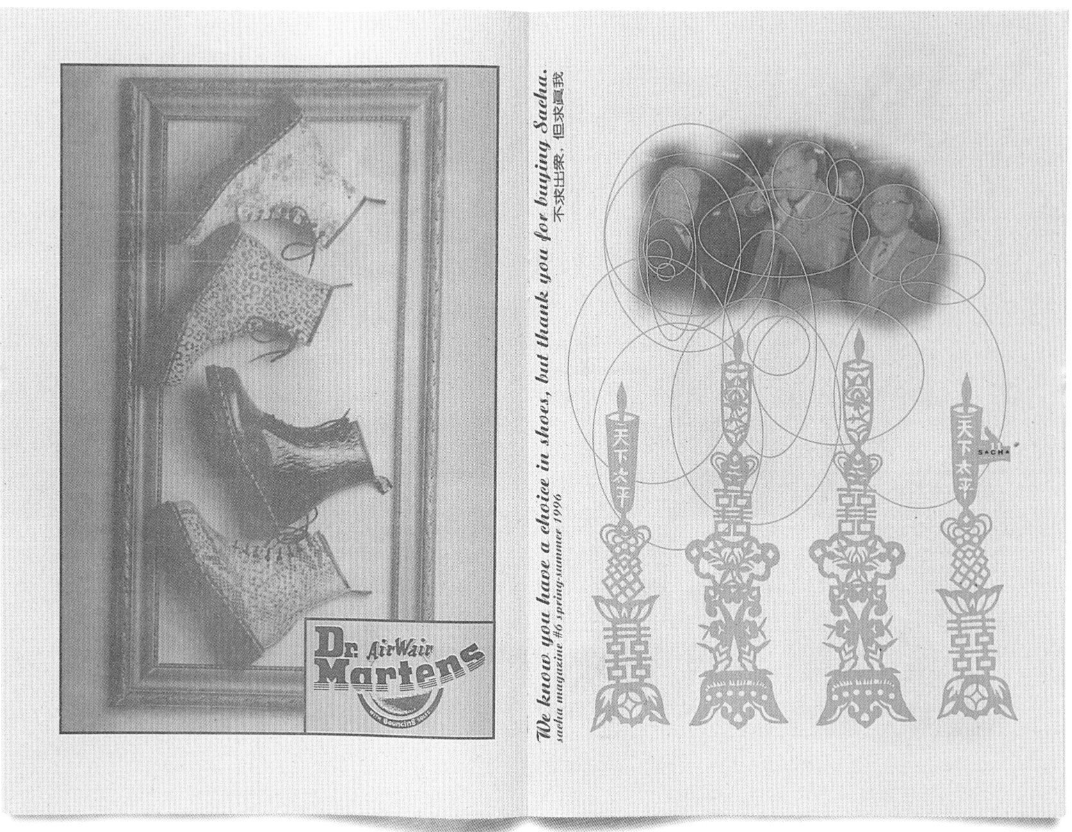

## Shoes

SACHA CL: Sacha Shoes CD, AD, D, I: Petra Janssen / Edwin Vollebergh P: Agent-X I: Liesbeth Verhoeven I, CW, DF: Studio Boot Netherlands 1996 *SIZE: 275×190*

## Shoes

ASIA PACIFIC LEATHER FAIR CL: Italian Trade Commission CD, AD: Eric Chan D, I: Francis Lee
DF: Eric Chan Design Co. Ltd. Hong Kong 1997 *SIZE: 260×160*

shoes
leather goods
from italy
spring & summer'98 collection

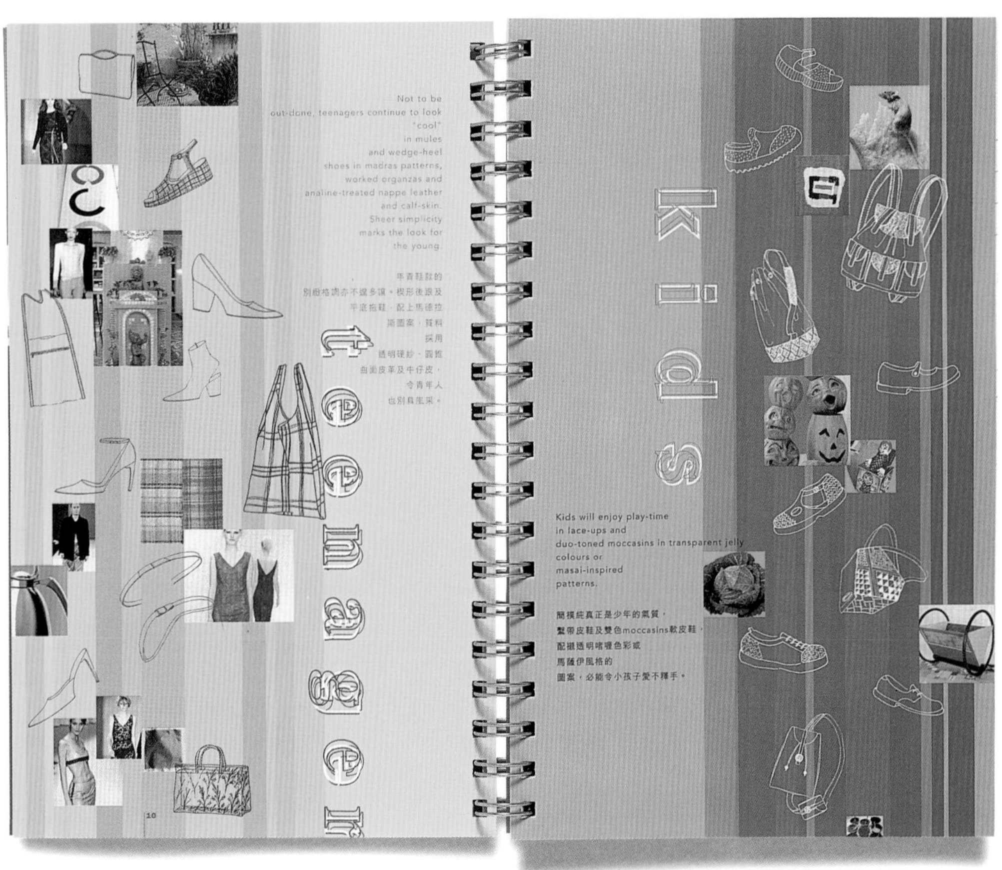
Not to be
out-done, teenagers continue to look
"cool"
in mules
and wedge-heel
shoes in madras patterns,
worked organzas and
analine-treated nappe leather
and calf-skin.
Sheer simplicity
marks the look for
the young.
kids
Kids will enjoy play-time
in lace-ups and
duo-toned moccasins in transparent jelly
colours or
masai-inspired
patterns.
簡樸純真正是少年的氣質，
繫帶皮鞋及雙色moccasins軟皮鞋，
配襯透明啫喱色彩或
馬薩伊風格的
圖案，必能令小孩子愛不釋手。

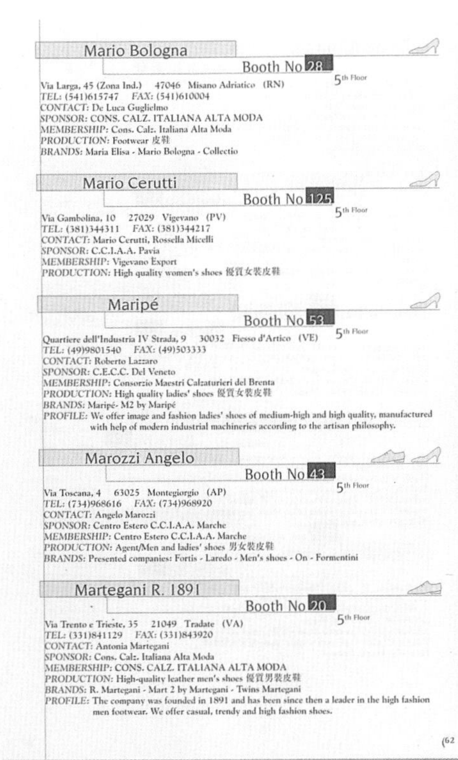

Mario Bologna
Booth No 28
5th Floor
Via Larga, 45 (Zona Ind.) 47046 Misano Adriatico (RN)
TEL: (541)615747 FAX: (541)610004
CONTACT: De Luca Guglielmo
SPONSOR: CONS. CALZ. ITALIANA ALTA MODA
MEMBERSHIP: Cons. Calz. Italiana Alta Moda
PRODUCTION: Footwear 皮鞋
BRANDS: Maria Elisa - Mario Bologna - Collectio

Mario Cerutti
Booth No 125
5th Floor
Via Gambolina, 10 27029 Vigevano (PV)
TEL: (381)344311 FAX: (381)344217
CONTACT: Mario Cerutti, Rossella Micelli
SPONSOR: C.C.I.A.A. Pavia
MEMBERSHIP: Vigevano Export
PRODUCTION: High quality women's shoes 優質女裝皮鞋

Maripé
Booth No 53
5th Floor
Quartiere dell'Industria IV Strada, 9 30032 Fiesso d'Artico (VE)
TEL: (49)9801540 FAX: (49)503333
CONTACT: Roberto Lazzaro
SPONSOR: C.E.C.C. Del Veneto
MEMBERSHIP: Consorzio Maestri Calzaturieri del Brenta
PRODUCTION: High quality ladies' shoes 優質女裝皮鞋
BRANDS: Maripé- M2 by Maripé
PROFILE: We offer image and fashion ladies' shoes of medium-high and high quality, manufactured with help of modern industrial machineries according to the artisan philosophy.

Marozzi Angelo
Booth No 43
5th Floor
Via Toscana, 4 63025 Montegiorgio (AP)
TEL: (734)968616 FAX: (734)968920
CONTACT: Angelo Marozzi
SPONSOR: Centro Estero C.C.I.A.A. Marche
MEMBERSHIP: Centro Estero C.C.I.A.A. Marche
PRODUCTION: Agent/Men and ladies' shoes 男女裝皮鞋
BRANDS: Presented companies: Fortis - Laredo - Men's shoes - On - Formentini

Martegani R. 1891
Booth No 20
5th Floor
Via Trento e Trieste, 35 21049 Tradate (VA)
TEL: (331)841129 FAX: (331)843920
CONTACT: Antonia Martegani
SPONSOR: Cons. Calz. Italiana Alta Moda
MEMBERSHIP: CONS. CALZ. ITALIANA ALTA MODA
PRODUCTION: High-quality leather men's shoes 優質男裝皮鞋
BRANDS: R. Martegani - Mart 2 by Martegani - Twins Martegani
PROFILE: The company was founded in 1891 and has been since then a leader in the high fashion men footwear. We offer casual, trendy and high fashion shoes.

(62

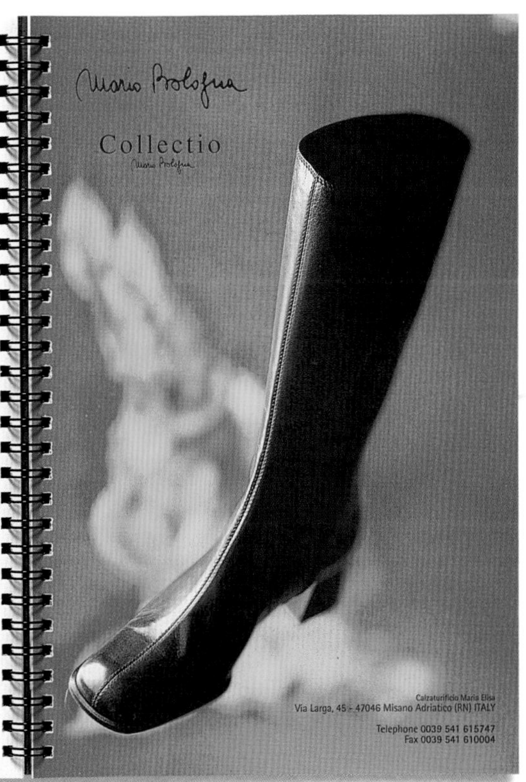
Mario Bologna
Collectio
Calzaturificio Maria Elisa
Via Larga, 45 - 47046 Misano Adriatico (RN) ITALY
Telephone 0039 541 615747
Fax 0039 541 610004

autumn & winter collection
SHOES & LEATHER
goods from Italy

## Shoes

ASIA PACIFIC LEATHER FAIR CL: Italian Trade Commission CD, AD: Eric Chan D, I: Lo Chi Ming P: Stephen Cheung
DF: Eric Chan Design Co. Ltd. Hong Kong 1997 *SIZE: 254×181*

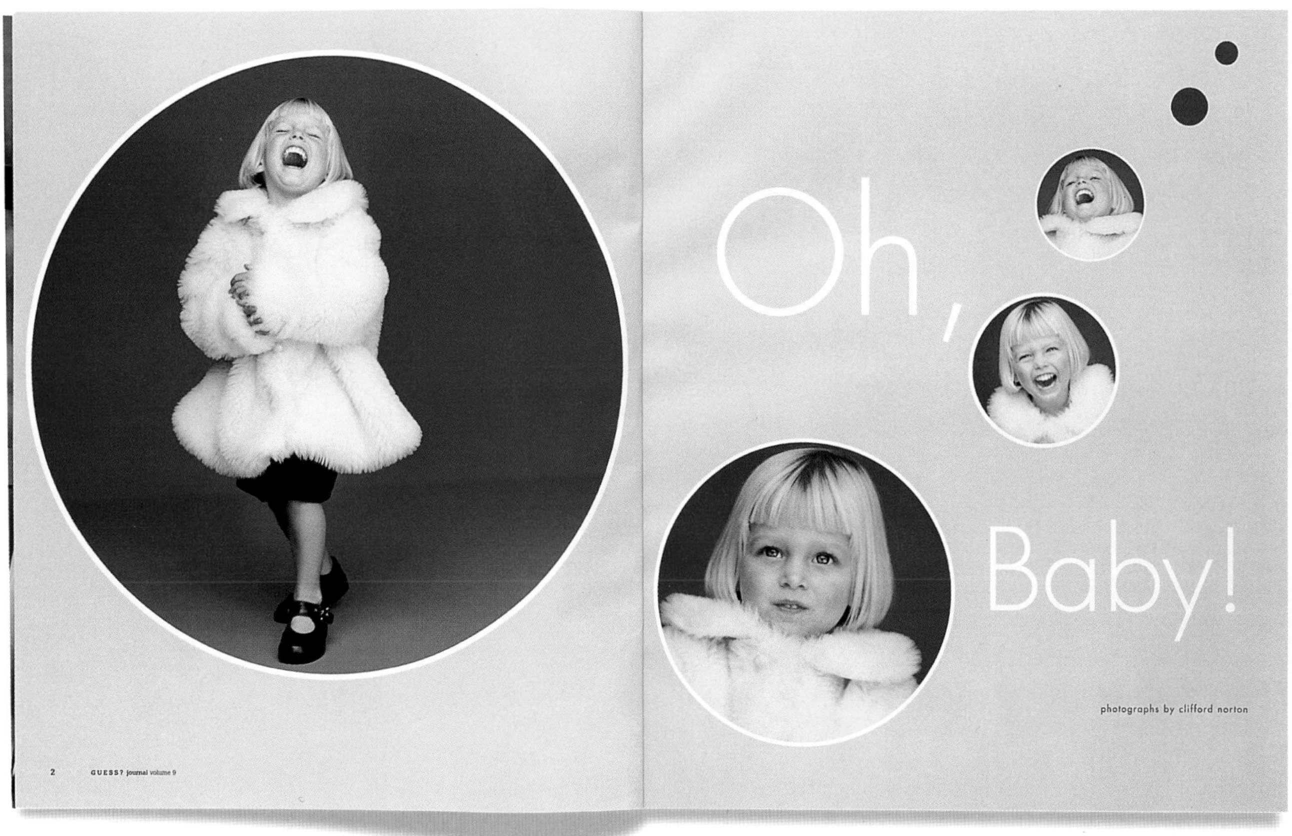
Oh,
Baby!
photographs by clifford norton
2 GUESS? journal volume 9

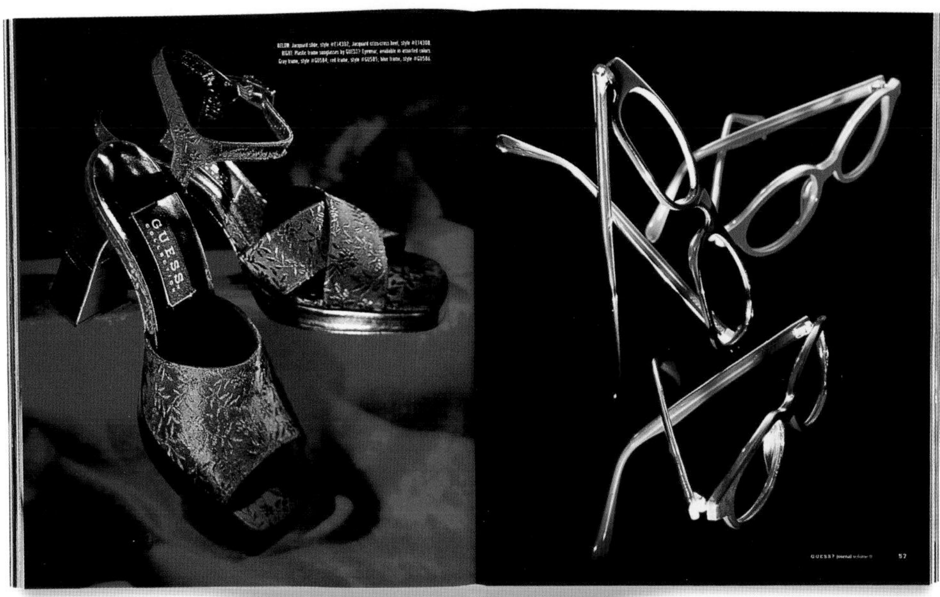


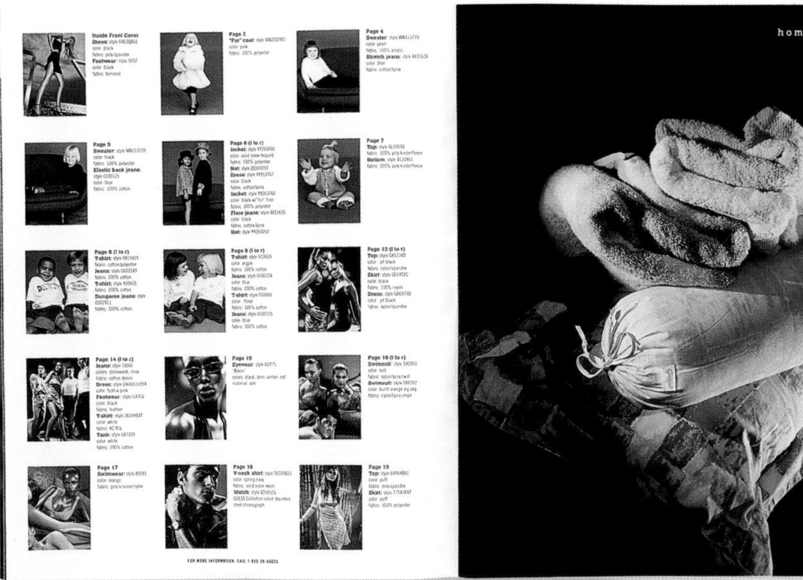


**Ladies' & Men's Wear**

GUESS? CL: Guess?, Inc. AD: Paul Marciano D: Leslie Oki P: Dah Len / Michael Hurd CW: Emily Corey USA 1998 *SIZE: 305×260*

**Page 53**
**Jacket:** style HW9560D134
color: rinse
fabric: 100% cotton
**Shirt:** style 8331WT35
color: indigo
fabric: 100% cotton
**Jean:** style HW1030D134/NOW
color: rinse
fabric: 100% cotton

**Page 54 (l to r)**
**Flannel Shirt:** style 88432B73
color: charcoal/bordeaux
fabric: 100% cotton
**Striped Shirt:** style 71436B51
fabric: cotton
**Shirt:** style 81455
color: white
fabric: pima poplin

**Page 58**
**Vest:** style 5656AW79
color: mist
fabric: cotton
**Shirt:** style 75385
color: white
fabric: 100% cotton
**Pant:** style 42130
color: black
fabric: cotton/lycra stretch

**Page 60**
**Shirt:** style 71436B51
color: navy striped oxford
fabric: cotton
**Jean:** style 001
color: rinse
fabric: 100% cotton

**Page 64 (l to r)**
**Shirt:** style 75385
color: white
fabric: cotton
**Dress:** style 63666T81
color: black
fabric: English rose

**Page 65**
**Sweater:** style G50PX
color: 553T
fabric: wool blend

**Page 65 (l to r)**
**Dress:** style 63666T81
color: black
fabric: English rose
**Sweater:** style 6536RT07
color: charcoal/multi
fabric: cotton blend
**Pant:** style 7P061
color: smoke
fabric: stretch sateen

**Page 74**
**Shirt:** style 16404EXV
color: rinse
fabric: 100% cotton

**Page 75**
**Jacket:** style 10874
color: rinse
fabric: 100% cotton
**Jean:** style 1060
color: rinse
fabric: 100%cotton

**Page 76**
**Shirt:** style 2146XMAA
color: grey heather
fabric: 100% cotton
**Jean:** style 1060
color: rinse
fabric: 100% cotton

**Page 77**
**Shirt:** style 21444ATN
color: rouge
fabric: 100% cotton
**Jean:** Premium Denim
color: rinse
fabric: 100% cotton

**Page 78**
**Tank:** style G82292C
color: black
fabric: stretch mesh
**Jean:** Premium Denim
color: rinse
fabric: 100% cotton
**Footwear:** style 9242 "Ilsa"
color: black
fabric: leather

**Page 79**
**Shirt:** style 5843BT40
color: G. I. green
fabric: 100% cotton
**Jacket:** style 24423
color: black
fabric: leather

**Page 80**
**Shirt:** style 81428M23
color: white
fabric: 100% cotton
**5-Pocket Jean:** style 43050A
color: white
fabric: 100% cotton

**Page 81**
**Top:** style 6446PT97
color: grey heather/black
fabric: 100% cotton
**Jean:** style 1060
color: rinse
fabric: 100% cotton

FOR MORE INFORMATION, CALL 1-800-39-GUESS

Rugged and serene, the earth moves to the
rhythm of wide open spaces.
There are no limits, and nothing to hold back.

In the silence that decides the fate of imagination,
the energy of possibility sets the heart free.
GUESS

**Ladies' & Men's Wear**

GUESS? CL: Guess?, Inc. AD: Paul Marciano D: Leslie Oki P: Pablo Alfaro / Daniela Federici
CW: Emily Corey USA 1998 *SIZE: 305×260*

MACPHEE
HARMONIE
FAKE MOUTON VEST ¥16,000
RIB TURTLENECK ¥9,800
PRINT SKIRT ¥12,000
SHIRT JACKET ¥11,000
VELVET PANTS ¥13,000
MUFFLER ¥7,900

TOMORR

OWLAND

**Ladies' Wear**

TOMORROWLAND CL, CD: Tomorrowland Co., Ltd. AD: Tsuyoshi Hirano P: Frédéric Jacquet Japan 1998 *SIZE: 245×170*

FLOWING PANTS
¥18,000
SHORT BOOTS
¥24,000

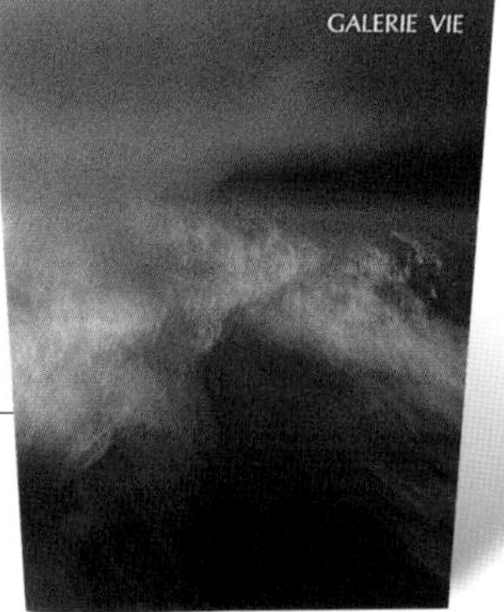
GALERIE VIE

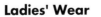

## Ladies' Wear

GALERIE VIE CL: Tomorrowland Co., Ltd. AD: Strange Fruits Inc. P: Koji Udo Japan 1998 *SIZE: 250×170*

**Ladies' Wear**

4°C CL: F. D. C. Products Inc. AD, DF: Stoïque + Co P: Yoshihiro Kawaguchi Japan 1997 *SIZE: 234×187*

## Ladies' Wear

DES PRÉS CL: Tomorrowland Co., Ltd. AD: M P: Junji Hata Japan 1998 *SIZE: 250×170*

DES PRÉS

## Ladies' Wear

GEORGIOU CL: Georgiou CD, AD, D: Andrew Janson P: Ron Derhacopian
Agency: Benenson Janson USA 1998 *SIZE: 292×219*

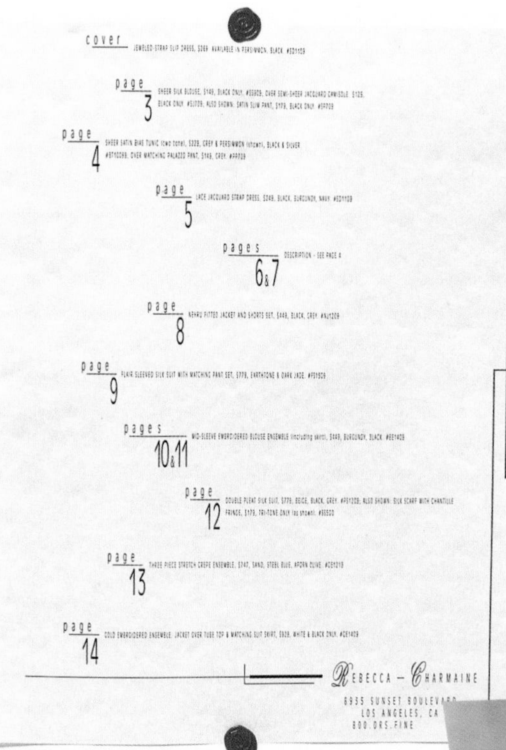

cover JEWELED-STRAP SLIP DRESS, $269. AVAILABLE IN PERSIMMON, BLACK. #SD1109

page 3 SHEER SILK BLOUSE, $149, BLACK ONLY. #SS909, OVER SEMI-SHEER JACQUARD CAMISOLE, $129, BLACK ONLY. #SJ709. ALSO SHOWN: SATIN SLIM PANT, $179, BLACK ONLY. #SP709

page 4 SHEER SATIN BIAS TUNIC (two tone), $229, GREY & PERSIMMON (shown), BLACK & SILVER #ST10099, OVER MATCHING PALAZZO PANT, $149, GREY. #PP709

page 5 LACE JACQUARD STRAP DRESS, $249, BLACK, BURGUNDY, NAVY. #SD1109

pages 6&7 DESCRIPTION - SEE PAGE 4

page 8 NEHRU FITTED JACKET AND SHORTS SET, $449, BLACK, GREY. #NJ1209

page 9 FLAIR SLEEVED SILK SUIT WITH MATCHING PANT SET, $779, EARTHTONE & DARK JADE. #FS1909

pages 10&11 MID-SLEEVE EMBROIDERED BLOUSE ENSEMBLE (including skirt), $449, BURGUNDY, BLACK. #EE1409

page 12 DOUBLE PLEAT SILK SUIT, $779, BEIGE, BLACK, GREY. #PS1209; ALSO SHOWN: SILK SCARF WITH CHANTILLE FRINGE, $179, TRI-TONE ONLY (as shown). #SS509

page 13 THREE PIECE STRETCH CREPE ENSEMBLE, $747, SAND, STEEL BLUE, ACORN OLIVE. #CE1210

page 14 GOLD EMBROIDERED ENSEMBLE: JACKET OVER TUBE TOP & MATCHING SLIT SKIRT, $929, WHITE & BLACK ONLY. #GE1409

REBECCA – CHARMAINE
8935 SUNSET BOULEVARD
LOS ANGELES, CA
800.DRS.FINE

**Ladies' Wear**

REBECCA-CHARMAINE CL: Rebecca-Charmaine CD, AD, D: Andrew Janson P: Robert Brinkman
Agency: Benenson Janson USA 1998 *SIZE: 398×304*

this page
EXPERT RIBBED MERINO WOOL MOCK TURTLENECK SWEATER

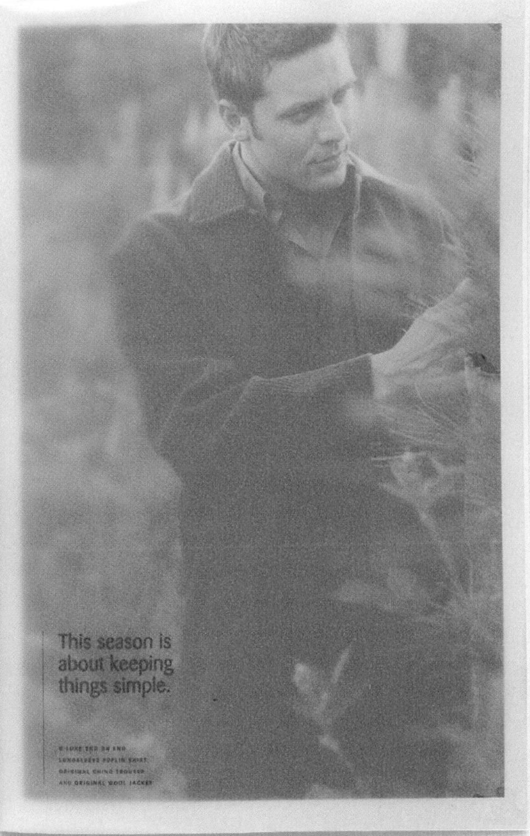
This season is about keeping things simple.

Comfort is the new rule.
opposite RELAXED LAMBSWOOL TURTLENECK BY EXPERT
below CASHMERE CAMISOLE AND CARDIGAN BY EXPERT

simple, sexy, evening chic
this page
top SEMI-TRANSPARENT EVENING DRESS
WITH ASYMETRIC BACK STRAP BY EXPERT
bottom STRETCH VELVET V-NECK EVENING DRESS BY EXPERT
opposite page
SEMI-TRANSPARENT EVENING DRESS
WITH ASYMETRIC BACK STRAP BY EXPERT (FRONT VIEW)

the pleasure of quiet relaxation

Enjoy the easy, peaceful moments.
The ultimate in comfort.
Index
2 RIBBED MERINO WOOL MOCK
TURTLENECK SWEATER
4 RELAXED LAMBSWOOL TURTLENECK
6 SOFT MOHAIR CAMISOLE
7 SILVER METALLIC CAMISOLE
AND CARDIGAN
EVERGREEN


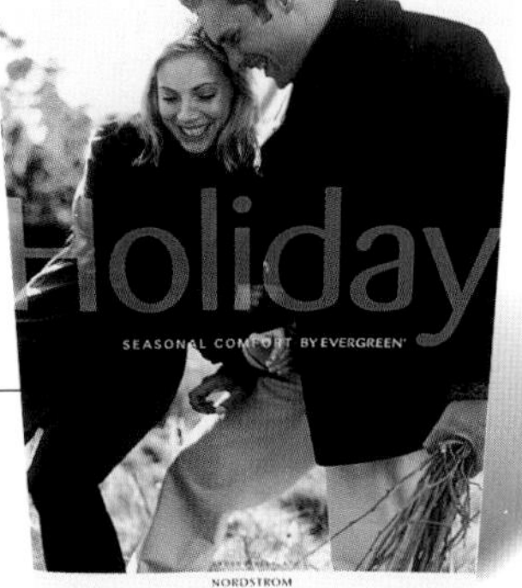

Holiday
NORDSTROM


## Ladies' & Men's Wear

NORDSTROM CL: Evergreen CD, AD: Franco Vendramin D: Steve McCluskey P: Heather Favell
DF: Novaidea Creative Resources Italy 1998 *SIZE: 229×153*

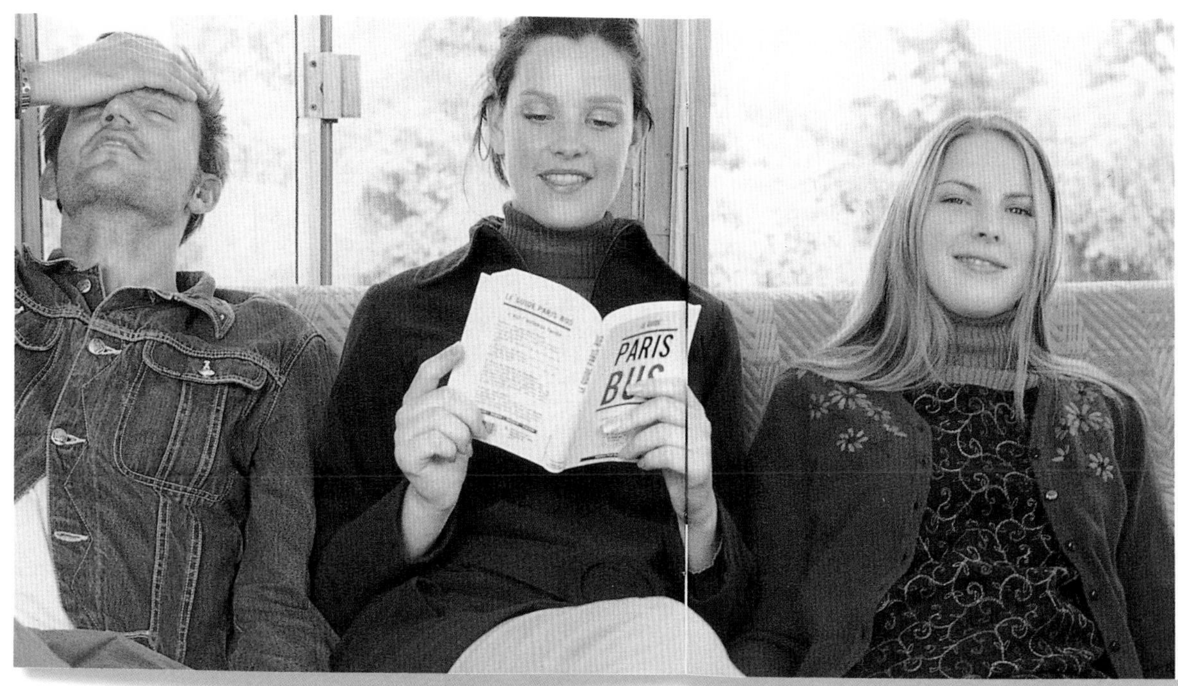
PARIS BUS
left／jacket no.14376 ¥22,000
turtle neck sweater no.93404 ¥5,900
pants no 16500 ¥8,900
right／cardigan no.93448 ¥8,900
jumper dress no.17199 ¥14,800
turtle neck sweater no.93402 ¥5,900

jumper skirt no.17201 ¥14,800 turtle neck sweater no.93405 ¥4,900 pants no.16522 ¥7,900 suede bag no.90813 ¥5,900

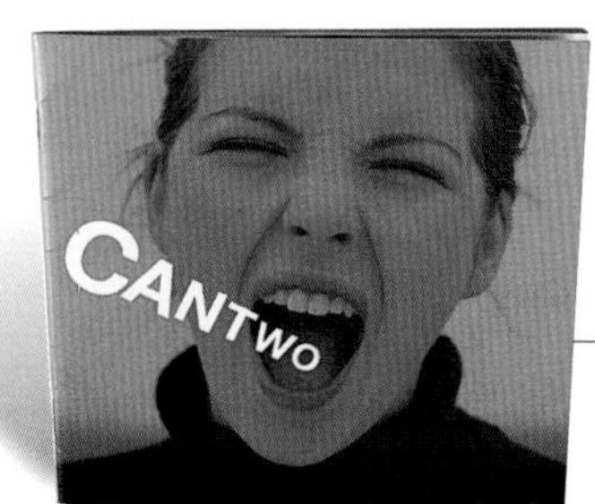
CANTWO

## Ladies' Wear

CANTWO CL: Tokyo Can Co., Ltd. CD: Mikiko Shimizu AD: Glüe P: Fred Aufray Japan 1997 *SIZE: 140×148*

## Ladies' Wear

MONTE OVEST CL: Monte Ovest Co., Ltd. CD: Kaoru Tatsui AD, D: Yasunori Wada P: Yuji Shibuya DF: Wada-P!! Associates Japan 1997 *SIZE: 296×210*

## Ladies' Wear

A. O. BY ATSUKI ONISHI CL: P/X Co., Ltd. P: Toshio Hagiri Japan 1996 *SIZE: 296×210*

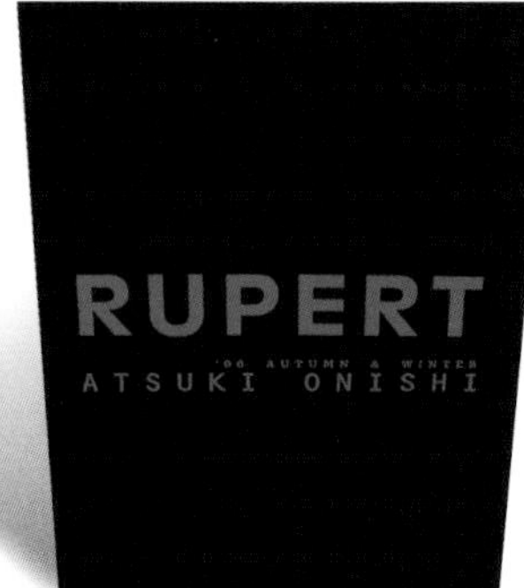


## Men's Wear

RUPERT CL: P/X Co., Ltd. P: Toshio Hagiri / Masumi Seki / Andrew Taylor Japan 1996 *SIZE: 296×210*

## Men's Wear

MEN'S TENORAS CL: Tenoras Co., Ltd CD, AD: Hiroshi Endo D: Takashi Machida P: Tiziano Bertola
CW: Kazushi Kikuchi / Akiko Suematsu DF: T & Wave Co., Ltd. Japan 1998 *SIZE: 297×210*

左から ブルゾン 50-54206 95 ¥29,000
シャツ 50-84415 963 ¥25,000
パンツ 50-74403 51 ¥19,000
シャツ 50-84417 993 ¥25,000
パンツ 50-74402 51 ¥19,000
左：シャツジャケット 50-84211 953 ¥35,000
ベスト 50-24204 943 ¥29,000
シャツ 50-84202 943 ¥25,000
パンツ 50-74205 951 ¥21,000
右：ニット 50-14205 21 ¥33,000
パンツ 50-74205 51 ¥21,000

DOLCE
The Perfect Blend of
トレーナー 151-33103 手前から：06(白) 912(グレー)
133(カラシ) 173(オレンジ) 183(パープル) 13(黒) ¥13,000

UNCLE DOLCE
ニット 151-13503 ¥25,000
トレーナー 151-33107 ¥17,000
フリース 151-33502 ¥25,000

DOLCE
DOLCE

## Men's Wear

DOLCE CL: World Co., Ltd. AD, D: Toshiyuki Kojima P: Masayuki Hayashi ST: Kaoru Watanabe DF: Kojima Design Office Japan 1997 *SIZE: 257×182*

FIT FOR WOMEN
RABAT
BISSAU
FREETOWN
DAKAR

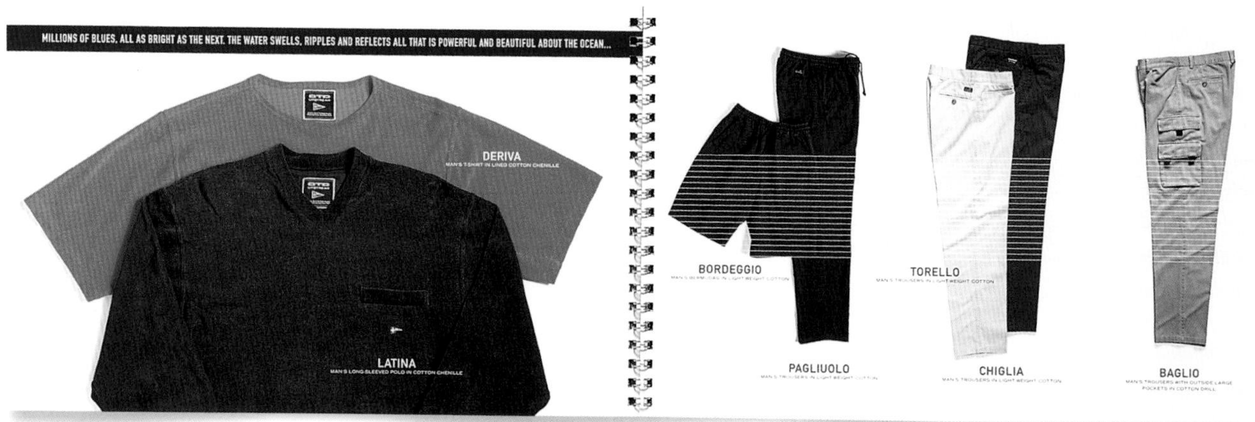
MILLIONS OF BLUES, ALL AS BRIGHT AS THE NEXT. THE WATER SWELLS, RIPPLES AND REFLECTS ALL THAT IS POWERFUL AND BEAUTIFUL ABOUT THE OCEAN...
DERIVA
LATINA
BORDEGGIO
TORELLO
PAGLIUOLO
CHIGLIA
BAGLIO

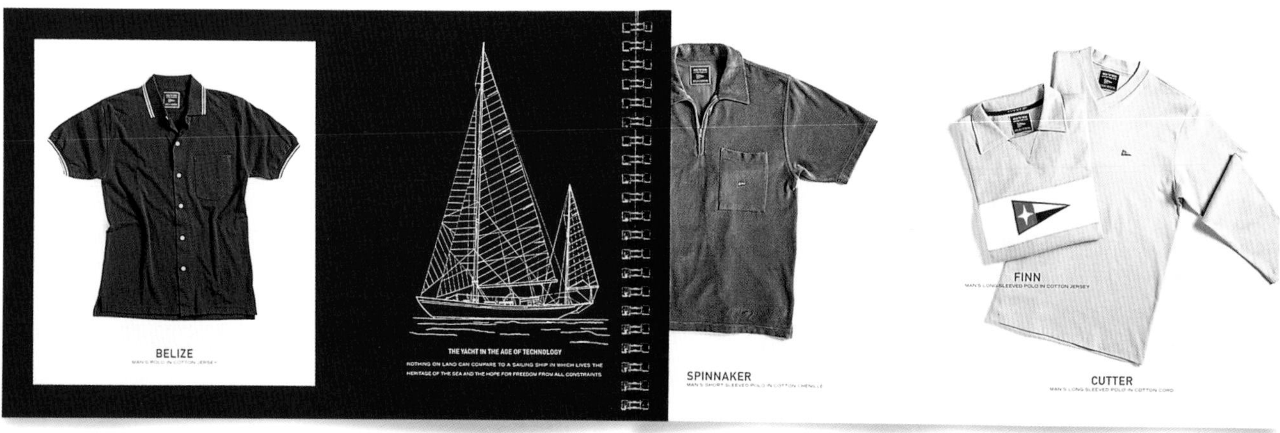
BELIZE
THE YACHT IN THE AGE OF TECHNOLOGY
SPINNAKER
FINN
CUTTER

CTD
UPSTREAM

## Ladies' & Men's Wear

CTD UPSTREAM CL: Dolomite CD, AD: Franco Vendramin D: Michele Pietrobon P: Faust Trevisan
DF: Novaidea Creative Resources Italy 1998 *SIZE: 153×229*

Easy Answers with
Originals BY EVERGREEN
The Perfect Pique Polo.
Pure and Simple.
The ultra fine cotton. The ideal fit. The flawless construction and extra-long tails. There's all-day comfort from collar to hem. Add in a full spectrum of all-occasion colors, and you've got what is unquestionably the perfect polo. The answer is Evergreen.
It's as easy as that.
27.50

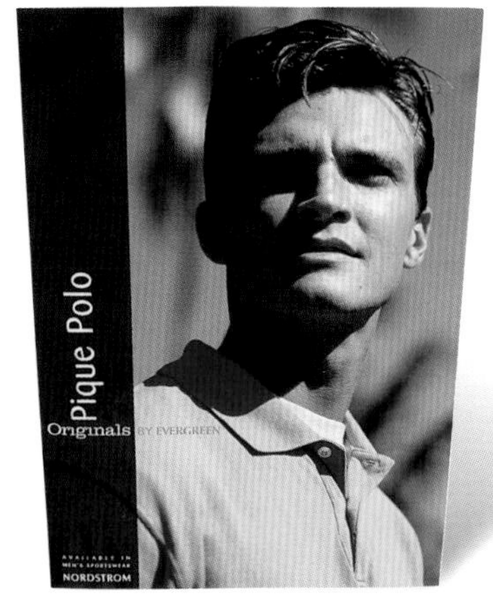

Pique Polo
Originals BY EVERGREEN
NORDSTROM

Easy Answers with
Originals BY EVERGREEN
The Perfect Chino Shirt.
Pure and Simple.
The perfect fit. The soft-washed cotton. The extra-long tails. All the right colors, and just the right price. This long-sleeve button down has "Favorite Shirt" written all over it. Stock your closet with these and stop wondering what to reach for each day. The answer is Evergreen.
It's as easy as that.
39.50

Chino Shirt
Originals BY EVERGREEN
NORDSTROM

Easy Answers with
Originals BY EVERGREEN
The Perfect Chino Walkshort.
Pure and Simple.
The feel of pure cotton. The comfortable cut. The detailed construction that ensures durability. You'll have both the right look and room to move. And a surprising choice of just the right colors. Walk right into summer in these perfect shorts. The answer is Evergreen. It's as easy as that.
27.50

Chino Walkshort
Originals BY EVERGREEN
NORDSTROM

**Ladies' & Men's Wear**

NORDSTROM CL: Nordstrom CD, AD: Franco Vendramin D: Steve McCluskey P: Daniela Federici DF: Novaidea Creative Resources Italy 1998 *SIZE: 230×157*

door het postorderbedrijf Mail&Female erotische lingerie voor vrouwen te
ontwerpen. De lijn die hieruit ontstaat - "Love from Holland" - is zo succes-
vol, dat ze in 1993 met steun van het ministerie van WVC haar eigen lingerielijn "Undressed by Marlies Dekkers" begint. Een jaar later wordt deze al
uitgebreid met een lingerielijn voor mannen. > De pers blijft haar
intussen belangstellend volgen, vooral vanwege haar spraakmakende optre-
dens en shows waarin ze op haar complexe vrouwbeelden voortbouwt. Maar in
de loop der jaren heeft Dekkers steeds minder entourage en spektakel nodig.
Het beeld van de zelfbewuste, uitdagende en erotische vrouw begint zich
helder uit te kristalliseren in de ontwerpen zelf en in de wijze waarop deze
gefotografeerd worden. De reportage in het septembernummer van Playboy
1993, in samenwerking met fotografe Inez van Lamsweerde, is daar een goe
voorbeeld van, evenals de latere fotoseries met Peter Wagenaar. Steeds zorg
de geraffineerde lingerie, goedgekozen poses en fraaie achtergrond ervoor
dat de sterk sensuele vrouw nergens een ordinaire pin-up of pornoster wo
> Tegelijkertijd maakt Dekkers zakelijk furore. "Undressed" is te koo
exclusieve lingeriezaken in binnen- en buitenland. Wanneer ze eind 1994
de bodyfashion-branche uitgeroepen wordt tot "lingeriedraagster" van he
jaar, levert dat een samenwerkingsverband op met de lingerieketen
Hunkemöller. De collectie die ze hiervoor ontwerpt bevat herkenbare, zi
kuisere elementen. Onder de naam "Seduced" brengt Hunkemöller de li
van Marlies Dekkers vanaf 1995 binnen het bereik van een groot publi
14000
1400
owards each other, there is room for women to manifest themselves as seducers in a
context of equality. Hence seduction gets a different tension and meaning." >
With her lingerie Dekkers does not only want to present a defiant self-confident erotic
woman, but at the same time she wants to question our manners and ideas about
seduction. > "Because after the topless period and feminism things have become
very boring", according to Dekkers. This is why she wants to reintroduce the tension
between men and women, but then in a modern way. "I consider it as a task of our
generation to capture the lost eroticism again."
1. Exhibition Catalogue Fashion and Art,
Museum of Fine Arts [ Brussels, 1996 ]
2. José Teunissen, The aggressive glamour of Véronique Leroy
in Items 6, 1994
Nudity in itself is not exiting. Eroticism
excellent tool for this."
[ Marlies Dekkers ]
256

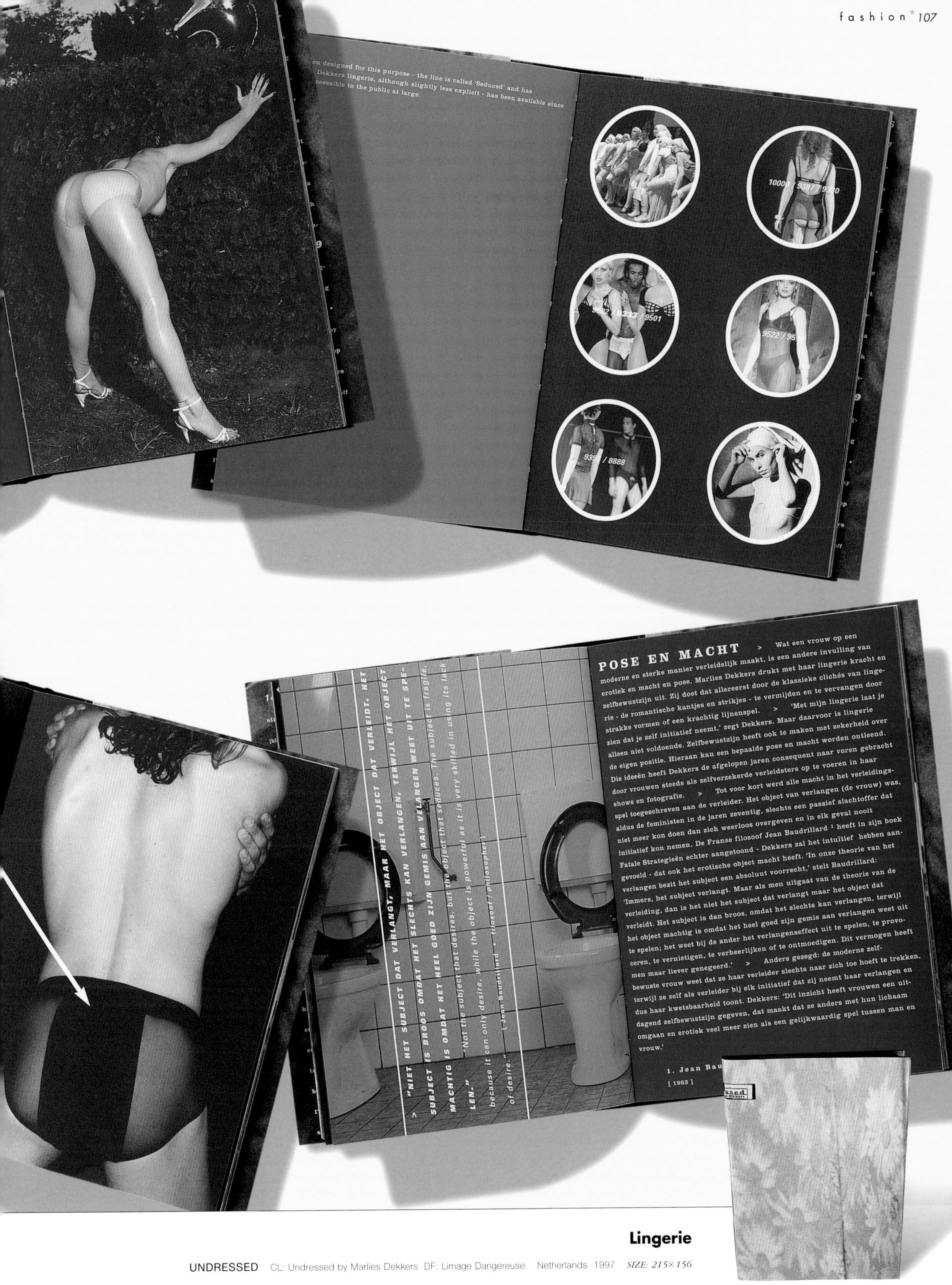

on designed for this purpose - the line is called 'Seduced' and has
Dekkers lingerie, although slightly less explicit - has been available since
ccessible to the public at large.

10000 / 9387 / 9510

9522 / 8333 / 9501

9522 / 95

939 / 8888

> "NIET HET SUBJECT DAT VERLANGT, MAAR HET OBJECT DAT VERLEIDT. HET
SUBJECT IS BROOS OMDAT HET SLECHTS KAN VERLANGEN, TERWIJL HET SPE-
MACHTIG IS OMDAT HET HEEL GOED ZIJN GEMIS AAN VERLANGEN WEET UIT TE SPE-
LEN." - Not the subject that desires, but the object that seduces. The subject is fragile,
because it can only desire, while the object is powerful as it is very skilled in using its lack
of desire." - Jean Baudrillard - filosoof / philosopher)

## POSE EN MACHT > Wat een vrouw op een
moderne en sterke manier verleidelijk maakt, is een andere invulling van
erotiek en macht en pose. Marlies Dekkers drukt met haar lingerie kracht en
zelfbewustzijn uit. Zij doet dat allereerst door de klassieke clichés van lingerie - de romantische kantjes en strikjes - te vermijden en te vervangen door
strakke vormen of een krachtig lijnenspel. > 'Met mijn lingerie laat je
zien dat je zelf initiatief neemt,' zegt Dekkers. Maar daarvoor is lingerie
alleen niet voldoende. Zelfbewustzijn heeft ook te maken met zekerheid over
de eigen positie. Hieraan kan een bepaalde pose en macht worden ontleend.
Die ideeën heeft Dekkers de afgelopen jaren consequent naar voren gebracht
door vrouwen steeds als zelfverzekerde verleidsters op te voeren in haar
shows en fotografie. > Tot voor kort werd alle macht in het
spel toegeschreven aan de verleider. Het object van verlangen (de vrouw) was,
aldus de feministen in de jaren zeventig, slechts een passief slachtoffer dat
niet meer kon doen dan zich weerloos overgeven en in elk geval nooit
initiatief kon nemen. De Franse filosoof Jean Baudrillard [1] heeft in zijn boek
Fatale Strategieën echter aangetoond - Dekkers zal het intuïtief hebben aan-
gevoeld - dat ook het erotische object macht heeft. 'In onze theorie van het
verlangen bezit het subject een absoluut voorrecht,' stelt Baudrillard:
'Immers, het subject verlangt. Maar als men uitgaat van de theorie van de
verleiding, dan is het niet het subject dat verlangt maar het object dat
verleidt. Het subject is dan broos, omdat het slechts kan verlangen, terwijl
het object machtig is omdat het heel goed zijn gemis aan verlangen weet uit
te spelen; het weet bij de ander het verlangenseffect uit te spelen, te provo-
ceren, te vernietigen, te verheerlijken of te ontmoedigen. Dit vermogen heeft
men maar liever genegeerd.' > Anders gezegd: de moderne zelfbewuste vrouw weet dat ze haar verleider slechts naar zich toe hoeft te trekken,
terwijl ze zelf als verleider bij elk initiatief dat zij neemt haar verlangen en
dus haar kwetsbaarheid toont. Dekkers: 'Dit inzicht heeft vrouwen een uit-
dagend zelfbewustzijn gegeven, dat maakt dat ze anders met hun lichaam
omgaan en erotiek veel meer zien als een gelijkwaardig spel tussen man en
vrouw.'

1. Jean Bau
[ 1983 ]

## Lingerie

UNDRESSED CL: Undressed by Marlies Dekkers DF: Limage Dangereuse Netherlands 1997 *SIZE: 215×156*

**Ladies' Wear**

GIRLIE WEAR CL: Girliewear CD, AD, D, I, CW: Skip Bolen DF: Skip Bolen Studio USA 1997 *SIZE: 216×138*

**Ladies' Wear**

METALICUS CL: Metalicus AD, D: Andrew Hoyne D: Natasha Schroter P: Marcus Struzina DF: Hoyne Design Australia 1997 *SIZE: 170×102*

Fiorucci
DOWN TO EARTH
EETY JEANS
WINTER '98 - '99
FIORUCCI
F368 TNE Metal
FAD6 TD4 Oregon
F165 TNE Fruit
F302 TN5 Linda
F865 TD4 Aurora
F101 TN5 Easy
Elio Fiorucci thanks
F 378 TNX Manlin
FAB4 TP9 Paster
F175 TP1 Noris
FIORUCCI
You are my sunshine!!
A FROG?
I'D ASKED FOR
A PRINCE!
FIORUCCI
UNA TI
SPAZ

F377 TNW Mec
FAC8 TR0 Pasha
FB63 T04 Iris
F160 TNB Stones
FAC4 T08 Carlitos
F473 TNW Rabia
FA85 TG3 Papaya
FB63 T04 Florida
F171 TNW Sullivan
FF11 T04 Summersby
FA83 TG2 Palmer
F176 TP1 Nefer
FIORUCCI

**Ladies' Wear**

FIORUCCI CL: Fiorucci Srl Italy 1998 *SIZE: 171×120, 200×151, 250×161*

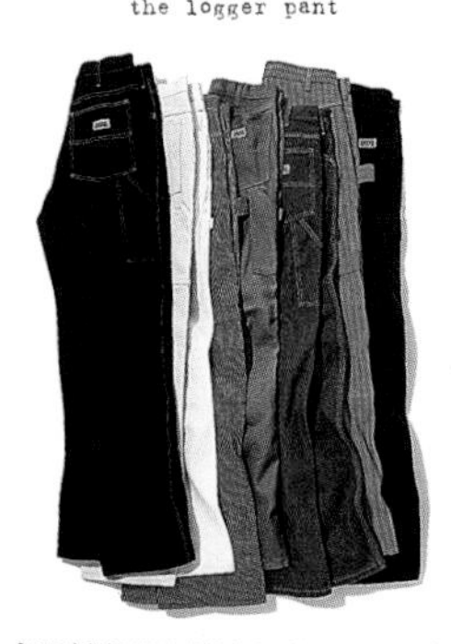

triple-knit hats

**Use your head.** Hearty, worsted spun acrylic. One size. USA. $15 each.
Top row (left to right): **RPM.** #250. **SEVEN TWENTY.** #251. **TRIPLE EIGHT.** #252.
Middle row (left to right): **CRUSH.** #253. **KILROY.** #254. **JACKSON.** #255.
Bottom row (left to right): **ORBIT.** #256. **THREE SIXTY.** #257. **OZONE.** #258.

1-800-432-7007
ORDER ANYTIME

**JOHNNY SHIRT.** Tricolor, long-sleeve rugby. Poly dazzle. S-XL. USA. #259. $40

**TAPED JACKET.** Lined with super-cozy fleece. Water/wind-resistant nylon oxford shell. Cargo chest pocket, Velcro®-seal cuffs, drawstring waist. 30". Polyfill. S-XL. USA. #260. $88

box fresh

**COLORBLOCK SHIRT.** Subprinted, long-sleeve vee neck. S-XL. Poly. USA. #261. $40

**BLOCK JACKET.** Toasty, soft fleece lining. Water/wind-resistant nylon oxford shell. Knit collar, storm cuffs, drawstring waist. 30" long. Polyfill. S-XL. USA. #262. $88

**SUBPRINT SHIRT.** Colorblocked, long-sleeve crew neck. S-XL. Poly. USA. #263. $40

**STRIPE JACKET.** Nylon oxford fights wind/water, polyfill interior keeps you warm. Wrap-around stripe. Adjustable, Velcro®-seal cuffs, drawstring waist. 30" long. S-XL. USA. #264. $88

17

## Ladies' and Men's Wear

GEAR TRIPLE EIGHT CL, DF: Gear Triple Eight CD, AD, CW: Robert Erskine CD, AD, D: Andrea Lew P: Mandy Schoch
USA 1997 *SIZE: 241×184*

**Ladies' and Men's Wear**

BEAMS CL: Beams Co., Ltd. AD, D, P: Mote Sinabel Japan 1998 *SIZE: 152×110*

Levi's
collection
printemps
- été '97
SPRing '97
TAPEZ : 3615 LEVIS
http : //www.levi.com.
Catalogue Levi Strauss
printemps-été '97
Conception : Marc Borgers
Photos Mode :
Geoffroy de Boisneau
Stylisme : Dominique Casalta
Photos Produits : Patrick Gries
Photos page 8 : Pascal Rougier
Illustrations p. 6 et 7 :
Angelo Di Marco
Production : Borgers Unltd
Imp. Lecerf - R.C.S. Pontoise B 672 044 971

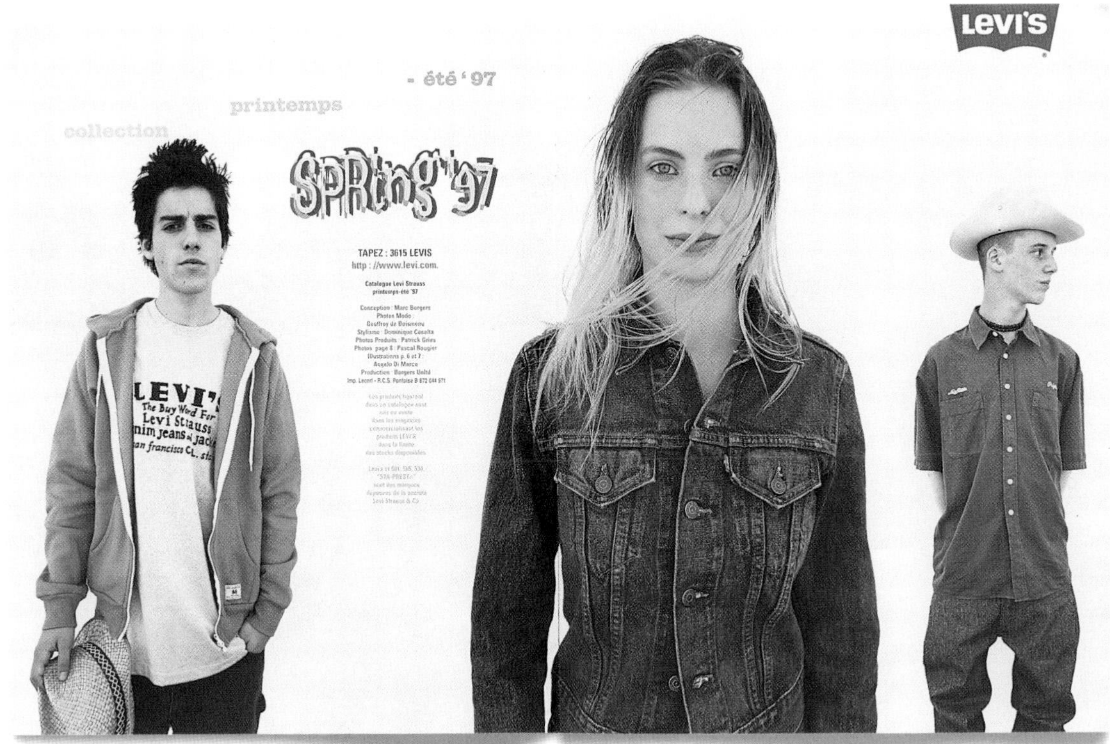

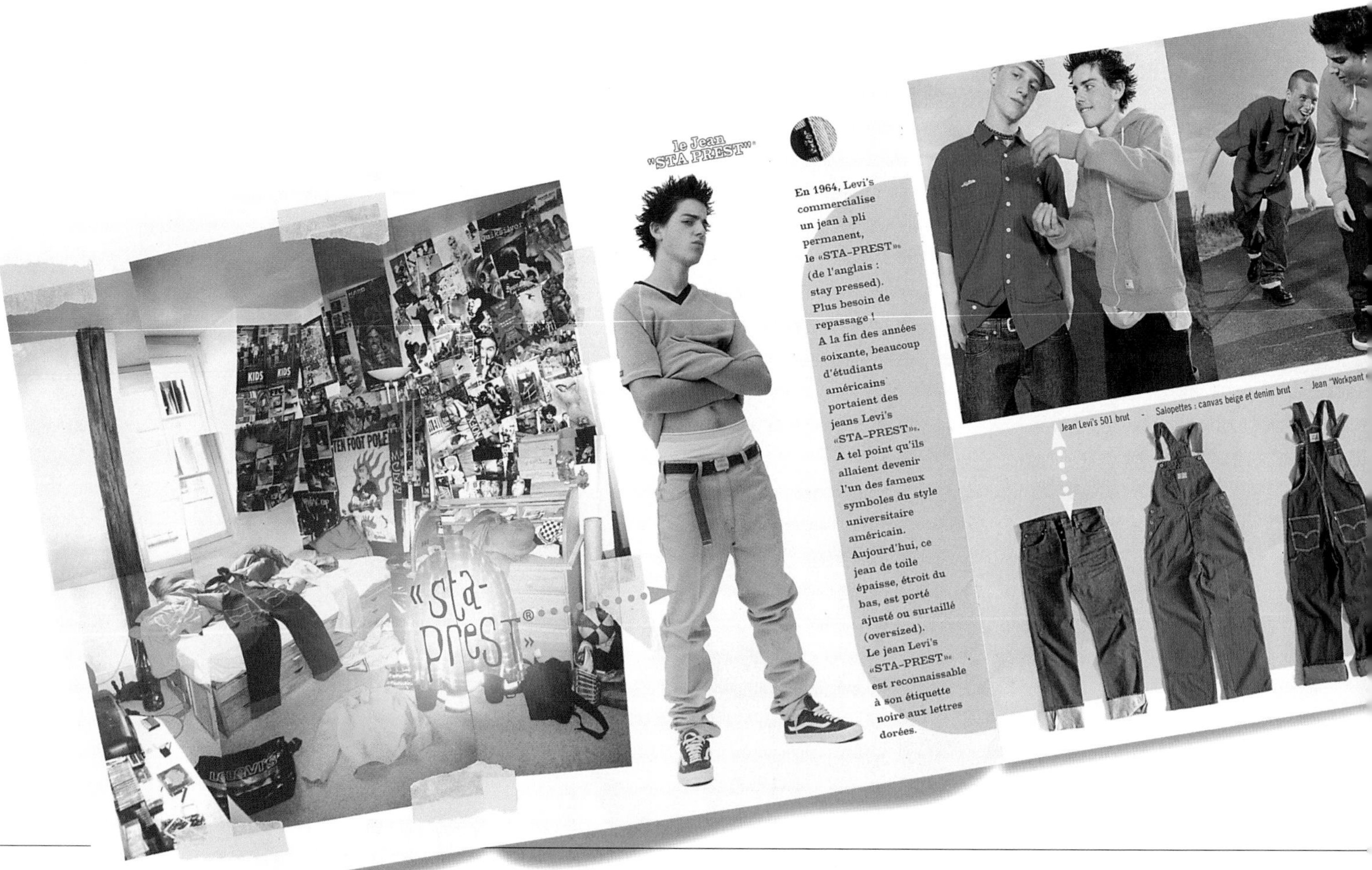

le Jean
"STA PREST"
«sta-prest»®
En 1964, Levi's commercialise un jean à pli permanent, le «STA-PREST®» (de l'anglais : stay pressed). Plus besoin de repassage ! A la fin des années soixante, beaucoup d'étudiants américains portaient des jeans Levi's «STA-PREST®». A tel point qu'ils allaient devenir l'un des fameux symboles du style universitaire américain. Aujourd'hui, ce jean de toile épaisse, étroit du bas, est porté ajusté ou surtaillé (oversized). Le jean Levi's «STA-PREST®» est reconnaissable à son étiquette noire aux lettres dorées.
Jean Levi's 501 brut - Salopettes : canvas beige et denim brut - Jean "Workpant"

artin, Max et Manu... Trois frères tellement jumeaux que
grain de beauté sur l'arrière de la cuisse gauche à la fossette du menton,
étaient interchangeables : mêmes yeux marrons rieurs, mêmes tignasses
nes, mêmes attitudes décontractées, mêmes façons de s'habiller...

petits, ils profitaient de cette ressemblance parfaite pour échapper aux punitions.
rt en maths, prenait la place de Max pendant ses "exams". Ou bien Manu, adroit
s, réparait les gaffes de Martin. Max, lui, était l'as du pinceau, du graff,
la famille. Il était passé directement des coloriages sur ses cahiers d'écolier à des
és remarqués sur les murs du quartier. Une galerie à la mode venait même de lui
accueillir sa première grande exposition!

Mais Max ne savait pas résister à la tentation. Dans le centre de la ville, il connaissait un grand mur vierge parfait pour graffer une dernière oeuvre sauvage! En pleine nuit, Max s'installa devant sa toile murale tel un Van Gogh urbain ayant abandonné ses pinceaux pour des bombes aérosol... Au petit matin, il finissait juste de donner la dernière touche de couleur à un immen-se dragon qui se dressait fier et fluo. Un passant, sur le chemin du travail, lui lança même un bravo admiratif...

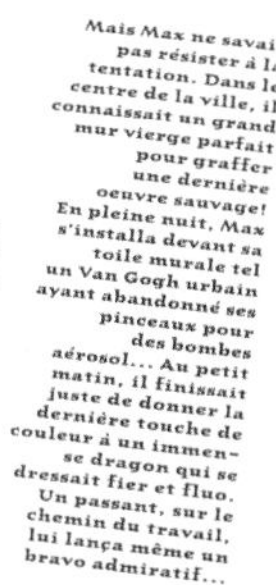

Des trois frères, **MANU** c'est le manuel. Il apprécie la souplesse de l'«**INDIGO VIEILLI**». Cette toile, certains la surnomment «moustache» en référence à l'usure spécifique des plis du bassin: *(Voir Détail)* on dirait effectivement les **moustaches** d'un chat! Un procédé quelque peu artisanal permet de mettre en valeur les contrastes du bleu. L'«Indigo Vieilli» existe en trois intensités de base : Foncé, bleu moyen et très clair.

L'artiste de la famille, c'est **MAX**. Il aime faire son jean lui-même, ça le distingue. Il porte le jean **«BRUT»** qu'il a acheté une taille plus grand. C'est l'indigo sous sa forme pure. La toile est raide, il faut la dompter et petit à petit marquer les formes de son corps dans le bleu foncé du denim. *Remarquez ici*, les bas sont retournés vers l'extérieur façon *«turn ups»*...

**MARTIN** le «matheux» porte un jean **«ONE WASH»**. Ce jean est coupé dans la toile classique du début du siècle, le tissage *"ring-ring"*, ultra-résistant. Ensuite, il est lavé une seule fois. Cela permet de porter un denim ultra foncé qui, avec le temps, se fait à votre corps. (Voir aussi les conseils-recette page suivante).

**Martin, Max et Manu...** Trois frères tellement jumeaux que du grain de beauté sur l'arrière de la cuisse gauche à la fossette du menton, ils étaient interchangeables : mêmes yeux marrons rieurs, mêmes tignasses brunes, mêmes attitudes décontractées, mêmes façons de s'habiller...

Déjà, tout petits, ils profitaient de cette ressemblance parfaite pour échapper aux punitions. Martin, fort en maths, prenait la place de Max pendant ses "exams". Ou bien Manu, adroit de ses mains, réparait les gaffes de Martin. Max, lui, était l'as du pinceau, du graff, l'artiste de la famille. Il était passé directement des coloriages sur ses cahiers d'écolier à des graffitis très remarqués sur les murs du quartier. Une galerie à la mode venait même de lui proposer d'accueillir sa première grande exposition!

Mais Max ne savait pas résister à la tentation. Dans le centre de la ville, il connaissait un grand mur vierge parfait pour graffer une dernière oeuvre sauvage! En pleine nuit, Max s'installa devant sa toile murale tel un Van Gogh urbain ayant abandonné ses pinceaux pour des bombes aérosol... Au petit matin, il finissait juste de donner la dernière touche de couleur à un immen-se dragon qui se dressait fier et fluo. Un passant, sur le chemin du travail, lui lança même un bravo admiratif...

Tant pis ! Max avait mal choisi son moment: c'était la «Semaine de Propreté»! Les trois frères furent convoqués au commissariat. Alignés devant un mur, ils souriaient. Même leurs amis n'étaient pas capable de les différencier. Et pourtant le témoin tendit la main en direction... du jean de Max : "C'est celui-là, le bon ! – Le mauvais ! lui répondit le flic, en pensant au délit.– Je parle du jean ! C'est celui-là qui a peint ce magnifique dragon !" Le policier se retourna. En effet, Max portait un jean «brut», alors que Martin avait sur les fesses le «one-wash» (lavé une fois) et Manu un «indigo vieilli»... Cela sautait aux yeux ! Les jumeaux ne se ressemblaient plus !

LEVI'S
catalogue
SPRing '97
LEVI'S

## Casual Wear

LEVI'S STRAUSS CL: Levi's Strauss CD, AD, D, CW: Marc Borgers P: Geoffroy de Boismenu I: Angelo Di Marco DF: Borgers Unlimited France 1997 *SIZE: 310×245*

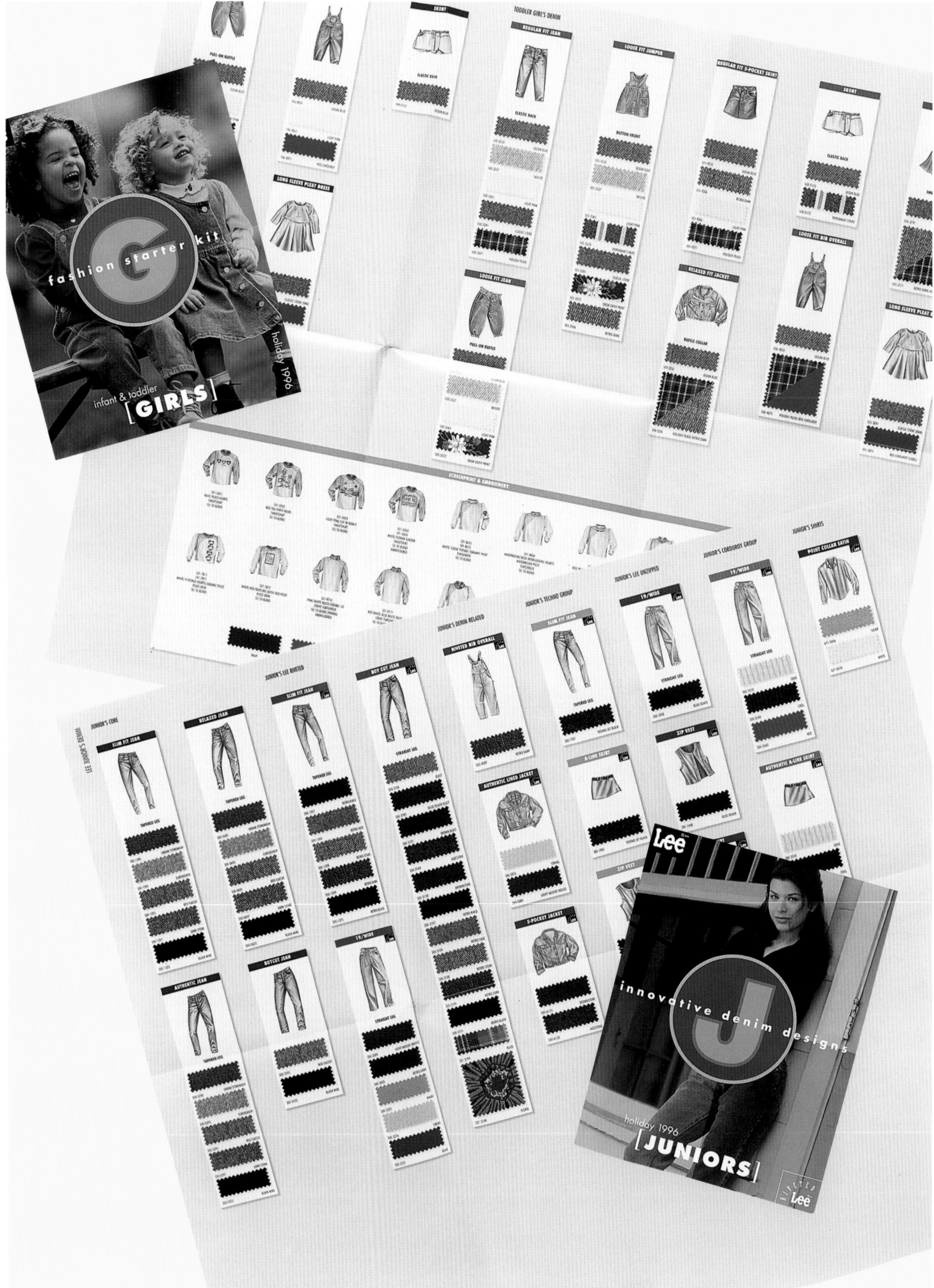


## Children's Clothes

LEE JEANS CL: Lee Jeans D: Joann Otto CW: Jeff Sobul DF: Muller + Company USA 1996 *SIZE: 280×216*

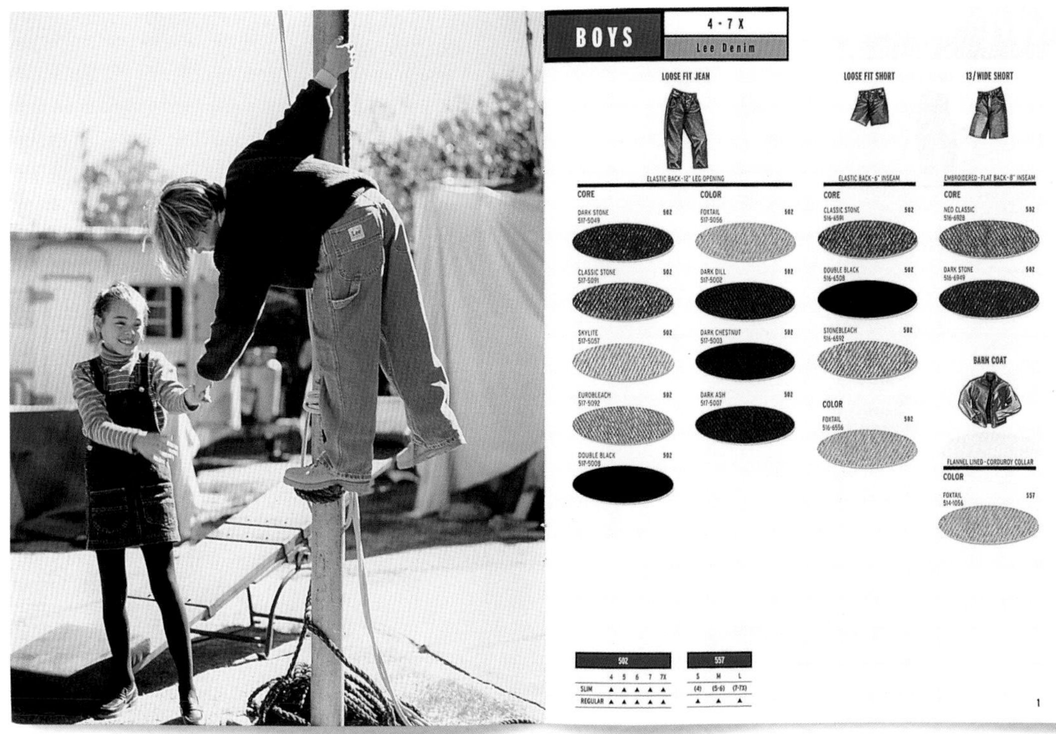

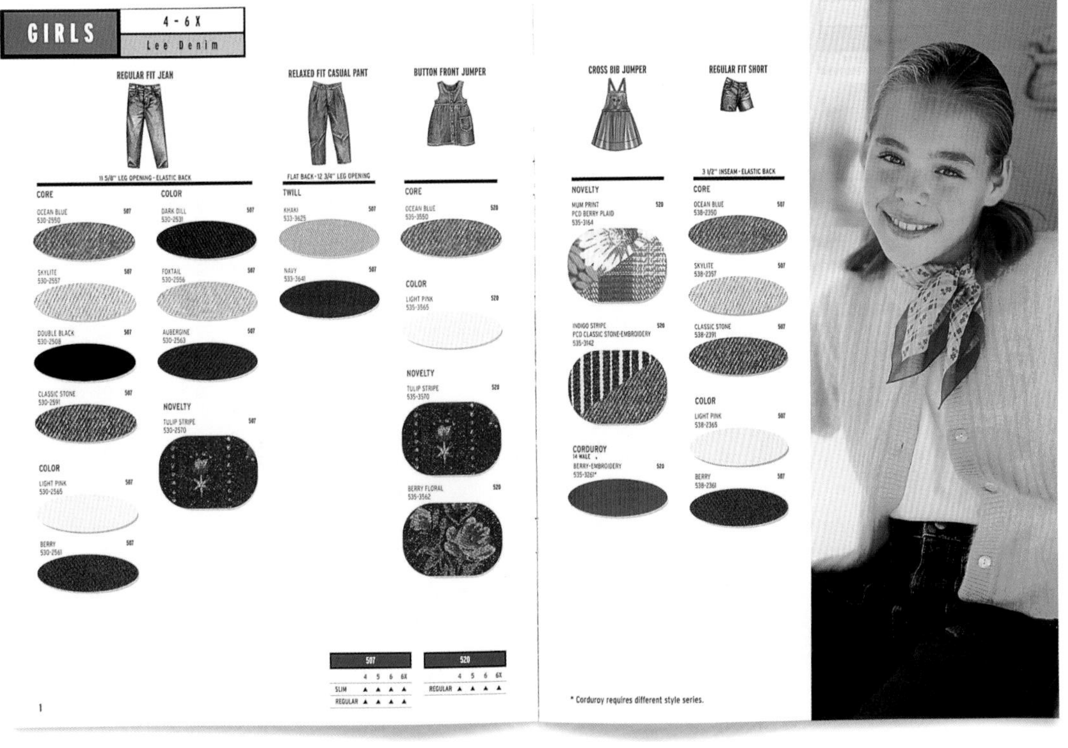

## Children's Clothes

LEE JEANS CL: Lee Jeans CD: John Muller AD: Susan Wilson D: Joann Otto / Jeff Miller / Denise Grojean P: Michael Regnier DF: Muller + Company USA 1996 *SIZE: 280×215*

36
photo: Pierre Choinière
cover
Sweater 48$
Page 2
Shirt 38$
Page 3
Blouse 38$
Pants 68$
Necklace 20$
Page 4
Polo Shirt 48$
Baithing Suit N/A
Page 5
Cardigan 48$
Skirt 58$
Page 6
Windbreaker 68$
Shirt 38$
Pants 38$
Page 7
T-Shirt 28$
Striped Beret 15$
Pullover 38$
Beret 12$
Page 8
Jacket 188$
Polo Shirt 42$
Pants 88$
T-Shirt 15$
Page 9
Jacket 48$
Polo Shirt 22$
Pants 78$
Sunglasses 18$
Page 10
Sweater 48$
Page 11
Sweater 48$
Page 12
T-Shirt 18$
Scarf (free with T-Shirt) Promo
Page 13
Striped T-Shirt 18$
Sweater with zip 38$
Page 14
Umbrella 25$
Blouse 32$
Sunglasses 10$
Capri Pants 42$
Page 16
Skirt 48$
Jacket 98$
Page 17
Top 48$
Pants 68$
Page 18
Top 48$
Skirt 48$
Page 19
T-Shirt 38$
Skirt 78$
Page 20
Shirt 38$
Sunglasses 18$
Page 21
Polo Shirt 42$
Blouse 48$
Belt 25$
all prices are in US dollars
Page 23
Overalls 88$
Beret 12$
Page 24
Pants 88$
Polo Shirt 38$
Belt 28$
Page 25
Polo Shirt 38$
Sunglasses 18$
Page 26
Jacket 118$
Page 28 & 29
Pants 68$
Dress 78$
Sunglasses 10$
Page 30
Polo Shirt 28$
Page 31
Jacket 168$
Shirt 48$
Tie 42$
Page 33
Jacket 118$
Pants 68$
Earrings 10$
Page 34
Blouse 38$
Necklace 20$
Pants 68$
Page 36
Shirt 48$
T-Shirt 38$
Sunglasses 18$
Earrings 10$
1230 ave of the Americas, N.Y.C., NY 10020
Roosevelt Field Shopping Center, Long Island, NY
Stamford Town Center, CT
South Shore Plaza, MA
Burlington Mall, MA

Tristan & AMERICA

## Ladies' Wear

TRISTAN & AMERICA CL: Tristan & America AD, D: Pol Baril / Denis Dulude P: Pierre Choinère
DF: K-O Creation Canada 1996 *SIZE: 140×139*

## Premium Goods

PEPSI CL: Pepsi-Cola CD, AD, D: John Norman AD, D: Mark Cantor AD: Michael Cory P: Peggy Sirota / Taka Studio I: Eric Pearl DF: Pinkhaus USA 1995 *SIZE: 175×176*

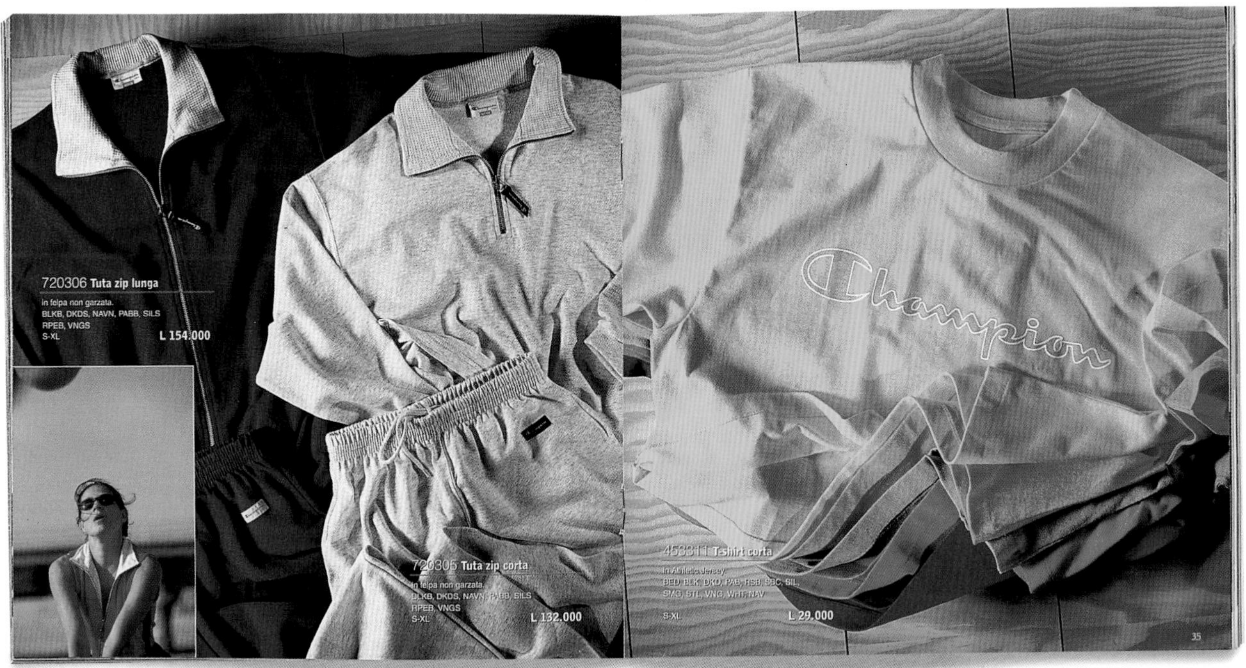

## Sportswear

CHAMPION U.S.A. CL: Champion U.S.A. CD, AD: Franco Vendramin D: Steve McCluskey P: Zucchi Ferruccio DF: Novaidea Creative Resources Italy 1997 *SIZE: 194×194*

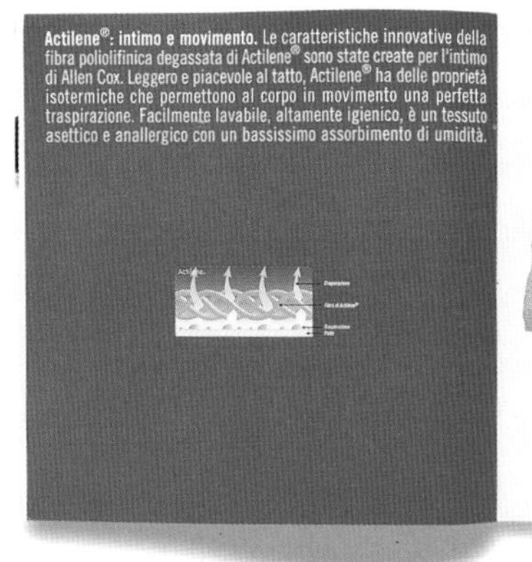
**Actilene®: intimo e movimento.** Le caratteristiche innovative della fibra poliolifinica degassata di Actilene® sono state create per l'intimo di Allen Cox. Leggero e piacevole al tatto, Actilene® ha delle proprietà isotermiche che permettono al corpo in movimento una perfetta traspirazione. Facilmente lavabile, altamente igienico, è un tessuto asettico e anallergico con un bassissimo assorbimento di umidità.

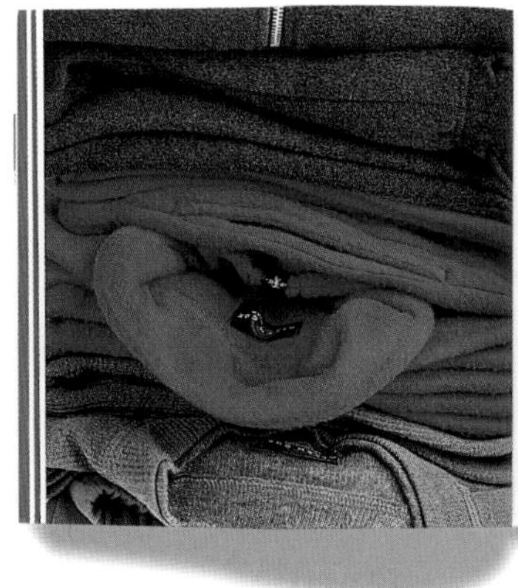
Allen Cox
corpi.
ACTIVEWEAR
in
movimento

ALLEN COX
COD. 5568 Boxer in jersey elasticizzato Thermocot elevato comfort segue ogni movimento del corpo

## Men's Underwear

ALLEN COX UNDERWEAR CL: Arcte AD, D: Giona Maiarelli P: Luca Castelli CW: Stefania Gaeta
DF: Maiarelli & Rathkopf Design Italy 1998 *SIZE: 300×320*

# recreation

sports

transportation

travel

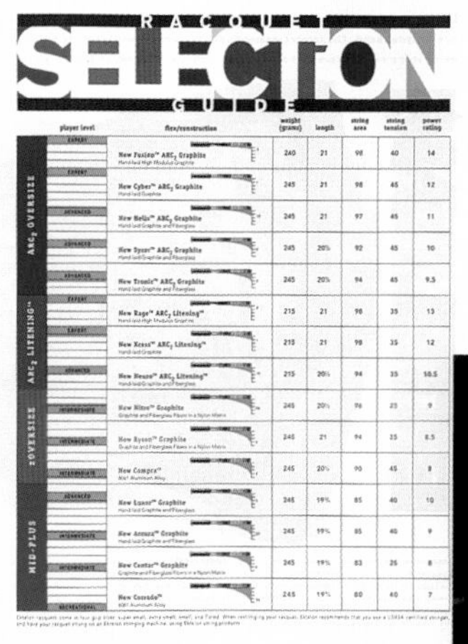

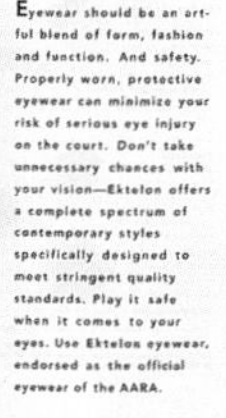

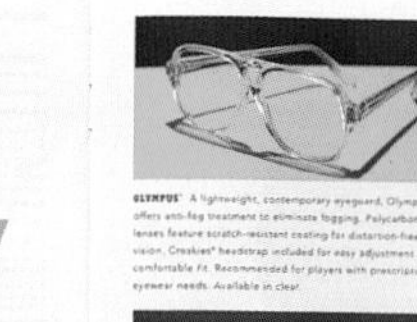

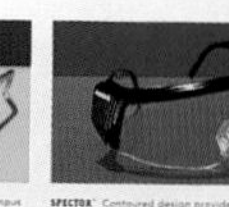

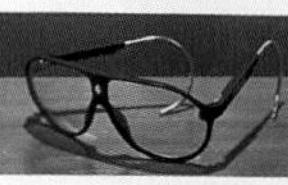

Tighten the wrist cord. Even up the strings. Inhale deeply. Before you know it, you're immersed in all-out, head-to-head competition. The sweat flies, and you're having a great time.

You're also getting a great workout. Racquetball is excellent exercise for those who are physically fit...and the ideal sport for those who want to be. Actor Eddie Murphy, Jeff Conine of the Florida Marlins and singer Kenny Loggins join the more than 10,000,000 people today who play racquetball to stay in shape. You too can achieve overall fitness by playing racquetball. Just check this out:

# RACQUETBALL IS FITNESS!

• **Caloric Consumption.** The action in racquetball is intense—play an hour and you'll burn more than 700 calories of energy. That's more calories per hour than cycling at 18 m.p.h., playing basketball, running an 8 1/2 minute mile or playing a game of tennis. Racquetball is a perfect sport for weight maintenance.

• **Total Muscle Tone.** The activity in racquetball involves all of the major muscle groups (leg, trunk, arm, back and stomach). The dynamics of the sport require that for every action, there is a split-second reaction. Because racquetball is so physically demanding, the sport is an excellent vehicle for developing and maintaining muscle tone.

• **Cardiovascular Workout.** A typical player makes over 1,200 explosive movements on the court during a one-hour workout, and covers nearly two miles in quick one and two-step bursts. Your heart rate increases and is maintained at 70%–80% of its maximum. This provides a low level cardiovascular fitness program, especially for lower level players, and a cardiovascular maintenance program for more skilled, advanced players.

• **Hand-Eye Coordination.** Racquetball offers an excellent way to improve hand-eye coordination. This is an important additional benefit of any exercise program, and is not available in many club workout activities.

• **Flexibility.** Developing endurance, joint flexibility and muscle strength is important in a comprehensive exercise program. The tremendous range of motion required to participate in racquetball forces muscles to stretch, resulting in flexibility. Many participating players also stretch in a pre-post game stretching program.

Racquetball provides definable and measurable fitness benefits. Whether you play competitively or just for fun, if you hit the court regularly you'll see an improvement in your physical condition and performance. What more could you ask of a sport that offers so much enjoyment?

| Activity | Calories/ Minute |
|---|---|
| Running (7 minute miles) | 17.4 |
| Racquetball | 13.7 |
| Cycling (racing) | 13.0 |
| Swimming (backstroke) | 13.0 |
| Swimming (crawl) | 12.0 |
| Basketball | 10.6 |
| Tennis | 8.4 |
| Cycling (leisure) | 7.7 |
| Golf | 6.5 |
| Walking | 6.3 |
| Volleyball | 3.9 |

Source: Michael O'Shea, Ph.D., Sports Training Institute

## Racquetball Rackets

TOTAL RACQUETBALL CL: Ektelon CD, AD, D: Jose' A. Serrano P: Carl Vanderschuit
DF: Mires Design Inc. USA 1994 *SIZE: 279×217*

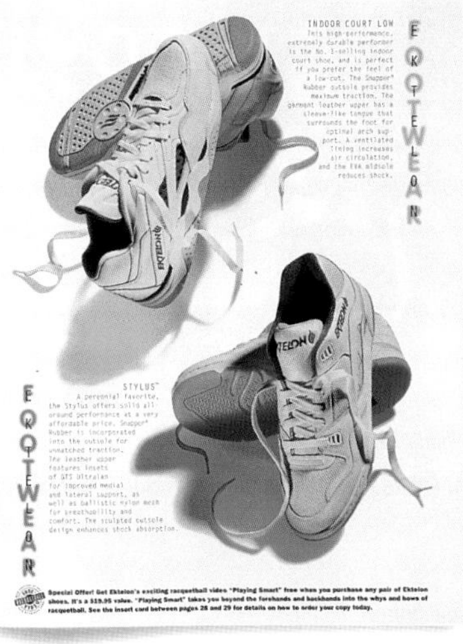

**Racquetball Rackets**

TOTAL RACQUETBALL CL: Ektelon CD, AD, D: Jose' A. Serrano P: Carl Vanderschuit
DF: Mires Design Inc. USA 1994 *SIZE: 279×217*

VEST KIT
DOWN PACK

PREMIER
SNOW WEAR/PREMIER/'97 COLLECTION
DOWN PACK
VEST KIT
Knit 2in1

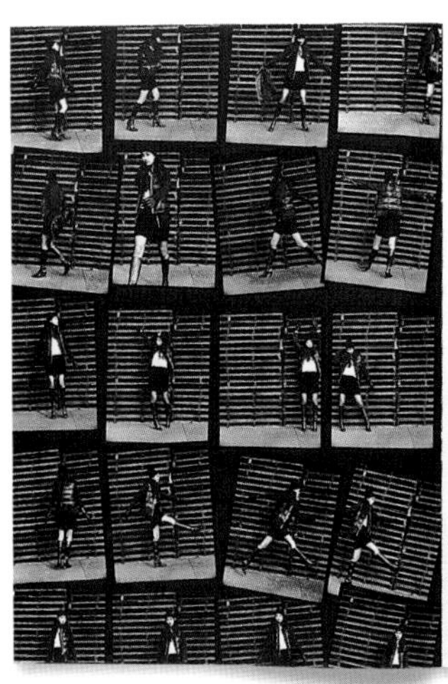

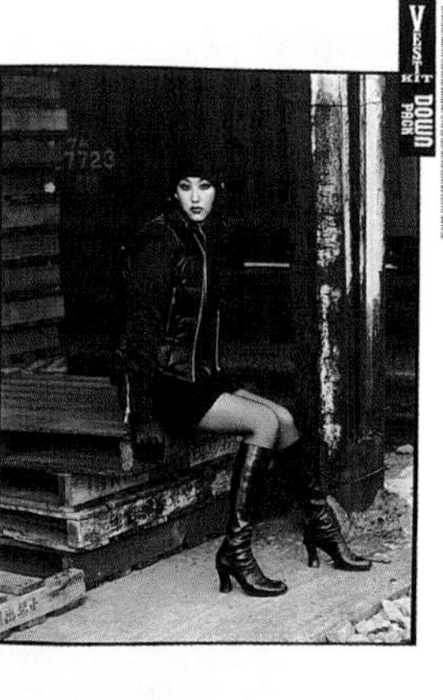

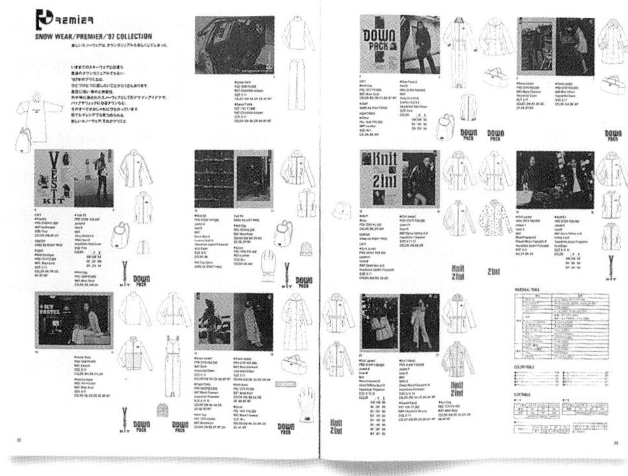

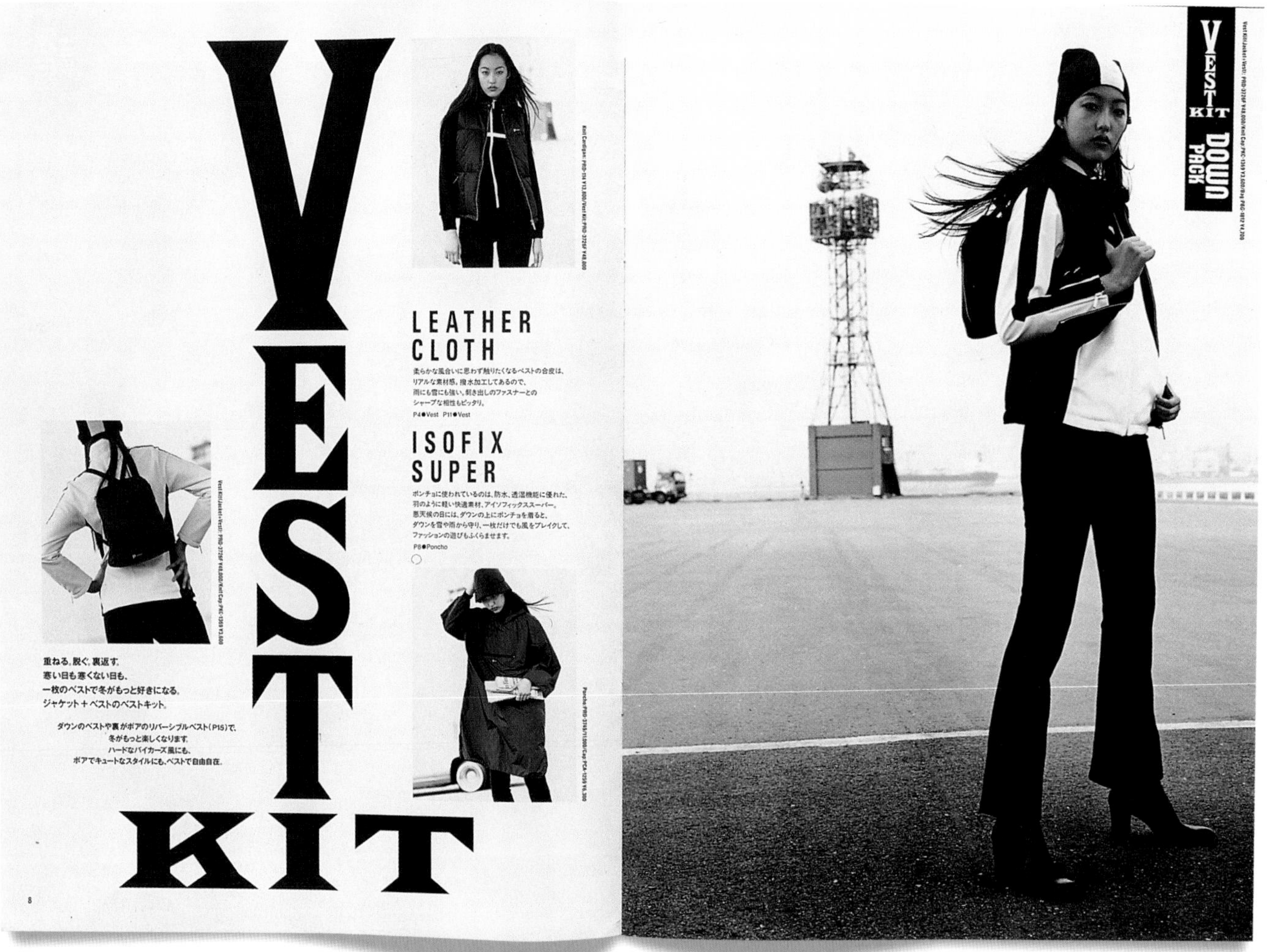

VEST
KIT
LEATHER
CLOTH
柔らかな風合いに思わず触りたくなるベストの合皮は、
リアルな素材感。撥水加工してあるので、
雨にも雪にも強い。剥き出しのファスナーとの
シャープな相性もピッタリ。
P4●Vest P11●Vest
ISOFIX
SUPER
ポンチョに使われているのは、防水、透湿機能に優れた、
羽のように軽い快適素材、アイソフィックススーパー。
悪天候の日には、ダウンの上にポンチョを着ると、
ダウンを雪や雨から守り、一枚だけでも風をブレイクして、
ファッションの遊びもふくらませます。
P8●Poncho
重ねる。脱ぐ。裏返す。
寒い日も寒くない日も、
一枚のベストで冬がもっと好きになる。
ジャケット＋ベストのベストキット。
ダウンのベストや裏がボアのリバーシブルベスト（P15）で、
冬がもっと楽しくなります。
ハードなバイカーズ風にも、
ボアでキュートなスタイルにも、ベストで自由自在。
8
VEST KIT
DOWN PACK

PREMIER
SNOW WEAR/PREMIER/'97 COLLECTION

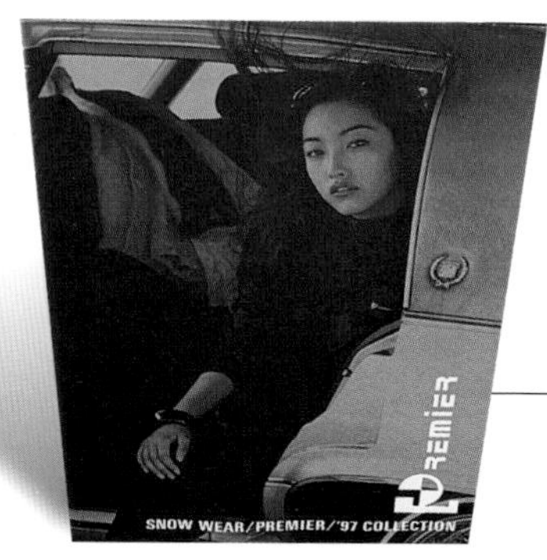

**Sportswear**

PREMIER CL: Descente., Ltd. AD, D: Motoko Naruse P: Hisashi Shimizu CW: Shinobu Matsuzuka
DF: Naruse Motoko Design Room Japan 1996 *SIZE: 363×257*

自分が宇宙の一部分だと実感する。
どんな自然を楽しみたいか、
数字と記号で選択できるシステム。
WARMTH SYSTEM
VERSATILITY SYSTEM
D.D. MULTI-FUNCTION GARMENT SYSTEM
900RVCP
900SDCP
900V2IN1
900CP
500R
300R

'97 D.D. WOMEN'S COLLECTION
RAID D.D.
TEAM D.D.
SOFT D.D.

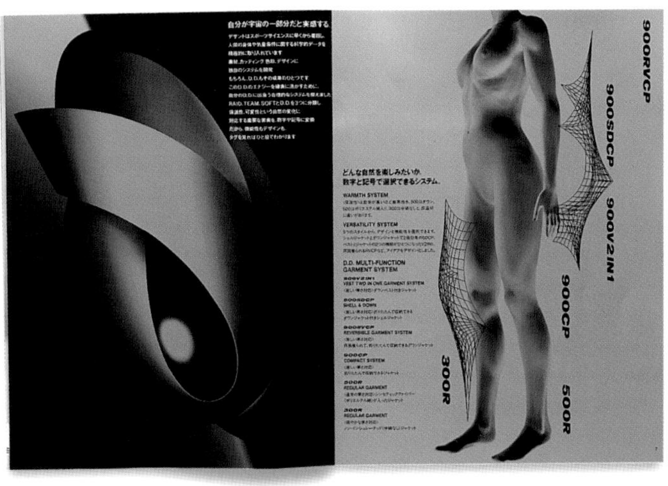

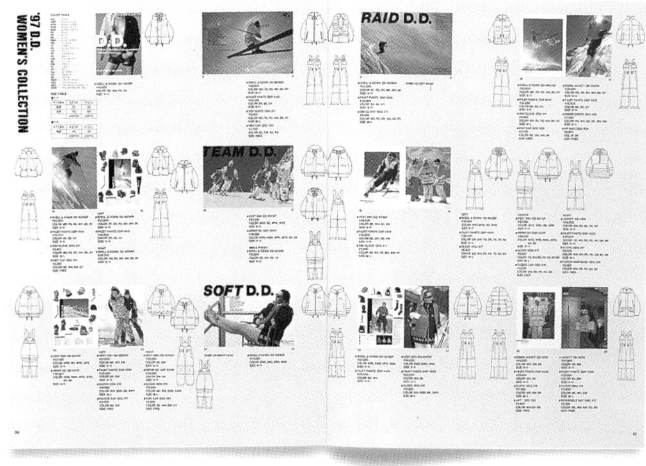

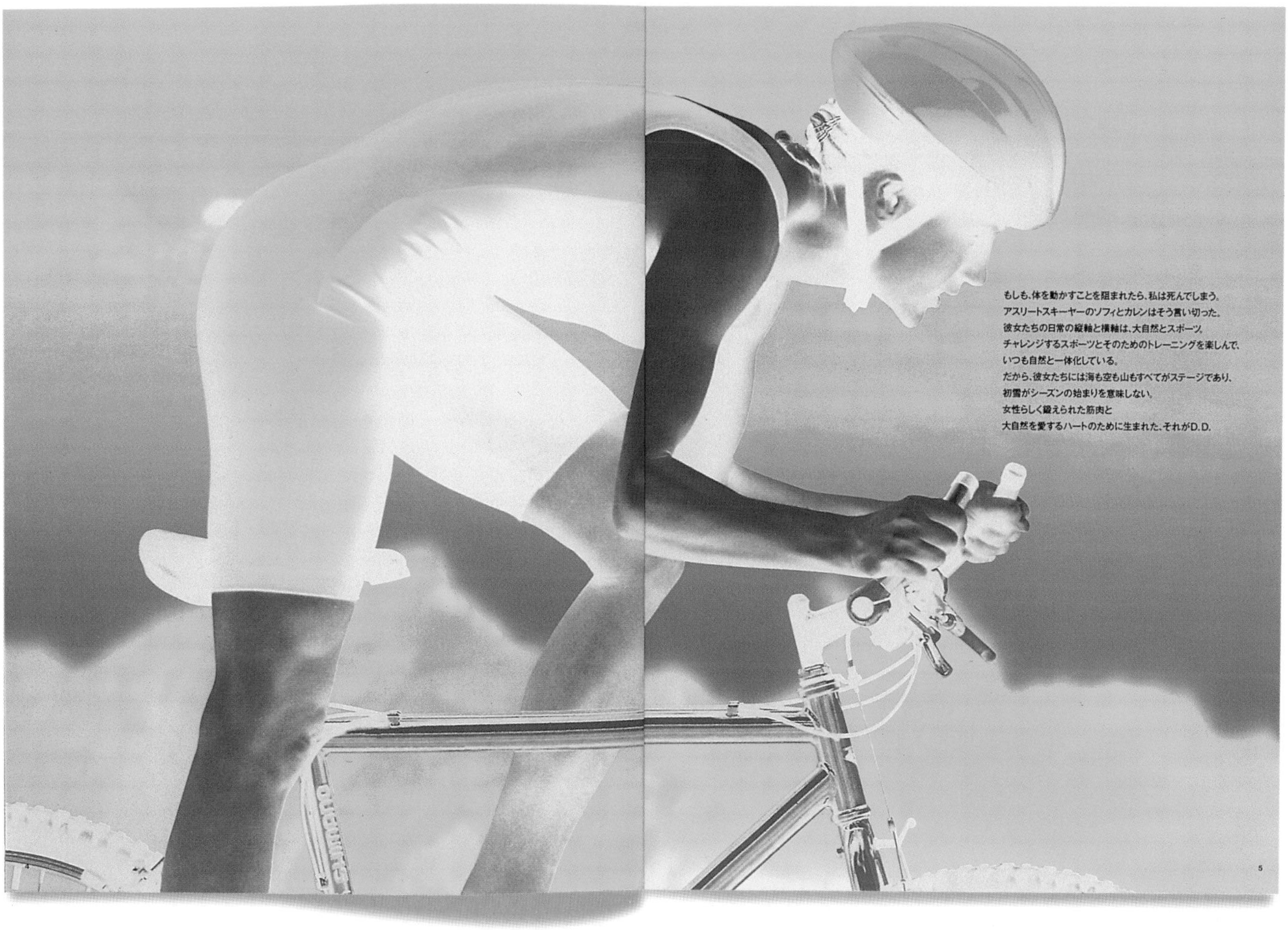

もしも、体を動かすことを阻まれたら、私は死んでしまう。
アスリートスキーヤーのソフィとカレンはそう言い切った。
彼女たちの日常の縦軸と横軸は、大自然とスポーツ。
チャレンジするスポーツとそのためのトレーニングを楽しんで、
いつも自然と一体化している。
だから、彼女たちには海も空も山もすべてがステージであり、
初雪がシーズンの始まりを意味しない。
女性らしく鍛えられた筋肉と
大自然を愛するハートのために生まれた、それがD.D.
5

DESCENTE DECOR
D.D.
The skier--poised between the sky and the earth
--aggressive and positive
'97 D.D. WOMEN'S COLLECTION

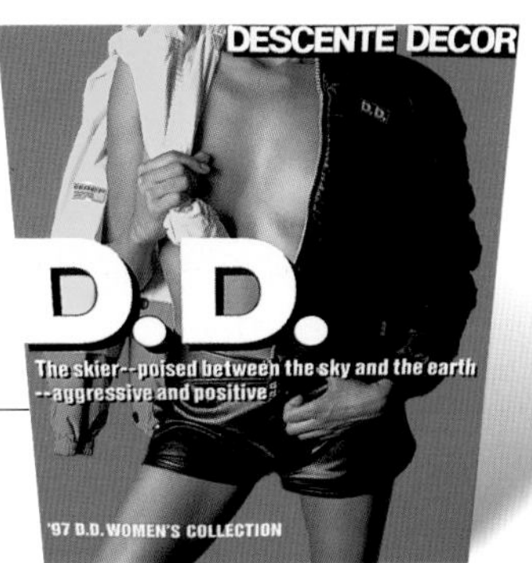

**Sportswear**

D. D. CL: Descente., Ltd. AD, D: Motoko Naruse P: Philip Fregnol / Kouichi Moriya / Kazu Nakamura CW: Shinobu Matsuzuka CG: Masayuki Itokazu DF: Naruse Motoko Design Room Japan 1996 *SIZE: 300×232*

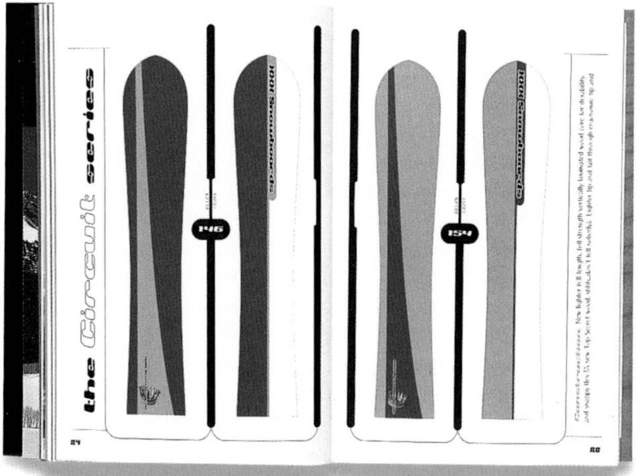
the Circuit series
146
154

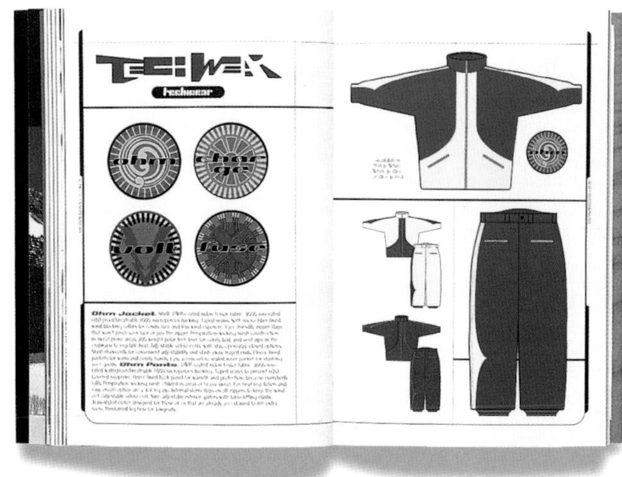
techwear

the Charge series

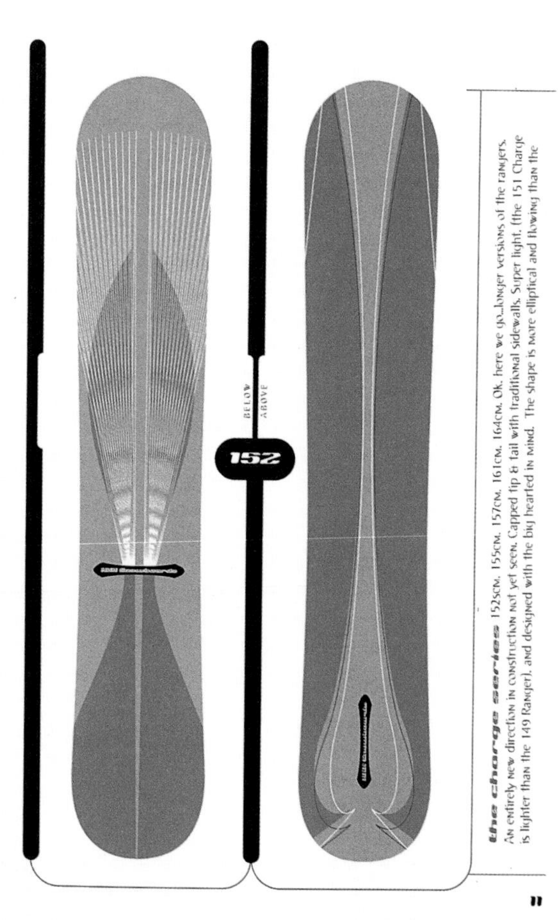
BELOW
ABOVE
152
the charge series 152cm, 155cm, 157cm, 161cm, 164cm. Ok, here we go...longer versions of the rangers.
An entirely new direction in construction not yet seen. Capped tip & tail with traditional sidewalls. Super light, (the 151 Charge
is lighter than the 149 Ranger), and designed with the big hearted in mind. The shape is more elliptical and flowing than the
11

## Snowboards

XXX CL, CW: XXX Snowboards CD, AD, D, I: Carlos Segura D, I: Colin Metcalf D: Laura Alberts P: Jeff Sciortino / Photonica I: Tony Klassen DF: Segura Inc. USA 1996 *SIZE: 194×133*

Table of Contents
98/99


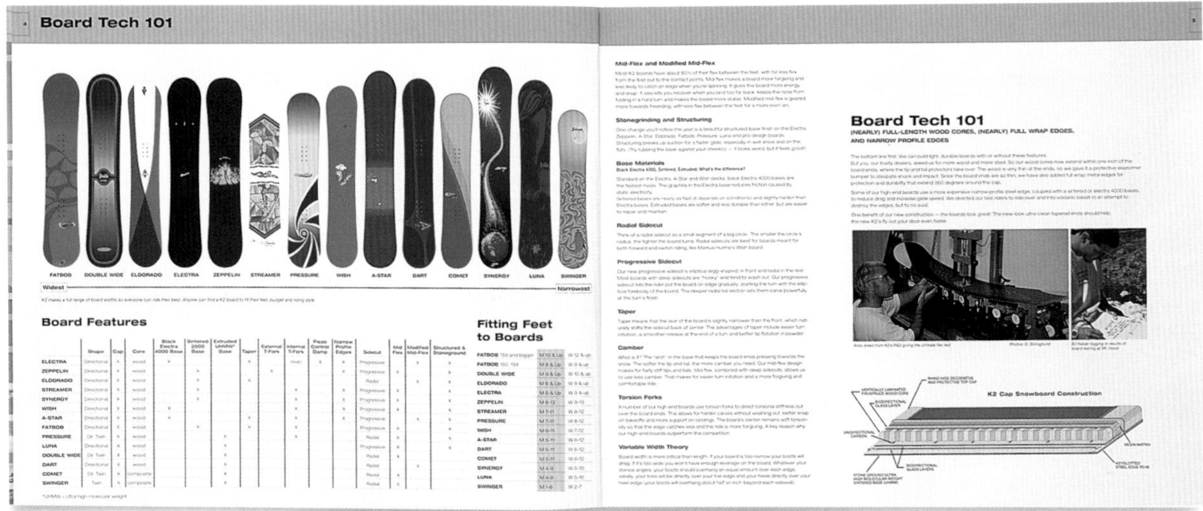

Board Tech 101
Board Features
Fitting Feet to Boards
Board Tech 101


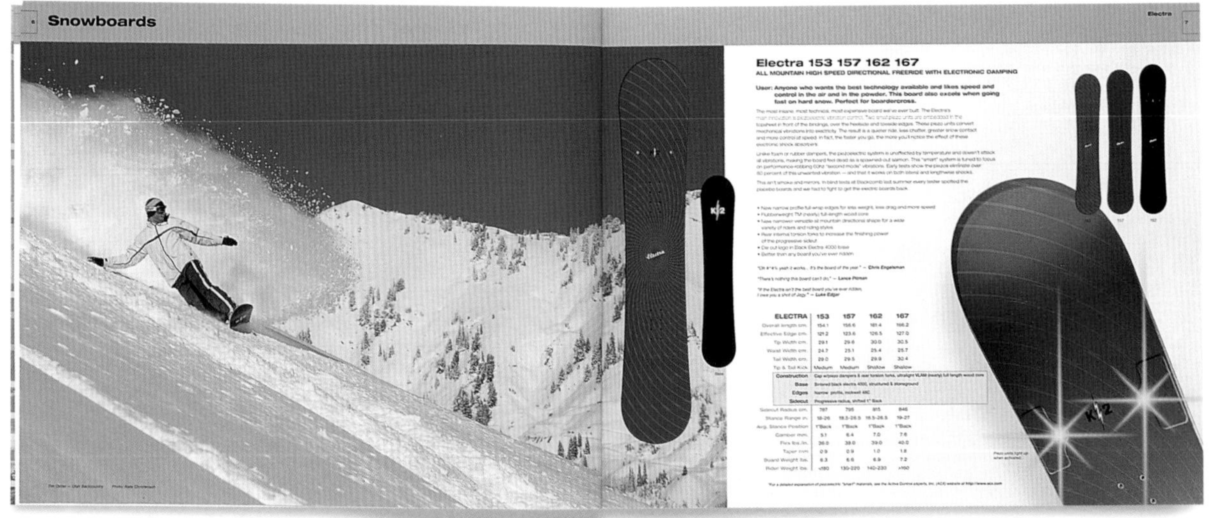

Snowboards
Electra 153 157 162 167

**Snowboards**

K2 SNOWBOARDS CL: K2 Snowboards CD: Hayley, Brent & Luke @ K2 Snowboards AD, D: Michael Strassburger D: Mark Atherton / Vittorio Costarella / Robynne Raye P: Jimmy Clark / Nils CW: John Erben DF: Modern Dog USA 1997 *SIZE: 233×293*

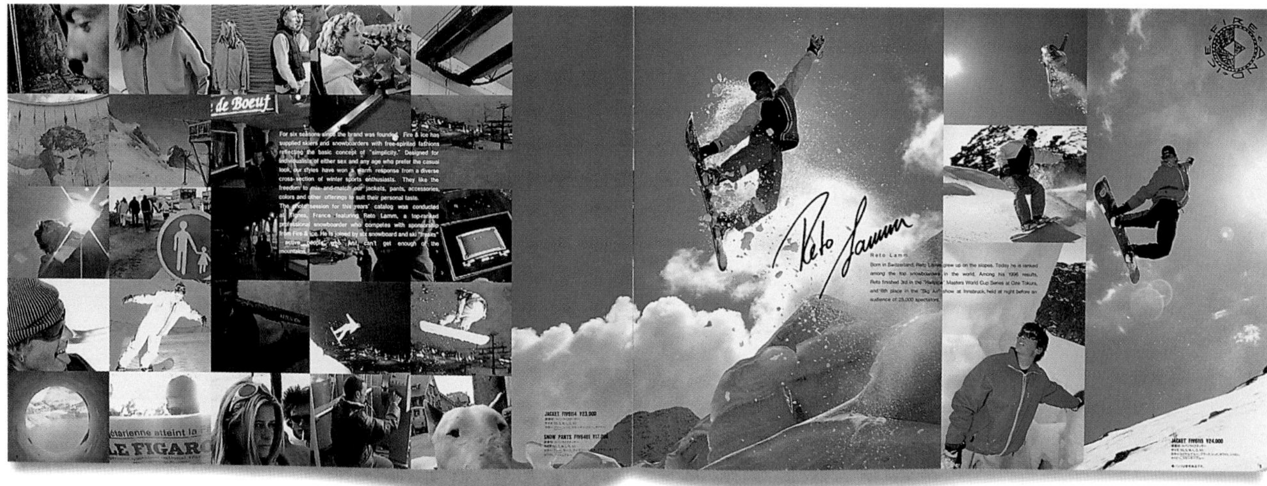

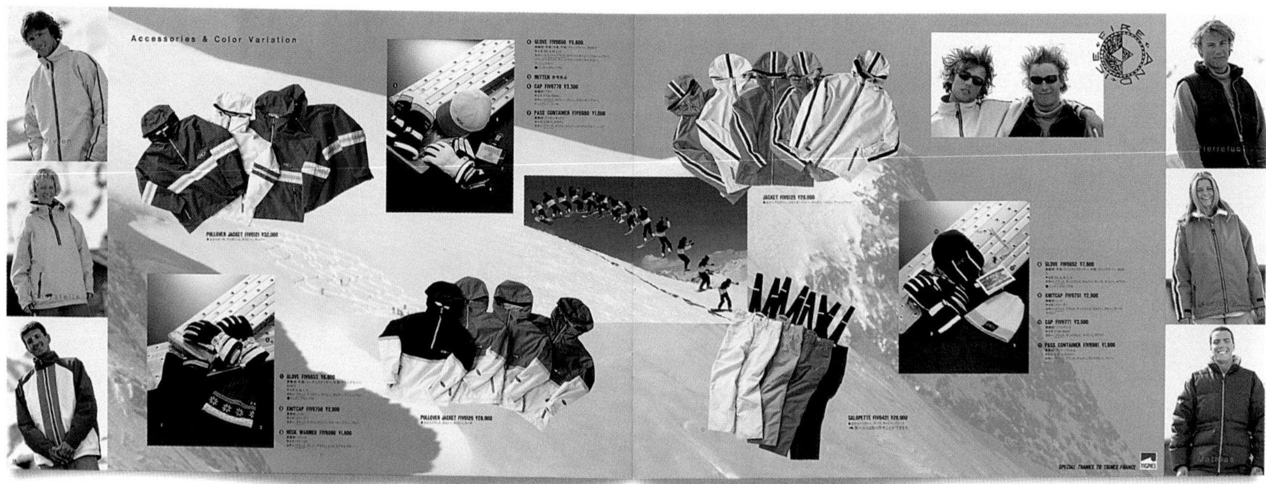

## Sports Equipment

FIRE & ICE CL: Phenix Co., Ltd. CD: Genyu Nakasone AD: Tetsuo Fujiwara D: Fumiko Arai P: Jean Marc Favre CW: Yoichi Sekiguchi DF: Stereo Studio Inc. Japan 1996 *SIZE: 256×363*

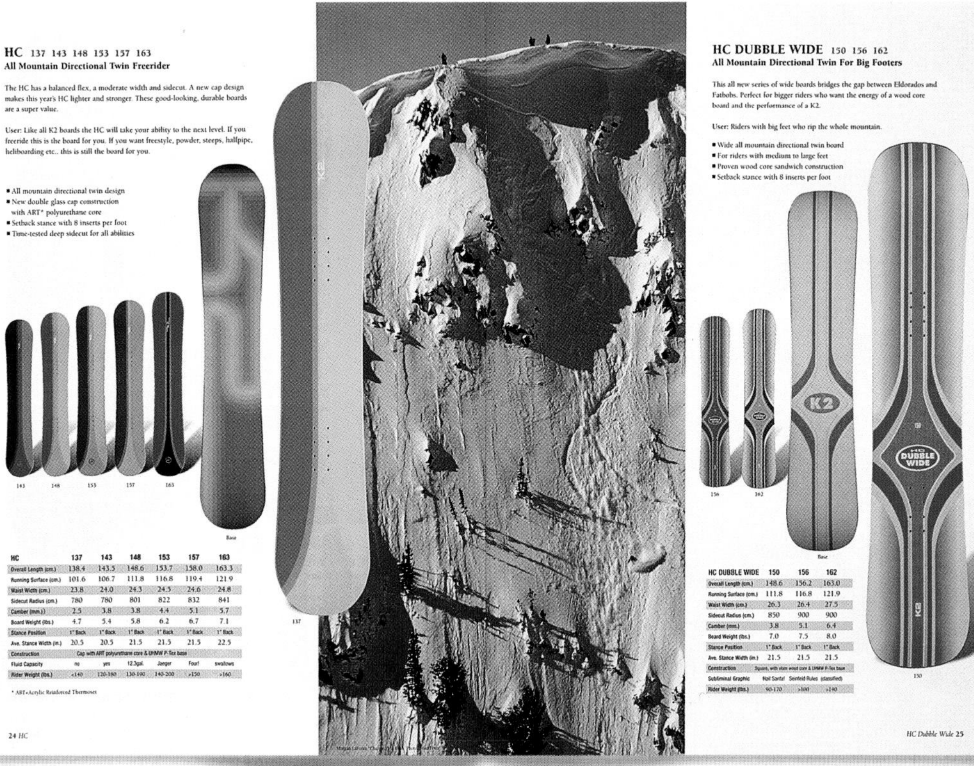

## HC 137 143 148 153 157 163
**All Mountain Directional Twin Freerider**

The HC has a balanced flex, a moderate width and sidecut. A new cap design makes this year's HC lighter and stronger. These good-looking, durable boards are a super value.

User: Like all K2 boards the HC will take your ability to the next level. If you freeride this is the board for you. If you want freestyle, powder, steeps, hallpipe, heliboarding etc., this is still the board for you.

- All mountain directional twin design
- New double glass cap construction with ART* polyurethane core
- Setback stance with 8 inserts per foot
- Time-tested deep sidecut for all abilities

143 148 153 157 163 Base 137

| HC | 137 | 143 | 148 | 153 | 157 | 163 |
|---|---|---|---|---|---|---|
| Overall Length (cm.) | 138.4 | 143.5 | 148.6 | 153.7 | 158.0 | 163.3 |
| Running Surface (cm.) | 101.6 | 106.7 | 111.8 | 116.8 | 119.4 | 121.9 |
| Waist Width (cm.) | 23.8 | 24.0 | 24.3 | 24.5 | 24.6 | 24.8 |
| Sidecut Radius (cm.) | 780 | 780 | 801 | 822 | 832 | 841 |
| Camber (mm.)) | 2.5 | 3.8 | 3.8 | 4.4 | 5.1 | 5.7 |
| Board Weight (lbs.) | 4.7 | 5.4 | 5.8 | 6.2 | 6.7 | 7.1 |
| Stance Position | 1" Back | 1" Back | 1" Back | 1" Back | 1" Back | 1" Back |
| Ave. Stance Width (in.) | 20.5 | 20.5 | 21.5 | 21.5 | 21.5 | 22.5 |
| Construction | Cap with ART polyurethane core & UHMW P-Tex base | | | | | |
| Fluid Capacity | no | yes | 12.3gal. | Jager | Four! | swallows |
| Rider Weight (lbs.) | <140 | 120-180 | 130-190 | 140-200 | >150 | >160 |

* ART=Acrylic Reinforced Thermoset

24 *HC*

## HC DUBBLE WIDE 150 156 162
**All Mountain Directional Twin For Big Footers**

This all new series of wide boards bridges the gap between Eldorados and Fatbobs. Perfect for bigger riders who want the energy of a wood core board and the performance of a K2.

User: Riders with big feet who rip the whole mountain.

- Wide all mountain directional twin board
- For riders with medium to large feet
- Proven wood core sandwich construction
- Setback stance with 8 inserts per foot

156 162 Base 150

| HC DUBBLE WIDE | 150 | 156 | 162 |
|---|---|---|---|
| Overall Length (cm.) | 148.6 | 156.2 | 163.0 |
| Running Surface (cm.) | 111.8 | 116.8 | 121.9 |
| Waist Width (cm.) | 26.3 | 26.4 | 27.5 |
| Sidecut Radius (cm.) | 850 | 900 | 900 |
| Camber (mm.) | 3.8 | 5.1 | 6.4 |
| Board Weight (lbs.) | 7.0 | 7.5 | 8.0 |
| Stance Position | 1" Back | 1" Back | 1" Back |
| Ave. Stance Width (in.) | 21.5 | 21.5 | 21.5 |
| Construction | Square, with slam wood core & UHMW P-Tex base | | |
| Subliminal Graphic | Hail Santa! | Seinfeld Rules | (classified) |
| Rider Weight (lbs.) | 90-170 | >100 | >140 |

*HC Dubble Wide* 25

## V-8

User: Turbo-charged nitro-burning freestyle huck farmers. The ultimate asymmetric soft binding, the all-new V-8 has rider tunable dampening to soften landings and squelch chatter. Add the most comfortable ankle strap ever, massive forward lean adjustment and lightweight twin-wall construction and you've got a winner.

- All-new asymmetrical baseplate with ultralight thinwall construction
- User tunable elastomer baseplate damping
- All-new ultrawide foam-injected ankle strap
- Tall or super-tall padded highback with adjustable offset
- Single screw forward lean adjustment (up to 30 degrees)
- OFR (one finger release) ratchet buckle
- EVA padded no-scissor toe strap
- Ultra-stiff adjustment disc with integrated washers
- 3 hole disc available

**Sizes** S-M (m 4-8) or M-L (m 9-14)

*"The new ratchet straps are really cool," says Josh Rosen, "way better than my old stuff."*

*"I use the V-4 because I like having a big, thick, deep heel cup," says Lance Pitman. "I also like having buckles instead of a ratchet buckle."*

## V-6

User: Same as above, only broker. An all mountain asymmetric that's similar to the V-8, but without a dampening system.

- All-new asymmetrical baseplate
- Ultralight thinwall Zytel construction
- Super-tall padded highback with adjustable offset
- Single screw forward lean adjustment (up to 30 degrees)
- EVA padded freeride ankle strap
- OFR (one finger release) ratchet buckle
- EVA padded no-scissor toe strap
- Ultra-stiff adjustment disc with integrated washers
- 3 hole disc available

**Sizes** S-M (m 4-8) or M-L (m 9-14)

## V-4

User: Freeriders of the planet. An update of K2's classic Freeride, this all mountain binding has a taller heelcup than our freestyle models and uses Zytel plastic ridiculous strength.

- Lightweight durable Zytel construction
- Supertall highback
- Single screw forward lean adjustment
- Classic freeride ankle strap
- EVA padded no-scissor toestrap
- Super-stiff resin disc

## V-2

User: Kids in general. An adjustable aluminum kids binding that grows as they do.

- Fits sizes 11-4, using a track-mounted highback
- Lightweight anodized aluminum baseplate
- Built-in forward lean
- Locking buckle

46 *Strap Bindings*

*Strap Bindings* 47

# Snowboards

K2 SNOWBOARDS CL: K2 Snowboards CD: Hayley, Luke & Brent @ K2 AD, D: Michael Strassburger D: Mark Atherton / Vittorio Costarella / Robynne Raye P: Doug Ogle / Jeff Curtis CW: John Erben DF: Modern Dog USA 1997 *SIZE: 279×198*

4

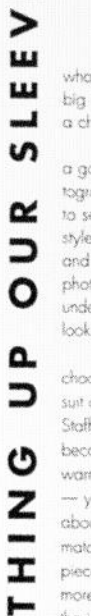


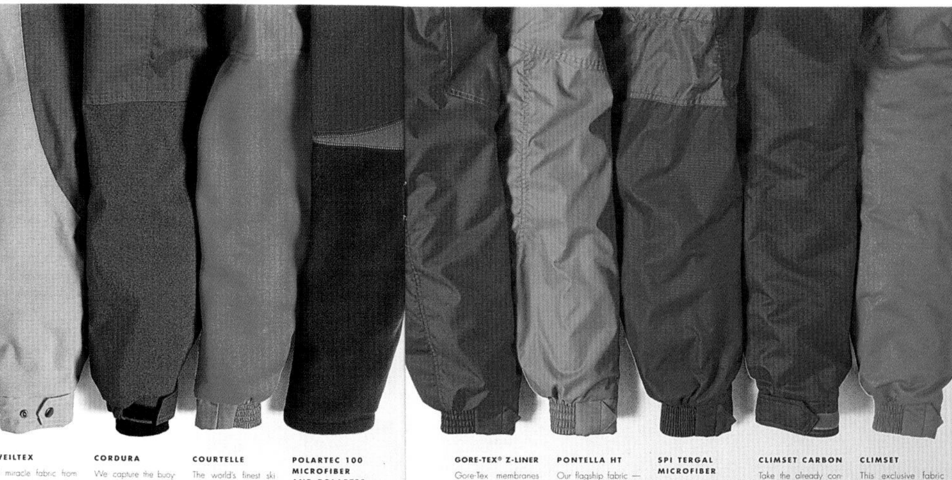

We know what you're thinking. This is a big catalog. How do I make a choice?

First impressions are a good start. Our studio photographs should make it easy to see at a glance which styles appeal to your taste and ambition. And our action photographs will help you understand how each garment looks around the mountains.

Second, you might choose between a one-piece suit or a two-piece ensemble. Staffers at Degré 7 prefer suits because they tend to be warmer and easier to wear — you never have to worry about whether your top matches the bottoms. Two-piece outfits, though, are more versatile. You can wear the jacket on the airplane, around town and back home. You'll find our pants and bibs more comfortable than competitors' because their empire waists fit high and snug.

Third, you should decide whether you tend to ski more in warmer, cooler, wetter or drier resorts. Our exclusive fabrics work extremely well in all climates, but each is biased slightly toward specific uses. If you lean toward cooler resorts or ones with wetter snow, then check out our Gore-Tex and Climset models. For warmer resorts or ones with drier snow, look at our Pontella HT and SPI Tergal microfiber models. All four fabrics are available in outfits lined with our famously toasty Courtelle insulation.

Our textile engineers and clothing designers are all dedicated alpinists. We know what you want because it's what we want.

**WEILTEX**

A miracle fabric from our textile laboratories in Besancon, this remarkable cloth looks and feels like the heavy twill of your favorite khaki trousers. Extremely tear- and water-resistant, it is exclusive to Degré 7 skiwear. Because of its luxury feel and back-country look, we use it in our Hickory line of suits and jackets. It has accents of Alcantara, a synthetic Italian fabric that looks and feels just like suede but is machine washable.

**CORDURA**

We capture the buoyant, youthful, hard-driving fervor of snowboarding in this functional, stylish shell fabric. This handsome new formulation of Cordura has a stiff, tough, knobby hand. Knees and shoulders of our snowboarding outfits are reinforced with Kevlar, and we use a new German-made coating called Schoeller Keprotec for waterproofness. We don't sell any Degré 7 snowboarding clothes in this catalog, but call us to ask for a dealer who does.

**COURTELLE**

The world's finest ski suit insulator, Courtelle is the prime reason Degré 7 suits are so comfortable that you feel as if you're skiing in pajamas. Its softly combed acrylic weave creates a microclimate that keeps you warm when it's cold out and cool when it's hot. Courtelle comes in two weights: The "middle-heavyweight," at 22 grams per square meter, is mostly for suits and pullovers; the "super-heavyweight", at 24 grams, is for jackets and parkas.

**POLARTEC 100 MICROFIBER AND POLARTEC 200 RECYCLED**

This is wool perfected — a plush, warm, two-sided fleece. Whether you're traversing a cliff in the Cariboos or bar-hopping in Barcelona, it'll never wear thin or stretch or smell. Its fibers are hydrophobic, so the fabric absorbs less than 1% of its weight in a snowstorm, never freezes and dries quickly. The 100-weight is a microfiber used in underwear. The 200-weight is largely recycled from post-consumer plastic waste.

**GORE-TEX® Z-LINER**

Gore-Tex membranes are the Mont Blanc of water-resistance — guaranteed to keep you dry. We start with a shell of rugged, water-resistant Pontella HT. While our competitors usually laminate the membrane to their shells with heat, we instead hang it naturally as a separate fabric just above the inside surface of the shell. This so-called Z-Liner then floats freely between the Pontella and our Courtelle insulation, working as a second skin to protect you from the wettest snow.

**PONTELLA HT**

Our flagship fabric — a highly breathable, water-resistant polyester that has the feel of cotton but the durability of canvas. We have improved it this year by employing a new poly thread that is thinner but stronger than the ones used in the past, allowing a denser weave. That, in addition to a long bath in DuPont's Teflon HT coating, makes our '96 Pontella highly water- and stain-resistant. The fabric is rip-stopped like a yacht's jib sail for extra strength.

**SPI TERGAL MICROFIBER**

The softest fabric available for technical ski-wear, our microfiber is as smooth as washed silk but tough as concrete. It's stronger than most microfibers because our fabric engineers figured out a way to reinforce it with little rip-stopping squares. It is bathed in Teflon HT for maximum water and stain repellence.

**CLIMSET CARBON**

Take the already considerable toughness of Climset, and multiply times three. We add carbon fibers — the stuff that keeps rocket wings stiff — to standard Climset to make this textile. We use it primarily in our back-country shells, since you'll be taking it where the rocks are hardest and the trees are sharpest.

**CLIMSET**

This exclusive fabric has a hard-guy appeal: A waterproof-breathable textile comprised of densely woven microfiber polyester, it is backed by a new kind of induction membrane that offers long lasting comfort and a soft hand. Climset feels like a silky modern update of the yellow rain slicker. Bulletproof and chic, we use it on our top-of-the-line outfits.

TO ORDER OR FIND YOUR NEAREST DEALER:
CALL TOLL FREE 1.800.877.3347

5

34
Bulle
Polartec 200 headband with earflaps
PAGE 31
PRICE $30
ITEM# G822
Blois
Climset/Polartec 200 kerchief-style headband
PAGE 11
PRICE $35
ITEM# G820
Benoit
Acrylic headband
PAGE 41
PRICE $30
ITEM# G821
Berat
Jacquard acrylic headband
Bip
Climset Polaire Climset cap
PAGE 21
PRICE $50
ITEM# G830
Boa
Polartec 200 hat
PAGE 15
PRICE $40
ITEM# G839
Bauer
Polartec 200 explorer's hat
PAGE 39
PRICE $50
ITEM# G835
Bingo
Polartec 200 neck gaitor/hat
PAGE 37
PRICE $30
ITEM# G838
Berni
Long Polartec 200 hat
PAGE 29
PRICE $40
ITEM# G837
Alex
Unisex Climset gloves
PAGE 7
PRICE $120
ITEM# G849
Brando
Reversible Polartec 200/Climset hat
PAGE 23
PRICE $55
ITEM# G836
Alban
Unisex Weiltex gloves for Hickory line
PAGE 19
PRICE $75
ITEM# G845
LEFT: Jim Jack bursts out of the powder at Alta. PHOTO: Lee Cohen
35
ACCESSORIES


POWDER PERFECT SKIWEAR FROM FRANCE ...AND OTHER ESSENTIALS FOR LIFE AT ALTITUDE

DEGRE 7

## Skiwear

DEGRE 7 CL: Degre 7 AD: Janèl Apple D: Maureen Agius P: Michael O' Connor / Scott Markewitz
CW: J. D. Markman DF: Kowalski Designworks, Inc. USA 1996 *SIZE: 275×217*

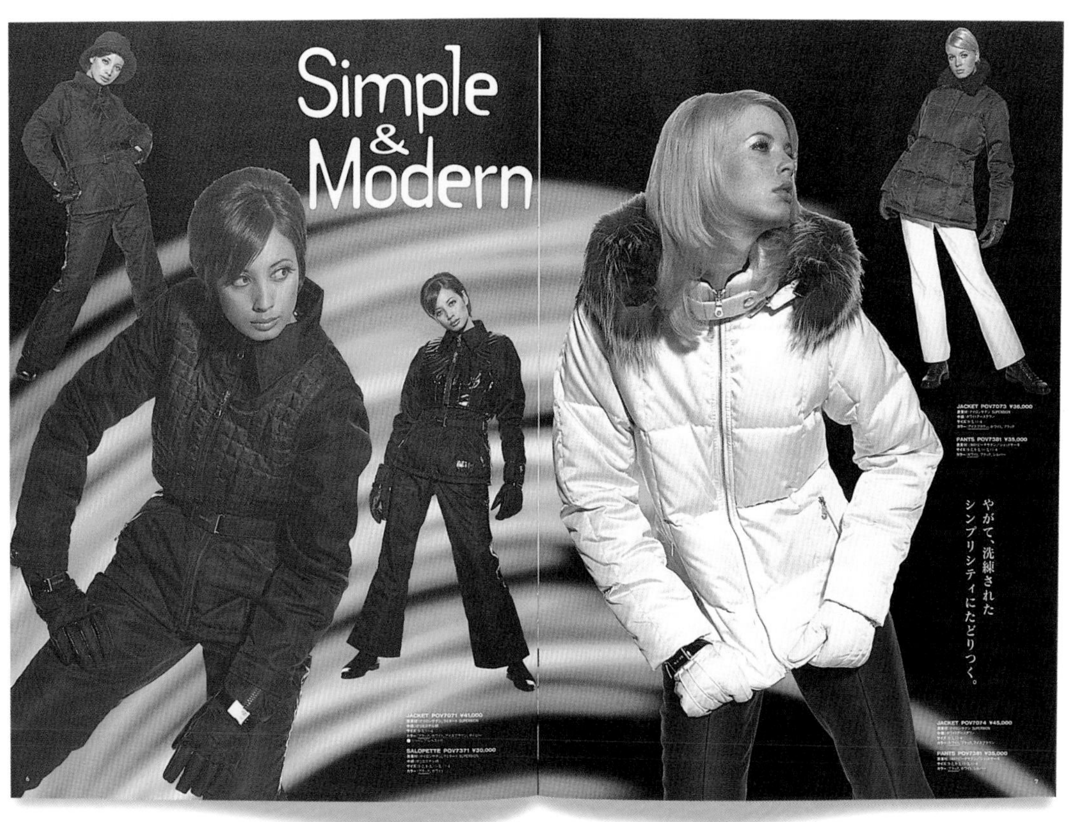

Simple & Modern
やがて、洗練された
シンプリシティにたどりつく。

nui
大人の女性に、とびきりのユーモアのセンス。

LINEA PALIO
LP
1996-1997
ski wear
collection


**Sports Equipment**

LINEA PALIO CL: Phenix Co., Ltd. CD: Genyu Nakasone AD: Tetsuo Fujiwara D: Chizuru Sugihara / Emi Shiratori
P: Peter Lindecke / Naohiro Isshiki CW: Hitomi Nouzu DF: Stereo Studio Inc. Japan 1996 *SIZE: 364×256*

GERMAN CYCLING DEVICE
PRODUCTS
98
ROTWILD by ADP ENGINEERING
CROSS SERIES

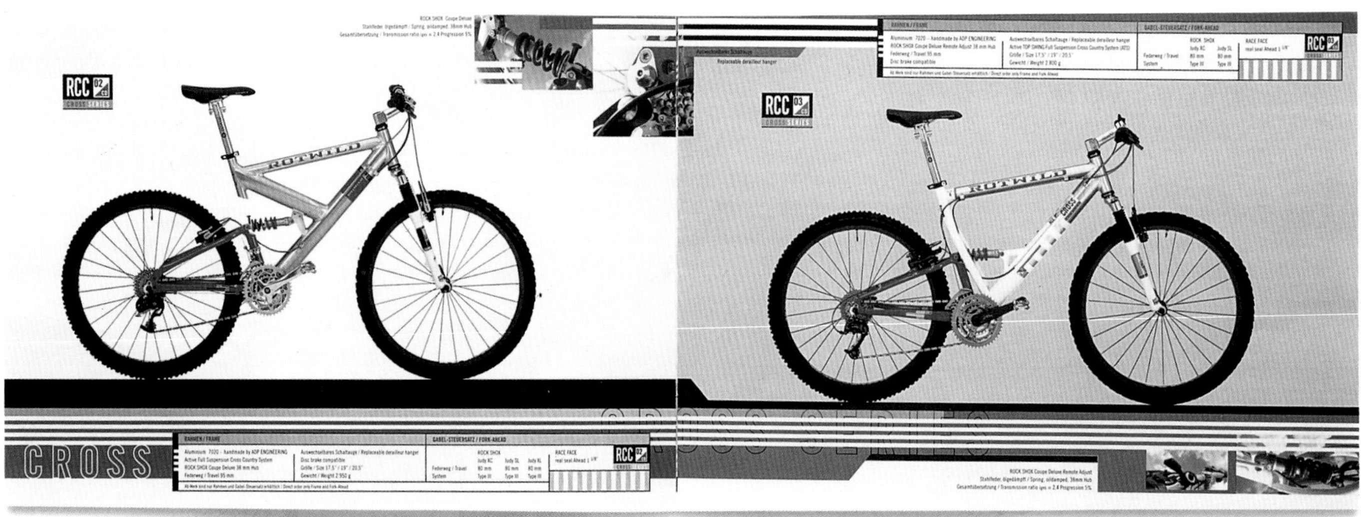
CROSS
CROSS SERIES

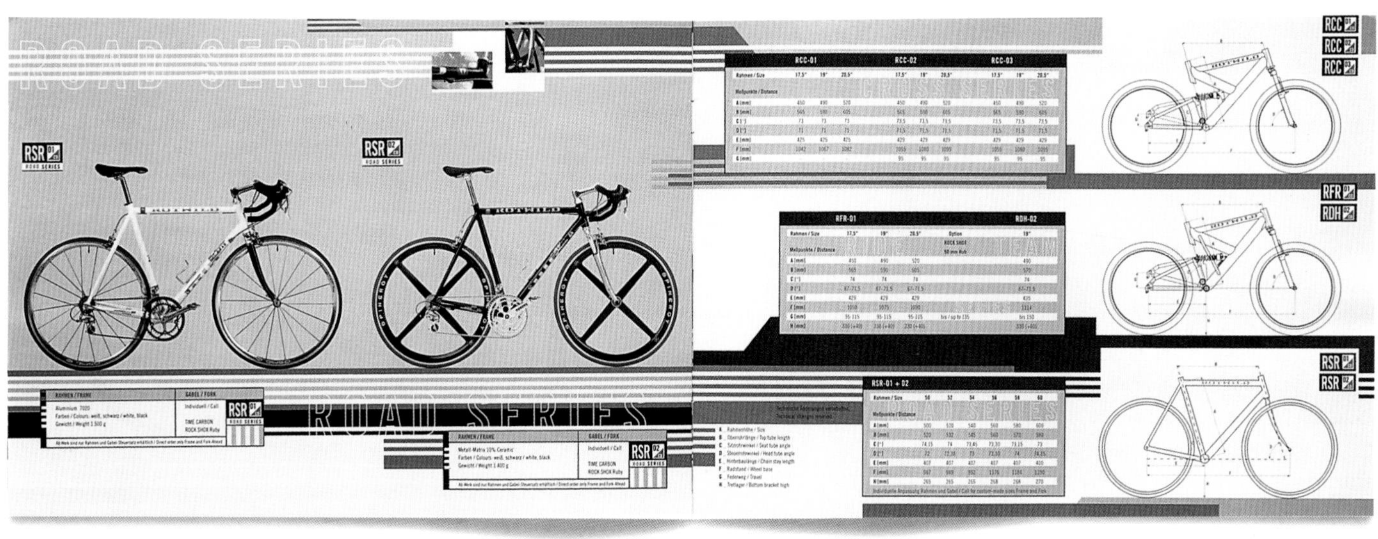

**Bicycle Components**

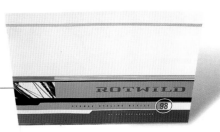

ROTWILD CL: ADP Engineering GmbH CD, AD: Ruediger Goetz AD: Heike Brockmann I: Juergen Winnerl
DF: Simon & Goetz Kommunikation GmbH Germany 1997 *SIZE: 210×297*

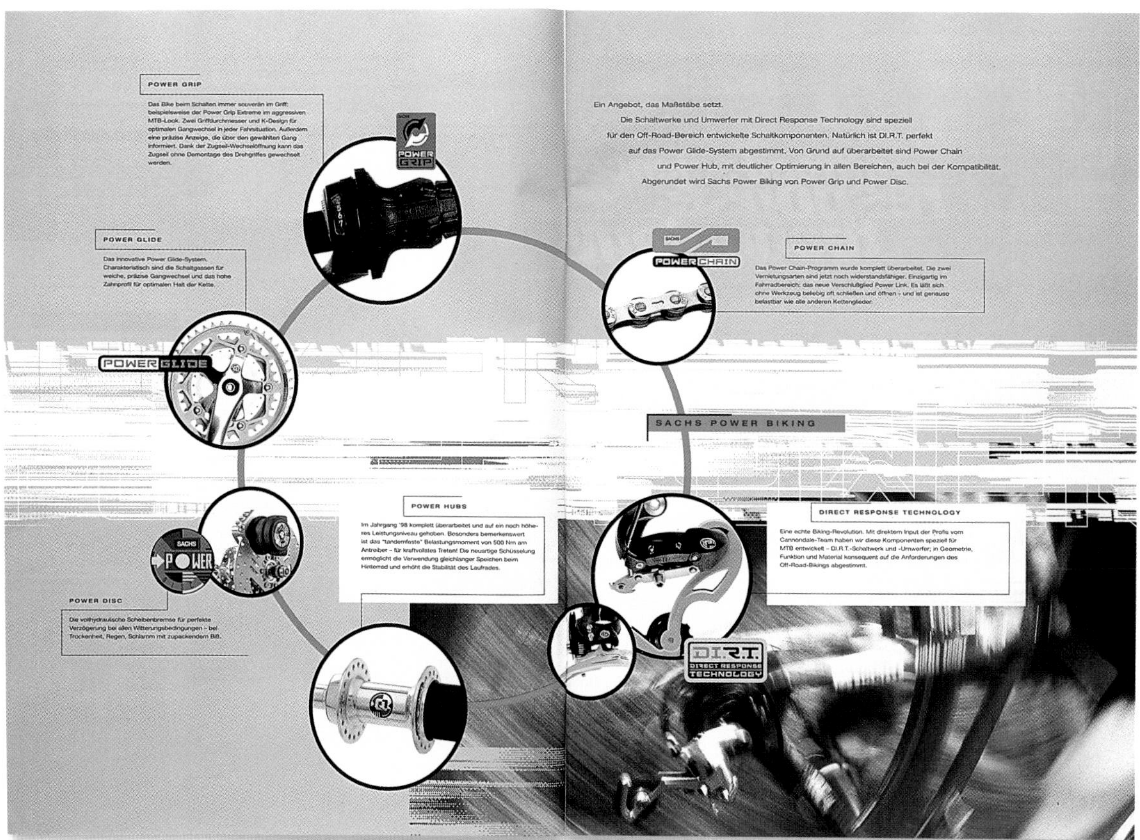
POWER GRIP
Das Bike beim Schalten immer souverän im Griff: beispielsweise der Power Grip Extreme im aggressiven MTB-Look. Zwei Griffdurchmesser und K-Design für optimalen Gangwechsel in jeder Fahrsituation. Außerdem eine präzise Anzeige, die über den gewählten Gang informiert. Dank der Zugseil-Wechselöffnung kann das Zugseil ohne Demontage des Drehgriffes gewechselt werden.
POWER GLIDE
Das innovative Power Glide-System. Charakteristisch sind die Schaltgassen für weiche, präzise Gangwechsel und das hohe Zahnprofil für optimalen Halt der Kette.
POWER GLIDE
POWER DISC
Die vollhydraulische Scheibenbremse für perfekte Verzögerung bei allen Witterungsbedingungen – bei Trockenheit, Regen, Schlamm mit zupackendem Biß.
POWER HUBS
Im Jahrgang '98 komplett überarbeitet und auf ein noch höheres Leistungsniveau gehoben. Besonders bemerkenswert ist das "tandemfeste" Belastungsmoment von 500 Nm am Antreiber – für kraftvollstes Treten! Die neuartige Schüsselung ermöglicht die Verwendung gleichlanger Speichen beim Hinterrad und erhöht die Stabilität des Laufrades.
Ein Angebot, das Maßstäbe setzt.
Die Schaltwerke und Umwerfer mit Direct Response Technology sind speziell
für den Off-Road-Bereich entwickelte Schaltkomponenten. Natürlich ist DI.R.T. perfekt
auf das Power Glide-System abgestimmt. Von Grund auf überarbeitet sind Power Chain
und Power Hub, mit deutlicher Optimierung in allen Bereichen, auch bei der Kompatibilität.
Abgerundet wird Sachs Power Biking von Power Grip und Power Disc.
POWER CHAIN
POWER CHAIN
Das Power Chain-Programm wurde komplett überarbeitet. Die zwei Vernietungsarten sind jetzt noch widerstandsfähiger. Einzigartig im Fahrradbereich: das neue Verschlußglied Power Link. Es läßt sich ohne Werkzeug beliebig oft schließen und öffnen – und ist genauso belastbar wie alle anderen Kettenglieder.
SACHS POWER BIKING
DIRECT RESPONSE TECHNOLOGY
Eine echte Biking-Revolution. Mit direktem Input der Profis vom Cannondale-Team haben wir diese Komponenten speziell für MTB entwickelt – DI.R.T.-Schaltwerk und -Umwerfer; in Geometrie, Funktion und Material konsequent auf die Anforderungen des Off-Road-Bikings abgestimmt.
DI.R.T.
DIRECT RESPONSE TECHNOLOGY

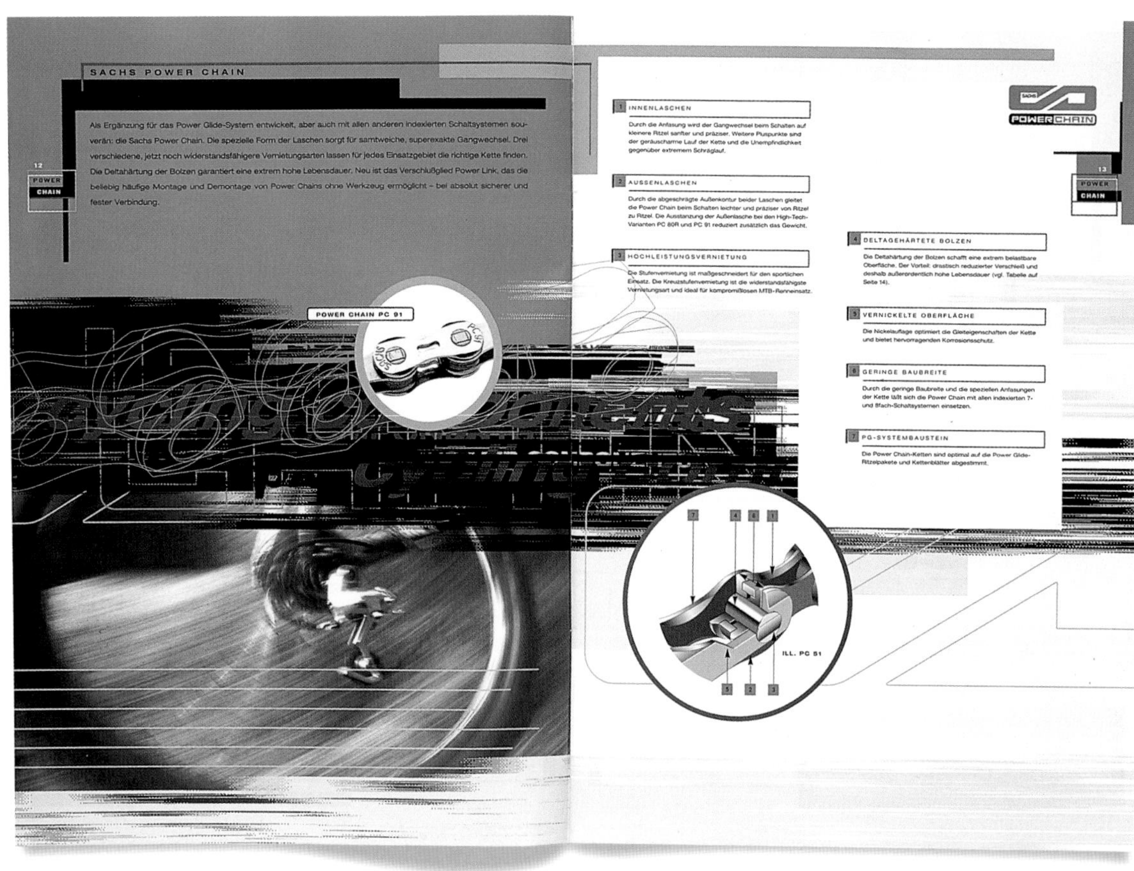
SACHS POWER CHAIN
Als Ergänzung für das Power Glide-System entwickelt, aber auch mit allen anderen indexierten Schaltsystemen souverän: die Sachs Power Chain. Die spezielle Form der Laschen sorgt für samtweiche, superexakte Gangwechsel. Drei verschiedene, jetzt noch widerstandsfähigere Vernietungsarten lassen für jedes Einsatzgebiet die richtige Kette finden. Die Deltahärtung der Bolzen garantiert eine extrem hohe Lebensdauer. Neu ist das Verschlußglied Power Link, das die beliebig häufige Montage und Demontage von Power Chains ohne Werkzeug ermöglicht – bei absolut sicherer und fester Verbindung.
12
POWER
CHAIN
POWER CHAIN PC 91
1 INNENLASCHEN
Durch die Anfasung wird der Gangwechsel beim Schalten auf kleinere Ritzel sanfter und präziser. Weitere Pluspunkte sind der geräuscharme Lauf der Kette und die Unempfindlichkeit gegenüber extremem Schräglauf.
2 AUSSENLASCHEN
Durch die abgeschrägte Außenkontur beider Laschen gleitet die Power Chain beim Schalten leichter und präziser von Ritzel zu Ritzel. Die Ausstanzung der Außenlasche bei den High-Tech-Varianten PC 80R und PC 91 reduziert zusätzlich das Gewicht.
3 HOCHLEISTUNGSVERNIETUNG
Die Stufenvernietung ist maßgeschneidert für den sportlichen Einsatz. Die Kreuzstufenvernietung ist die widerstandsfähigste Vernietungsart und ideal für kompromißlosen MTB-Renneinsatz.
POWER CHAIN
13
POWER
CHAIN
4 DELTAGEHÄRTETE BOLZEN
Die Deltahärtung der Bolzen schafft eine extrem belastbare Oberfläche. Der Vorteil: drastisch reduzierter Verschleiß und deshalb außerordentlich hohe Lebensdauer (vgl. Tabelle auf Seite 14).
5 VERNICKELTE OBERFLÄCHE
Die Nickelauflage optimiert die Gleiteigenschaften der Kette und bietet hervorragenden Korrosionsschutz.
6 GERINGE BAUBREITE
Durch die geringe Baubreite und die speziellen Anfasungen der Kette läßt sich die Power Chain mit allen indexierten 7- und 8fach-Schaltsystemen einsetzen.
7 PG-SYSTEMBAUSTEIN
Die Power Chain-Ketten sind optimal auf die Power Glide-Ritzelpakete und Kettenblätter abgestimmt.
ILL. PC 91

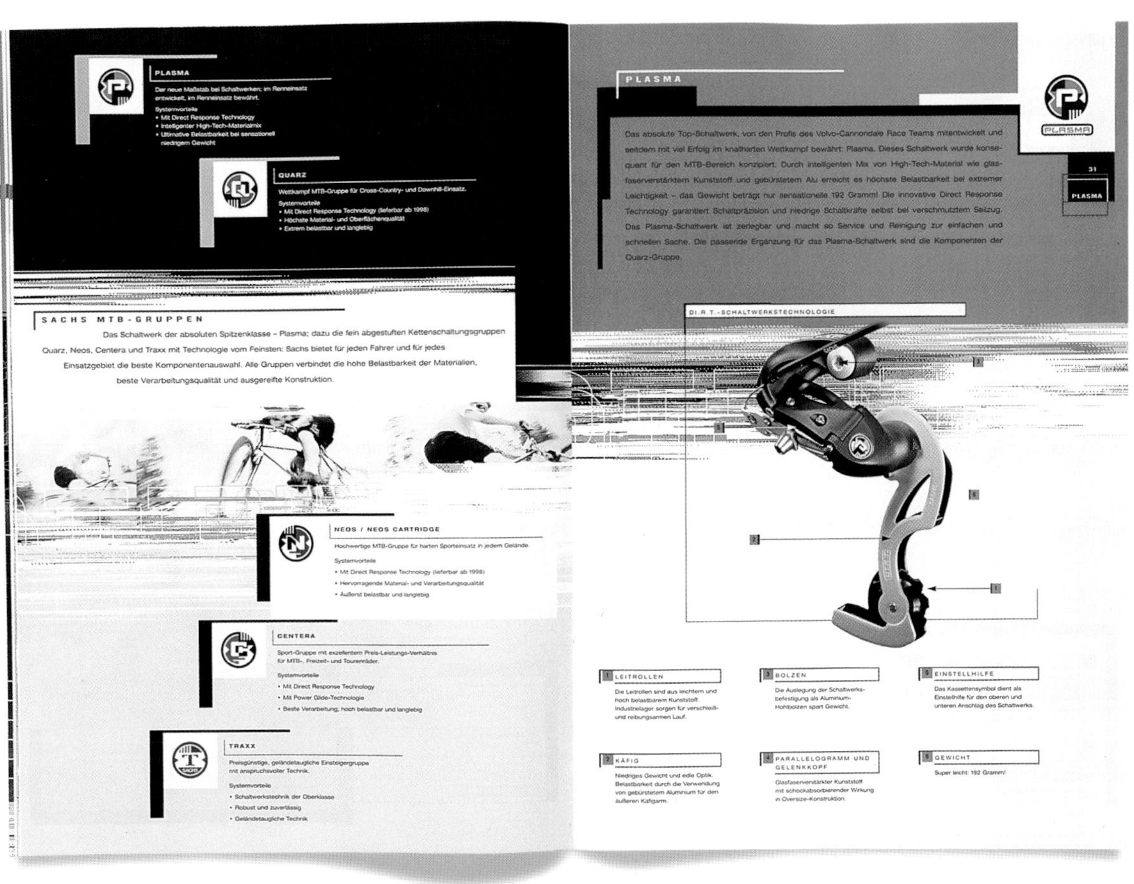

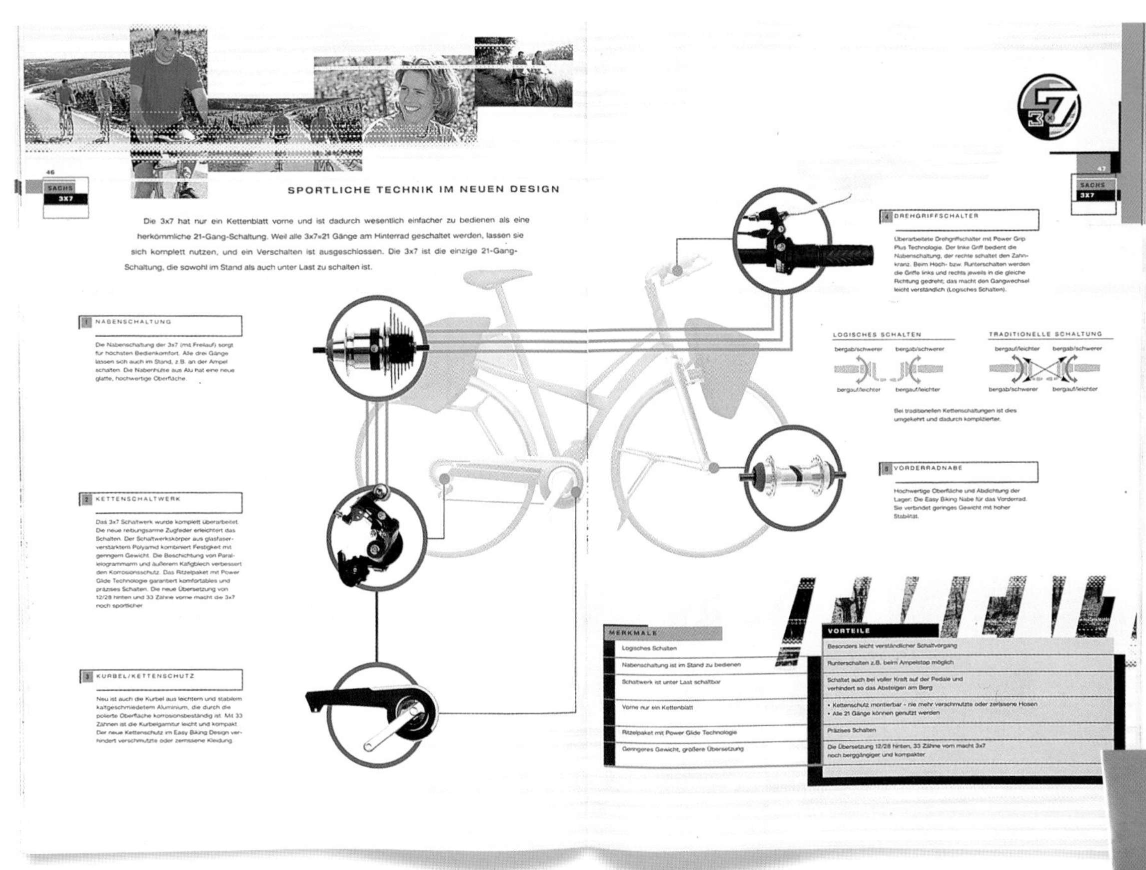

## Bicycle Components

SACHS CL: Sachs Bicycle Components CD: Ruediger Goetz AD: Christian Dekant I: Manuela Schmidt
DF: Simon & Goetz Kommunikation GmbH Germany 1997 *SIZE: 296×210*

## Bicycle Helmets & Accessories

GIRO CL: Giro Sport Design, Inc. AD, D: Jack Anderson D: David Bates / Mary Chin Hutchison P: Jim Cummins I: Todd Connor / Yutaka Sasaki DF: Hornall Anderson Design Works USA 1994 *SIZE: 136×216*

## Helmets & Pads For Aggresive Sports

PRO-TEC CL, P: Pro-Tec CD, AD, D, CW: Eric Ruffing CW: Randy Mello / Tom Aekely DF: 13th Floor USA 1997 *SIZE: 127×127*

## Helmets & Pads For Aggresive Sports

PRO-TEC CL, P: Pro-Tec CD, AD, D, CW: Eric Ruffing P: Rizzo / Slagerman / 13th Floor I: Miguel Parres / Tim Ward CW: Randy Mello DF: 13th Floor USA 1997 *SIZE: 177×126*

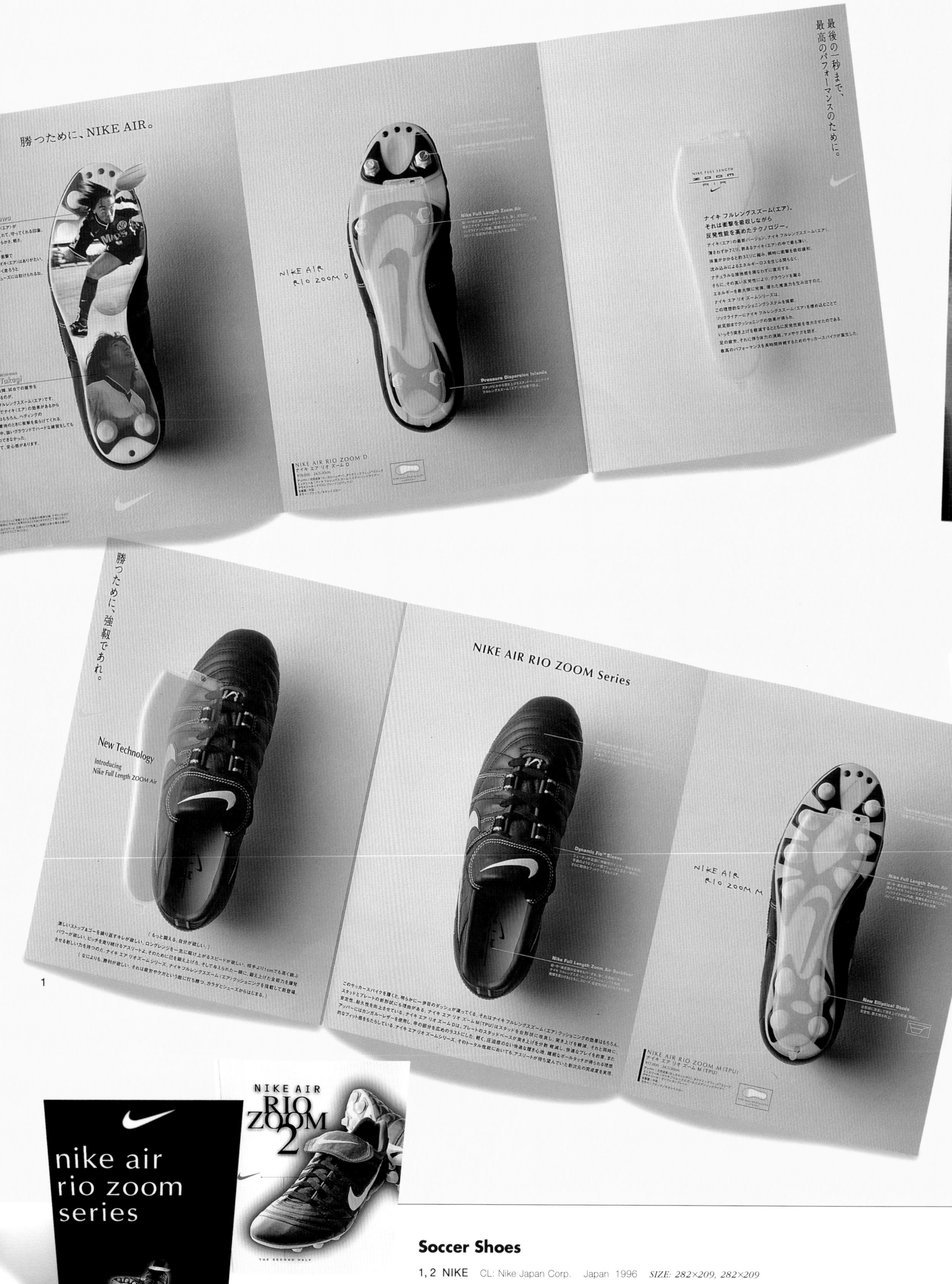


1

**Soccer Shoes**

1, 2 NIKE CL: Nike Japan Corp. Japan 1996 *SIZE: 282×209, 282×209*

Soccer

KICK OFF

THE FIRST HALF

その差は後半の足に出る。

New Technology
Cushioning
［クッショニング］

NIKE ATHLETE
Masami Ihara

井原はNIKEを履く。

NIKE AIR
RIO
ZOOM
2

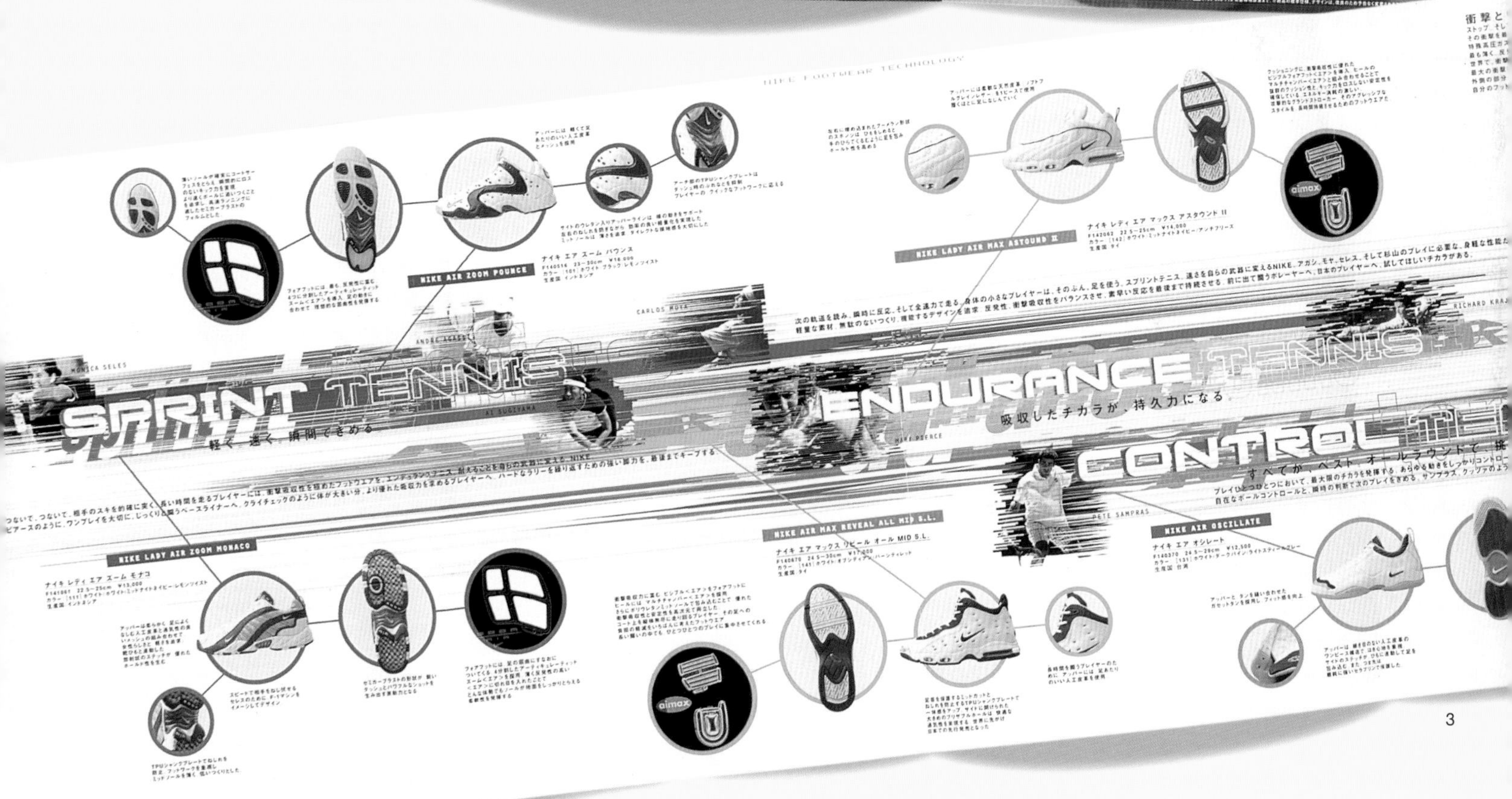

THE SECOND HALF

Nike Soccer

KICK OFF

THE FIRST HALF

その差は後半の足に出る。

New Technology
Lightweight
［ライトウエイト］

HALF TIME

NIKE ATHLETE
Takuya Takagi

高木はNIKEを履く。

NIKE AIR
RIO
ZOOM
2

THE SECOND HALF

Nike Soccer

KICK OFF

その差は後半の足に出る。

New Technology
Fitting
［フィッティング］

NIKE AIR RIO ZOOM SERIES

NIKE AIR RIO ZOOM 2 H.G.

NIKE AIR RIO ZOOM 2 S.G.

NIKE AIR RIO ZOOM 2 F.G.

NIKE ATHLETE
Takashi Hirano

平野はNIKEを履く。

NIKE AIR
RIO
ZOOM
2

THE SECOND HALF

2

衝撃と

NIKE AIR ZOOM POUNCE

ナイキ エア ズーム パウンス

NIKE LADY AIR MAX ASTOUND II

ナイキ レディ エア マックス アスタウンド II

MONICA SELES

ANDRE AGASSI

CARLOS MOYA

RICHARD KRAJICEK

SPRINT TENNIS

軽く、速く、瞬間できめる

ENDURANCE TENNIS

吸収したチカラが、持久力になる。

CONTROL TENNIS

すべてが、ベスト、オールラウンドで。

PETE SAMPRAS

NIKE LADY AIR ZOOM MONACO

ナイキ レディ エア ズーム モナコ

NIKE AIR MAX REVEAL ALL MID S.L.

ナイキ エア マックス リビール オール MID S.L.

NIKE AIR OSCILLATE

ナイキ エア オシレート

air max

3

NIKE TENNIS

Spring '96

## Tennis Shoes

3 NIKE CL: Nike Japan Corp. Japan 1996 *SIZE: 257×182*

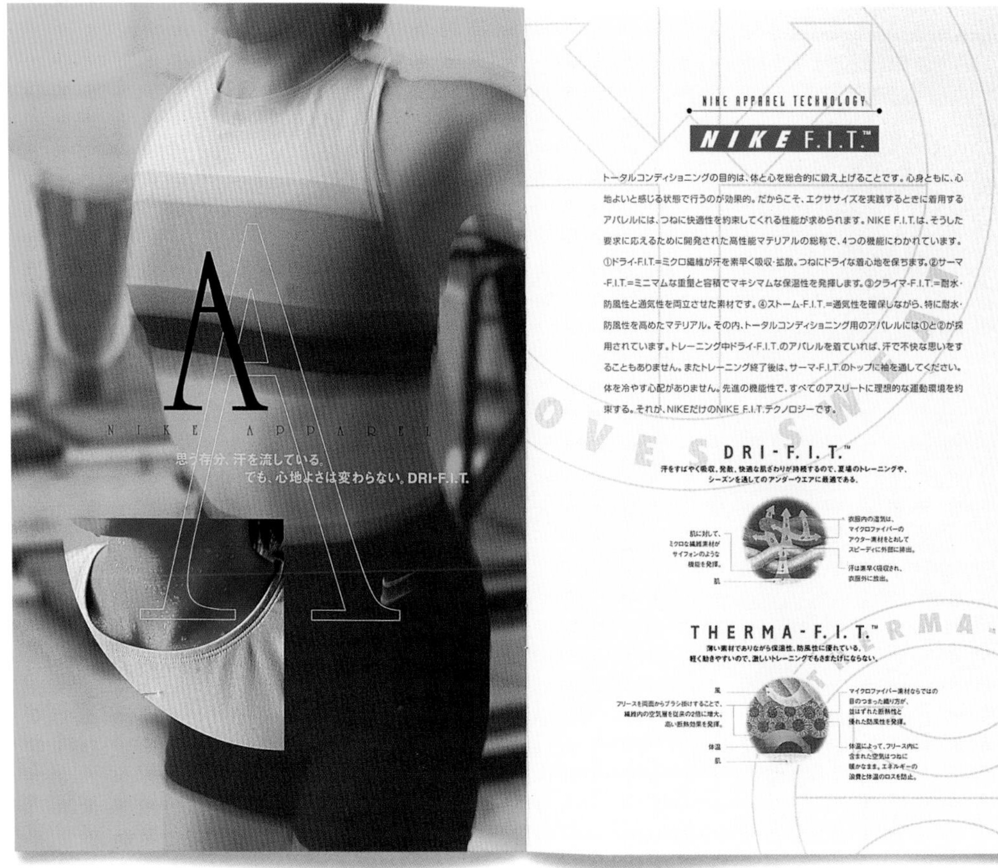


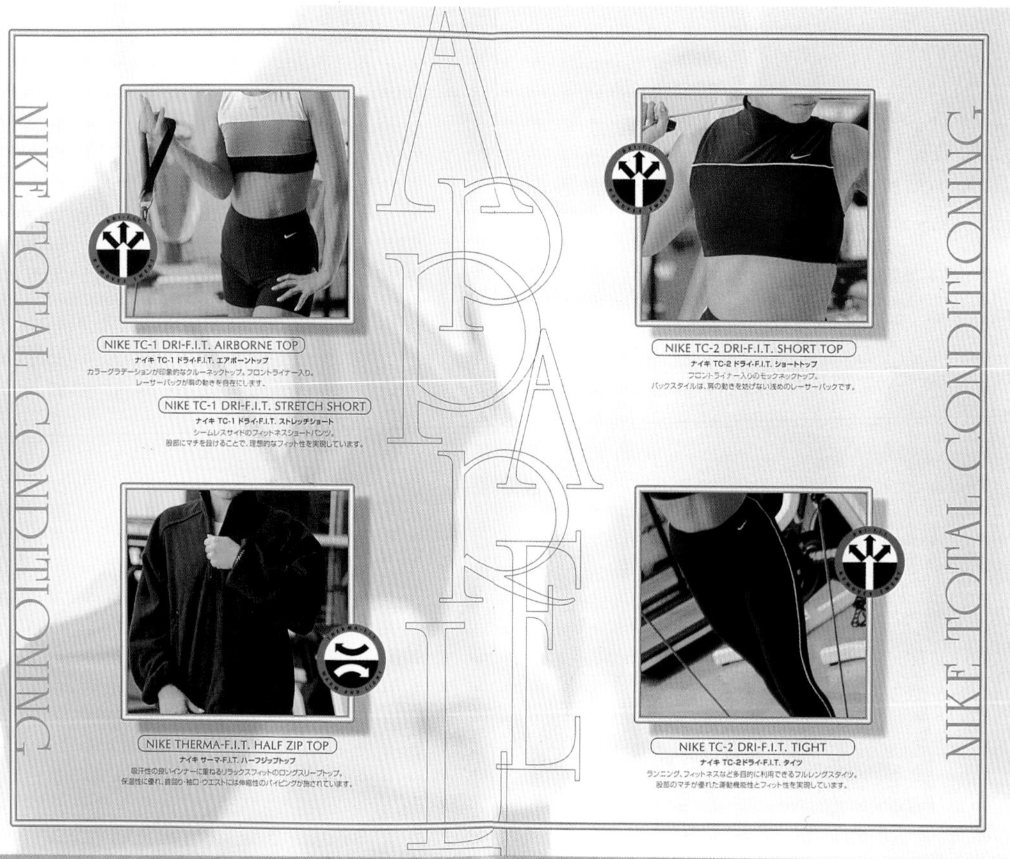


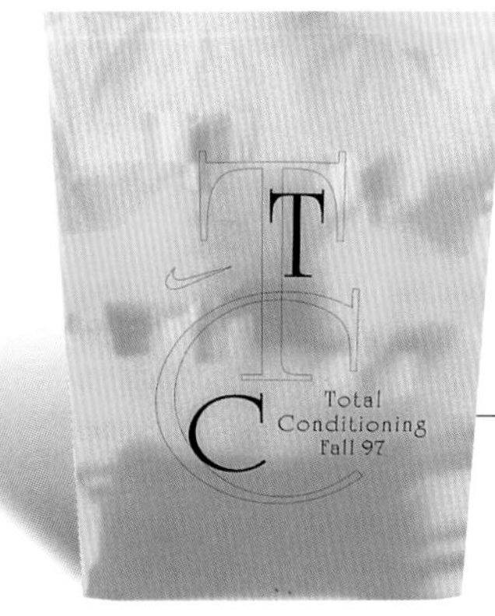


## Sportswear

NIKE CL: Nike Japan Corp Japan 1996 *SIZE: 257×164*

wave
BELL'S NEW RECREATIONAL SKATE HELMET OFFERS A SLEEK, AERO SHAPE AND HIP GRAPHICS THAT WILL TURN HEADS WHILE SKATING DOWN THE STRAND, IN THE PARK, OR THROUGH THE RACE COURSE.
★ EXCLUSIVE BELL HALF NELSON™ FIT STRAP PROVIDES A SNUG FIT AND HELPS ELIMINATE HELMET BOUNCE.
★ DESIGNED SPECIFICALLY FOR IN-LINE SKATING WITH EXTENDED REAR COVERAGE FOR ADDED PROTECTION AGAINST BACKWARD FALLS.
★ SEALED EDGE FIT PADS OFFER A COMFORTABLE, PLUSH INTERIOR.
★ 10 AIR-SUCKING VENTS.
★ CAM-LOCKS™ MAKE STRAP ADJUSTMENT EASIER THAN EVER.
★ NEW 3-D BELL LOGO.
chain link teal/green: #97208 - youth/adult S/M #97209 - youth/adult M/L
rip tide blue/black: #97210 - youth/adult S/M #97211 - youth/adult M/L
alien
RADICAL, ALIEN-LIKE SHAPE APPEALS TO SKATERS WHO WANT A BOLD, OUT-OF-THE ORDINARY DESIGN.
★ DURABLE MATTE FINISH HARDSHELL.
★ EXTENDED REAR COVERAGE.
★ PATENTED CAM-LOCKS™ MAKE STRAP ADJUSTMENT EASY.
black: #97807 - youth/adult (one size)
green: #97808 - youth/adult (one size)
torrent
CLASSIC HELMET DESIGN, POPULAR AMONG RECREATIONAL SKATERS.
★ EXTRA LARGE FRONT VENTS.
★ EXTENDED REAR COVERAGE.
★ VIBRANT SILK-SCREEN DESIGNS IN POPULAR COLORS.
screamin' mimi (purple/teal/black):
#97204 - youth/adult S/M
#97205 - youth/adult M/L
purple abyss:
#97206 - youth/adult S/M
#97207 - youth/adult M/L

protective gear
OUR NEW BELL PAD SETS COMBINE PROTECTION WITH VALUE-ADDED FEATURES AND THE QUALITY YOUR CUSTOMERS HAVE COME TO EXPECT FROM THE BELL BRAND.
wristguards
★ LIGHTWEIGHT VENTILATED MESH FABRIC FOR SUPER-BREATHABILITY.
★ DURABLE POLYPROPYLENE INJECTION MOLDED PLASTIC INSERTS HELP PROTECT AGAINST HYPEREXTENSION.
★ DOUBLE STITCHED LEATHER ENHANCES DURABILITY.
★ SHOCK-ABSORBING EVA FOAM.
wrist guards: #03444 - child
#03439 - youth/adult S/M
#03434 - youth/adult M/L
knee/elbowpads
★ MESH FABRIC OFFERS EXTRA BREATHABILITY.
★ CONTOURED PLASTIC CAP OFFERS SUPERIOR FIT AND PROTECTION.
★ THICK FOAM PADDING PROVIDES EXTRA COVERAGE.
★ SLEEVELESS DESIGN ALLOWS PADS TO BE PUT ON & TAKEN OFF EASILY.
★ WIDE REINFORCED ELASTIC STRAPS FOR EASY ADJUSTABILITY.
2 PACK - wrist guards / knee pads set:
#03443 - child
#03437 - youth/adult S/M
#03433 - youth/adult M/L
3 PACK - wrist guards / knee pads / elbow pads set:
#03442 - child
#03436 - youth/adult S/M
#03431 - youth/adult M/L
BELL HELMETS
league series
hockey
IDEAL FOR SERIOUS LEAGUE COMPETITION OR STREET PICK-UP GAMES, THIS HELMET OFFERS SUPERIOR PROTECTION, COMFORT AND FUNCTIONALITY.
★ HELMET MEETS AND EXCEEDS ASTM F1492 STANDARD.
★ HECC-APPROVED PIVOTING FACE CAGE.
★ ENERGY-ABSORBING, MULTIPLE-IMPACT LINER MADE OF POLYSAN - SAME MATERIAL USED INSIDE BELL RACE CAR HELMETS.
★ SCRATCH RESISTANT HARD ABS OUTERSHELL.
★ LETTER AND NUMBER STICKER KIT FOR TEAM CUSTOMIZING.
★ CUSHIONED CHIN CUP.
★ SOFT INNER FOAM PADDING.
★ EXTENDED REAR COVERAGE WITH RUBATEX™ PADDING.
black: #97219 youth/adult (one size)


BELL skate catalog 1997

**Bike & Skate Helmets**

BELL SKATE CL: Bell Sports, Inc. CD, AD, D: Eric Ruffing P: Scott Lightner CW: Diane Chamberlain DF: 13th Floor USA 1997 *SIZE: 293×229*

## Functional Anatomy: A short course on MontBell™ shell design.

When you buy a MontBell shell, you're getting years of outdoor experience. We've incorporated this extensive experience into the design and development of each MontBell shell.

The three shells on these two pages illustrate the functional features we've pioneered in our shell line. While not every shell includes every feature, you'll find the unique features of each style listed on the page number indicated in the chart at right.

MontBell: The difference is in the details.



## What's the best MontBell shell for me?

We understand that selecting an all-weather shell is a serious investment and we want to help you make the best decision.

Every MontBell outerwear shell is guaranteed to be waterproof. Period. You can select any of our shells with complete confidence that it will protect you from rain, wind and snow. And it will breathe, because we use only Gore-Tex® or DryTec™ waterproof, breathable fabrics in our winter shell line.

Our shells are also designed to be useful for a wide variety of activities and conditions, ranging form the extreme to the everyday.

Use the chart below to determine the degree of venting, fabric breathability and freedom of movement offered by each MontBell shell design. Higher ratings indicate improved comfort for highly aerobic activities such as backcountry and extreme skiing, mountaineering, climbing and cycling. Lower ratings are best for lower exertion activities like hiking, sailing, travel and golf. Wherever the spirit of adventure leads you, MontBell makes a shell to help you meet the challenge.

| STYLE | Venting | Breathability of fabric | Freedom of movement | Men's/Unisex weights (oz.) | Women's weights (oz.) | Price | Page | FABRIC |
|---|---|---|---|---|---|---|---|---|
| Tempest Parka | 3 | 3 | 3 | 20 | | $299 | 17 | 3-ply Gore-Tex |
| Tempest Full-Zip Pants | 3 | 3 | 3 | 19 | | $249 | 17 | 3-ply Gore-Tex |
| Freney Parka | 2 | 3 | 3 | 25 | 21 | $299 | 18 | 3-ply Gore-Tex |
| Alpine Pants | 3 | 3 | 2 | 26 | | $249 | 18 | 3-ply Gore-Tex |
| Cornice Parka | 3 | 3 | 3 | 28 | | $319 | 19 | 3-ply Gore-Tex |
| Cyclone Parka | 3 | 2 | 3 | 19.5 | | $249 | 20 | 3-layer DryTec |
| Cyclone Full-Zip Pants | 3 | 2 | 3 | 19 | | $169 | 21 | 3-layer DryTec |
| VersaLite Jacket | 2 | 2 | 2 | 8.5 | | $159 | 22 | 2-layer DryTec |
| VersaLite Pants | 2 | 2 | 2 | 6.5 | | $99 | 22 | 2-layer DryTec |
| Back Bowl Parka | 3 | 3 | 3 | 34 | | $339 | 34 | 2-ply Gore-Tex |
| All-Terrain Bib | 3 | 3 | 3 | 31 | | $289 | 35 | 2-ply Gore-Tex |
| Mountain Edge Anorak | 3 | 3 | 3 | 33 | | $319 | 35 | 2-ply Gore-Tex |
| All-Terrain Pants | 3 | 3 | 3 | 29 | 26 | $259 | 36 | 2-ply Gore-Tex |
| Chute Jacket | 3 | 3 | 3 | 27 | | $289 | 36 | 2-ply Gore-Tex |
| Powder Shot One-Piece | 3 | 3 | 3 | 51 | 47 | $499 | 37 | 2-ply Gore-Tex |
| Inside Edge Jacket | 2 | 2 | 3 | 29 | | $219 | 38 | 2-layer DryTec |
| Fall Line Parka | 2 | 2 | 3 | 32 | 26 | $249 | 39 | 2-layer DryTec |
| Fall Line Pants | 2 | 2 | 3 | 23 | 21 | $169 | 39 | 2-layer DryTec |
| Gore-Tex Raincoat | 2 | 3 | 2 | 19 | | $299 | 42 | 3-ply Gore-Tex |

1 = Low, 2 = Moderate, 3 = High

1-800-683-2002 mont·bell

14 15

### DriOn™ Zip T-neck

The permanent technical merits of DriOn in a versatile full-coverage T-neck design make this the first thing you should put on for a day of cold weather activity. Offering substantially more neck coverage than our Crewneck, its thin profiled T-neck collar will help prevent heat loss from your carotid artery. The mid-sternum coil zipper pulls down to dissipate heat when you want to. Close fitting, the unobtrusive flatstitched seams help you stay unencumbered while swinging an ice tool or planting a pole. A tone-on-tone embroidered MontBell wrist logo reminds you who to call for more DriOn when after a week you're still dry and don't smell like a barnyard animal. Made in USA.

**COLORS:** Dark Teal, Black, Ash
**SIZES:** unisex S-M-L-XL
**WT:** 8.3 oz. (234 grams)
**341557B** **$39**

Dark Teal Black Ash

### DriOn™ Long-Sleeve Crewneck

Crewnecks are perfect as a first layer. They offer clean lines and a completely unobtrusive design. Our close fitting DriOn Crewneck is an ideal base for an advanced layering system. Its permanent moisture control and anti-bacterial traits will keep up with you no matter where you go. In milder climates or seasons, the Crewneck makes a great top for running or cycling. Self fabric cuffs and low banded collar. Made in USA.

*Men's*
**COLORS:** Ash, Dark Teal, Black
**SIZES:** S-M-L-XL
**WT:** 8 oz. (226 grams)
**341517B** **$34**
*Women's*
**COLORS:** Ash, Dark Teal, Black
**SIZES:** S-M-L
**WT:** 8 oz. (226 grams)
**341527B** **$34**

1-800-683-2002 mont·bell

Ash Dark Teal Black

### DriOn™ Long-Leg Bottoms

Give your legs the protection and comfort they deserve. With self fabric cuffs and flat elasticized waistbands, DriOn Bottoms will lie smoothly under a shell or ski pants. The men's bottom has a self fabric fly and the women's, naturally, is sized and cut for women (sans the fly). Made in USA.

*Men's*
**COLORS:** Black, Ash, Dark Teal
**SIZES:** S-M-L-XL
**WT:** 7.5 oz. (212 grams)
**341537B** **$34**
*Women's*
**COLORS:** Black, Ash, Dark Teal
**SIZES:** S-M-L
**WT:** 7.5 oz. (212 grams)
**341547B** **$34**

Ash Dark Teal Black

## DriOn™: The most advanced, active underwear available.

24 25

mont·bell fall 1995

## Sportswear

MONTBELL CL: Montbell USA D: Carrie Wallahan P: David Belda CW: Paul Bousquet / Susan Quijano
DF: Kowalski Designworks, Inc. USA 1995 *SIZE: 265×217*

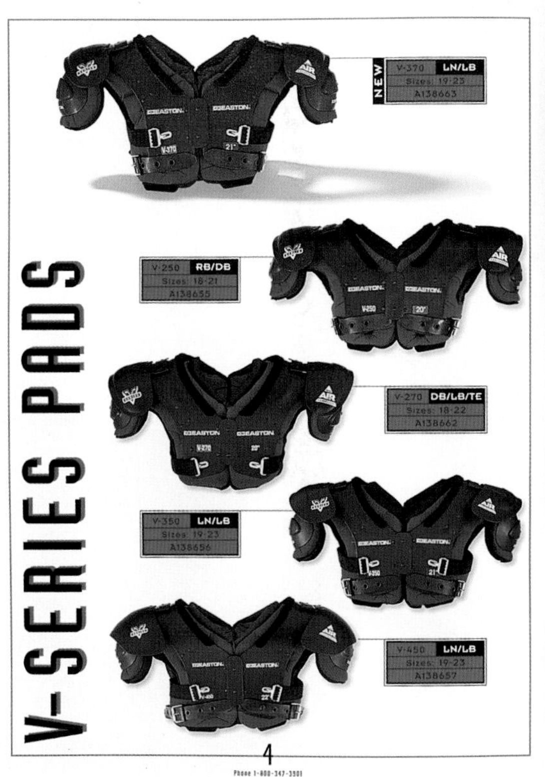

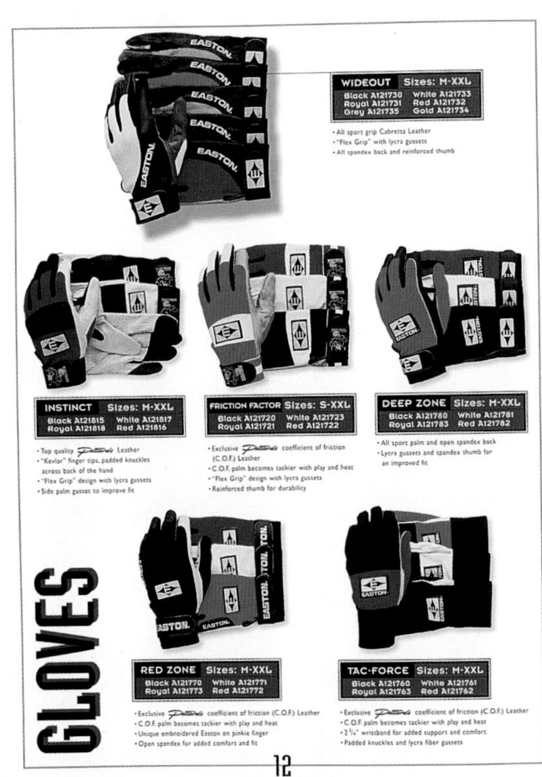

**Sports Equipment**

EASTON FOOTBALL CL, CW: Easton Sports D: Carrie Wallahan P: Color & Light
DF: Kowalski Designworks, Inc. USA 1996 *SIZE: 279×210*

## technical specifications

| | | |
|---|---|---|
| TYPE | | |
| YEAR | 1995 | |
| LENGTH O.A. | 24.0 m | 79'10" |
| LENGTH W.L. | 20.80 m | 68'30" |
| MAX BEAM | 5.80 m | 19'00" |
| DRAUGHT | 3.50 m | 11'60" |
| DISPLACEMENT | 27 tons | 59,525 lb |
| BALLAST | 11 tons | 24,250 lb |
| SAIL AREA | 308 m² | 3,315 ft² |
| ACCOMMODATION | 6+2 guests, + 2 crew. Owner's stateroom: 2 beds, head and shower. Guest cabin: 2 beds + 1 pullman, head and shower. Guest cabin: 2 beds + 1 pullman, head and shower. Crew cabin: 2 beds, head and shower. Saloon: tables and seats for 10. | |
| DESIGN | German Frers | |
| INTERIOR DESIGN | Tommaso Spadolini | |
| CONSTRUCTION | Maxi Dolphin, Italy ABS (American Bureau of Shipping) supervision and 100 A1 - Malta Cross classification (the highest) | |
| CONSTRUCTION TYPE | Advanced composite (Kevlar-epoxy-carbon fibre) | |
| RIG | Fractional, swept-back spreadered, wide based, no running backstays. | |
| SAIL INVENTORY | Wally full-battened main sail, Wally self-tacking jib, genoa, gennaker. | |
| DECK FINISH | Teak | |
| SPEED (ENGINE) | 10.00 kn | |

## technical details

| | |
|---|---|
| RIGGING | Rigg... |
| DECK HARDWARE | Harken |
| HYDRAULICS | Navtec-Cariboni |
| SAILS | North Sails |
| ENGINE | 175 HP, Yanmar 4LH-DTE |
| TRANSMISSION | Mechanical, Reggiani |
| PROPELLER | Gori 3 blades folding |
| GENERATOR | Kohler 18.5CCOZ, 15 kW |
| WATER-MAKER | H.E.M. osmosis, 200 l/hour, 52 gal/hour |
| AUTO PILOT | Robertson |
| AIR CONDITIONING | Condaria |
| PAINT | Awlgrip |
| ANCHOR WINDLASS | Lewmar |
| TENDER | Inflatable 8 persons, outboard 20 HP |
| GALLEY | 4 burners and oven on gimbals mountings. Trash compactor |
| REFRIGERATION | 1 freezer + 1 refrigerator |

## tanks

| | |
|---|---|
| FUEL | 2 for 550 l, 145 gal |
| FRESH WATER | |

## navigation and communication

| | |
|---|---|
| GPS | B&G |
| DEPTH-SOUNDER | B&G |
| WIND INSTRUMENTS | B&G (Hidra 2) |
| SPEEDOMETER | B&G |
| VHF | Shipmate RS-8300 |
| SSB | Sailor RE-2100 |
| CELLULAR | GSM Motorola |
| HI-FI RADIO | Pioneer |
| TV VCR | Sony |

# 100S

WALLY

# Relativity. More than a Theory

**According to Einstein, speed expands time. This is why your holidays on board a Wally Yacht stretch out, the courses shorten, and the 80 m² of your saloon will welcome your guests, your dreams and your moments of relaxation, in a comfort that is anything but relative.**

Wally Yachts increases performance without any reduction in luxury. The racing results show Wally Yachts regularly crossing finish lines well ahead of the "latest" cruising yachts to which they are often compared. Even more remarkable is that the Wally Yachts' performance is often superior to all-out maxi-racing boats.

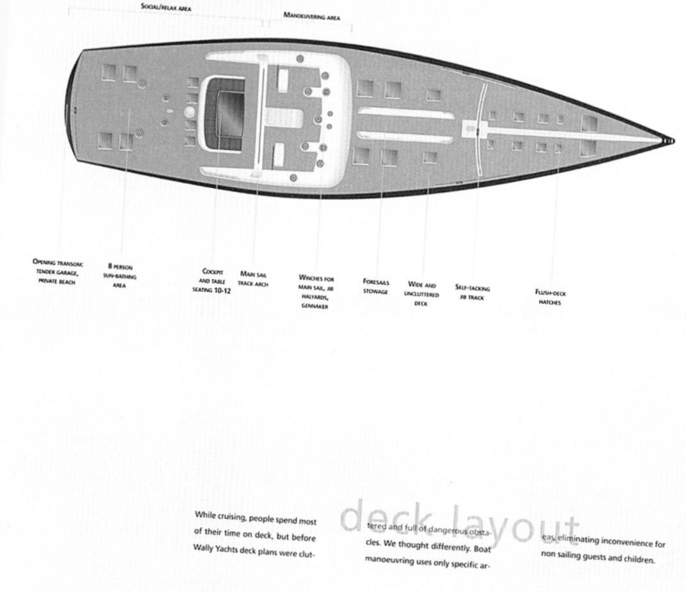
Social/relax area
Manoeuvering area
Opening transomc tender garage, private beach
8 person sun-bathing area
Cockpit and table seating 10-12
Main sail track arch
Winches for main sail, jib halyards, gennaker
Foresails stowage
Wide and uncluttered deck
Self-tacking jib track
Flush-deck hatches
deck layout
While cruising, people spend most of their time on deck, but before Wally Yachts deck plans were cluttered and full of dangerous obstacles. We thought differently. Boat manoeuvring uses only specific areas, eliminating inconvenience for non sailing guests and children.

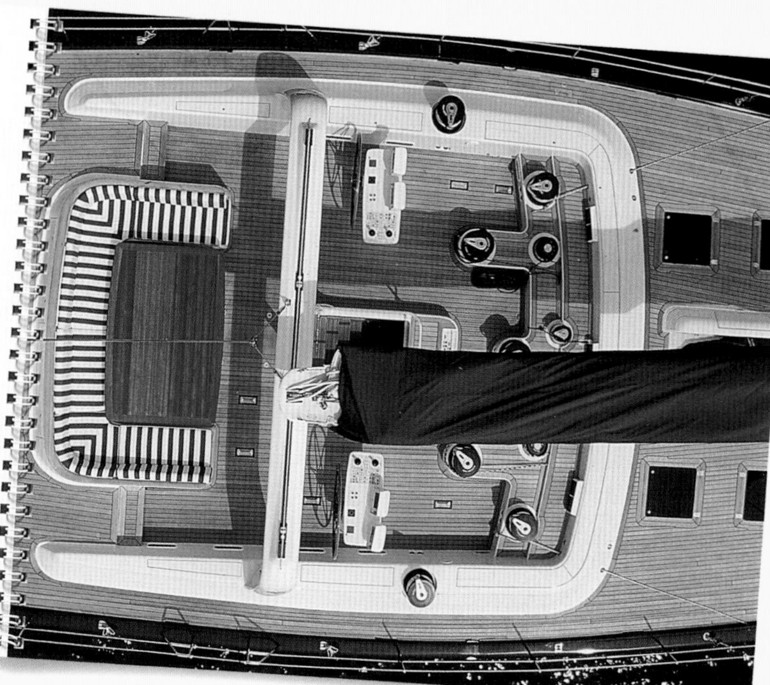

WALLY

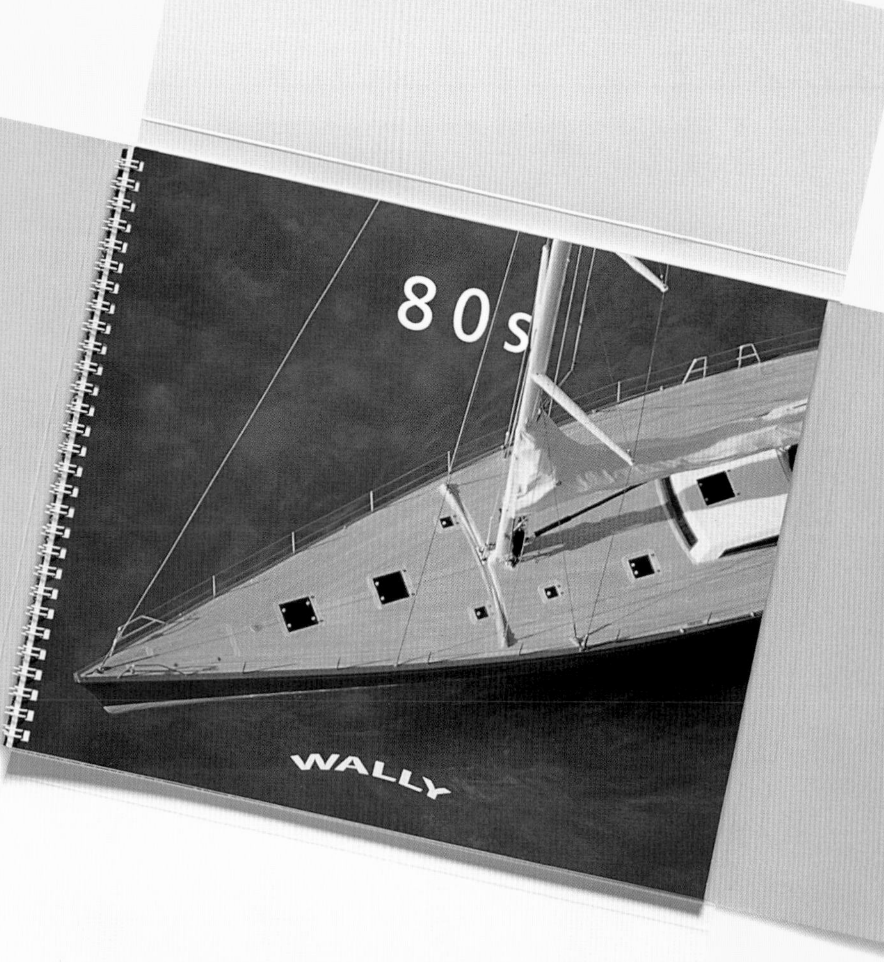
80s
WALLY

WALLY

## Custom Yachts

WALLY YACHTS CL: Wally Yachts CD, AD: Guido Grugnola D: Mario Piazza P: Carlo Borlenghi / Daniel Forster / Guy Gurney / Franco Pale / Billy Black I: Maurizia Merati CW: Monica Paolazzi / Andrea Di Gregorio DF: Industrial & Corporate Profiles srl Italy 1997 *SIZE: 250×302*

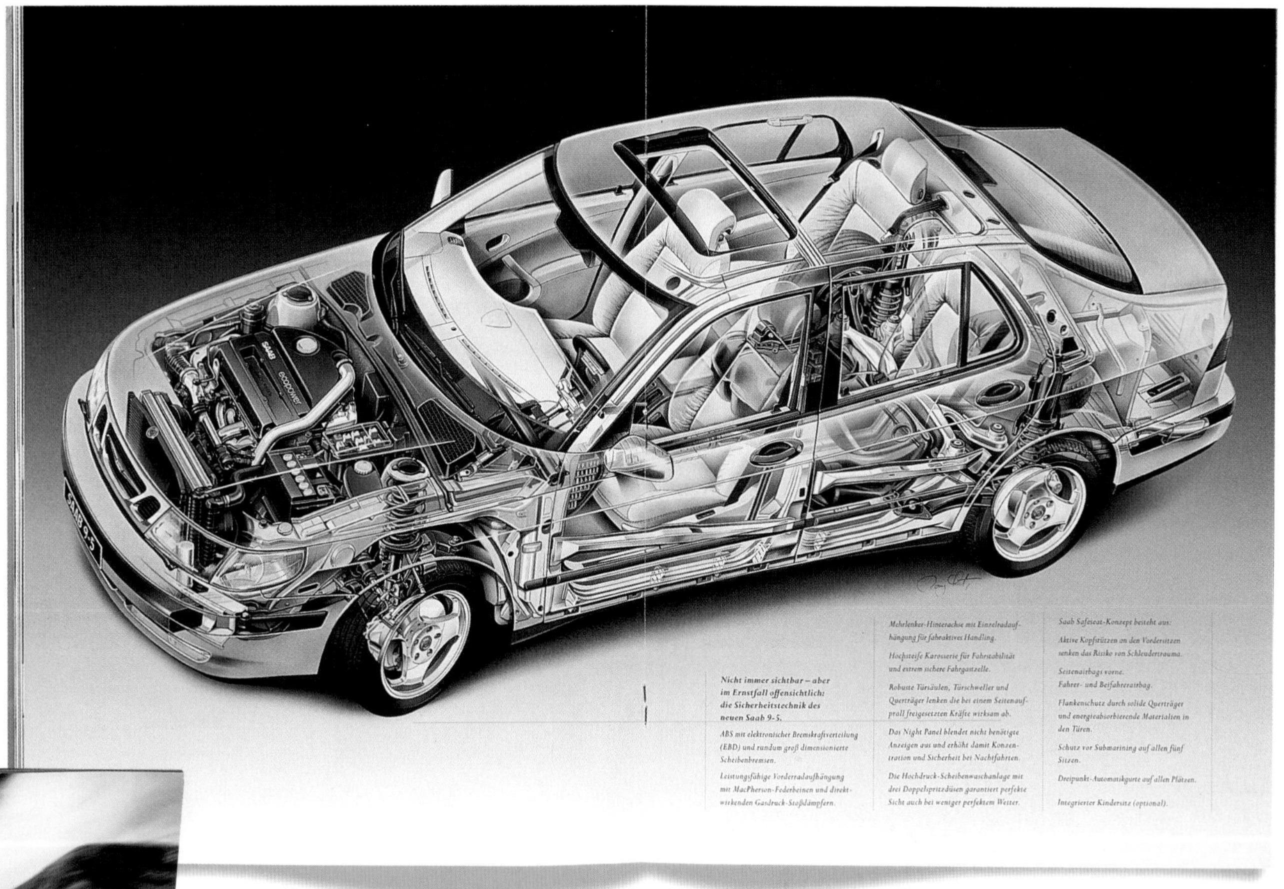


Der neue Saab 9-5

## Autos

SAAB CL: Saab CD, AD: Nelson Zancato AD: Flora Maffi D: Henrik Gustafsson / Susanna Bergendorf
P: Glen Percival / Mervyn Franklyn / Richard Svår I: Ronie Lutz CW: Lars Fritsch DF: Explicit Sweden 1997 *SIZE: 279×216*

Saab 9-3, 1998.
Equipment and features.

Standard equipment

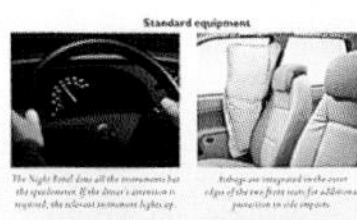

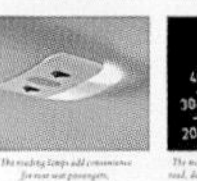

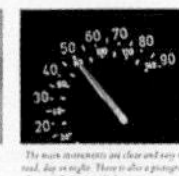

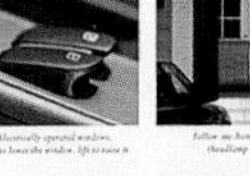

The first active protection against whiplash injuries.

The Saab Active Head Restraint (SAHR) was first introduced in the Saab 9-5, as part of the Saab Safeseat concept. It is now also standard in the Saab 9-3. The system is ingeniously simple, yet effective. It is activated by the weight and movement of the body in a rear-end collision. By sliding forwards and upwards, it cushions the head as it moves backwards, so that the cervical vertebrae are not angled as far back as they are with conventional head restraints.

**How to prepare for the unexpected**

We have analysed real-life accidents involving cars of all kinds for many years – aquiring experience to make our cars even safer.

The Saab 9-3 is designed to accommodate a wide spectrum of real-life crash situations, with the overall aim of reducing injuries to its occupants. Members and body panels should not just absorb energy by buckling, they should do so in a predictable manner.

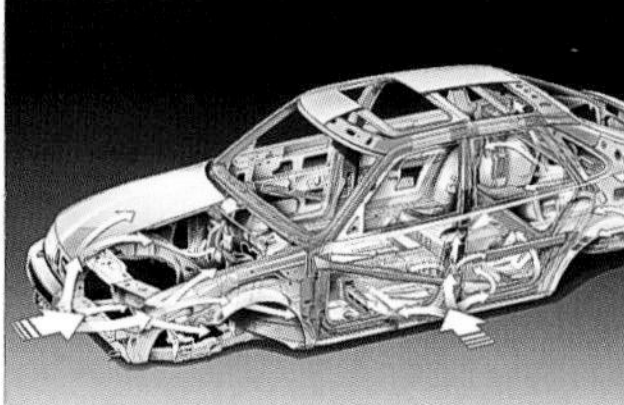

To protect the head and chest, there is additional protection in the form of a full-size airbag, which is standard on the driver's side and optional for the front seat passenger. Both front seats also feature built-in side airbags which are activated in a side-on collision. The doors have sturdy side impact members and energy-absorbent filling material to dissipate collision forces over a wide area.

22 23

"Engines, aerodynamic design, safety, handling and road feedback through seat and steering wheel – everything combines to make the Saab 9-3 a car for all the senses."

Einar Hareide, Head of design at Saab

## The Saab way.

It all started in 1947, when the aircraft manufacturer Saab introduced its first car. It looked different, with its extreme aerodynamic shape, and performed differently, with its transverse engine and front-wheel drive.

This aircraft heritage has led to a strong tradition of innovative design, reflected in features like the early application of turbo technology in passenger cars, direct ignition, seat heating, side impact protection and active head restraints, to mention just a few Saab innovations.

Get acquainted with the new Saab 9-3 and you will discover a great deal more about the Saab way of building cars.

**Autos**

SAAB CL: Saab CD, AD: Nelson Zancato AD: Flora Maffi AD: Henrik Gustafsson P: Mervyn Franklyn / Willie Von Recklinghausen / Richard Svår I: Ronie Lutz CW: Lars Hars Hedlund DF: Explicit Sweden 1997 *SIZE: 279×216*

WE CREATED THE M-CLASS ALL-ACTIVITY VEHICLE, KNOWING THAT ONE OF THE PLEASURES OF OWNING THIS TYPE OF VEHICLE IS CUSTOMIZING IT FOR YOUR OWN PARTICULAR NEEDS, PASTIMES AND SENSE OF STYLE. WE DEVELOPED THE ACCESSORIES TO LET YOU DO JUST THAT.

ROOF RACK BASIC CARRIER
Black protective-coated crossbars are aerodynamic and mount to the roof rails to form a solid main unit to which the various specialized carriers can be mounted.
Q 6 84 0022 $268
ROOF-MOUNTED BOARD RACK
This versatile rack can carry surfboards, snow-boards and windsurfers as well as small canoes or kayaks.
Q 6 84 0020 $115
SPORT LUGGAGE CONTAINER
Our sport luggage container is aerodynamically designed and adds 8.5 cu ft of weather-resistant storage space to the roof of your vehicle. It opens from both sides and is lockable.
Q 6 84 0021 $540
INTERIOR BIKE RACK
Sometimes it's best not to leave your bikes on the roof or rear of your vehicle, so we offer an interior bike rack that keeps two full-size bikes secure and safe from the elements. The rack is hinged so the second row seats can be reopened when bikes are removed. (Requires removal of bikes' front wheel.) Q 6 84 0023 $449

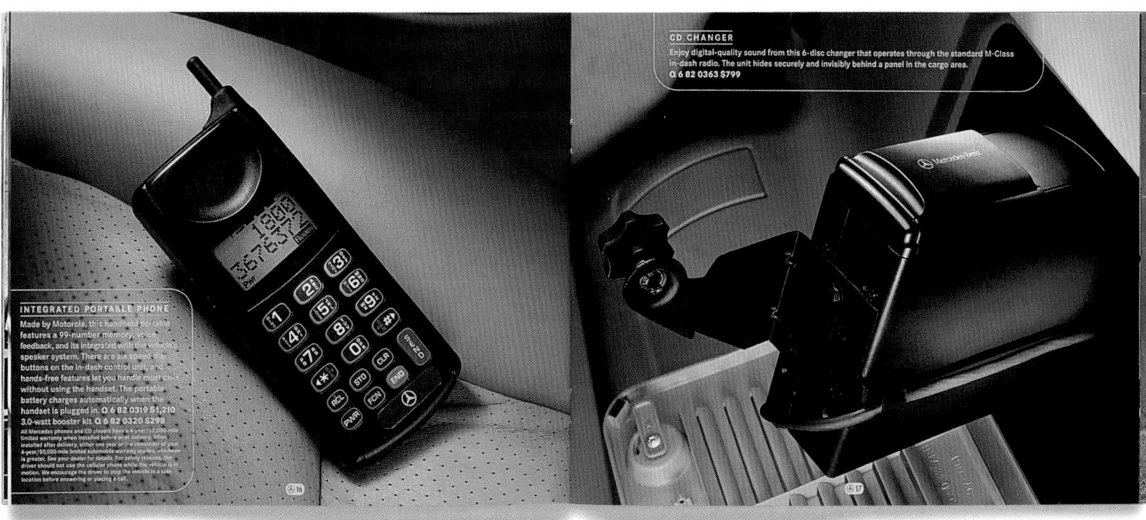
INTEGRATED PORTABLE PHONE
Made by Motorola, this handheld portable features a 99-number memory, voice feedback, and its integrated with the vehicle's speaker system. There are six speed-dial buttons on the in-dash control unit, and hands-free features let you handle most calls without using the handset. The portable battery charges automatically when the handset is plugged in. Q 6 82 0319 $1,210
3.0-watt booster kit Q 6 82 0320 $298
CD CHANGER
Enjoy digital-quality sound from this 6-disc changer that operates through the standard M-Class in-dash radio. The unit hides securely and invisibly behind a panel in the cargo area.
Q 6 82 0363 $799

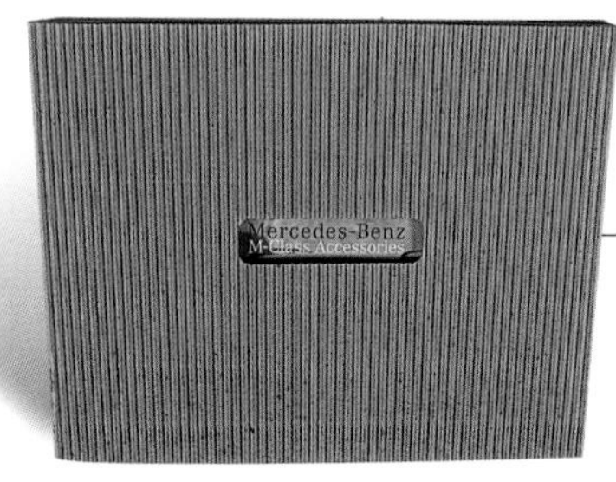
Mercedes-Benz
M-Class Accessories

## Automotive Accessories

MERCEDES-BENZ CL: Mercedes-Benz N. A. CD, AD: Joel Fuller AD, D: Todd Houser P: Brian Garland CW: Frank Cunningham DF: Pinkhaus USA 1997 *SIZE: 178×214*

## Automotive Accessories

MERCEDES-BENZ CL: Mercedes-Benz N. A. CD, AD, D: Kristin Johnson P: Scott Williamson / Steve Shaw CW: Frank Cunningham DF: Pinkhaus USA 1997 *SIZE: 178×215*

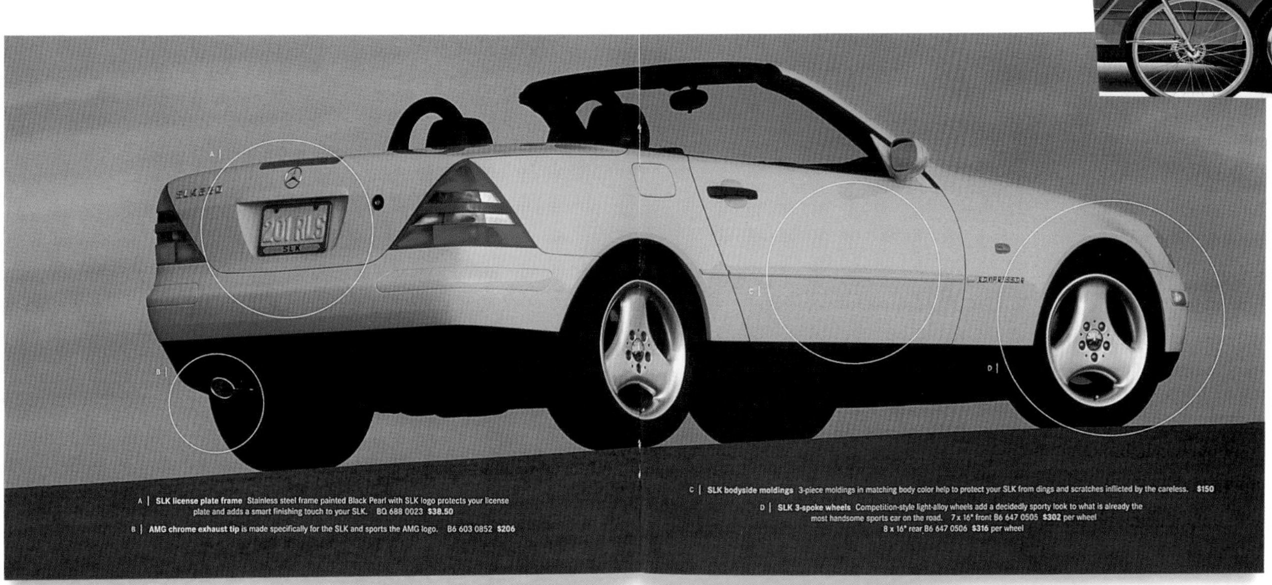
A | SLK license plate frame Stainless steel frame painted Black Pearl with SLK logo protects your license plate and adds a smart finishing touch to your SLK. BQ 688 0023 $38.50
B | AMG chrome exhaust tip is made specifically for the SLK and sports the AMG logo. B6 603 0852 $206
C | SLK bodyside moldings 3-piece moldings in matching body color help to protect your SLK from dings and scratches inflicted by the careless. $150
D | SLK 3-spoke wheels Competition-style light-alloy wheels add a decidedly sporty look to what is already the most handsome sports car on the road. 7 x 16" front B6 647 0505 $302 per wheel
8 x 16" rear B6 647 0506 $316 per wheel

## Automotive Accessories

TOUCAN INDUSTRIES CL: Toucan Industries Inc. CD, AD, I: Nigel Walker D: Emily Yeung CW: Mark Allen DF: That's Nice L.L.C. USA 1997 *SIZE: 305×229*

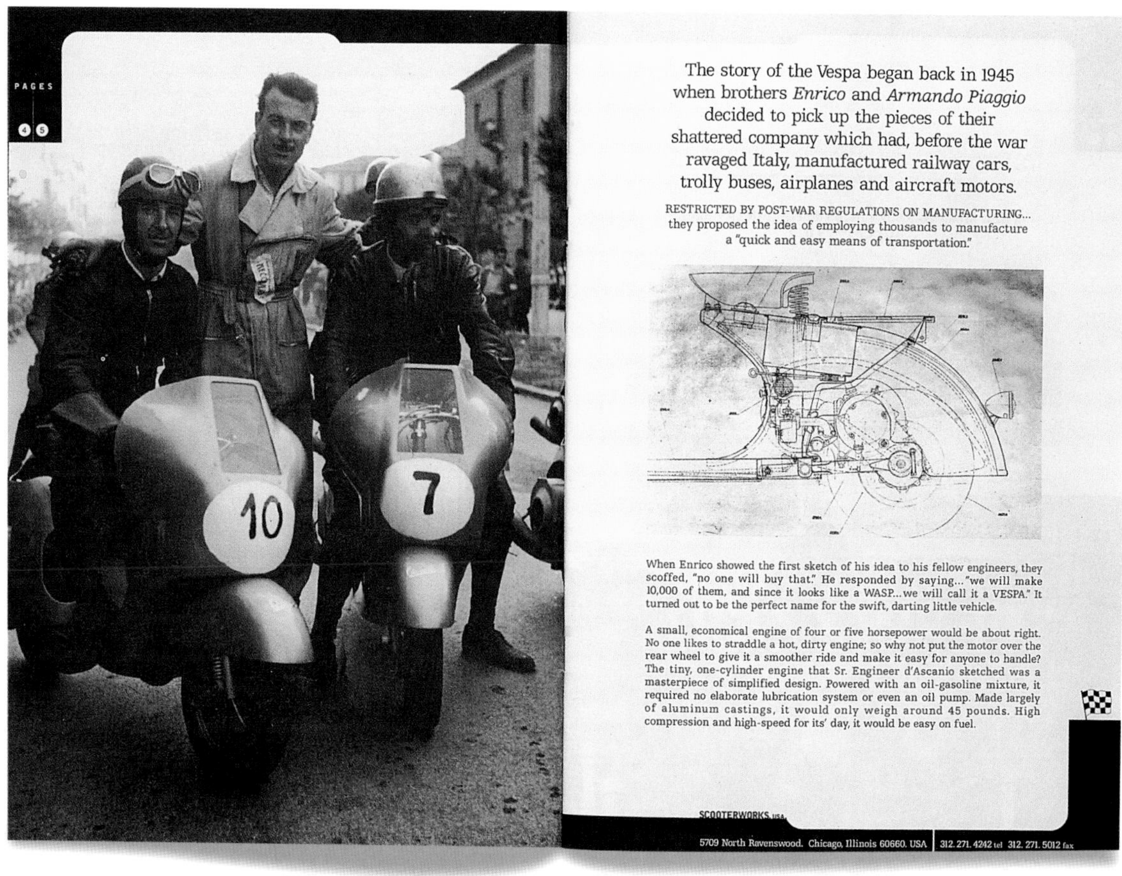


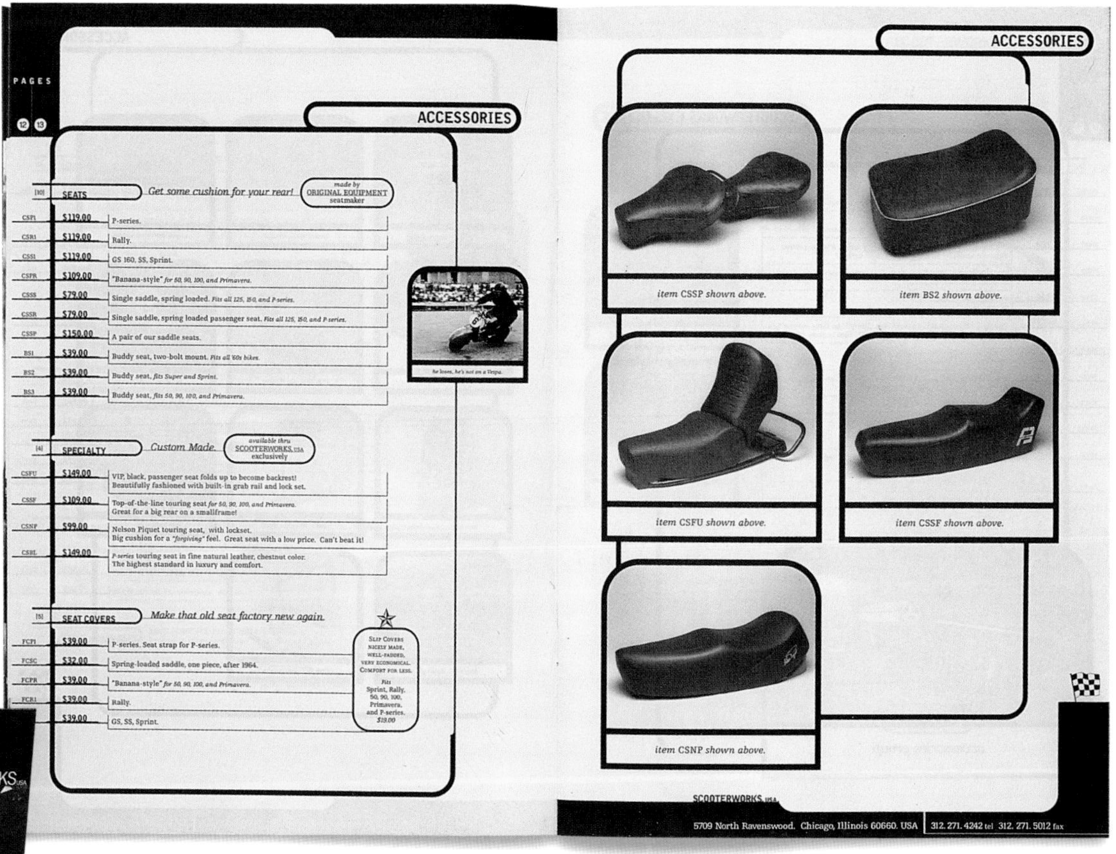


## Scooters

VESPA CL, CW: Scooterworks CD, AD, D: Carlos Segura DF: Segura Inc. USA 1995 *SIZE: 274×189*

As Baja's most well-respected and successful off road tour operator, Baja Off Road Tours has over eight years experience in taking both the seasoned off road rider as well as the novice on safe, memorable trips. Baja Off Road Tours is endorsed by the Governor of Baja California, the Secretary of Tourism for Baja California, and the Policia Federal De Caminos, or Federal Highway Patrol. There is no other off road tour operator in Baja, or Mexico for that matter, with the credentials and experience of Baja Off Road Tours. Baja Off Road Tours is recognized as the leader by Team Green, Kawasaki's amateur racing department and by Kawasaki Motors Corp., U.S.A.
Baja Off Road Tours has been featured in Men's Journal, Cycle News, Cycle World, Dirt Bike, Dirt Rider and Kawasaki's Team Green News and has been televised on ESPN, ESPN2, EXTRA!, Motoworld and Motoworld 2. In addition to all this enthusiastic coverage Baja Off Road Tours has also been featured in European and Japanese magazines.
where the pavement stops
chris haines baja off-road tours begin


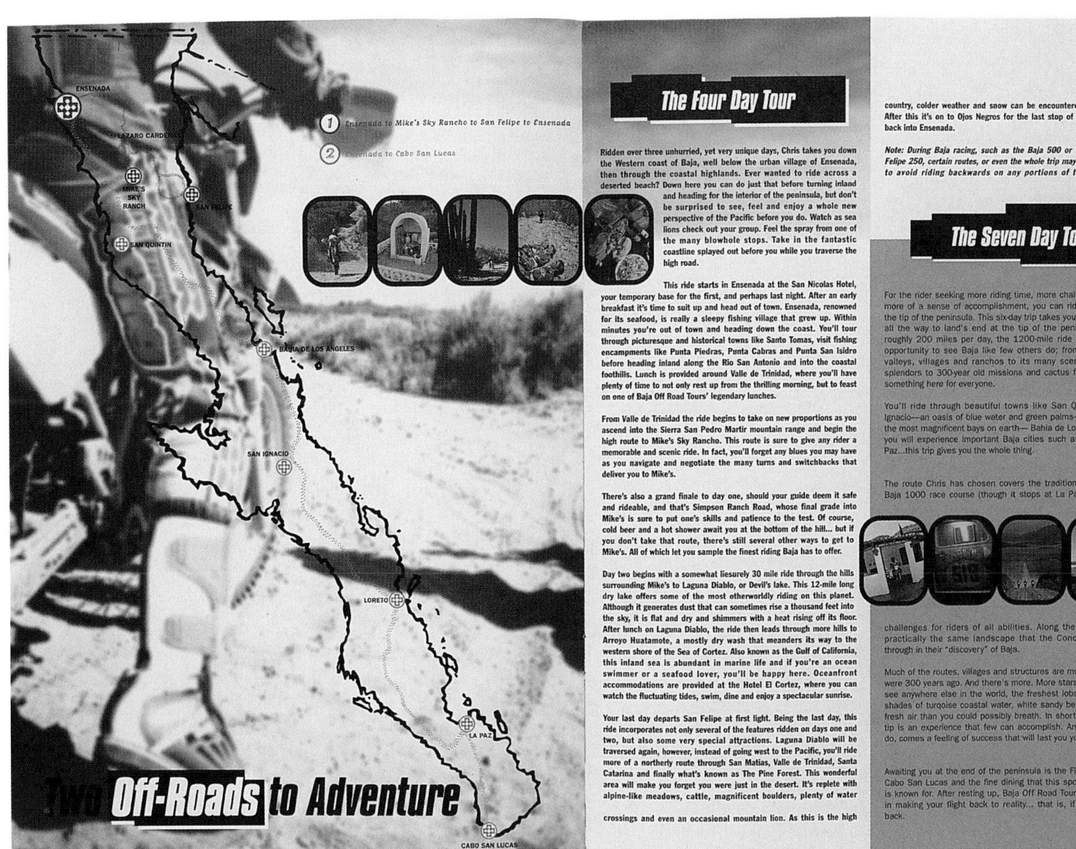


## The Four Day Tour

Ridden over three unhurried, yet very unique days, Chris takes you down the Western coast of Baja, well below the urban village of Ensenada, then through the coastal highlands. Ever wanted to ride across a deserted beach? Down here you can do just that before turning inland and heading for the interior of the peninsula, but don't be surprised to see, feel and enjoy a whole new perspective of the Pacific before you do. Watch as sea lions check out your group. Feel the spray from one of the many blowhole stops. Take in the fantastic coastline splayed out before you while you traverse the high road.

This ride starts in Ensenada at the San Nicolas Hotel, your temporary base for the first, and perhaps last night. After an early breakfast it's time to suit up and head out of town. Ensenada, renowned for its seafood, is really a sleepy fishing village that grew up. Within minutes you're out of town and heading down the coast. You'll tour through picturesque and historical towns like Santo Tomas, visit fishing encampments like Punta Piedras, Punta Cabras and Punta San Isidro before heading inland along the Rio San Antonio and into the coastal foothills. Lunch is provided around Valle de Trinidad, where you'll have plenty of time to not only rest up from the thrilling morning, but to feast on one of Baja Off Road Tours' legendary lunches.

From Valle de Trinidad the ride begins to take on new proportions as you ascend into the Sierra San Pedro Martir mountain range and begin the high route to Mike's Sky Rancho. This route is sure to give any rider a memorable and scenic ride. In fact, you'll forget any blues you may have as you navigate and negotiate the many turns and switchbacks that deliver you to Mike's.

There's also a grand finale to day one, should your guide deem it safe and rideable, and that's Simpson Ranch Road, whose final grade into Mike's is sure to put one's skills and patience to the test. Of course, cold beer and a hot shower await you at the bottom of the hill... but if you don't take that route, there's still several other ways to get to Mike's. All of which let you sample the finest riding Baja has to offer.

Day two begins with a somewhat liesurely 30 mile ride through the hills surrounding Mike's to Laguna Diablo, or Devil's lake. This 12-mile long dry lake offers some of the most otherworldly riding on this planet. Although it generates dust that can sometimes rise a thousand feet into the sky, it is flat and dry and shimmers with a heat rising off its floor. After lunch on Laguna Diablo, the ride then leads through more hills to Arroyo Huatamote, a mostly dry wash that meanders its way to the western shore of the Sea of Cortez. Also known as the Gulf of California, this inland sea is abundant in marine life and if you're an ocean swimmer or a seafood lover, you'll be happy here. Oceanfront accommodations are provided at the Hotel El Cortez, where you can watch the fluctuating tides, swim, dine and enjoy a spectacular sunrise.

Your last day departs San Felipe at first light. Being the last day, this ride incorporates not only several of the features ridden on days one and two, but also some very special attractions. Laguna Diablo will be traversed again, however, instead of going west to the Pacific, you'll ride more of a northerly route through San Matias, Valle de Trinidad, Santa Catarina and finally what's known as The Pine Forest. This wonderful area will make you forget you were just in the desert. It's replete with alpine-like meadows, cattle, magnificent boulders, plenty of water crossings and even an occasional mountain lion. As this is the high country, colder weather and snow can be encountered here in winter. After this it's on to Ojos Negros for the last stop of the trip and then back into Ensenada.

*Note: During Baja racing, such as the Baja 500 or 1000, or the San Felipe 250, certain routes, or even the whole trip may be run in reverse to avoid riding backwards on any portions of the race course.*

## The Seven Day Tour

For the rider seeking more riding time, more challenges and even more of a sense of accomplishment, you can ride all the way to the tip of the peninsula. This six-day trip takes you from Ensenada, all the way to land's end at the tip of the peninsula. Covering roughly 200 miles per day, the 1200-mile ride gives riders the opportunity to see Baja like few others do; from its peaks and valleys, villages and ranchos to its many scenic and cultural splendors to 300-year old missions and cactus forests—there is something here for everyone.

You'll ride through beautiful towns like San Quintin and San Ignacio—an oasis of blue water and green palms—through one of the most magnificent bays on earth— Bahia de Los Angeles— and you will experience important Baja cities such as Loreto and La Paz...this trip gives you the whole thing.

The route Chris has chosen covers the traditional point-to-point Baja 1000 race course (though it stops at La Paz) and provides challenges for riders of all abilities. Along the way you'll see practically the same landscape that the Conquistadors rode through in their "discovery" of Baja.

Much of the routes, villages and structures are much the way they were 300 years ago. And there's more. More stars than you'll ever see anywhere else in the world, the freshest lobster tacos, three shades of turqoise coastal water, white sandy beaches and more fresh air than you could possibly breath. In short, the ride to the tip is an experience that few can accomplish. And for do, comes a feeling of success that will last you your wh

Awaiting you at the end of the peninsula is the Finister Cabo San Lucas and the fine dining that this sport-fish is known for. After resting up, Baja Off Road Tours will in making your flight back to reality... that is, if you w back.

baja off road

## Motorcycle Tours

BAJA TOURS CL: Chris Haines Baja Tours CD, AD, D, P, CW: Mike Salisbury D, I: Mary Ellen McGough CW: Vince Iorio DF: Mike Salisbury Communications USA 1997 *SIZE: 295×209*

l'avion ou le train*
+ les transferts*
+ l'hébergement
+ les repas à volonté
+ le vin à table
+ les soirées-spectacles
+ la fête
+ le night-club
+ les forfaits ski
+ les cours de sport
+ le matériel et l'encadrement
+ le Mini-Club
* sur certaines destinations
au Club c'est tout compris
Ils seront vos hôtes cet hiver dans tous nos villages:
Les chefs de villages
l'Europe en douceur
France ✱ Espagne ✱ Canaries

à partir de 4 990F
la semaine de séjour. Vol compris au départ de Paris.
Village accueillant les enfants à tout âge.
Encadrement à partir de 2 ans.
Coral Beach
Israël
Entre les fonds de la mer Rouge, célèbres pour leur beauté, et le désert millénaire, un village très chaleureux, idéal en famille ou entre amis.
Bienvenue au Club
Au bord de la mer Rouge, à 10 mn en voiture du centre d'Eilat. Aéroport : Ovda, à 75 km.
Températures moyennes
N D J F M A
Max 28 23 21 23 26 31
Min 16 12 10 11 12 14
nuits fraîches en déc. et janv.
Décalage horaire : + 1 h.
Sports à volonté
Gymnastique, salle de musculation, volley, beach-volley.
Avec cours d'initiation : plongée libre, planche à voile, tir à l'arc, 4 tennis en dur, dont 2 éclairés.
Partez à la découverte
Vous souhaitez visiter Jérusalem, Massada, le désert du Néguev et pousser une pointe jusqu'en Jordanie ? Nous vous proposons un programme varié d'excursions* d'une demi-journée à 2 jours.
Pour préparer vos vacances
Consultez le Guide des prix page 27.
Vos enfants au village, Trident page 12.
* Avec supplément.
Un site de rêve pour fans de plongée libre.
Découverte
Chefs de village : leur savoir-faire ; le "savoir-fête"
Brésiliens, canadiens, marocains, suisses, belges, français, tunisiens... ils sont une centaine à travers le monde à partager les mêmes valeurs : gentillesse, générosité, imagination, professionnalisme, enthousiasme. Ce sont les Chefs de village. Voici les six petits derniers. Leur histoire, leur coup de foudre pour le Club. Demain ils deviendront eux aussi de grands Chefs de villages comme les 83 autres qui transforment jour après jour les 78 villages que nous vous présentons dans les pages qui suivent, en une fête de tous les instants... Choisissez votre destination... Pour le reste votre Chef de village et son équipe de GO s'occupent de tout.
Olivier Rapin
30 ans, architecte d'intérieur, menuisier-charpentier. Olivier rêve d'être prof de gym et lorsqu'il réussit ses examens de fin d'études, ses parents lui offrent une semaine de vacances au Club Med à Djerba. De retour en Suisse, Olivier résistera un mois et demi exactement avant de repartir au Club Med. Tour à tour, moniteur de natation et de ski, Olivier devient coordinateur des sports puis Chef de village, en 1998.
Patrick Serva
34 ans, électromécanicien. 1986 : Patrick organise des spectacles, danse et joue les mannequins à l'occasion. Patrick discute avec un ami : « Et si tu venais travailler au Club Med ? » Il se retrouve à St-Moritz avec un job... de danseur. Il sera animateur, responsable animation puis coordinateur des sports.
Scott «Teach» Mayer
30 ans, diplômé d'Harvard en littérature anglaise et américaine. Scott voulait faire un break de six mois entre ses études et ses débuts dans l'enseignement. Au Club par exemple, comme G.O... Il passe six mois à Sandpiper comme moniteur Mini-Club. Son contrat achevé, Scott décide de prolonger ses vacances le temps de découvrir l'Europe puis l'Asie. Quand il se réveille, il est trop tard : « mon ancien métier n'était plus adapté à mes nouveaux intérêts».
Thierry Buche
33 ans, diplômé en arts graphiques En 87, son copain André part en Yougoslavie comme G.O. Thierry passe à Paris proposer ses services comme moniteur de ski nautique. « Il nous faut un décorateur pour la Yougoslavie ». Envoyé à Pompadour pour un essai, il réussit son examen de passage et rejoint son copain à Sveti Marko. Moniteur de ski l'hiver, de ski nautique l'été, il embarque aujourd'hui pour de nouvelles aventures avec le Club Med.
Chris «hammer» Keeley
38 ans, diplômé en marketing. Ne l'appelez plus jamais Chris, son nom c'est Hammer. C'est du moins celui que lui a donné un speaker, lors d'un match de baseball à Vancouver. Pour le jeune Keeley, la vie se résume alors à deux activités majeures : son métier d'agent immobilier et la fête. Tout naturellement Hammer se retrouve G.M. à Tahiti. C'était en 89. Depuis, il n'a pas quitté le Club.
Eric Leje
Club Med
98/99

**Package Tours**

CLUB MED CL: Club Med K. K. Japan 1998 *SIZE: 298×210*

AA-VE

Challenge · Pride · Success

## Teenage Adventure Programs

AMERICA'S ADVENTURE CL: America's Adventure / Venture Europe D: Carrie Wallahan P: David Belda
DF: Kowalski Designworks, Inc. USA 1996 *SIZE: 305×229*

12

# AMAZING ACTION & ACTIVITIES

## Day & Night, We Do it Right

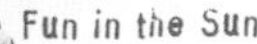

### Fun in the Sun

As the innovative leader in active student travel each program is action-packed with a great variety and choice of activities. If you are not familiar with an activity, don't worry we'll show you how. Every tour is equipped with a full set of athletic gear.

**Daytime activities include:** Mountain biking, whitewater rafting, jet boating, rollerblading, water skiing, snow skiing, hiking, aquabiking, horseback riding, sea kayaking, snorkeling, snowboarding, swimming, inner-tubing, canoeing, alpine sliding, snow-mobiling, rock climbing, bouldering, whirlyball, volleyball, soccer, football, basketball, frisbee, hackeysack, tennis, aquariums, zoos, interactive museums, college visits, TV studios, and much more.

"We did so many wonderful activities and toured sights that were incredible. Everything was well organized and fun. This trip was filled with non-stop action and incredible experiences."
**Dara Gordon**
**Beverly Hills, California**

13

### We do it right at Night

When the sun goes down, we just keep on going.

**Nighttime excitement includes:** Theme parks, dance clubs, T.V. tapings, baseball games, water parks, famous restaurants like Hard Rock and Planet Hollywood, comedy clubs, Broadway shows and summer stock theater, movies, laser rock, Q-Zar laser tag, bumper boats, batting cages, ice skating, roller skating, rock 'n bowl, mini-golf, go-carting, campfires, s'mores and much more.

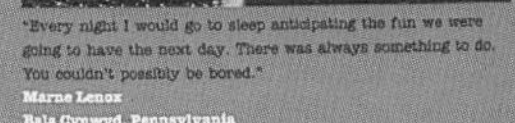
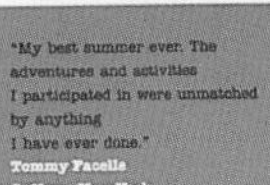

"Every night I would go to sleep anticipating the fun we were going to have the next day. There was always something to do. You couldn't possibly be bored."
**Marne Lenox**
**Bala Cynwyd, Pennsylvania**

"My best summer ever. The adventures and activities I participated in were unmatched by anything I have ever done."
**Tommy Facelle**
**Suffern, New York**

32

# THE BEST SUMMER OF MY LIFE

### COMMENTS FROM LAST SUMMER

With thousands of alumni it's not possible to list everyone, so here is a small sampling of the hundreds of ecstatic reviews we received last summer. Additional references from your area are available upon request.

"This was the most amazing summer ever in my entire life. We did everything from hiking in the canyons to Disneyland and Universal, we were busy every second. All of the new things I did, such as putting up a tent, rafting, snorkeling, kayaking, touching the dolphins and the ropes course, will always be remembered. The people made the trip. The counselors were also phenomenal. They were very kind and caring."
Carly Abel • Livingston, New Jersey

"I enjoyed making and meeting new friends. I learned so much not only about respect, but about our country. It was a memorable, incredible experience."
Hallie Gelb • Orange, Ohio

"Thank you so much for all that you have done to make Rachel's Musiker Tour a great experience. Your staff is to be recommended for their support to her as well as the entire Musiker Family. Thanks again for everything."
Elaine and Bob Minkoff
Potomac, Maryland

"This tour was one of the most incredible things I have ever done. There is no one else that I would rather have shared this with than 40 new friends."
Beth Taranto • Atlanta, Georgia

"I loved it. It was a great experience for bonding, working in teams, overcoming fears, seeing and trying new things. It is definitely a growing and maturing trip."
Tara Schwarz • Highland Park, Illinois

"I had many high expectations of the summer and the tour. All of them were met or exceeded. Thank you so much for a wonderful summer."
Alison Malmon • Potomac, Maryland

"The tour offered me an opportunity to expand my horizons, meet neat and interesting people, and explore the limits of my abilities. Having spent a total of six weeks with these people, I feel that I have formed a bond that goes beyond common friendship."
Leon Chao • Arlington, Virginia

"I made a lot of new friends. The stops were so much fun!"
Marilyn Sheets • Scottsdale, Arizona

"I bonded like crazy with people from all over the country. This tour allows you to do that while exposing you to new experiences of the country."
Crystal Sands • Fort Lee, New Jersey

"My summer was awesome! I had a lot of fun with my new friends from all over the world."
Marisa Laura Barretto
Sao Paulo, Brazil

"Everyday got better and better. I met a lot of great people and saw a lot of wonderful things."
Patricia De Raeymaeker • Brussels, Belgium

"Through the many activities we did, we all were able to get to know more about each other. I made a bunch of great new friends with whom I hope to stay close to."
Zoe Levy • Riverdale, New York

33

"I came away with a feeling that I have met some of the most special people. I have had the summer with new experiences, memories and a new family. Thank you, Musiker!"
Lindsay Abramowitz
Woodcliff Lake,
New Jersey

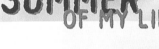

"I thought it was great. The tour could not have been better."
Dave Vangrov • Orlando, Florida

"Everyone was really nice and got along great. It felt like a big family. Everything was well organized."
Joey Gartner • New York, New York

"This tour was the best way to discover America. I met great people and it was one of the best experiences I ever had."
Edward Marchal • Paris, France

"I had a phat time."
Cory Kwiat • Muttontown, New York

"It was a very good experience because I saw a lot of new things and met a lot of nice, new people."
Mark de Frahan • Brussels, Belgium

"A once in a lifetime experience that I can look back on as one of my most memorable experiences."
Jason Rappaport • Boca Raton, Florida

"I saw extraordinary sights, made lifetime friends and now have a completely different view of America."
Kristin Hendricks • McLean, Virginia

"It was amazing! I loved walking away with over 40 new best friends and thousands of memories."
Lauren Mermel • Great Neck, New York

"Musiker was by far the coolest summer experience I have ever been a part of."
Jonathan Frank • Bethesda, Maryland

"This was the best summer I've ever had. I met a lot of people and got to know them. I wish this trip could be my life."
Dayo Chou • Douglaston, New York

MUSIKER TOURS 1998

Active Student Tours & Adventure Programs

## Student Tour & Adventure Program

MUSIKER TOURS CL: Musiker Tours, Inc. AD: Krysten Bonzelet D: Ann Leonardi P: Markham Johnson / Paul Goldberg / Donna Smith CW: Robert Musiker DF: Kowalski Designworks, Inc. USA 1997 *SIZE: 305×229*

Sea Kayaking in Fiji
Paddling Palau

Royal Inca

Since 1978 Wilderness Travel has been in the business of making dreams come true. We have taken intrepid travelers into the heart of remote Himalayan kingdoms and brought them nose-to-nose with friendly fur seals in the Galápagos Islands. This year we want to take you! Whether you long to find yourself on the summit of Mount Kilimanjaro or on the terrace of a cafe in Provence, your journey begins right here among these pages.

**Choose from an enormous variety of destinations and activities**

With over 100 adventures on seven continents, we have a trip to suit your every travel whim: from high mountain treks and luxurious inn-to-inn hikes, to sea kayaking in Palau and explorations of the rainforest in the Amazon Basin.

Our 1999 program features a fantastic range of adventures, from easy cultural tours to rugged backcountry treks. There are safaris, hikes, cruises, and adventures that offer a combination of activities. And we have trips to destinations around the globe, from Antarctica to Zimbabwe.

Overwhelmed by the choices? Don't be. You can request a comprehensive detailed itinerary for any of our adventures to help you choose the one that's right for you. Our office staff is available to discuss any aspect of your trip, destination, or interest; we are also happy to give you the names of guests who have been on a particular trip or traveled with a specific trip leader. We're here every step of the way to help you select, prepare for, and enjoy your ideal adventure.

**Superb leadership is our hallmark**

Our trip leaders are naturalists, authors, photographers—and, perhaps most importantly, terrific travel companions. No other company places such a strong emphasis on leadership—but we believe it's the key to a successful trip. Traveling in the company of a guide who knows the language, customs, and natural history of a place really brings you "into" the adventure, and helps you reach a new level of participation. Adventuring with a seasoned, committed trip leader—each of whom has an abiding love for his or her corner of the world—and that rare ability to deal with the unexpected in a resourceful manner—makes for an unforgettable travel experience.

**Handcrafted itineraries**

Each of our trips has been carefully crafted to capture the best of a particular destination. This means traveling at an appropriate pace, ensuring proper acclimatization, choosing the ideal campsites, and simply knowing those hidden, off-the-beaten-path places that make for an exceptional journey. Both in the field and at our home office in Berkeley, our staff members are experts in the art of itinerary design. We will be happy to discuss logistics with you if you're interested in the "why" of it all, or you can leave it to us and be confident in the knowledge that a great deal of thought and more than 20 years of experience have gone into planning every adventure.

## THE BEST IN Adventure Travel

**Getting you ready for adventure**

We are a company of dedicated travelers, and we love sharing insights gained from our own adventures abroad. Our area experts are always ready to help you decide which trip is right for you, and how best to get prepared. In addition, well before you leave you'll receive detailed pre-departure information for your trip, including packing lists, medical information, and specifics on everything from visas to photography. We also include reading lists to fire up your imagination for the journey ahead.

Finally, we oversee all of your arrangements, including air travel and trip extensions, from your first discussions with us until you're safely home again. We'll do the work so you can focus on preparing for and then enjoying your trip!

**References available upon request**

Our high percentage of repeat clientele means we deliver on our promises of excellence. But you don't have to take our word for it. Call about any trip in our program and we'll be happy to refer you to a client who's been there with us.

4 About Wilderness Travel    Photo credits—Above: Andy Freeberg • Opposite page, clockwise from top left: Galen Rowell, Andy Freeberg, Brian McGilloway, David Robbins, Markham Johnson

"...What keeps me coming back to Wilderness Travel is the quality of your leaders. In Provence, Annie Hawkins and James Fuss were a perfect team. Annie was both efficient and irresistibly charming—opening our eyes to the sensualité of France. James was cheerful, amusing, and incredibly knowledgeable about the local cuisine. This was my third trip with Wilderness. I still fondly remember the camaraderie shared with Richard Munro on the Tour du Mt. Blanc. And the once in a lifetime experience I shared with my son in Tanzania with Godfrey Mbise, who told me, 'I will not forget you, Mama'—nor I he. And now when I think of those red fields of poppies, I will certainly recall wonderful moments shared with Annie and James."
Jennifer S. Huntley • Country Walks in Provence/May '98

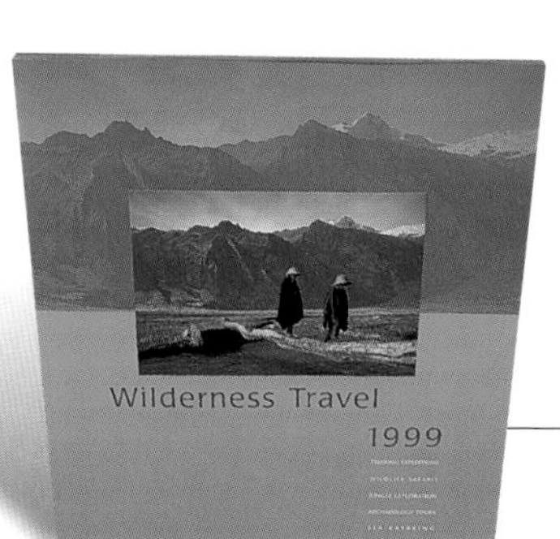
Wilderness Travel
1999

## Package Tours

WILDERNESS TRAVEL CL: Wilderness Travel AD, I: Krysten Bonzelet D, I: Amanda Bellows CW: Scott Senauke/ Rachel Eve Radway
DF: Kowalski Designworks, Inc. USA 1998 *SIZE: 305×229*

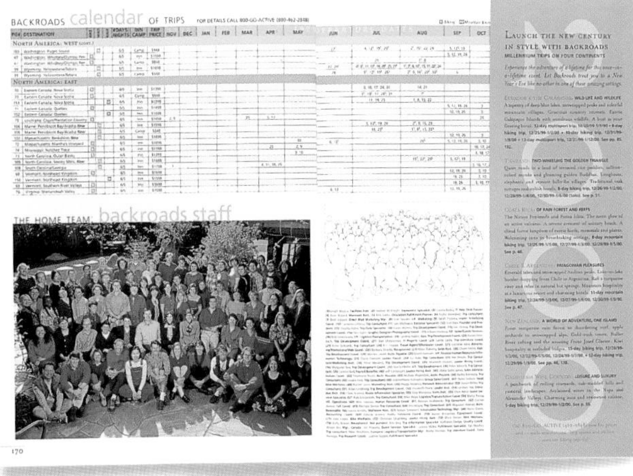

IT'S NOT HOW far YOU GO...
...IT'S how YOU GET THERE.
Active travel is the difference between looking at life and living it. Stand spellbound on the North Rim of the Grand Canyon after a spectacular 40-mile bike ride. Breathe in the scent of rosemary as you hike to a Tuscan hill town. Listen to the chatter of monkeys overhead as you raft down a Costa Rican river. Rather than experiencing the world as though it were a museum with everything framed behind glass windows, Backroads invites you to experience the world. Bike. Walk. Hike. Kayak. Raft. Snorkel. Ski. 150 itineraries. 90 destinations. The choice is yours.

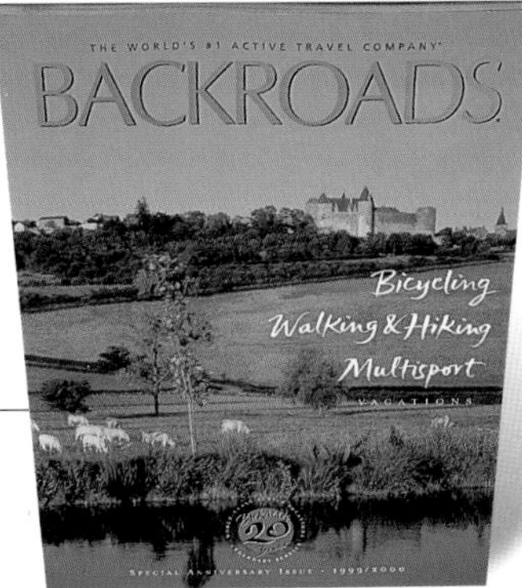

BACKROADS
Bicycling
Walking & Hiking
Multisport
VACATIONS

## Active Travel Vacations

BACKROADS CL: Backroads AD: Janél Apple D: Carrie Wallahan / Derrick Wynes Calligraphy: Lily Lee
DF: Kowalski Designworks, Inc. USA 1998 *SIZE: 305×229*

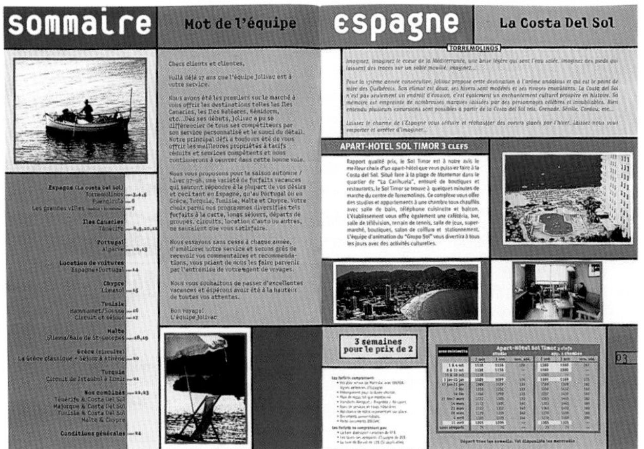


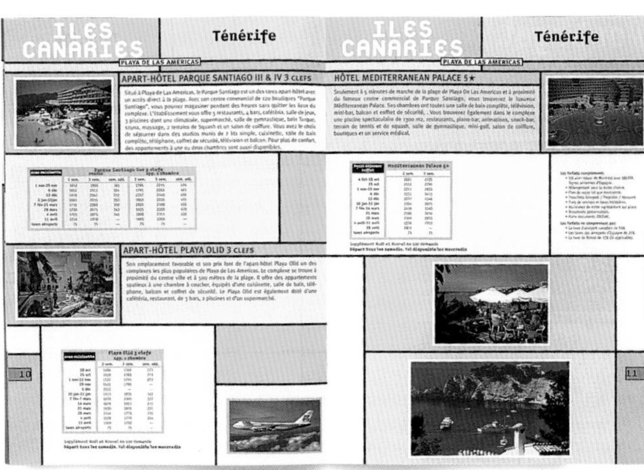


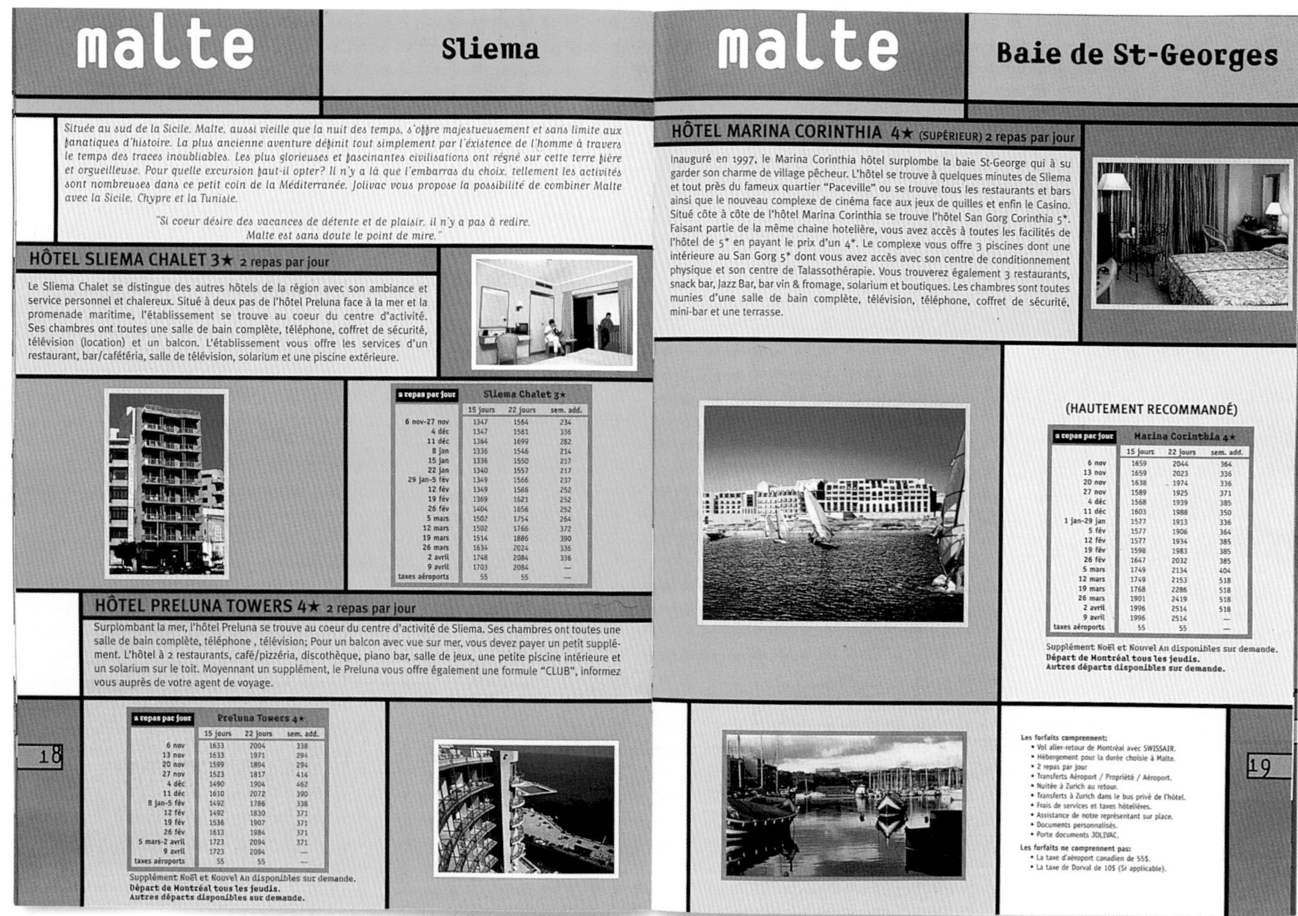

# malte
## Sliema

*Située au sud de la Sicile, Malte, aussi vieille que la nuit des temps, s'offre majestueusement et sans limite aux fanatiques d'histoire. La plus ancienne aventure définit tout simplement par l'existence de l'homme à travers le temps des traces inoubliables. Les plus glorieuses et fascinantes civilisations ont régné sur cette terre fière et orgueilleuse. Pour quelle excursion faut-il opter? Il n'y a là que l'embarras du choix, tellement les activités sont nombreuses dans ce petit coin de la Méditerranée. Jolivac vous propose la possibilité de combiner Malte avec la Sicile, Chypre et la Tunisie.*

*"Si coeur désire des vacances de détente et de plaisir, il n'y a pas à redire. Malte est sans doute le point de mire."*

### HÔTEL SLIEMA CHALET 3★ 2 repas par jour

Le Sliema Chalet se distingue des autres hôtels de la région avec son ambiance et service personnel et chaleureux. Situé à deux pas de l'hôtel Preluna face à la mer et la promenade maritime, l'établissement se trouve au coeur du centre d'activité. Ses chambres ont toutes une salle de bain complète, téléphone, coffret de sécurité, télévision (location) et un balcon. L'établissement vous offre les services d'un restaurant, bar/cafétéria, salle de télévision, solarium et une piscine extérieure.

| 2 repas par jour | Sliema Chalet 3★ | | |
|---|---|---|---|
| | 15 jours | 22 jours | sem. add. |
| 6 nov-27 nov | 1347 | 1564 | 234 |
| 4 déc | 1347 | 1581 | 336 |
| 11 déc | 1364 | 1699 | 282 |
| 8 jan | 1336 | 1546 | 214 |
| 15 jan | 1336 | 1550 | 217 |
| 22 jan | 1340 | 1557 | 217 |
| 29 jan-5 fév | 1349 | 1566 | 237 |
| 12 fév | 1349 | 1586 | 252 |
| 19 fév | 1369 | 1621 | 252 |
| 26 fév | 1404 | 1656 | 252 |
| 5 mars | 1502 | 1754 | 264 |
| 12 mars | 1502 | 1766 | 372 |
| 19 mars | 1514 | 1886 | 390 |
| 26 mars | 1634 | 2024 | 336 |
| 2 avril | 1748 | 2084 | 336 |
| 9 avril | 1703 | 2084 | — |
| taxes aéroports | 55 | 55 | — |

### HÔTEL PRELUNA TOWERS 4★ 2 repas par jour

Surplombant la mer, l'hôtel Preluna se trouve au coeur du centre d'activité de Sliema. Ses chambres ont toutes une salle de bain complète, téléphone , télévision; Pour un balcon avec vue sur mer, vous devez payer un petit supplément. L'hôtel à 2 restaurants, café/pizzéria, discothèque, piano bar, salle de jeux, une petite piscine intérieure et un solarium sur le toit. Moyennant un supplément, le Preluna vous offre également une formule "CLUB", informez vous auprès de votre agent de voyage.

| 2 repas par jour | Preluna Towers 4★ | | |
|---|---|---|---|
| | 15 jours | 22 jours | sem. add. |
| 6 nov | 1633 | 2004 | 338 |
| 13 nov | 1633 | 1971 | 294 |
| 20 nov | 1599 | 1894 | 294 |
| 27 nov | 1523 | 1817 | 414 |
| 4 déc | 1490 | 1904 | 462 |
| 11 déc | 1610 | 2072 | 390 |
| 8 jan-5 fév | 1492 | 1786 | 338 |
| 12 fév | 1492 | 1830 | 371 |
| 19 fév | 1536 | 1907 | 371 |
| 26 fév | 1613 | 1984 | 371 |
| 5 mars-2 avril | 1723 | 2094 | 371 |
| 9 avril | 1723 | 2094 | — |
| taxes aéroports | 55 | 55 | — |

Supplément Noël et Nouvel An disponibles sur demande.
**Départ de Montréal tous les jeudis.**
**Autres départs disponibles sur demande.**

18

# malte
## Baie de St-Georges

### HÔTEL MARINA CORINTHIA 4★ (SUPÉRIEUR) 2 repas par jour

Inauguré en 1997, le Marina Corinthia hôtel surplombe la baie St-George qui à su garder son charme de village pêcheur. L'hôtel se trouve à quelques minutes de Sliema et tout près du fameux quartier "Paceville" ou se trouve tous les restaurants et bars ainsi que le nouveau complexe de cinéma face aux jeux de quilles et enfin le Casino. Situé côte à côte de l'hôtel Marina Corinthia se trouve l'hôtel San Gorg Corinthia 5*. Faisant partie de la même chaine hotelière, vous avez accès à toutes les facilités de l'hôtel de 5* en payant le prix d'un 4*. Le complexe vous offre 3 piscines dont une intérieure au San Gorg 5* dont vous avez accès avec son centre de conditionnement physique et son centre de Talassothérapie. Vous trouverez également 3 restaurants, snack bar, Jazz Bar, bar vin & fromage, solarium et boutiques. Les chambres sont toutes munies d'une salle de bain complète, télévision, téléphone, coffret de sécurité, mini-bar et une terrasse.

(HAUTEMENT RECOMMANDÉ)

| 2 repas par jour | Marina Corinthia 4★ | | |
|---|---|---|---|
| | 15 jours | 22 jours | sem. add. |
| 6 nov | 1659 | 2044 | 364 |
| 13 nov | 1659 | 2023 | 336 |
| 20 nov | 1638 | 1974 | 336 |
| 27 nov | 1589 | 1925 | 371 |
| 4 déc | 1568 | 1939 | 385 |
| 11 déc | 1603 | 1988 | 350 |
| 1 jan-29 jan | 1577 | 1913 | 336 |
| 5 fév | 1577 | 1906 | 364 |
| 12 fév | 1577 | 1934 | 385 |
| 19 fév | 1598 | 1983 | 385 |
| 26 fév | 1647 | 2032 | 385 |
| 5 mars | 1749 | 2134 | 404 |
| 12 mars | 1749 | 2153 | 518 |
| 19 mars | 1768 | 2286 | 518 |
| 26 mars | 1901 | 2419 | 518 |
| 2 avril | 1996 | 2514 | 518 |
| 9 avril | 1996 | 2514 | — |
| taxes aéroports | 55 | 55 | — |

Supplément Noël et Nouvel An disponibles sur demande.
**Départ de Montréal tous les jeudis.**
**Autres départs disponibles sur demande.**

**Les forfaits comprennent:**
- Vol aller-retour de Montréal avec SWISSAIR.
- Hébergement pour la durée choisie à Malte.
- 2 repas par jour
- Transferts Aéroport / Propriété / Aéroport.
- Nuitée à Zurich au retour.
- Transferts à Zurich dans le bus privé de l'hôtel.
- Frais de services et taxes hôtelières.
- Assistance de notre représentant sur place.
- Documents personnalisés.
- Porte documents JOLIVAC.

**Les forfaits ne comprennent pas:**
- La taxe d'aéroport canadien de 55$.
- La taxe de Dorval de 10$ (Si applicable).

19

**Package Tours**

JOLIVAC CL: Jolivac CD, AD, D: Denis Dulude D: Pol Baril DF: K-O Creation Canada 1997 *SIZE: 276×205*

## Outdoor Adventure Race

ECO CHALLENGE CL: Eco Challenge Lifestyles Inc. CD, AD: Rick Seireeni D, I: Tanja Richter P: Dan Campbell I: Heejo Seok DF: Studio Seireeni, Inc. USA 1997 *SIZE: 291×225*

## Package Tours

JALPAK CL: Jalpak Co., Ltd. CD: Yu Akinaga AD: Sachiyo Hayashi Japan 1998 *SIZE: 297×209*

## Package Tours

PLAY GUIDE TOUR KS CL: Play Guide Tour KS Inc. AD, D: Katsue Okutomi Japan 1998 *SIZE: 297×212*

### 南極半島・フォークランド諸島の見どころ

南シェトランド諸島から南極半島にかけては、多くの観光探検・上陸地点があります。
また、今年からフォークランドも仲間入り。さらに見どころ充実です。
それらのうちから代表的なものをご紹介いたします。
天候や波の状況を見ながら、毎日エキスペディション・リーダーが上陸ポイントを決定いたします。

エレラ海峡

岩場でひとやすみのアデリーペンギン

ネコハーバー

リビングストン島

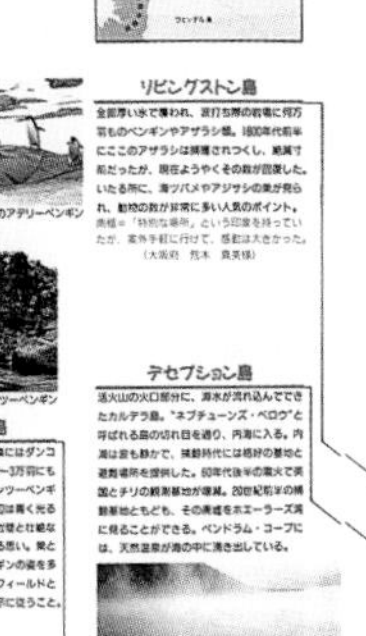

クーバービル島

デセプション島

ボランティアポイント

キングジョージ島

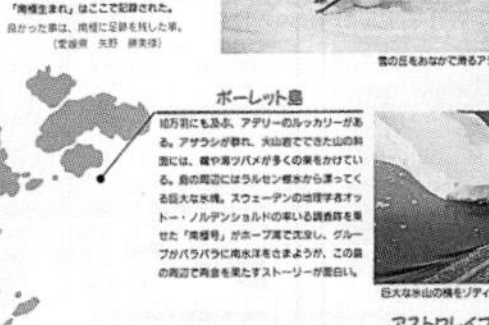

ノイマイヤ海峡

スタンレー

ホープ湾

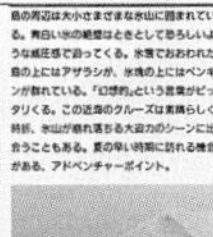

ポーレット島

お客様の声

パラダイスベイ

ルメア海峡

アストロレイブ島

ピーターマン島

アルミランテ・ブラウン

---

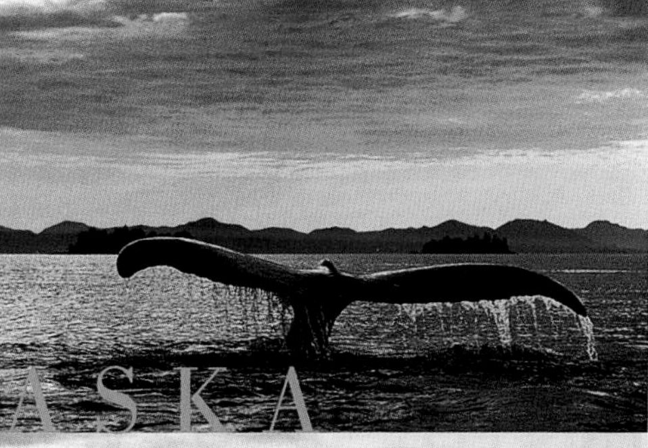

What's your pleasure?

Holland America offers you two wonderful ways to experience the splendors of Alaska. Both itineraries include the incomparable Inside Passage, an incredible waterway through some of the world's most spectacular scenery. You see it all from the vantage point of your fabulous floating resort.

**National Park Rangers alert you to the sights in Glacier Bay *(above)*. Watch a whale wag his tail *(top right)*. Your Inside Passage cruise is one scenic treat after another *(bottom right)*.**

# ON TO ALASKA

CHOOSE YOUR ROUTE

**A CLASSIC CRUISE**

Our Glacier Bay Inside Passage Cruise is a favorite of cruise connoisseurs. In seven days, you will sail round-trip from Vancouver, B.C., with a day in Glacier Bay at midpoint of the voyage. You go ashore and get close to the real Alaska at the ports of Juneau, Skagway and Ketchikan, where you may add new dimensions to your holiday with dozens of optional adventures like flightseeing, river rafting, canoeing, fishing and touring to native villages.

Everything about the Glacier Bay Inside Passage Cruise is unforgettable, but nothing will live as long in your memory as the magical day cruising Glacier Bay National Park. As you sail ever deeper into the fjord, densely forested slopes change to rugged, rocky crests: this is the newer part of the bay, where nature has not yet had time to clothe the land exposed by retreating glaciers. Like frozen rivers, glaciers flow to the bay, where the icebergs they have spawned bob and float. The National Park Service Rangers who have joined the ship point out harbor seals sunning on ice floes, mountain goats like balls of fluff high on the cliff. Maybe you'll see a humpback whale breaching, or a school of leaping orcas.

**DISCOVER THE GLACIERS**

Choose the Glacier Discovery Cruise between Vancouver, B.C. and Seward/Anchorage if you wish a leisurely seven-day voyage, highlighted by the dazzling glacial giants of Southcentral Alaska. Feast your eyes on the multiple glaciers of remote College Fjord, and the massive icy face of Hubbard Glacier in Wrangell-St. Elias National Park. On some cruises you're privileged to visit Valdez with its picturesque backdrop of mountains – the "Switzerland of Alaska." Some include a day cruising Glacier Bay. Every cruise includes stops at Ketchikan, Juneau and Sitka, where you have ample time for a variety of shore excursions. And every Glacier Discovery Cruise takes you through the enchanting Inside Passage, with maximum opportunity to enjoy the delights of cruising.

10 11

## Cruise Tours

HOLLAND AMERICA LINE CL: Holland America Line AD, D: John Hornall D: Julie Lock / Patt Dietz / Virginia Le DF: Hornall Anderson Design Works, Inc. USA 1997 *SIZE: 275×212*

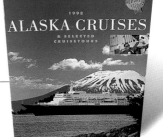

## Spa

LUDWIGSTORFF SPA CL: Ludwigstorff Spa CD, AD, D, I: Lothar Ämilian Heinzle DF: Atelier Heinzle Austria 1997 *SIZE: 210×199*

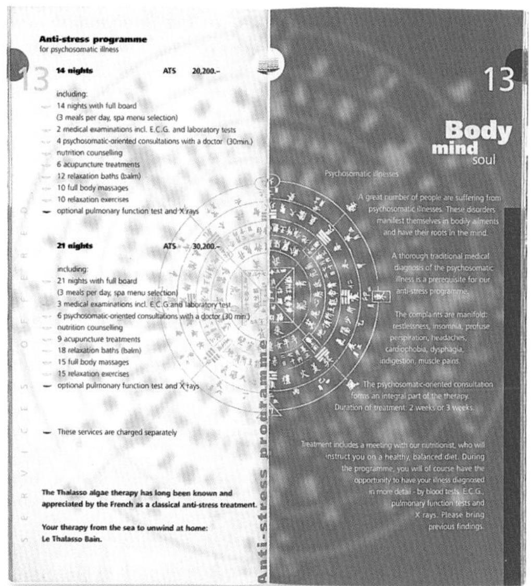

## Package Tours

TOP FIT CL: Top Fit Sport-Freizeit Und Trainingsreisen CD: Markus Friebe DF: Convex Design Group Germany 1998 *SIZE: 297×210*

# hobby

toys

musical instruments

stationery, tools & crafts

books & software

1-800-367-6372
A | Our child's motorsport
jumpsuit is a comfortable
and practical, washable
one piece outfit in soft brushed
cotton twill. Red or Black
S (2T), M (3T), L (4T)
D9701 6101 $49.50
REMEMBER YOUR FIRST MERCEDES?
B | Our child's cap is super-soft
sueded pique with an adjustable strap.
Made in the USA. Fits ages 6 to 12
961 999 7102 $16
C | Our child's M-Class T-shirt is
made with the finest quality
organically grown cotton, ring-spun
for extra softness. This could be the
softest, most comfortable T-shirt
your child has ever worn.
S-L D9801 4400 $15
D | Our eco-cotton infant/toddler jumpsuit
is also made from organically grown cotton, and
no bleaches, chemicals or sizing were used
in the manufacturing process. Exceptionally soft.
9-24 mo. Natural D9801 4500 $39.50
E | Being a toddler shouldn't stop you
from owning a Mercedes. To a tot, a Bobby Benz
in the garage is better than a pony in the barn.
Some assembly required.
Age 1½-3 B6 600 5800 $89
23

1-800-367-6372
S-LK 230
A DAY AT THE RACES
A | This SLK pedal car is perfect for little racers 2 to 5 years old. It even looks good parked under the piano.
Some assembly required. B6 600 5805 $295
24
B | It might come as a surprise
that Mercedes vehicles aren't
for the road alone. In fact, the
farms of Europe have long relied
on Mercedes commercial
vehicles like our front loader.
This replica is pedal-operated
with a hand-operated front loader
and a seat that adjusts
to three positions for different
leg lengths. Made in Germany.
Some assembly required.
Recommended for ages 3½ to 7.
A950 999 1404 $295
C | Winner's circle T-shirt is
100% combed cotton with our
Motorsport logo on the front and
"Powered by Mercedes-Benz"
on the back, with images of our
victorious racing cars. Children's
sizes S-L. (Adult T-shirt page 51)
D9701 4102 $12
D | For years, the Mercedes
Unimog has been an all-purpose
workhorse – the little truck that
can do anything. Our Unimog
pedal truck is a replica of unusual
quality that makes the sound
of a real truck engine when you
press the horn, and has a seat
adjustable to three positions
to accommodate different
leg lengths. Made in Germany.
Some assembly required.
Recommended for ages 3½ to 7.
A950 999 1504 $395
25

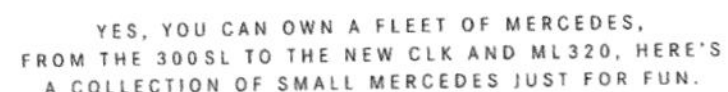
YES, YOU CAN OWN A FLEET OF MERCEDES,
FROM THE 300SL TO THE NEW CLK AND ML320, HERE'S
A COLLECTION OF SMALL MERCEDES JUST FOR FUN.

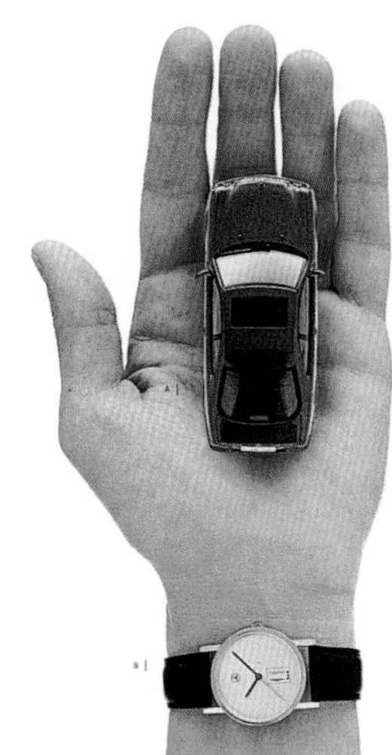

A | The new **CLK coupe** is a stunning design, with flowing lines and a muscular attitude. Its cousin, the CLK-GTR is already making history on the racing circuit. 1:43 scale. Mineral Green B6 600 5740 **$24** Quartz Blue B6 600 5739 **$24**

B | Our **SLK quartz watch** features a high-sheen chrome-plated housing, a silver-plated face and a black leather strap. Water-tight to 3 ATM B6 600 4018 **$58**

C | **SLK diecast replica** is a lovingly detailed 1:43 scale model. A car you can study from every angle. Brilliant Silver B6 600 5721 **$22.50**

D | The **SLK diecast model** is a perfect replica with a retractable hard top. 1:18 scale. Brilliant Silver B6 600 5204 **$34.50** Sunburst Yellow A950 999 3204 **$34.50**

E | The **ML320** combines vault-like strength and Mercedes engineering and takes the sport utility vehicle to the next level. 1:24 scale. Brilliant Silver A950 999 3604 **$14.95**

F | The new **CLK coupe** continues the tradition of the 300 CE, 560 SEC and other legendary Mercedes coupes. Available in 1:18 scale. B6 600 5221 **$34.50**

G | **SLK diecast replica** is a lovingly detailed 1:43 scale model. Imperial Red B6 600 5722 **$22.50**

H | The new **ML320** was designed from the ground up to be the ultimate sport utility vehicle. 1:24 scale. Black A950 999 3704 **$14.95**

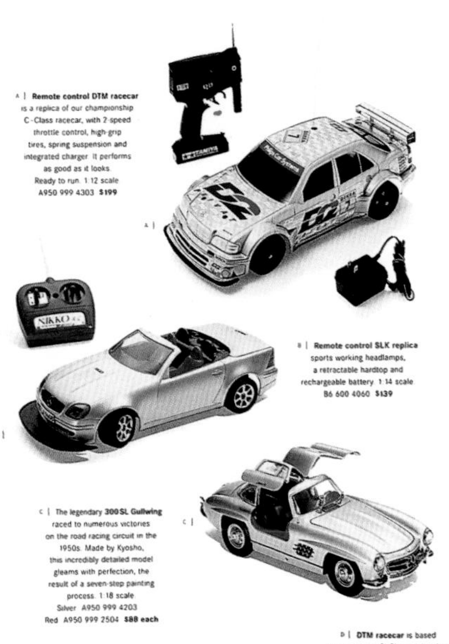

A | **Remote control DTM racecar** is a replica of our championship C-Class racecar, with 2-speed throttle control, high-grip tires, spring suspension and integrated charger. It performs as good as it looks. Ready to run. 1:12 scale A950 999 4303 **$199**

B | **Remote control SLK replica** sports working headlamps, a retractable hardtop and rechargeable battery. 1:14 scale B6 600 4060 **$139**

C | The legendary **300SL Gullwing** raced to numerous victories on the road racing circuit in the 1950s. Made by Kyosho, this incredibly detailed model gleams with perfection, the result of a seven-step painting process. 1:18 scale Silver A950 999 4203 Red A950 999 2504 **$88 each**

D | **DTM racecar** is based on our sporty C-Class sedan, but with technological refinements that make it closer to a Formula One racecar in performance. A finely detailed replica of our Touring Car competition racecar from Paul's Model Art. 1:43 scale A950 999 0004 **$42.50**

48

1-800-367-6372

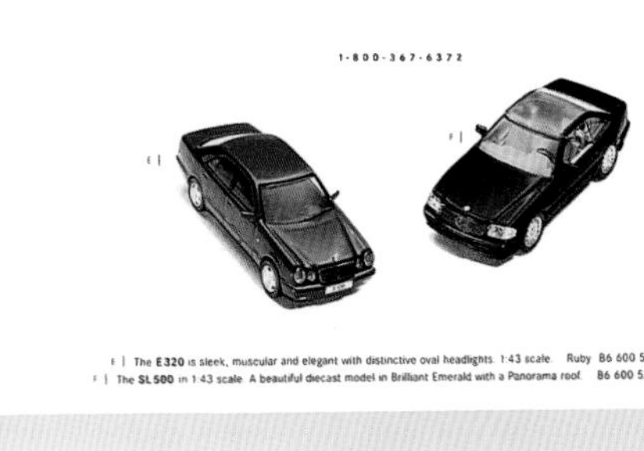

E | The **E320** is sleek, muscular and elegant with distinctive oval headlights. 1:43 scale. Ruby B6 600 5719 **$22**
F | The **SL500** in 1:43 scale. A beautiful diecast model in Brilliant Emerald with a Panorama roof. B6 600 5723 **$32.50**

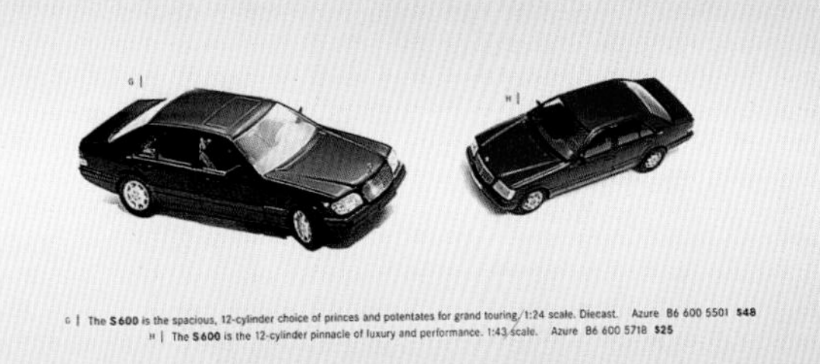

G | The **S600** is the spacious, 12-cylinder choice of princes and potentates for grand touring. 1:24 scale. Diecast. Azure B6 600 5501 **$48**
H | The **S600** is the 12-cylinder pinnacle of luxury and performance. 1:43 scale. Azure B6 600 5718 **$25**

I | The spacious, versatile interior of the new **E320 Wagon** is wrapped in a sleek, aerodynamic design. 1:43 scale. Black B6 600 5725 **$24**
J | The **C-Class** sets a new standard in value, safety and performance. 1:43 scale. Brilliant Emerald B6 600 5717 **$22**

49

Mercedes-Benz

## Toys

**MERCEDES-BENZ** CL: Mercedes-Benz N. A. CD, AD: Kristin Johnson AD, D: Caroline Keavy D: Beth Wood P: Steve Shaw / Eric Huang / Scott Williamson CW: Frank Cunningham DF: Pinkhaus USA 1997 *SIZE: 279×216*

ACTIVITÉS MANUELLES

Les premiers pas

Par la variété des techniques, l'enfant multiplie les manipulations, précise ses gestes et affine sa sensibilité. Ces livres pratiques donnent les conseils de base et des modèles très simples pour réaliser les premières œuvres.

Dessain & Tolra. Collection Premiers pas. L'unité, 70 F

Découpages. Pliages. Pochoirs.


Découpages
Pliages
Pochoirs
0/6 ans


Une ferme en construction

Nature & découvertes propose des activités manuelles qui permettent aux enfants d'apprendre à se servir de leurs mains et développer leur esprit créatif. Cette ferme complète demande concentration et minutie pour assembler les éléments en carton puis peindre le toit, les murs, le sol...

Ferme 99,50 F

Peintures 49,50 F

Pinceaux en mousse 15 F

Cahier de coloriage

Conçus spécialement pour Nature & découvertes, ces dessins naturalistes offrent des contours bien marqués. L'enfant apportera toute son attention pour colorier les espaces sans déborder.

29,50 F

10

Les artistes en herbe de 6 à 9 ans


Les petits explorateurs se posent mille énigmes. Pour trouver les réponses, leurs sources privilégiées seront les expériences de terrain, les premiers livres documentaires et "les grands".

Sortez... Faites-leur découvrir de nouveaux horizons : bord de rivière et bord de mare, prairie à plat ventre et nez en l'air... Tous les espaces se différencient par divers objets ramenés dans la "boîte à trésors" de l'enfant : petits cailloux, plumes, coquille d'escargot vide... Dans son carnet d'explorateur, l'enfant notera en vrac ses sensations et toutes les impressions ressenties. Y seront aussi consignées les innombrables questions posées.

Parents, guidez ces écrivains débutants et surtout, ne répondez pas à toutes leurs questions ! Indiquez leur des outils pour qu'ils puissent les résoudre par eux-mêmes...

*Réseau École et Nature*

11

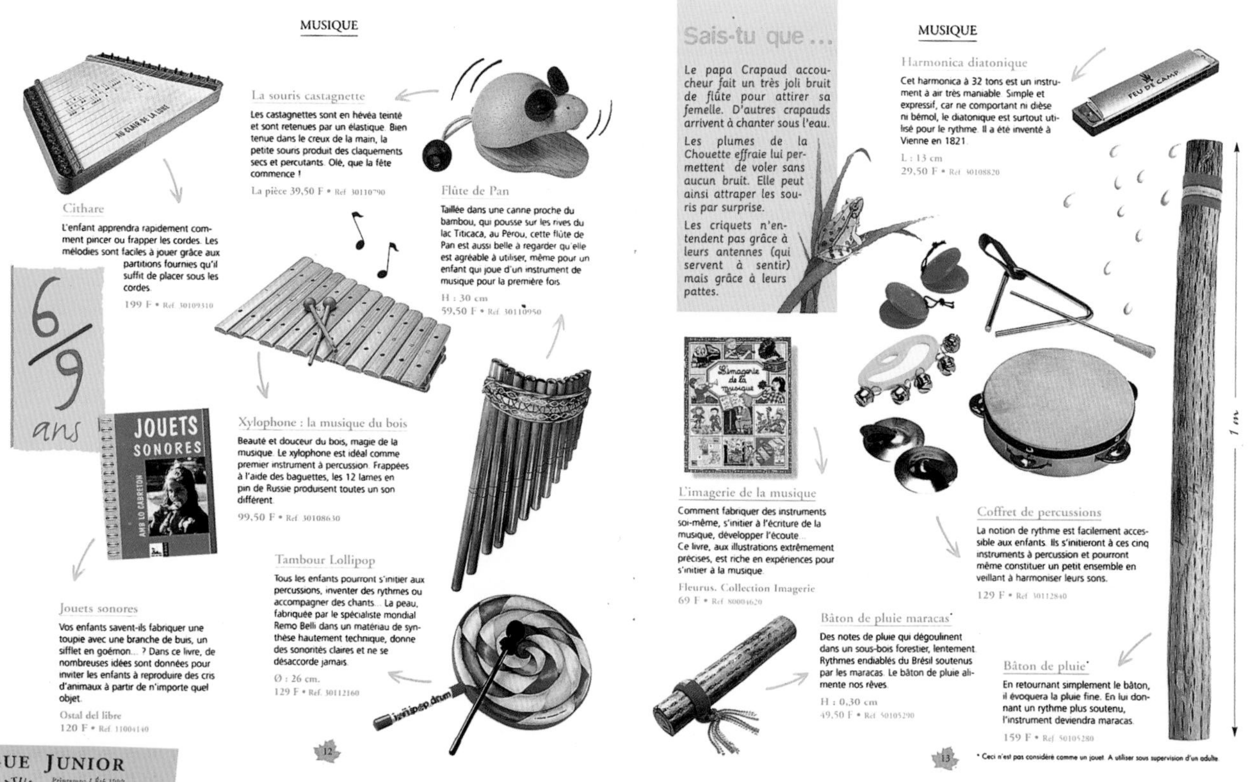

MUSIQUE

Cithare

L'enfant apprendra rapidement comment pincer ou frapper les cordes. Les mélodies sont faciles à jouer grâce aux partitions fournies qu'il suffit de placer sous les cordes.

199 F

La souris castagnette

Les castagnettes sont en hévéa teinté et sont retenues par un élastique. Bien tenue dans le creux de la main, la petite souris produit des claquements secs et percutants. Olé, que la fête commence !

La pièce 39,50 F

Flûte de Pan

Taillée dans une canne proche du bambou, qui pousse sur les rives du lac Titicaca, au Pérou, cette flûte de Pan est aussi belle à regarder qu'elle est agréable à utiliser, même pour un enfant qui joue d'un instrument de musique pour la première fois.

H : 30 cm 59,50 F

Xylophone : la musique du bois

Beauté et douceur du bois, magie de la musique. Le xylophone est idéal comme premier instrument à percussion. Frappées à l'aide des baguettes, les 12 lames en pin de Russie produisent toutes un son différent.

99,50 F

Tambour Lollipop

Tous les enfants pourront s'initier aux percussions, inventer des rythmes ou accompagner des chants... La peau, fabriquée par le spécialiste mondial Remo Belli dans un matériau de synthèse hautement technique, donne des sonorités claires et ne se désaccorde jamais.

Ø : 26 cm. 129 F

Jouets sonores

Vos enfants savent-ils fabriquer une toupie avec une branche de buis, un sifflet en goémon... ? Dans ce livre, de nombreuses idées sont données pour inviter les enfants à reproduire des cris d'animaux à partir de n'importe quel objet.

Ostal del libre 120 F


6/9 ans
JOUETS SONORES


12

Sais-tu que...

Le papa Crapaud accoucheur fait un très joli bruit de flûte pour attirer sa femelle. D'autres crapauds arrivent à chanter sous l'eau.

Les plumes de la Chouette effraie lui permettent de voler sans aucun bruit. Elle peut ainsi attraper les souris par surprise.

Les criquets n'entendent pas grâce à leurs antennes (qui servent à sentir) mais grâce à leurs pattes.

MUSIQUE

Harmonica diatonique

Cet harmonica à 32 tons est un instrument à air très maniable. Simple et expressif, car ne comportant ni dièse ni bémol, le diatonique est surtout utilisé pour le rythme. Il a été inventé à Vienne en 1821.

L : 13 cm 29,50 F

L'imagerie de la musique

Comment fabriquer des instruments soi-même, s'initier à l'écriture de la musique, développer l'écoute... Ce livre, aux illustrations extrêmement précises, est riche en expériences pour s'initier à la musique.

Fleurus. Collection Imagerie 69 F

Coffret de percussions

La notion de rythme est facilement accessible aux enfants. Ils s'initieront à ces cinq instruments à percussion et pourront même constituer un petit ensemble en veillant à harmoniser leurs sons.

129 F

Bâton de pluie maracas*

Des notes de pluie qui dégoulinent dans un sous-bois forestier, lentement. Rythmes endiablés du Brésil soutenus par les maracas. Le bâton de pluie alimente nos rêves.

H : 0,30 cm 49,50 F

Bâton de pluie*

En retournant simplement le bâton, il évoquera la pluie fine. En lui donnant un rythme plus soutenu, l'instrument deviendra maracas.

159 F


1 m


* Ceci n'est pas considéré comme un jouet. A utiliser sous supervision d'un adulte.

13

CATALOGUE JUNIOR

Printemps / Été 1998

Nouvelle édition

Découvrir le Monde et la Nature en s'amusant...

**Nature-Inspired Goods**

NATURE & DÉCOUVERTES CL: Nature & Découvertes CD, AD, D, P, I, DF: The En' Print Team France 1998 *SIZE: 255×210*

Here it is! The 1998 AlphaBet Soup WisH BOOK. The best Of the best: The coolest of cool. These Are the toys on every kid's Wish List. If you dOn't see what you're looking for in here, chances are you'll find it at one of our stores. Just ask! March to a different drummer. Get into the GROOVE. Come on — it's time to play!
Alphabet Soup
— leading the way in great toys!


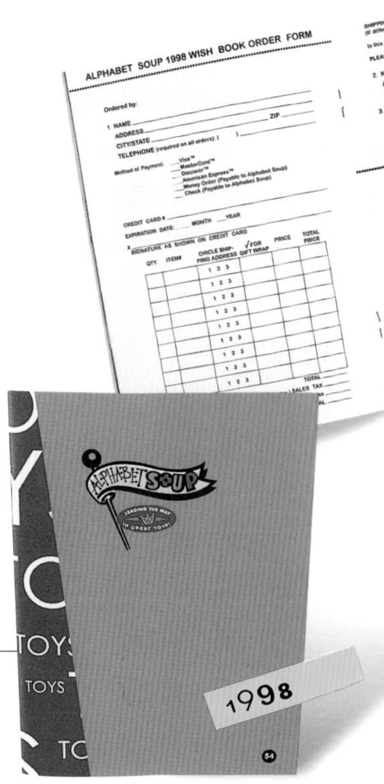

**Toys**

ALPHABET SOUP CL: Alphabet Soup CD, AD, D: John Sayles P: Bill Nellans CW: Mary Langen DF: Sayles Graphic Design USA 1997 *SIZE: 178×127*

## LEGO® legetøj til babyer og børn i førskolealderen

Børn lærer gennem leg, og indenfor de 2 første leveår lærer de mere end i resten af deres liv. Derfor laver vi ikke kun legetøj, som underholder, men også legetøj som udvikler børns basale evner. Du finder LEGO PRIMO og LEGO DUPLO legetøjet på siderne 2 - 17.

## Specielt til piger

Piger fra 5 års alderen elsker at lege rolleleg med far, mor og børn, og de er vilde med alle mulige små, søde dekorationer og tilbehør. De to pigeserier Belville og LEGO SCALA er udviklet med dette in mente, så nu kan I vælge på side 20 - 27.

## Mest for drenge

Pigerne har også lov til at komme ind i de mange andre LEGO universer, men drengene er mere vilde med at bygge disse actionfyldte modeller og lege cowboys og indianere, aliens fra det ydre rum, dykke ned i havets dybder, lege konger og eventyrer samt udfordre deres kunnen med nogle teknisk avancerede konstruktioner. Begynd på side 28 og se de mange, mange modeller, som kan bygges og skilles og bygges om til noget nyt i én uendelighed.

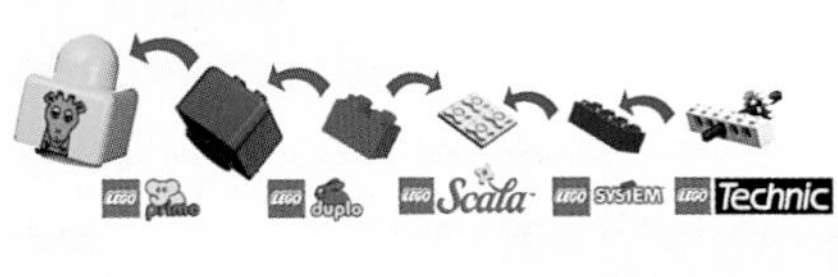

LEGO elementer kan håndvaskes i lunkent vand. Max 40°C. Undtaget er elektriske dele, og de følgende LEGO PRIMO elementer: dromedar, palme og tog.

http://www.LEGO.com

2

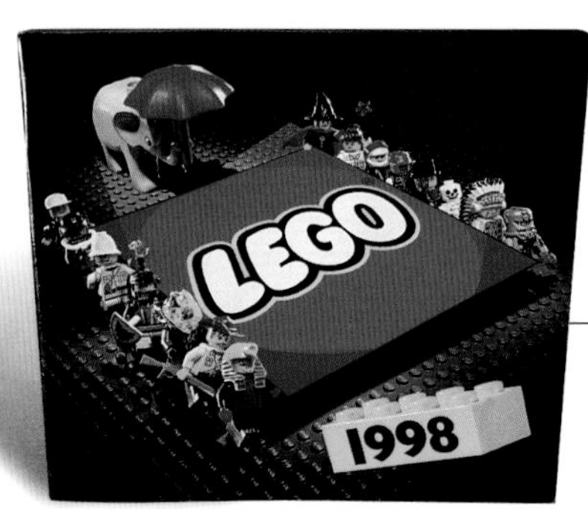


**Toys**

LEGO CL: Lego Japan Japan 1998 *SIZE: 195×210*

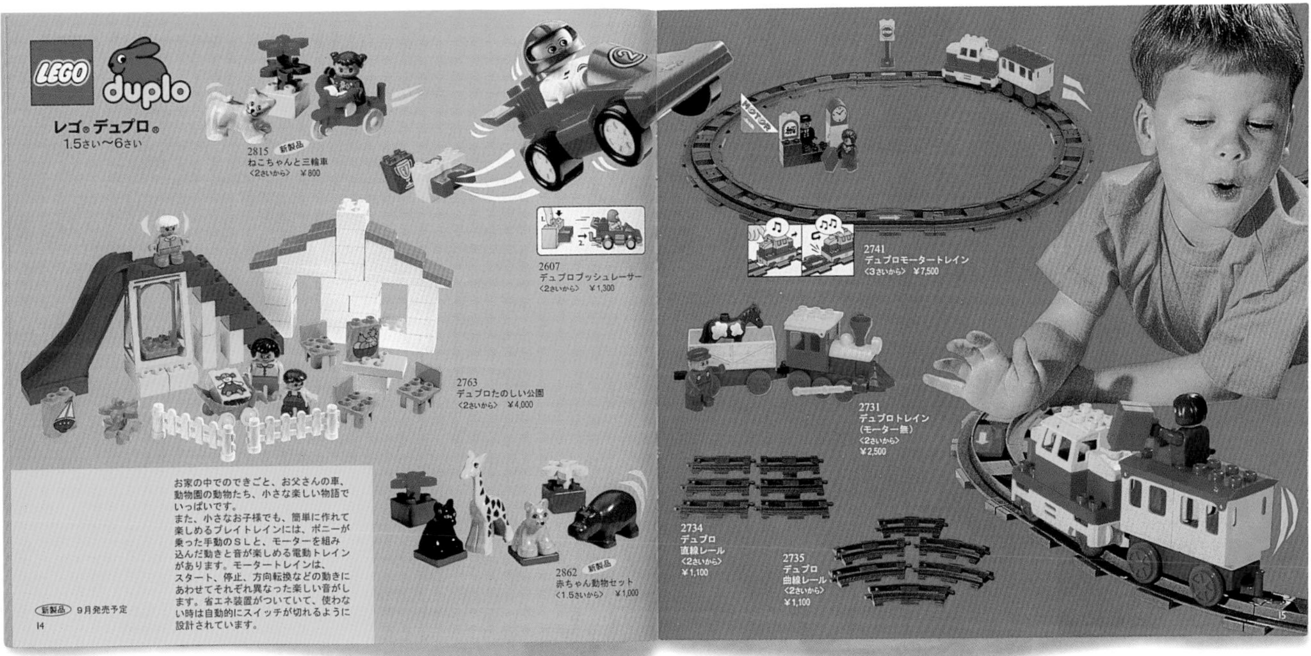


**Toys**

LEGO CL: Lego Japan Japan 1998 *SIZE: 195×210*

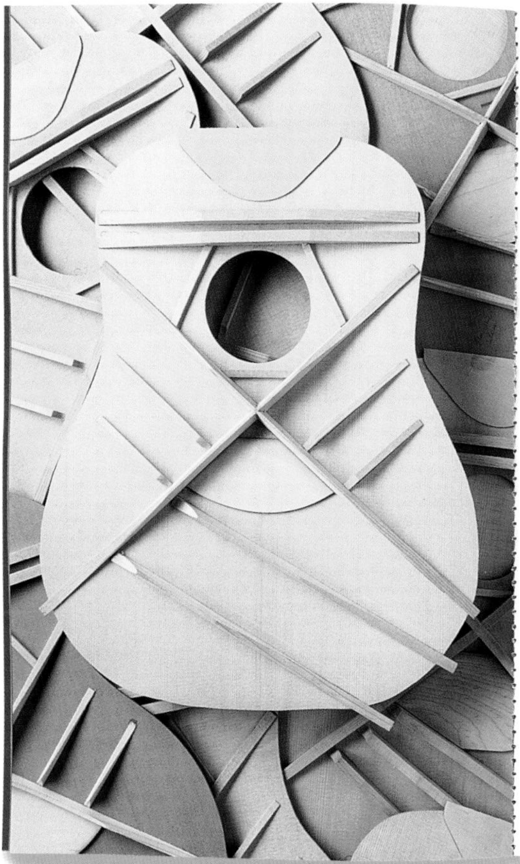

SIX HUNDRED SERIES
600 SERIES
TOP | SITKA SPRUCE
BACK SIDES | BIG LEAF MAPLE
BINDING | WHITE PLASTIC
INLAY | PEARL 'LEAF PATTERN'
MODEL 655ce
JUMBO
600 series Curly maple is perhaps the most visually exciting wood found on guitars. We use stains and a gloss finish to accentuate its dramatic figure, and we complement the wood with deluxe binding and inlay. Maple Taylors are favorites with guitarists who amplify their acoustic sound. Controlled overtones and even response from the lowest to the highest notes provide an ideal signal source for the Fishman dual-source pickup system. It's the perfect recipe for a contemporary stage guitar. The 600 Series now comes in a natural finish, or in stunning transparent colors—amber, red, black, blue, or green.
PAGE TWENTY-THREE

SIX HUNDRED SERIES
MODEL 610ce
MODEL 615ce
JUMBO
MODEL 614ce
GRAND AUDITORIUM
MODEL 612ce
GRAND CONCERT

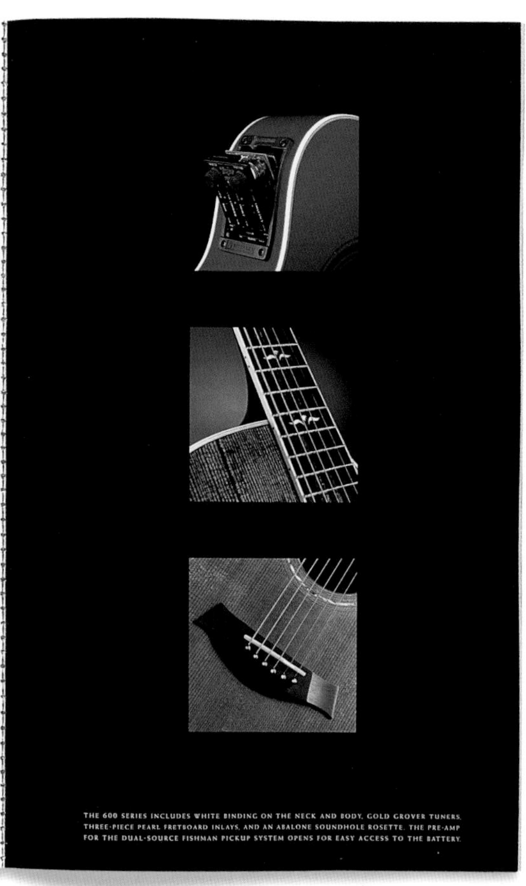
THE 600 SERIES INCLUDES WHITE BINDING ON THE NECK AND BODY, GOLD GROVER TUNERS, THREE-PIECE PEARL FRETBOARD INLAYS, AND AN ABALONE SOUNDHOLE ROSETTE. THE PRE-AMP FOR THE DUAL-SOURCE FISHMAN PICKUP SYSTEM OPENS FOR EASY ACCESS TO THE BATTERY.

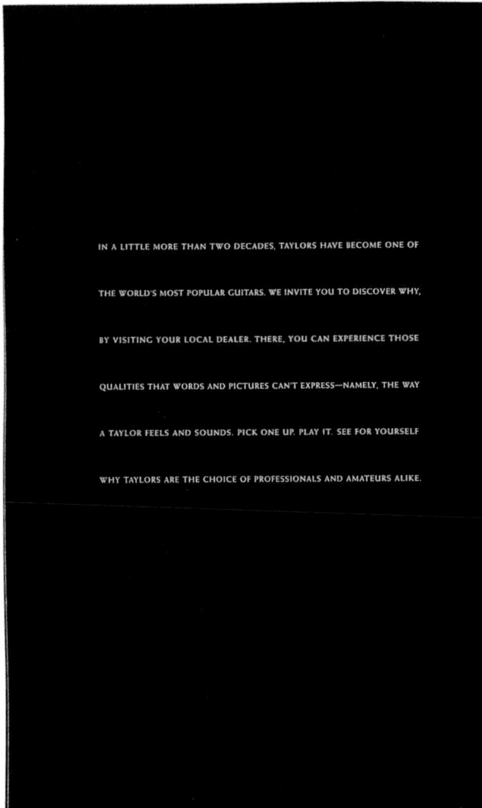


SPECIFICATIONS

SERIES 300

| | |
|---|---|
| BACK/SIDES | Sapele Mahogany |
| TOP | Sitka Spruce |
| SOUNDHOLE ROSETTE | Plastic |
| NECK | Mahogany |
| FRETBOARD | Ebony |
| FRETBOARD INLAY | Pearl Dots |
| HEADSTOCK OVERLAY | Indian Rosewood |
| BINDING | Black Plastic |
| BRIDGE | Ebony |
| NUT & SADDLE | Tusq |
| TUNING MACHINES | Chrome-Plated Grovers |
| SCALE LENGTH | 25 1/2 inches |
| TRUSS ROD | Adjustable |
| NUMBER OF FRETS | 20 |
| FINISH | Satin with Gloss Top |
| CASE | SKB Molded Hardshell |

| | | 310 | 310-CE | 312-CE | 314 | 314-CE | 355 |
|---|---|---|---|---|---|---|---|
| TYPE/SIZE OF GUITAR | 6-String Dreadnought | • | • | | | | |
| | 6-String Grand Concert | | | • | | | |
| | 6-String Grand Auditorium | | | | • | • | |
| | 12-String Jumbo | | | | | | • |
| STRINGS* | Med. Gauge/Phosphor Bronze | • | • | | | | |
| | Light Gauge/Phosphor Bronze | | | • | • | • | • |
| NECK WIDTH AT NUT | 1 11/16 inches | • | • | | | | |
| | 1 3/4 inches | | | • | • | • | |
| | 1 7/8 inches | | | | | | • |
| BRACING | Scalloped, X-Brace | • | • | • | • | • | |
| | Tapered, X-Brace | | | | | | • |
| CUTAWAY | None | • | | | • | | • |
| | Venetian | | • | • | | • | |
| ELECTRONICS | None | • | | | • | | • |
| | Fishman® Prefix™ | | • | • | | • | |
| BODY WIDTH | 15 inches | | | • | | | |
| | 16 inches | • | • | | • | • | |
| | 17 inches | | | | | | • |
| BODY LENGTH | 19 1/2 inches | | | • | | | |
| | 20 inches | • | • | | • | • | |
| | 21 inches | | | | | | • |
| BODY DEPTH | 4 1/8 inches | | | • | | | |
| | 4 5/8 inches | • | • | | • | • | • |
| OVERALL LENGTH | 40 1/2 inches | | | • | | | |
| | 41 inches | • | • | | • | • | |
| | 43 inches | | | | | | • |

SERIES 400

| | |
|---|---|
| BACK/SIDES | Ovangkol |
| TOP | Sitka Spruce |
| SOUNDHOLE ROSETTE | Plastic |
| NECK | Mahogany |
| FRETBOARD | Ebony |
| FRETBOARD INLAY | Pearl Dots |
| HEADSTOCK OVERLAY | Indian Rosewood |
| BINDING | White Plastic |
| BRIDGE | Ebony |
| NUT & SADDLE | Tusq |
| TUNING MACHINES | Chrome-Plated Grovers |
| SCALE LENGTH | 25 1/2 inches |
| TRUSS ROD | Adjustable |
| NUMBER OF FRETS | 20 |
| BRACING | Scalloped, X-brace |
| FINISH | Satin with Gloss Top |
| CASE | SKB Molded Hardshell |

| | | 410 | 410-CE | 412-CE | 414 | 414-CE | 415 |
|---|---|---|---|---|---|---|---|
| TYPE/SIZE OF GUITAR | 6-String Dreadnought | • | • | | | | |
| | 6-String Grand Concert | | | • | | | |
| | 6-String Grand Auditorium | | | | • | • | |
| | 6-String Jumbo | | | | | | • |
| STRINGS* | Med. Gauge/Phosphor Bronze | • | • | | | | • |
| | Light Gauge/Phosphor Bronze | | | • | • | • | |
| NECK WIDTH AT NUT | 1 11/16 inches | • | • | | | | • |
| | 1 3/4 inches | | | • | • | • | |
| CUTAWAY | None | • | | | • | | • |
| | Venetian | | • | • | | • | |
| ELECTRONICS | None | • | | | • | | • |
| | Fishman® Prefix™ | | • | • | | • | |
| BODY WIDTH | 15 inches | | | • | | | |
| | 16 inches | • | • | | • | • | |
| | 17 inches | | | | | | • |
| BODY LENGTH | 19 1/2 inches | | | • | | | |
| | 20 inches | • | • | | • | • | |
| | 21 inches | | | | | | • |
| BODY DEPTH | 4 1/8 inches | | | • | | | |
| | 4 5/8 inches | • | • | | • | • | • |
| OVERALL LENGTH | 40 1/2 inches | | | • | | | |
| | 41 inches | • | • | | • | • | |
| | 42 inches | | | | | | • |

## Acoustic Guitars

TAYLOR GUITARS CL: Taylor Guitars CD, AD, D: Scott Mires D: Gale Spitzley P: Chris Wimpey I: Tracy Sabin CW: Richard Johnston / Andrea May / Kurt Listug / John D'Agostino DF: Mires Design, Inc. USA 1998 *SIZE: 321×203*

## We started making

We started making guitars without a preconceived notion that they should look like some other brand, or that they should follow turn of the century ideas. Bob brought a fresh, common sense approach to an old world craft and, in the process, started trends that changed the way American guitars are built → Bob has been a real pioneer in the application of CAD/CAM technology to guitar making. But once the computer controlled machines are finished turning out incredibly accurate wooden parts, small teams of guitarmakers take over. There are no assembly lines at Taylor. Instead, each member of every team performs many different tasks in building one of our guitars. They're proud of what they build, and it shows → Even the business side of Taylor Guitars is not just business as usual. Though his work is not visible to the guitar player, Kurt is also an innovator. He has organized Taylor's growth so our company runs efficiently without needing lots of people who do not actively build guitars. When you buy a Taylor, you're paying for fine woods and skilled guitar builders, not middle management → But our most important innovations apply to Taylor instruments themselves. Most companies reserve features like scalloped top bracing and ebony fretboards and bridges for their deluxe models. We put this kind of quality into every Taylor, and we're the only guitarmakers to build our own cases, but that's another story in itself → Considering the success Taylor Guitars has enjoyed, you would think the desire to innovate and improve would have slowed. But at Taylor, there are constant improvements in the details: closer tolerances, a smoother finish that's environmentally safe, and less waste of natural resources. Through careful design, such changes have actually improved all our instruments. Our biggest challenge in the past year, along with the introduction of several new models, has been to design two completely new types of instruments. One is a small and inexpensive Taylor for children, or for travel. The other is a radical new Acoustic Bass, the largest instrument we've ever built → We invite you to look at our new Taylor guitars. Look carefully, up close. More importantly, we'd like you to take the time to play several different new Taylors. We've put a lot of ourselves into them, but guitars just seem like objects until they're used to play music. That's where you come in. In your own way, you're the one who completes the final step in turning what we build into a guitar.

*It begins with a careful design and accurately machined parts. But only people with experience and dedication to the craft can complete the building of a Taylor guitar.*

OFFICIAL
STRING UP
GUITAR TEST
STOOL

Four Hundred Series Here are some excellent choices for your first real acoustic guitar–all solid woods and 100% American-made. Though most popular with serious beginners and intermediate players, even more advanced guitarists on a budget often choose a 400 Series Taylor as a second guitar for alternate tunings or duets with friends. This year we've added the mahogany Dreadnought 450, putting our 12-string experience and reputation into the most affordable Taylor 12-string ever offered. → We designed the 400 Series to cut costs without cutting tone, volume, or playability. Many people are drawn to the satin finish and no frills appearance, however, and the most frequent response is "I love the look!" Of course, everyone loves the way these Taylors play and sound, thanks to scalloped top bracing and ebony fretboard and bridge. Perhaps the hardest part is choosing between the mahogany and maple versions.
Pictured from left to right: models 410, 412, 450, 422, and 420.

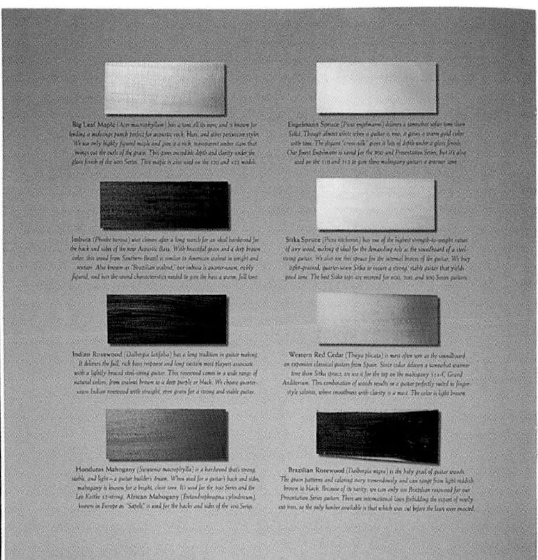
Big Leaf Maple
Engelmann Spruce
Imbuia
Sitka Spruce
Indian Rosewood
Western Red Cedar
Honduran Mahogany
Brazilian Rosewood

## Which one?

Which one? For 1997 we're offering more models than ever before, but how do you decide which Taylor is right for you? Here are some general rules about tone in relation to different guitar bodies and wood selections. Remember that such comparisons are relative, and only you can decide which of our guitars best suits your needs. **Dreadnoughts** Since Dreadnoughts are the best known steel string guitars, we'll use these models for comparison. With its wide waist and deep sides, the Dreadnought offers a large soundboard and body cavity in a compact, efficient shape. This design emphasizes bass response and offers incredible volume. Rosewood Taylor Dreadnoughts like the 810 are known for a warm tone with deep bass and lots of sustain, while mahogany and maple versions (510 & 610) have a brighter sound. **Grand Concerts** Dreadnoughts aren't for everyone, and Taylor was one of the first to offer a full range of medium sized guitars. Grand Concerts have a more intimate and balanced response that is treasured by fingerstyle players. The cutaway versions (612-C, 812-C & 912-C) are popular with acoustic-electric players as they fit close to the body and allow maximum mobility on stage. The cutaway gives access to the entire fretboard, allowing full use of Taylor's legendary low action and accurate intonation even in the highest positions. The mahogany 512 and rosewood 712 are more traditional non-cutaway shapes. **Grand Auditorium** The Grand Auditorium, Bob's newest design, offers the best of both the Dreadnought's power and the Grand Concert's balanced tone. Though as wide and deep as a Dreadnought, their narrow waist allow these models to sit lower in your lap. The sharper curve at the waist tightens the soundboard in front of the bridge, giving more treble response to balance the powerful bass. This is the first year we've offered cutaway versions of the Grand Auditorium, making the 514-C, 614-C, 814-C and 914-C the newest Taylors. See if you don't agree that this beautiful shape captures the best of our other three body sizes in one exceptional, all around guitar. **Jumbos** For players who prefer the extra deep resonance of an oversized guitar, we offer Jumbo six-string models in both maple and rosewood (the 615 and 815-C). Their power is felt almost as much as heard, and these Taylors can fill a room with sound. They're especially effective in the hands of strong players with a hard, percussive style. We've always used Jumbos for most twelve-string models, as the full bass response from the deep body balances the additional treble strings.

Dreadnought

Grand Concert

Grand Auditorium

Jumbo

Taylor Guitars
1997 Catalog

## Guitars

TAYLOR GUITARS CL: Taylor Guitars CD, AD, D: Scott Mires P: Chris Wimpey DF: Mires Design Inc. USA 1997 *SIZE: 279×279*

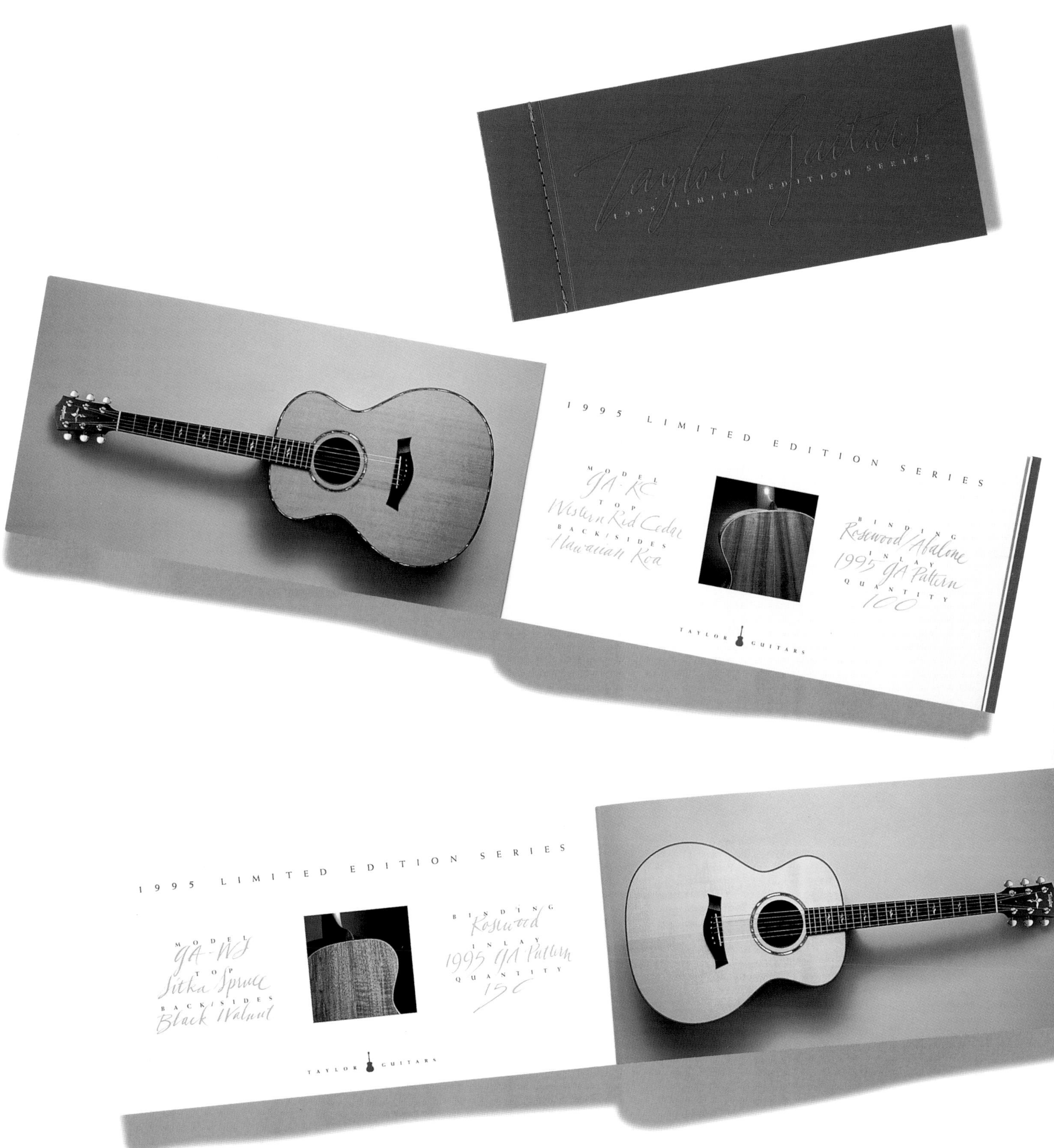


## Guitars

TAYLOR GUITARS CL: Taylor Guitars CD, AD, D: Scott Mires D: Miguel Perez P: Chris Wimpey Calligraphy: Judythe Sieck CW: John Robertson / Bob Taylor DF: Mires Design Inc. USA 1996 *SIZE: 102×237*

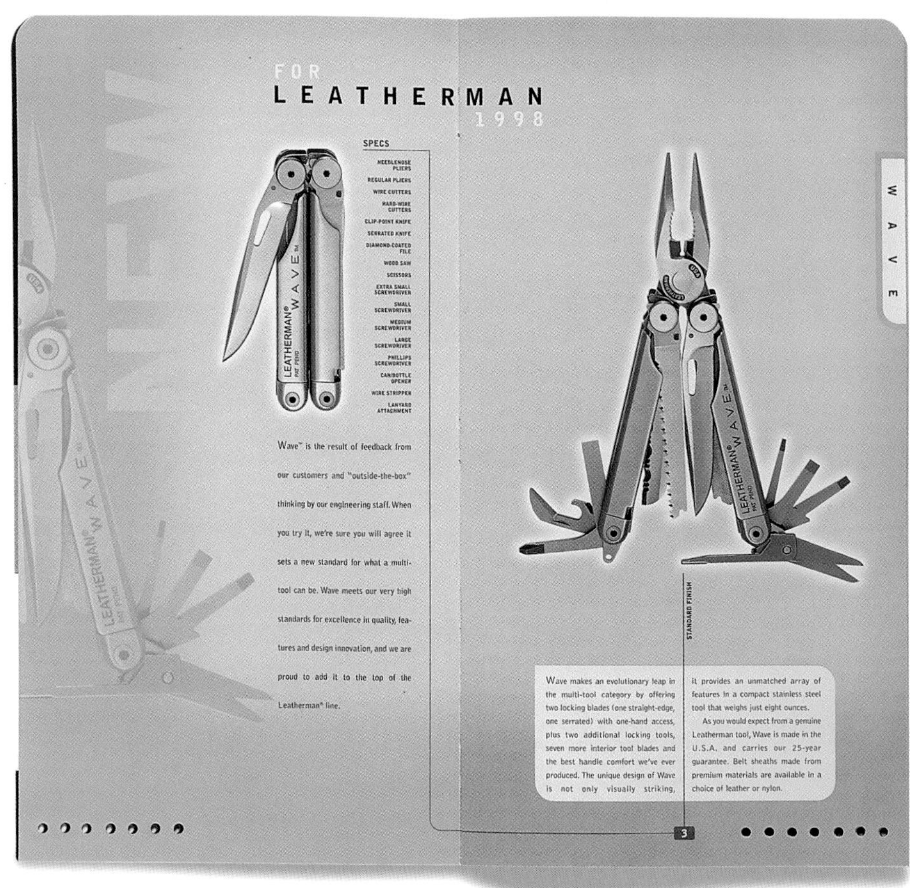
FOR
LEATHERMAN
1998
NEW
SPECS
NEEDLENOSE PLIERS
REGULAR PLIERS
WIRE CUTTERS
HARD-WIRE CUTTERS
CLIP-POINT KNIFE
SERRATED KNIFE
DIAMOND-COATED FILE
WOOD SAW
SCISSORS
EXTRA SMALL SCREWDRIVER
SMALL SCREWDRIVER
MEDIUM SCREWDRIVER
LARGE SCREWDRIVER
PHILLIPS SCREWDRIVER
CAN/BOTTLE OPENER
WIRE STRIPPER
LANYARD ATTACHMENT
Wave™ is the result of feedback from our customers and "outside-the-box" thinking by our engineering staff. When you try it, we're sure you will agree it sets a new standard for what a multi-tool can be. Wave meets our very high standards for excellence in quality, features and design innovation, and we are proud to add it to the top of the Leatherman® line.
WAVE
STANDARD FINISH
Wave makes an evolutionary leap in the multi-tool category by offering two locking blades (one straight-edge, one serrated) with one-hand access, plus two additional locking tools, seven more interior tool blades and the best handle comfort we've ever produced. The unique design of Wave is not only visually striking, it provides an unmatched array of features in a compact stainless steel tool that weighs just eight ounces.
As you would expect from a genuine Leatherman tool, Wave is made in the U.S.A. and carries our 25-year guarantee. Belt sheaths made from premium materials are available in a choice of leather or nylon.
3

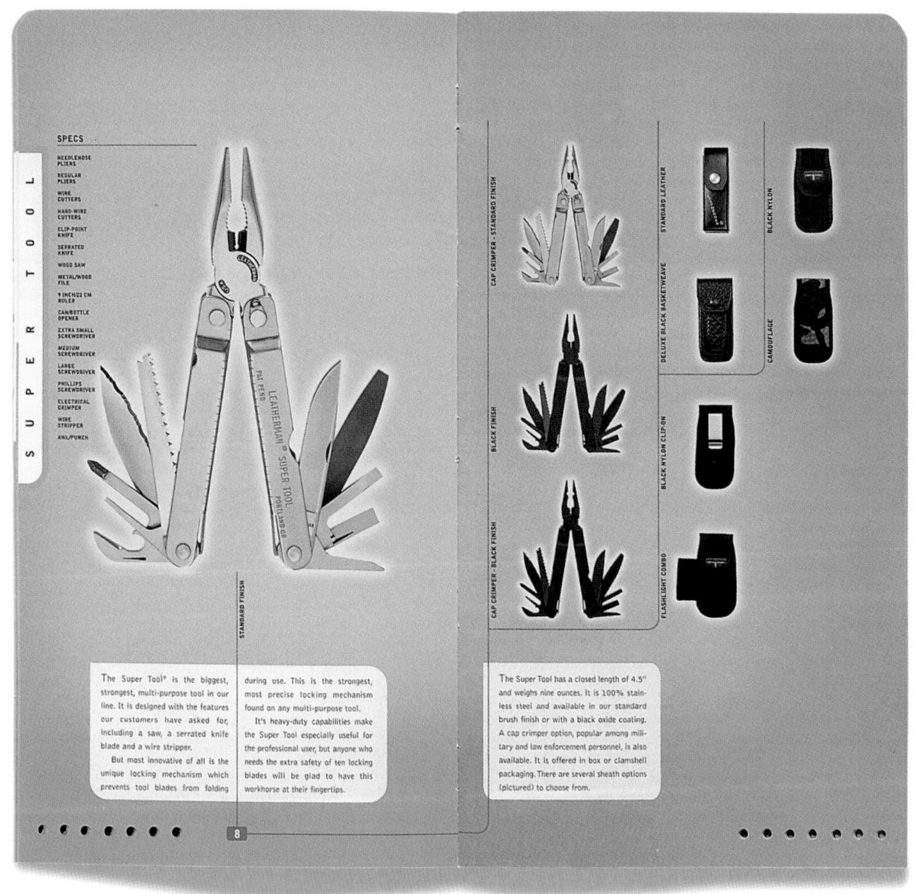
SPECS
NEEDLENOSE PLIERS
REGULAR PLIERS
WIRE CUTTERS
HARD-WIRE CUTTERS
CLIP-POINT KNIFE
SERRATED KNIFE
WOOD SAW
METAL/WOOD FILE
9 INCH/22 CM RULER
CAN/BOTTLE OPENER
EXTRA SMALL SCREWDRIVER
MEDIUM SCREWDRIVER
LARGE SCREWDRIVER
PHILLIPS SCREWDRIVER
ELECTRICAL CRIMPER
WIRE STRIPPER
AWL/PUNCH
SUPER TOOL
STANDARD FINISH
The Super Tool® is the biggest, strongest, multi-purpose tool in our line. It is designed with the features our customers have asked for, including a saw, a serrated knife blade and a wire stripper.
But most innovative of all is the unique locking mechanism which prevents tool blades from folding during use. This is the strongest, most precise locking mechanism found on any multi-purpose tool.
It's heavy-duty capabilities make the Super Tool especially useful for the professional user, but anyone who needs the extra safety of ten locking blades will be glad to have this workhorse at their fingertips.
8
CAP CRIMPER - STANDARD FINISH
BLACK FINISH
CAP CRIMPER - BLACK FINISH
STANDARD LEATHER
DELUXE BLACK BASKETWEAVE
BLACK NYLON CLIP-ON
FLASHLIGHT COMBO
BLACK NYLON
CAMOUFLAGE
The Super Tool has a closed length of 4.5" and weighs nine ounces. It is 100% stainless steel and available in our standard brush finish or with a black oxide coating. A cap crimper option, popular among military and law enforcement personnel, is also available. It is offered in box or clamshell packaging. There are several sheath options (pictured) to choose from.

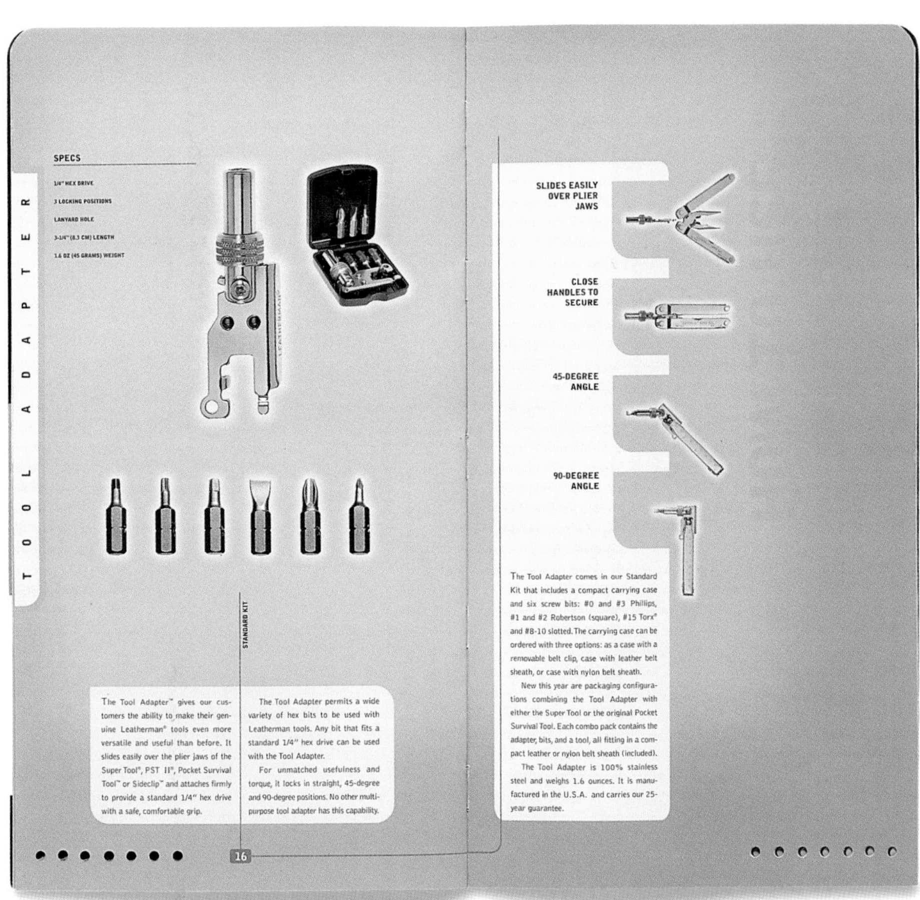

TOOL ADAPTER
SPECS
1/4" HEX DRIVE
3 LOCKING POSITIONS
LANYARD HOLE
3-1/4" (8.3 CM) LENGTH
1.6 OZ (45 GRAMS) WEIGHT
STANDARD KIT
The Tool Adapter™ gives our customers the ability to make their genuine Leatherman® tools even more versatile and useful than before. It slides easily over the plier jaws of the Super Tool®, PST II®, Pocket Survival Tool™ or Sideclip™ and attaches firmly to provide a standard 1/4" hex drive with a safe, comfortable grip.
The Tool Adapter permits a wide variety of hex bits to be used with Leatherman tools. Any bit that fits a standard 1/4" hex drive can be used with the Tool Adapter.
For unmatched usefulness and torque, it locks in straight, 45-degree and 90-degree positions. No other multi-purpose tool adapter has this capability.
16
SLIDES EASILY OVER PLIER JAWS
CLOSE HANDLES TO SECURE
45-DEGREE ANGLE
90-DEGREE ANGLE
The Tool Adapter comes in our Standard Kit that includes a compact carrying case and six screw bits: #0 and #3 Phillips, #1 and #2 Robertson (square), #15 Torx® and #8-10 slotted. The carrying case can be ordered with three options: as a case with a removable belt clip, case with leather belt sheath, or case with nylon belt sheath.
New this year are packaging configurations combining the Tool Adapter with either the Super Tool or the original Pocket Survival Tool. Each combo pack contains the adapter, bits, and a tool, all fitting in a compact leather or nylon belt sheath (included).
The Tool Adapter is 100% stainless steel and weighs 1.6 ounces. It is manufactured in the U.S.A. and carries our 25-year guarantee.

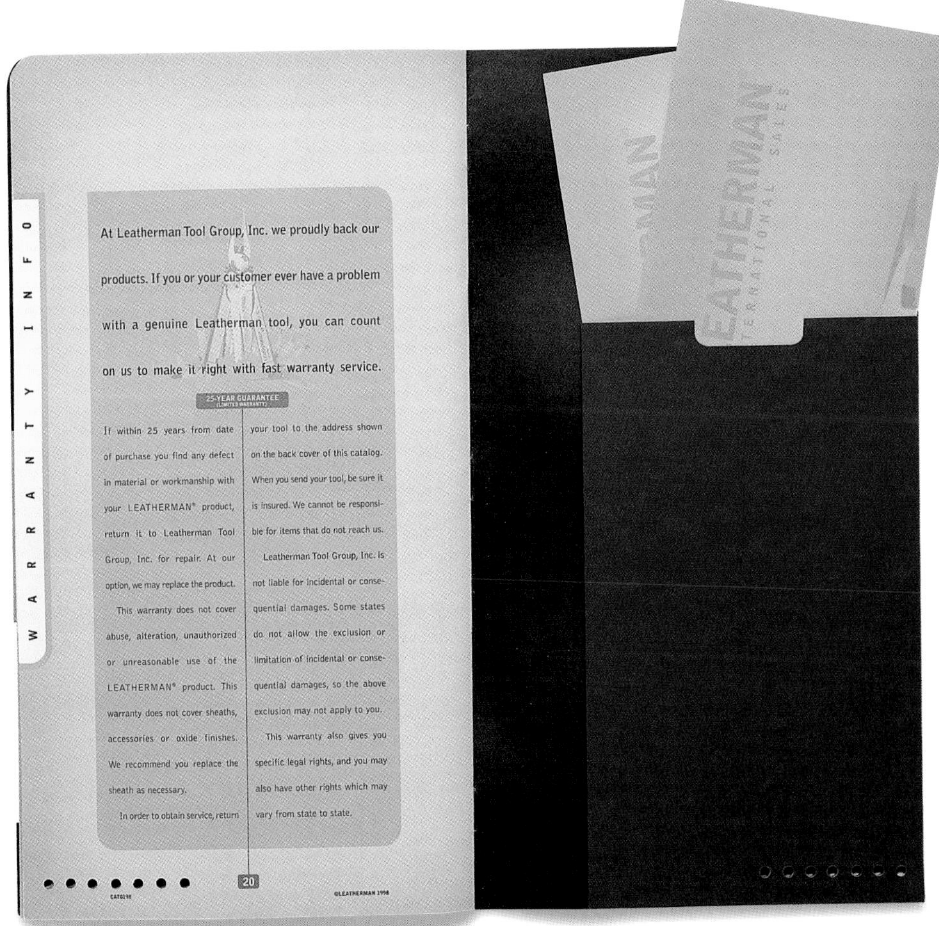

WARRANTY INFO
At Leatherman Tool Group, Inc. we proudly back our products. If you or your customer ever have a problem with a genuine Leatherman tool, you can count on us to make it right with fast warranty service.
25-YEAR GUARANTEE (LIMITED WARRANTY)
If within 25 years from date of purchase you find any defect in material or workmanship with your LEATHERMAN® product, return it to Leatherman Tool Group, Inc. for repair. At our option, we may replace the product.
This warranty does not cover abuse, alteration, unauthorized or unreasonable use of the LEATHERMAN® product. This warranty does not cover sheaths, accessories or oxide finishes. We recommend you replace the sheath as necessary.
In order to obtain service, return your tool to the address shown on the back cover of this catalog. When you send your tool, be sure it is insured. We cannot be responsible for items that do not reach us.
Leatherman Tool Group, Inc. is not liable for incidental or consequential damages. Some states do not allow the exclusion or limitation of incidental or consequential damages, so the above exclusion may not apply to you.
This warranty also gives you specific legal rights, and you may also have other rights which may vary from state to state.
20
LEATHERMAN INTERNATIONAL SALES

LEATHERMAN® 1998

## Multi-Purpose Compact Tools

LEATHERMAN CL, CW: Leatherman Tools AD: Jack Anderson AD, D: David Bates D: Lisa Cerveny P: Condit Studio I: Jack Unruh DF: Hornall Anderson Design Works, Inc. USA 1997 *SIZE: 280×152*

## Connecting System

CONNECTORS - FOR - CL: For. S.P.A. CD, AD, D, DF: Kuni-Graphic Design Company Italy 1997 *SIZE: 297×210*

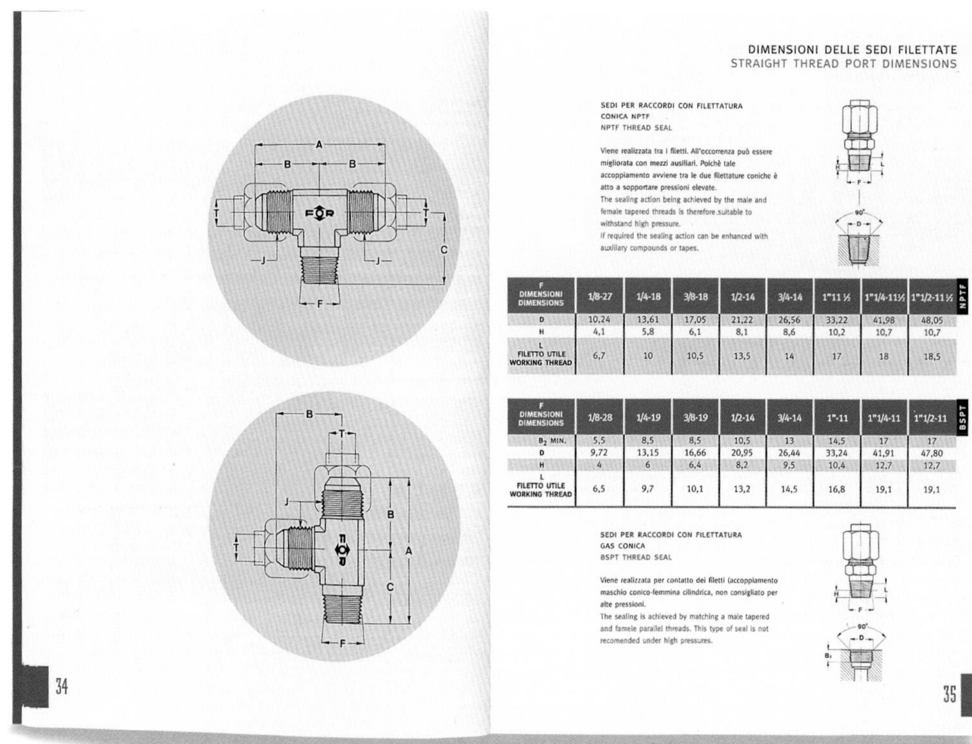

DIMENSIONI DELLE SEDI FILETTATE
STRAIGHT THREAD PORT DIMENSIONS

SEDI PER RACCORDI CON FILETTATURA
CONICA NPTF
NPTF THREAD SEAL

Viene realizzata tra i filetti. All'occorrenza può essere migliorata con mezzi ausiliari. Poichè tale accoppiamento avviene tra le due filettature coniche è atto a sopportare pressioni elevate.
The sealing action being achieved by the male and female tapered threads is therefore suitable to withstand high pressure.
If required the sealing action can be enhanced with auxiliary compounds or tapes.

| F DIMENSIONI DIMENSIONS | 1/8-27 | 1/4-18 | 3/8-18 | 1/2-14 | 3/4-14 | 1"11 ½ | 1"1/4-11½ | 1"1/2-11½ |
|---|---|---|---|---|---|---|---|---|
| D | 10,24 | 13,61 | 17,05 | 21,22 | 26,56 | 33,22 | 41,98 | 48,05 |
| H | 4,1 | 5,8 | 6,1 | 8,1 | 8,6 | 10,2 | 10,7 | 10,7 |
| L FILETTO UTILE WORKING THREAD | 6,7 | 10 | 10,5 | 13,5 | 14 | 17 | 18 | 18,5 |

NPTF

| F DIMENSIONI DIMENSIONS | 1/8-28 | 1/4-19 | 3/8-19 | 1/2-14 | 3/4-14 | 1"-11 | 1"1/4-11 | 1"1/2-11 |
|---|---|---|---|---|---|---|---|---|
| $B_2$ MIN. | 5,5 | 8,5 | 8,5 | 10,5 | 13 | 14,5 | 17 | 17 |
| D | 9,72 | 13,15 | 16,66 | 20,95 | 26,44 | 33,24 | 41,91 | 47,80 |
| H | 4 | 6 | 6,4 | 8,2 | 9,5 | 10,4 | 12,7 | 12,7 |
| L FILETTO UTILE WORKING THREAD | 6,5 | 9,7 | 10,1 | 13,2 | 14,5 | 16,8 | 19,1 | 19,1 |

BSPT

SEDI PER RACCORDI CON FILETTATURA
GAS CONICA
BSPT THREAD SEAL

Viene realizzata per contatto dei filetti (accoppiamento maschio conico-femmina cilindrica, non consigliato per alte pressioni.
The sealing is achieved by matching a male tapered and famele parallel threads. This type of seal is not recomended under high pressures.

34

35

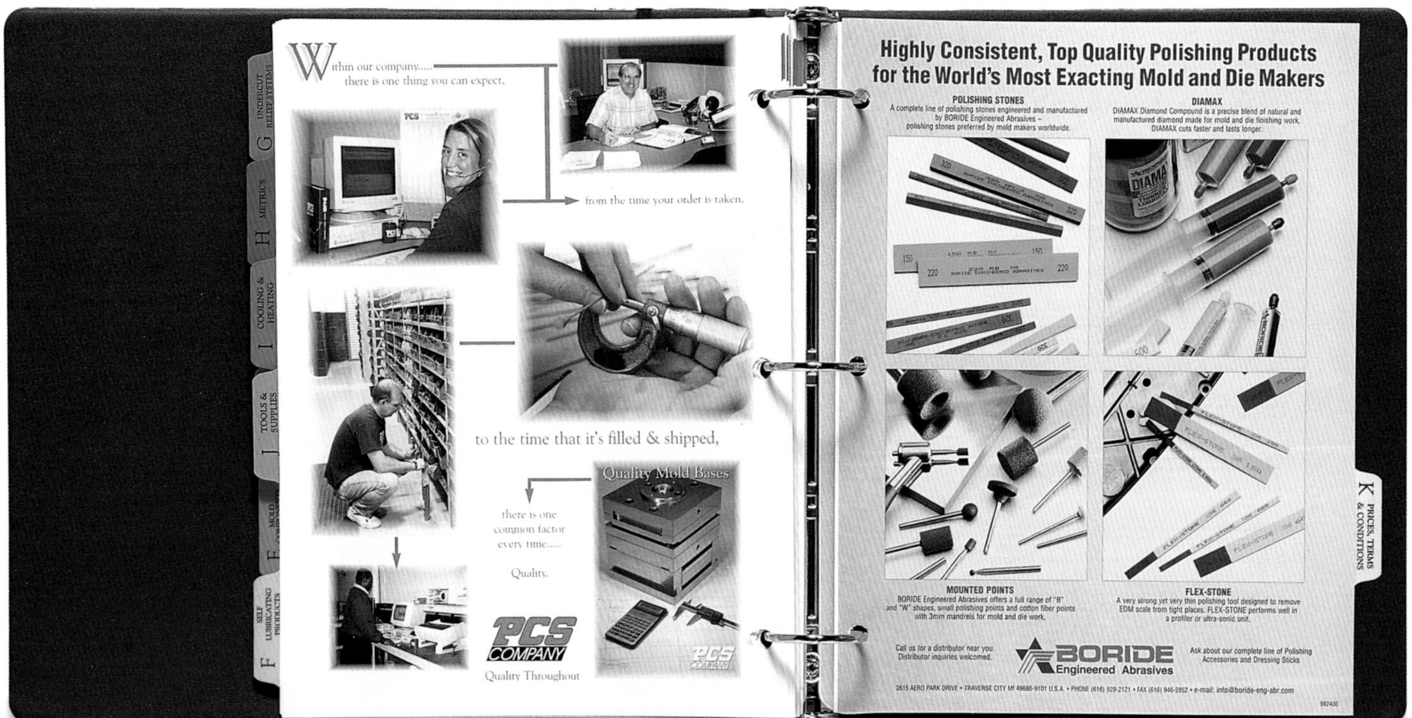

Within our company..... there is one thing you can expect,

from the time your order is taken,

to the time that it's filled & shipped,

there is one common factor every time.....

Quality.

Quality Mold Bases

PCS COMPANY
Quality Throughout

Highly Consistent, Top Quality Polishing Products for the World's Most Exacting Mold and Die Makers

POLISHING STONES
A complete line of polishing stones engineered and manufactured by BORIDE Engineered Abrasives – polishing stones preferred by mold makers worldwide.

DIAMAX
DIAMAX Diamond Compound is a precise blend of natural and manufactured diamond made for mold and die finishing work. DIAMAX cuts faster and lasts longer.

MOUNTED POINTS
BORIDE Engineered Abrasives offers a full range of "B" and "W" shapes, small polishing points and cotton fiber points with 3mm mandrels for mold and die work.

FLEX-STONE
A very strong yet very thin polishing tool designed to remove EDM scale from tight places. FLEX-STONE performs well in a profiler or ultra-sonic unit.

Call us for a distributor near you. Distributor inquiries welcomed.

BORIDE Engineered Abrasives

Ask about our complete line of Polishing Accessories and Dressing Sticks

2615 AERO PARK DRIVE • TRAVERSE CITY MI 49686-9101 U.S.A. • PHONE (616) 929-2121 • FAX (616) 946-2852 • e-mail: info@boride-eng-abr.com

982400



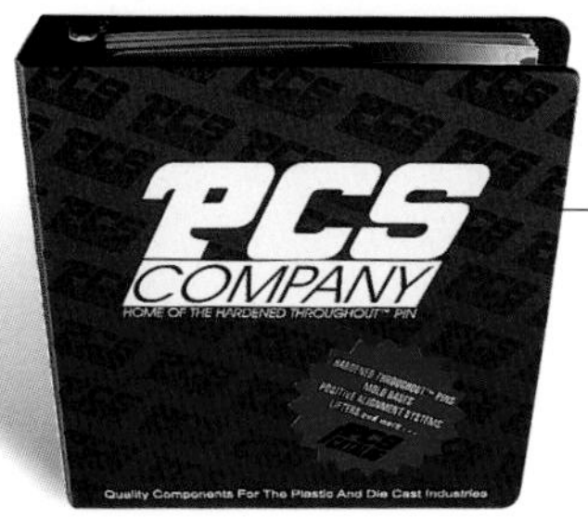



## Plastic Mold Components

PCS CL: PCS Company CD: Dwight A. Zahringer AD: Julia Dyer D: Edwardo Bonaducci P: Cazzo Slinger CW: Jim Stuart / Debra Downs DF: PCS Design Labitory Inc. USA 1997 *SIZE: 292×270*

# Tools

PROJAHN GOLD CL: Projahn Praezisionswerkzeuge GmbH AD, D: Bert Projahn P: Cornelia Koch
DF: Bert Projahn Typografie Germany 1997 *SIZE: 297×210*

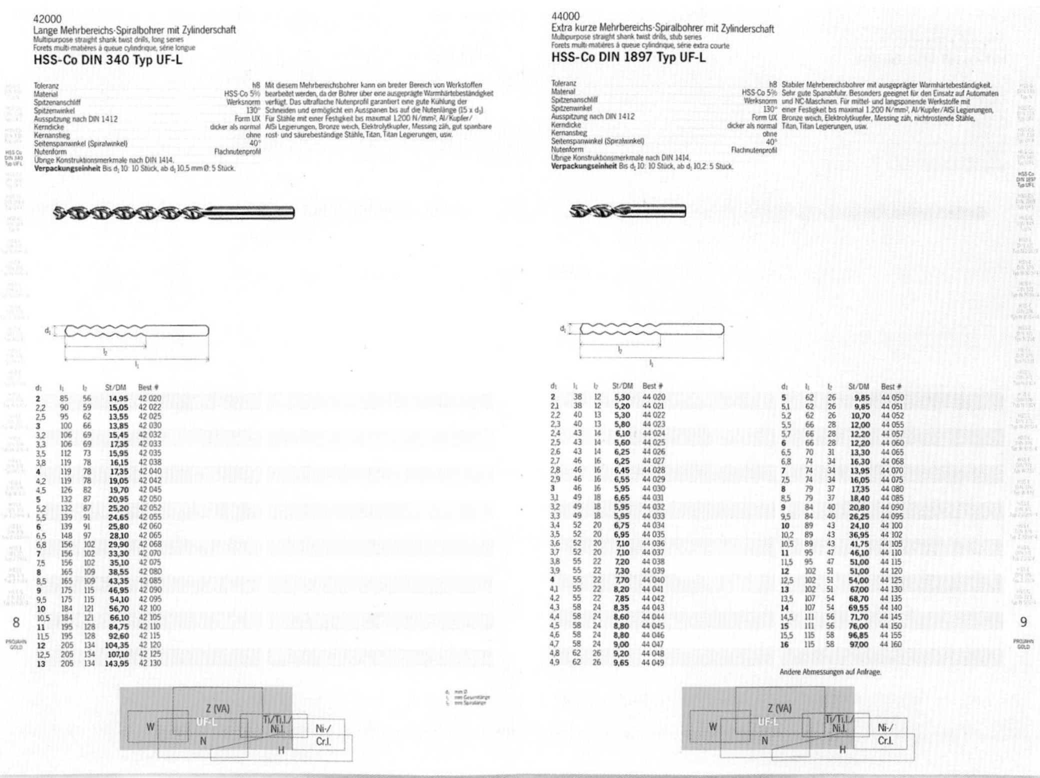

42000
Lange Mehrbereichs-Spiralbohrer mit Zylinderschaft
Multipurpose straight shank twist drills, long series
Forets multi-matières à queue cylindrique, série longue
**HSS-Co DIN 340 Typ UF-L**

| | |
|---|---|
| Toleranz | h8 |
| Material | HSS-Co 5% |
| Spitzenanschliff | Werksnorm |
| Spitzenwinkel | 130° |
| Ausspitzung nach DIN 1412 | Form UX |
| Kerndicke | dicker als normal |
| Kernanstieg | ohne |
| Seitenspanwinkel (Spiralwinkel) | 40° |
| Nutenform | Flachnutenprofil |

Mit diesem Mehrbereichsbohrer kann ein breiter Bereich von Werkstoffen bearbeitet werden, da der Bohrer über eine ausgeprägte Warmhärtebeständigkeit verfügt. Das ultraflache Nutenprofil garantiert eine gute Kühlung der Schneiden und ermöglicht ein Ausspanen bis auf die Nutenlänge (15 x $d_1$). Für Stähle mit einer Festigkeit bis maximal 1.200 N/mm², Al/Kupfer/AlSi Legierungen, Bronze weich, Elektrolytkupfer, Messing zäh, gut spanbare rost- und säurebeständige Stähle, Titan, Titan Legierungen, usw.

Übrige Konstruktionsmerkmale nach DIN 1414.
**Verpackungseinheit** Bis $d_1$ 10: 10 Stück, ab $d_1$ 10,5 mm Ø: 5 Stück.

| $d_1$ | $l_1$ | $l_2$ | St/DM | Best # |
|---|---|---|---|---|
| **2** | 85 | 56 | **14,95** | 42 020 |
| 2,2 | 90 | 59 | **15,05** | 42 022 |
| 2,5 | 95 | 62 | **13,55** | 42 025 |
| **3** | 100 | 66 | **13,85** | 42 030 |
| 3,2 | 106 | 69 | **15,45** | 42 032 |
| 3,3 | 106 | 69 | **17,35** | 42 033 |
| 3,5 | 112 | 73 | **15,95** | 42 035 |
| 3,8 | 119 | 78 | **16,15** | 42 038 |
| **4** | 119 | 78 | **17,35** | 42 040 |
| 4,2 | 119 | 78 | **19,05** | 42 042 |
| 4,5 | 126 | 82 | **19,70** | 42 045 |
| **5** | 132 | 87 | **20,95** | 42 050 |
| 5,2 | 132 | 87 | **25,20** | 42 052 |
| 5,5 | 139 | 91 | **24,65** | 42 055 |
| **6** | 139 | 91 | **25,80** | 42 060 |
| 6,5 | 148 | 97 | **28,10** | 42 065 |
| 6,8 | 156 | 102 | **29,90** | 42 068 |
| **7** | 156 | 102 | **33,30** | 42 070 |
| 7,5 | 156 | 102 | **35,10** | 42 075 |
| **8** | 165 | 109 | **38,55** | 42 080 |
| 8,5 | 165 | 109 | **43,35** | 42 085 |
| **9** | 175 | 115 | **46,95** | 42 090 |
| 9,5 | 175 | 115 | **54,10** | 42 095 |
| **10** | 184 | 121 | **56,70** | 42 100 |
| 10,5 | 184 | 121 | **66,10** | 42 105 |
| **11** | 195 | 128 | **84,75** | 42 110 |
| 11,5 | 195 | 128 | **92,60** | 42 115 |
| **12** | 205 | 134 | **104,35** | 42 120 |
| 12,5 | 205 | 134 | **107,10** | 42 125 |
| **13** | 205 | 134 | **143,95** | 42 130 |

8 PROJAHN GOLD

44000
Extra kurze Mehrbereichs-Spiralbohrer mit Zylinderschaft
Multipurpose straight shank twist drills, stub series
Forets multi-matières à queue cylindrique, série extra courte
**HSS-Co DIN 1897 Typ UF-L**

| | |
|---|---|
| Toleranz | h8 |
| Material | HSS-Co 5% |
| Spitzenanschliff | Werksnorm |
| Spitzenwinkel | 130° |
| Ausspitzung nach DIN 1412 | Form UX |
| Kerndicke | dicker als normal |
| Kernanstieg | ohne |
| Seitenspanwinkel (Spiralwinkel) | 40° |
| Nutenform | Flachnutenprofil |

Stabiler Mehrbereichsbohrer mit ausgeprägter Warmhärtebeständigkeit. Sehr gute Spanabfuhr. Besonders geeignet für den Einsatz auf Automaten und NC-Maschinen. Für mittel- und langspanende Werkstoffe mit einer Festigkeit bis maximal 1.200 N/mm², Al/Kupfer/AlSi Legierungen, Bronze weich, Elektrolytkupfer, Messing zäh, nichtrostende Stähle, Titan, Titan Legierungen, usw.

Übrige Konstruktionsmerkmale nach DIN 1414.
**Verpackungseinheit** Bis $d_1$ 10: 10 Stück, ab $d_1$ 10,2: 5 Stück.

| $d_1$ | $l_1$ | $l_2$ | St/DM | Best # |
|---|---|---|---|---|
| **2** | 38 | 12 | **5,30** | 44 020 |
| 2,1 | 38 | 12 | **5,20** | 44 021 |
| 2,2 | 40 | 13 | **5,30** | 44 022 |
| 2,3 | 40 | 13 | **5,80** | 44 023 |
| 2,4 | 43 | 14 | **6,10** | 44 024 |
| 2,5 | 43 | 14 | **5,60** | 44 025 |
| 2,6 | 43 | 14 | **6,25** | 44 026 |
| 2,7 | 46 | 16 | **6,25** | 44 027 |
| 2,8 | 46 | 16 | **6,45** | 44 028 |
| 2,9 | 46 | 16 | **6,55** | 44 029 |
| **3** | 46 | 16 | **5,95** | 44 030 |
| 3,1 | 49 | 18 | **6,65** | 44 031 |
| 3,2 | 49 | 18 | **5,95** | 44 032 |
| 3,3 | 49 | 18 | **5,95** | 44 033 |
| 3,4 | 52 | 20 | **6,75** | 44 034 |
| 3,5 | 52 | 20 | **6,95** | 44 035 |
| 3,6 | 52 | 20 | **7,10** | 44 036 |
| 3,7 | 52 | 20 | **7,10** | 44 037 |
| 3,8 | 55 | 22 | **7,20** | 44 038 |
| 3,9 | 55 | 22 | **7,30** | 44 039 |
| **4** | 55 | 22 | **7,70** | 44 040 |
| 4,1 | 55 | 22 | **8,20** | 44 041 |
| 4,2 | 55 | 22 | **7,85** | 44 042 |
| 4,3 | 58 | 24 | **8,35** | 44 043 |
| 4,4 | 58 | 24 | **8,60** | 44 044 |
| 4,5 | 58 | 24 | **8,80** | 44 045 |
| 4,6 | 58 | 24 | **8,80** | 44 046 |
| 4,7 | 58 | 24 | **9,00** | 44 047 |
| 4,8 | 62 | 26 | **9,20** | 44 048 |
| 4,9 | 62 | 26 | **9,65** | 44 049 |

| $d_1$ | $l_1$ | $l_2$ | St/DM | Best # |
|---|---|---|---|---|
| **5** | 62 | 26 | **9,85** | 44 050 |
| 5,1 | 62 | 26 | **9,85** | 44 051 |
| 5,2 | 62 | 26 | **10,70** | 44 052 |
| 5,5 | 66 | 28 | **12,00** | 44 055 |
| 5,7 | 66 | 28 | **12,20** | 44 057 |
| **6** | 66 | 28 | **12,20** | 44 060 |
| 6,5 | 70 | 31 | **13,30** | 44 065 |
| 6,8 | 74 | 34 | **16,30** | 44 068 |
| **7** | 74 | 34 | **13,95** | 44 070 |
| 7,5 | 74 | 34 | **16,05** | 44 075 |
| **8** | 79 | 37 | **17,35** | 44 080 |
| 8,5 | 79 | 37 | **18,40** | 44 085 |
| **9** | 84 | 40 | **20,80** | 44 090 |
| 9,5 | 84 | 40 | **26,25** | 44 095 |
| **10** | 89 | 43 | **24,10** | 44 100 |
| 10,2 | 89 | 43 | **36,95** | 44 102 |
| 10,5 | 89 | 43 | **41,75** | 44 105 |
| **11** | 95 | 47 | **46,10** | 44 110 |
| 11,5 | 95 | 47 | **51,00** | 44 115 |
| **12** | 102 | 51 | **51,00** | 44 120 |
| 12,5 | 102 | 51 | **54,00** | 44 125 |
| **13** | 102 | 51 | **67,00** | 44 130 |
| 13,5 | 107 | 54 | **68,70** | 44 135 |
| **14** | 107 | 54 | **69,55** | 44 140 |
| 14,5 | 111 | 56 | **71,70** | 44 145 |
| **15** | 111 | 56 | **76,00** | 44 150 |
| 15,5 | 115 | 58 | **96,85** | 44 155 |
| **16** | 115 | 58 | **97,00** | 44 160 |

Andere Abmessungen auf Anfrage.



9 PROJAHN GOLD

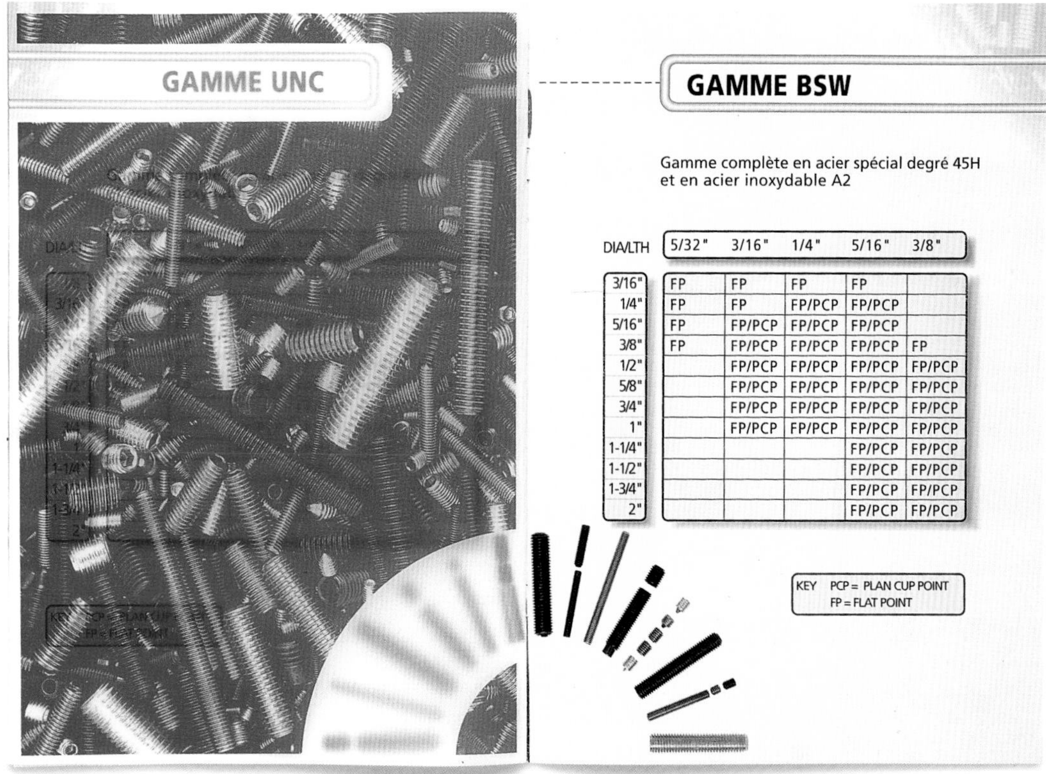

GAMME UNC

GAMME BSW

Gamme complète en acier spécial degré 45H
et en acier inoxydable A2

| DIA/LTH | 5/32" | 3/16" | 1/4" | 5/16" | 3/8" |
|---|---|---|---|---|---|
| 3/16" | FP | FP | FP | FP | |
| 1/4" | FP | FP | FP/PCP | FP/PCP | |
| 5/16" | FP | FP/PCP | FP/PCP | FP/PCP | |
| 3/8" | FP | FP/PCP | FP/PCP | FP/PCP | FP |
| 1/2" | | FP/PCP | FP/PCP | FP/PCP | FP/PCP |
| 5/8" | | FP/PCP | FP/PCP | FP/PCP | FP/PCP |
| 3/4" | | FP/PCP | FP/PCP | FP/PCP | FP/PCP |
| 1" | | FP/PCP | FP/PCP | FP/PCP | FP/PCP |
| 1-1/4" | | | | FP/PCP | FP/PCP |
| 1-1/2" | | | | FP/PCP | FP/PCP |
| 1-3/4" | | | | FP/PCP | FP/PCP |
| 2" | | | | FP/PCP | FP/PCP |

KEY PCP = PLAN CUP POINT
FP = FLAT POINT

# Socket Set Screws

SOCKET SET SCREWS CL: Omas CD, D: Ivano Gozzi P: Massimo Ceccoli CW: Loretta Montironi
DF: B & AR Communication San Marino 1997 *SIZE: 297×210*

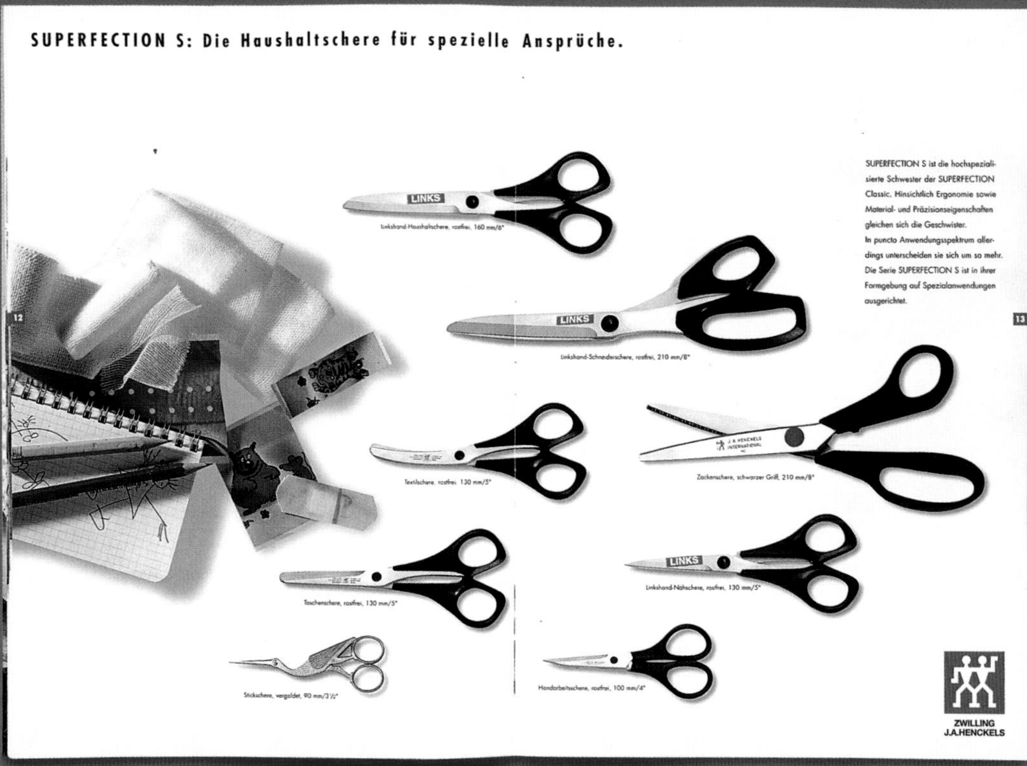
SUPERFECTION S: Die Haushaltschere für spezielle Ansprüche.
LINKS
LINKS
LINKS
SUPERFECTION S ist die hochspezialisierte Schwester der SUPERFECTION Classic. Hinsichtlich Ergonomie sowie Material- und Präzisionseigenschaften gleichen sich die Geschwister.
In puncto Anwendungsspektrum allerdings unterscheiden sie sich um so mehr. Die Serie SUPERFECTION S ist in ihrer Formgebung auf Spezialanwendungen ausgerichtet.
12
13
ZWILLING
J.A.HENCKELS

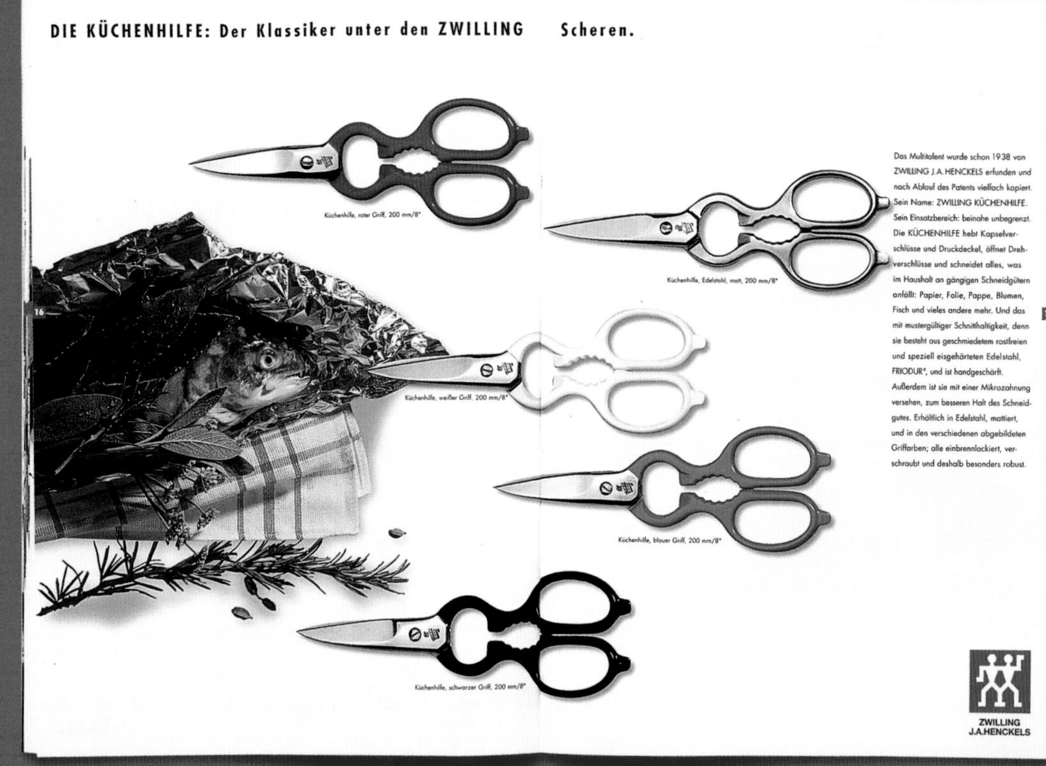
DIE KÜCHENHILFE: Der Klassiker unter den ZWILLING Scheren.
Das Multitalent wurde schon 1938 von ZWILLING J.A.HENCKELS erfunden und nach Ablauf des Patents vielfach kopiert. Sein Name: ZWILLING KÜCHENHILFE. Sein Einsatzbereich: beinahe unbegrenzt. Die KÜCHENHILFE hebt Kapselverschlüsse und Druckdeckel, öffnet Drehverschlüsse und schneidet alles, was im Haushalt an gängigen Schneidgütern anfällt: Papier, Folie, Pappe, Blumen, Fisch und vieles andere mehr. Und das mit mustergültiger Schnitthaltigkeit, denn sie besteht aus geschmiedetem rostfreien und speziell eisgehärteten Edelstahl, FRIODUR®, und ist handgeschärft. Außerdem ist sie mit einer Mikrozahnung versehen, zum besseren Halt des Schneidgutes. Erhältlich in Edelstahl, mattiert, und in den verschiedenen abgebildeten Griffarben; alle einbrennlackiert, verschraubt und deshalb besonders robust.
16
17
ZWILLING
J.A.HENCKELS

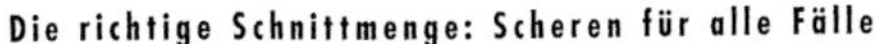

Die richtige Schnittmenge: Scheren für alle Fälle.

**Küchenhilfe**
Kräftige Schere für viele Zwecke. Ideal zum Schneiden aller Schneidgüter im Küchenbereich.

**Vielzweckschere**
Mittelgroße, stabile Schere. Wegen ihrer Vielseitigkeit und leichten Handhabung ideal für alle normalen Schneidarbeiten im Haushalt.

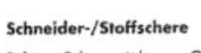

**Schneider-/Stoffschere**
Robuste Schere mit langen Griffaugen und kräftigen Scherenblättern, besonders zum Schneiden von Stoffen geeignet. Erhältlich in unterschiedlichen Größen – passend für die entsprechenden Stoffqualitäten.

**Papierschere**
Lange, schlanke Schere, die mit wenigen Schnitten große Papierstücke schneidet.

**Designschere**
Erfüllt alle Anforderungen, die an eine zweckmäßige Schere gestellt werden. Unterscheidet sich von herkömmlichen Ausführungen allerdings durch die moderne Optik.

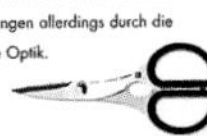

**Näh-, Stick- und Handarbeitschere**
Feine, spitze Schere. Ist leicht und handlich zum Auftrennen von Nähten sowie zum Schneiden von Garnen und Fäden.

**Bastel-/Hobbyschere**
Kleine, handliche Schere mit runder Spitze. Damit können auch Kinder gefahrlos schneiden.

**Geflügelschere**
Schweres Schneidwerkzeug, stabil und kraftvoll. Knochenbrecher und gezahnte Schneide zerteilen mühelos Hähnchen, Puten, Enten oder Gänse.

**Nagelschere**
Scharfe, schnittige Schere mit gebogener Schneide, die den Fingernagel sauber bis in die Ecken formt und kürzt.

**Hautschere**
Sehr zarte, feine Schere mit gebogener dünner Schneide zum Entfernen störender Häutchen.

**Friseurschere**
Schere mit glatter Wate oder Mikrozahnung, in unterschiedlichen Größen und Gewichten. Die Mikrozahnung faßt die Haare und hält sie fest, so daß sie beim Schneiden nicht aus der Schere rutschen.

**Effilierschere**
Schere mit einer oder zwei gezahnten Schneiden. Je feiner die Zahnung ist, desto stärker werden die Haare ausgedünnt.

**Zackenschere**
Zackig ausgefräste, exakt aufeinander eingeschliffene Schneidblätter zum fransenfreien Zuschneiden von Stoff.

**Textilschere**
Kleine, handliche Schere mit runder Spitze, die nicht im Schneidgut – z. B. Mullbinden – hängenbleibt.

**Taschenschere**
Kleine, handliche Schere mit runder Spitze. Wie bei der Bastelschere besteht keine Verletzungsgefahr.

Besondere Kennzeichen: Zahlreiche Qualitätsmerkmale.

Die perfekte Bearbeitung durch den qualifizierten Scherenspezialisten ist eines der entscheidendsten Merkmale für die Güte einer Qualitätsschere von ZWILLING J.A.HENCKELS. Schließlich soll sie ein Leben lang das funktionstüchtige Werkzeug sein und bleiben. Folgende Charakterzüge sind deshalb unbedingt beim Kauf zu beachten:

**Die Spitzen** sollen im geschlossenen Zustand gleichmäßig abschließen und bis zum letzten Millimeter sauber schneiden. Je feiner die Schneidanforderung, desto schlanker muß die Spitzenform zulaufen.
**Der Abzug** entscheidet über die Qualität der Schneidleistung. Billige Scheren können oft nur ein Material gut schneiden, während Qualitätsinstrumente bei verschiedenen Materialien immer optimale Schneidleistung zeigen.
**Das Finish** bestimmt die Qualität der gesamten Oberflächenbearbeitung einer rundum sauber verarbeiteten Schere.
**Der Gang** – das Verhalten beim Öffnen und Schließen – ist das Hauptkriterium für die Funktionstüchtigkeit der Schere. Dabei berühren sich die Schneiden einer guten Schere vom Ansatz bis zur Spitze immer nur an einem Punkt: Im geschlossenen Zustand liegen nur die Spitzen aneinander. Am besten erkennt man das, wenn man eine Schere von der Seite betrachtet und zwischen den Schneiden durchschauen kann.
**Die Schraube** ist ein leicht erkennbares und wesentliches Merkmal einer Qualitätsschere. Mit ihr reguliert der Spezialist bei der Montage den Scherengang. Nach langer Schnittzeit kann die verschraubte Schere leicht vom Fachmann demontiert und für die nächsten Jahre wieder geschärft werden. Dabei wird der Gang mit der Schraube wieder optimal justiert.

**Die Scherenauge**
platz für die Finge
feiner die Arbeiten,
ger der benötigte
größer bzw. klein
Dabei unterscheid
zwischen Rund- (
scheren) und Lan
Stoffscheren).
Die Innenform d
arbeitet sein, d
der natürlichen
glatt-rund ausg
schliffen ist.

Selbstverständl
Fachleute auf
kriterien. Ori
den hier gen
Qualitätsme
sicher, mit ei
richtige Wa

Das Finish · Der Abzug · Der Gang · Die Spitzen · Die Schraube

**Scissors**

ZWILLING J. A. HENCKELS CL: Zwilling J. A. Henckels Japan Ltd. Japan 1998 *SIZE: 297×210*

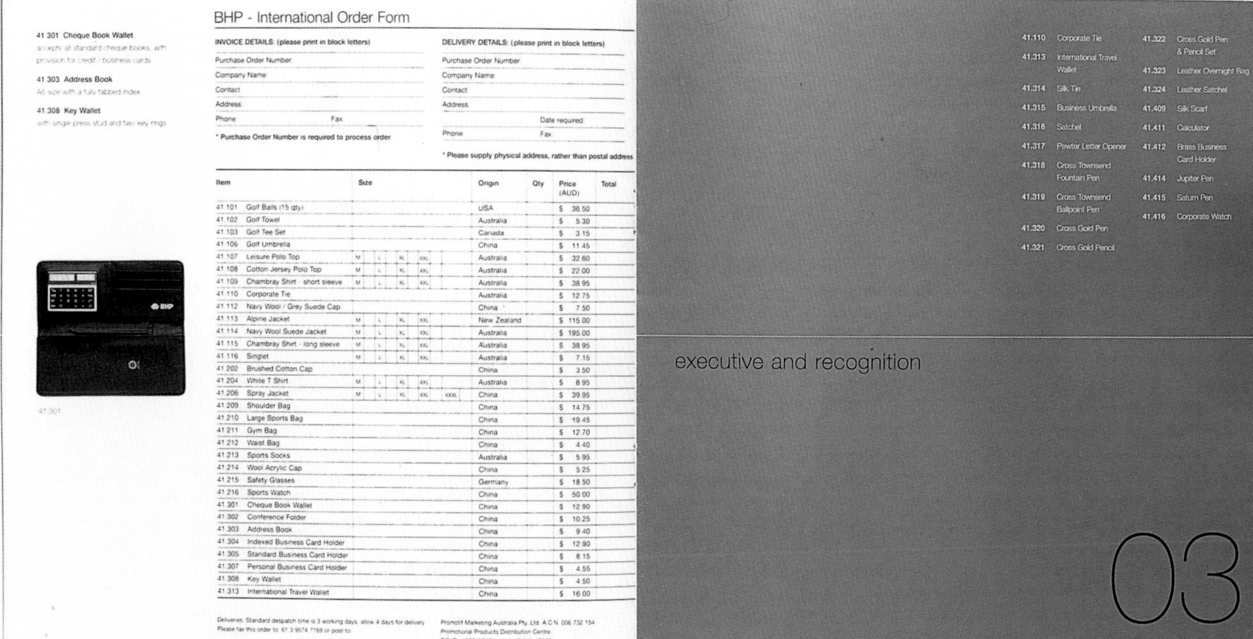
41.301 **Cheque Book Wallet**
accepts all standard cheque books, with provision for credit / business cards

41.303 **Address Book**
A5 size with a fully tabbed index

41.308 **Key Wallet**
with single press stud and two key rings

41.301

BHP - International Order Form

**INVOICE DETAILS: (please print in block letters)**

Purchase Order Number:
Company Name:
Contact:
Address:
Phone: Fax:

*** Purchase Order Number is required to process order**

**DELIVERY DETAILS: (please print in block letters)**

Purchase Order Number:
Company Name:
Contact:
Address:
Date required:
Phone: Fax:

*** Please supply physical address, rather than postal address**

| Item | Size | Origin | Qty | Price (AUD) | Total |
|---|---|---|---|---|---|
| 41.101 Golf Balls (15 qty) | | USA | | $ 36.50 | |
| 41.102 Golf Towel | | Australia | | $ 5.30 | |
| 41.103 Golf Tee Set | | Canada | | $ 3.15 | |
| 41.106 Golf Umbrella | | China | | $ 11.45 | |
| 41.107 Leisure Polo Top | M L XL XXL | Australia | | $ 32.60 | |
| 41.108 Cotton Jersey Polo Top | M L XL XXL | Australia | | $ 22.00 | |
| 41.109 Chambray Shirt - short sleeve | M L XL XXL | Australia | | $ 38.95 | |
| 41.110 Corporate Tie | | Australia | | $ 12.75 | |
| 41.112 Navy Wool / Grey Suede Cap | | China | | $ 7.50 | |
| 41.113 Alpine Jacket | M L XL XXL | New Zealand | | $ 115.00 | |
| 41.114 Navy Wool Suede Jacket | M L XL XXL | Australia | | $ 195.00 | |
| 41.115 Chambray Shirt - long sleeve | M L XL XXL | Australia | | $ 38.95 | |
| 41.116 Singlet | M L XL XXL | Australia | | $ 7.15 | |
| 41.202 Brushed Cotton Cap | | China | | $ 3.50 | |
| 41.204 White T Shirt | M L XL XXL | Australia | | $ 8.95 | |
| 41.206 Spray Jacket | M L XL XXL XXXL | China | | $ 39.95 | |
| 41.209 Shoulder Bag | | China | | $ 14.75 | |
| 41.210 Large Sports Bag | | China | | $ 19.45 | |
| 41.211 Gym Bag | | China | | $ 12.70 | |
| 41.212 Waist Bag | | China | | $ 4.40 | |
| 41.213 Sports Socks | | Australia | | $ 5.95 | |
| 41.214 Wool Acrylic Cap | | China | | $ 5.25 | |
| 41.215 Safety Glasses | | Germany | | $ 18.50 | |
| 41.216 Sports Watch | | China | | $ 50.00 | |
| 41.301 Cheque Book Wallet | | China | | $ 12.90 | |
| 41.302 Conference Folder | | China | | $ 10.25 | |
| 41.303 Address Book | | China | | $ 9.40 | |
| 41.304 Indexed Business Card Holder | | China | | $ 12.90 | |
| 41.305 Standard Business Card Holder | | China | | $ 8.15 | |
| 41.307 Personal Business Card Holder | | China | | $ 4.55 | |
| 41.308 Key Wallet | | China | | $ 4.50 | |
| 41.313 International Travel Wallet | | China | | $ 16.00 | |

Deliveries: Standard despatch time is 3 working days, allow 4 days for delivery
Please fax this order to: 61 3 9574 7188 or post to:

Promotif Marketing Australia Pty. Ltd. A.C.N. 006 732 154
Promotional Products Distribution Centre
P.O. Box 939, Mt Waverley, Victoria, 3149

41.110 Corporate Tie
41.313 International Travel Wallet
41.314 Silk Tie
41.315 Business Umbrella
41.316 Satchel
41.317 Pewter Letter Opener
41.318 Cross Townsend Fountain Pen
41.319 Cross Townsend Ballpoint Pen
41.320 Cross Gold Pen
41.321 Cross Gold Pencil
41.322 Cross Gold Pen & Pencil Set
41.323 Leather Overnight Bag
41.324 Leather Satchel
41.409 Silk Scarf
41.411 Calculator
41.412 Brass Business Card Holder
41.414 Jupiter Pen
41.415 Saturn Pen
41.416 Corporate Watch

executive and recognition

03

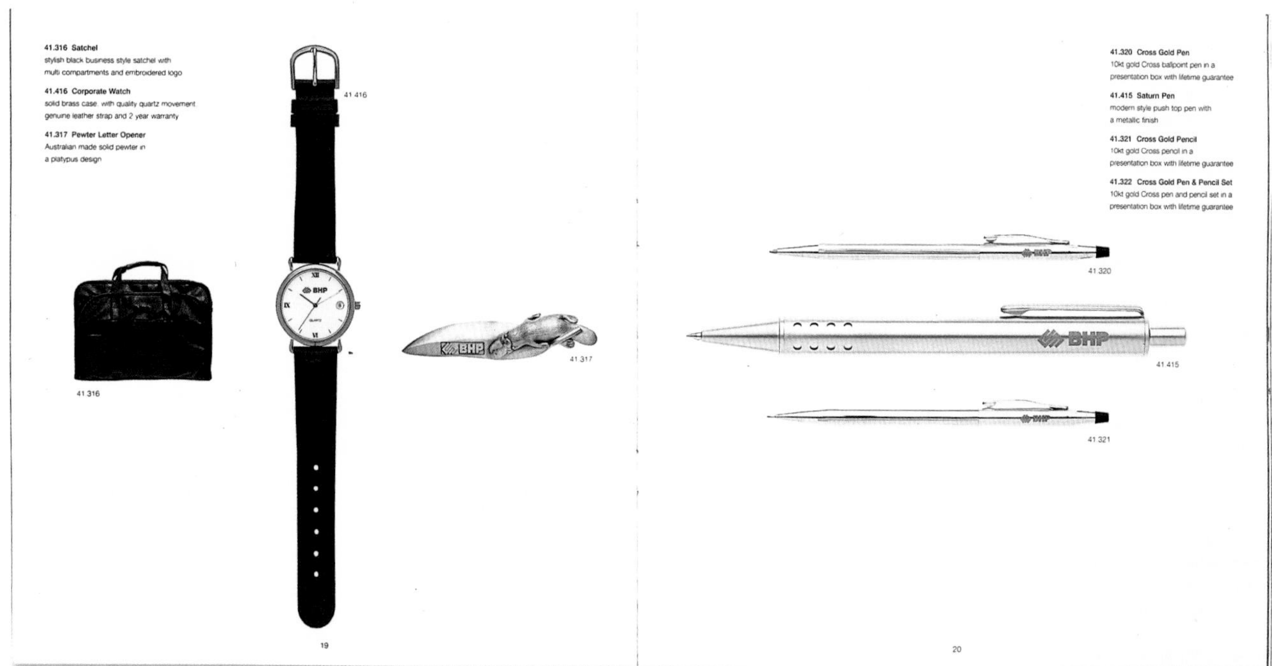
41.316 **Satchel**
stylish black business style satchel with multi compartments and embroidered logo

41.416 **Corporate Watch**
solid brass case, with quality quartz movement genuine leather strap and 2 year warranty

41.317 **Pewter Letter Opener**
Australian made solid pewter in a platypus design

41.316

41.416

41.317

19

41.320 **Cross Gold Pen**
10kt gold Cross ballpoint pen in a presentation box with lifetime guarantee

41.415 **Saturn Pen**
modern style push top pen with a metallic finish

41.321 **Cross Gold Pencil**
10kt gold Cross pencil in a presentation box with lifetime guarantee

41.322 **Cross Gold Pen & Pencil Set**
10kt gold Cross pen and pencil set in a presentation box with lifetime guarantee

41.320

41.415

41.321

20

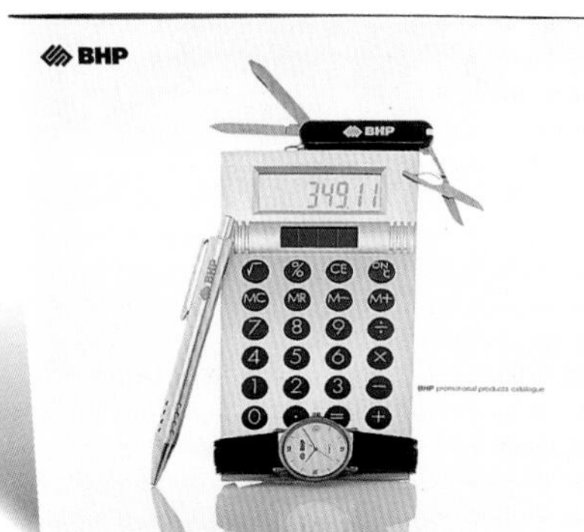


## Stationery

BHP CL: BHP CD: Fabio Ongarato AD: Ronnen Goren D: Dylan Griffith P: Dieu Tan
DF: Fabio Ongarato Design Australia 1997 *SIZE: 210×210*

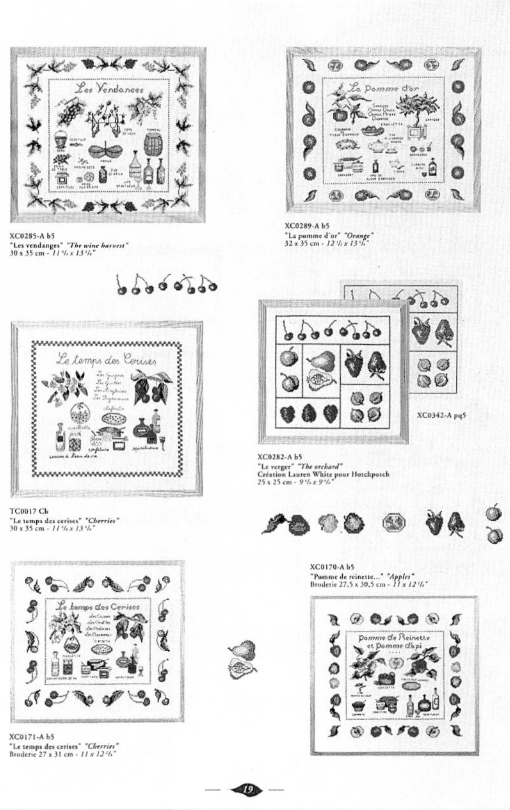


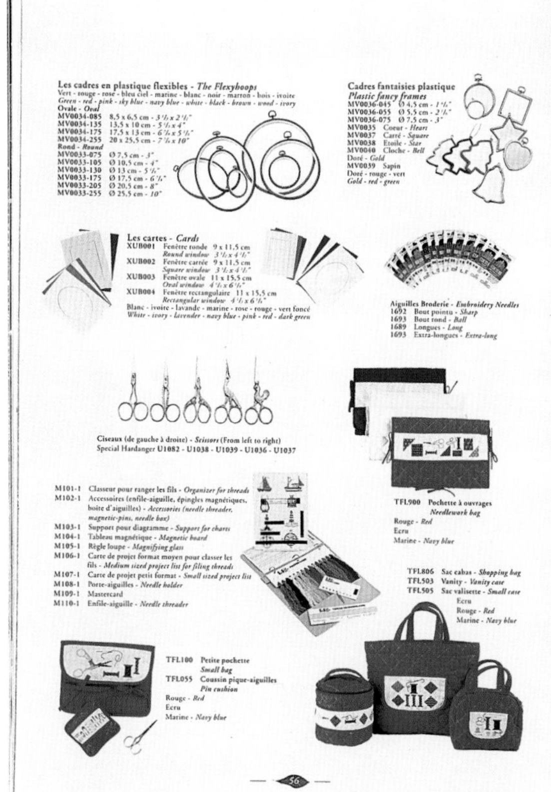

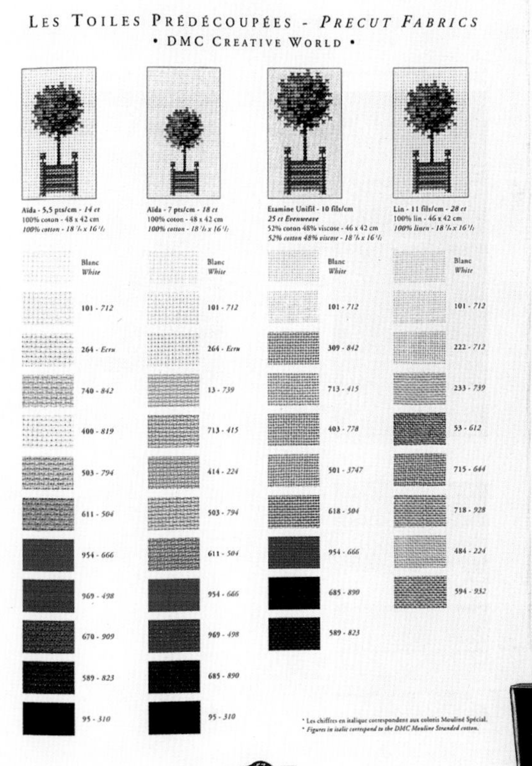


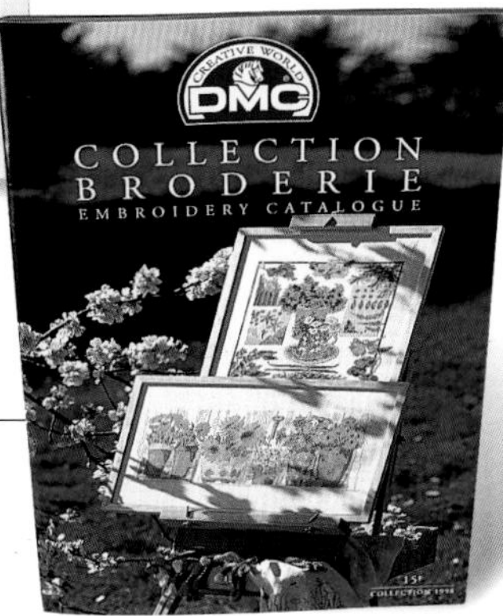


## Embroidery

DMC EMBROIDERY CL: DMC Embroidery CD: Patrick Bouju AD: Nathalie Berthelot P: Christophe Dugied DF: Small Is Beautiful! France 1998 *SIZE: 297×210*

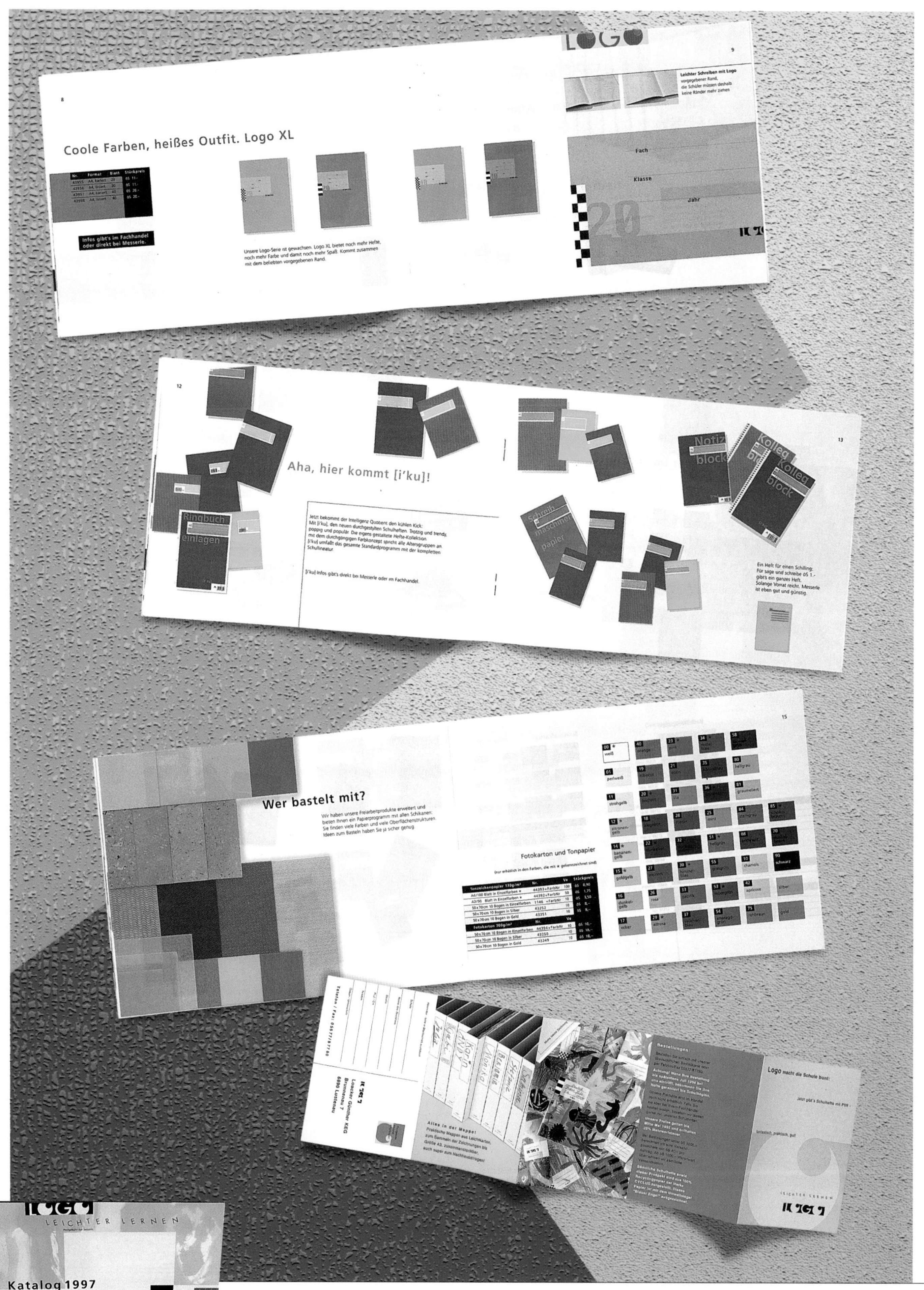


## Stationery

LOGO + I:KU CL: Messerle GmbH CD, AD: Sandro Scherling / Sigi Ramoser D: Klaus Österle P: Harald Peter CW: Hermann Brändle DF: Atelier Für Text Und Gestaltung Austria 1997 *SIZE: 148×210, 148×105*

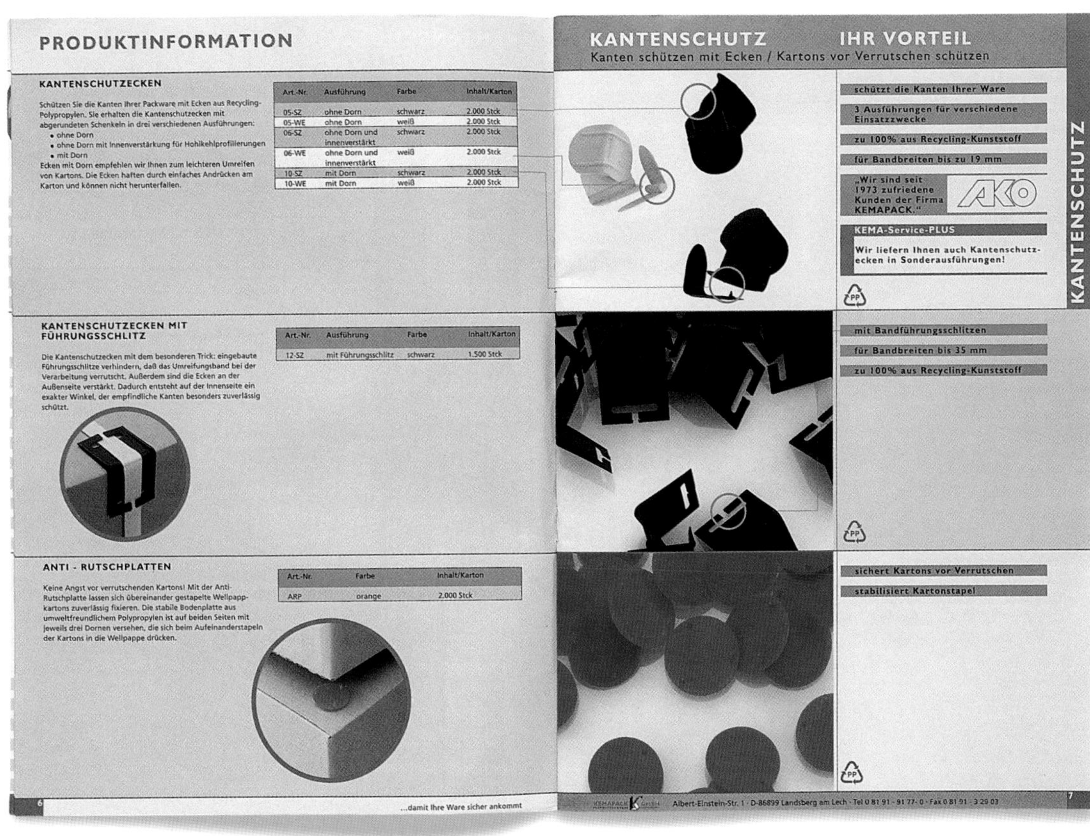

## PRODUKTINFORMATION

### KANTENSCHUTZECKEN

Schützen Sie die Kanten Ihrer Packware mit Ecken aus Recycling-Polypropylen. Sie erhalten die Kantenschutzecken mit abgerundeten Schenkeln in drei verschiedenen Ausführungen:

- ohne Dorn
- ohne Dorn mit Innenverstärkung für Hohlkehlprofilierungen
- mit Dorn

Ecken mit Dorn empfehlen wir Ihnen zum leichteren Umreifen von Kartons. Die Ecken haften durch einfaches Andrücken am Karton und können nicht herunterfallen.

| Art.-Nr. | Ausführung | Farbe | Inhalt/Karton |
|---|---|---|---|
| 05-SZ | ohne Dorn | schwarz | 2.000 Stck |
| 05-WE | ohne Dorn | weiß | 2.000 Stck |
| 06-SZ | ohne Dorn und innenverstärkt | schwarz | 2.000 Stck |
| 06-WE | ohne Dorn und innenverstärkt | weiß | 2.000 Stck |
| 10-SZ | mit Dorn | schwarz | 2.000 Stck |
| 10-WE | mit Dorn | weiß | 2.000 Stck |

### KANTENSCHUTZECKEN MIT FÜHRUNGSSCHLITZ

Die Kantenschutzecken mit dem besonderen Trick: eingebaute Führungsschlitze verhindern, daß das Umreifungsband bei der Verarbeitung verrutscht. Außerdem sind die Ecken an der Außenseite verstärkt. Dadurch entsteht auf der Innenseite ein exakter Winkel, der empfindliche Kanten besonders zuverlässig schützt.

| Art.-Nr. | Ausführung | Farbe | Inhalt/Karton |
|---|---|---|---|
| 12-SZ | mit Führungsschlitz | schwarz | 1.500 Stck |

### ANTI - RUTSCHPLATTEN

Keine Angst vor verrutschenden Kartons! Mit der Anti-Rutschplatte lassen sich übereinander gestapelte Wellpappkartons zuverlässig fixieren. Die stabile Bodenplatte aus umweltfreundlichem Polypropylen ist auf beiden Seiten mit jeweils drei Dornen versehen, die sich beim Aufeinanderstapeln der Kartons in die Wellpappe drücken.

| Art.-Nr. | Farbe | Inhalt/Karton |
|---|---|---|
| ARP | orange | 2.000 Stck |

6 ...damit Ihre Ware sicher ankommt

## KANTENSCHUTZ — IHR VORTEIL

Kanten schützen mit Ecken / Kartons vor Verrutschen schützen

- schützt die Kanten Ihrer Ware
- 3 Ausführungen für verschiedene Einsatzzwecke
- zu 100% aus Recycling-Kunststoff
- für Bandbreiten bis zu 19 mm

„Wir sind seit 1973 zufriedene Kunden der Firma KEMAPACK." AKO

KEMA-Service-PLUS

Wir liefern Ihnen auch Kantenschutzecken in Sonderausführungen!

PP

- mit Bandführungsschlitzen
- für Bandbreiten bis 35 mm
- zu 100% aus Recycling-Kunststoff

PP

- sichert Kartons vor Verrutschen
- stabilisiert Kartonstapel

PP

KANTENSCHUTZ

KEMAPACK GmbH Albert-Einstein-Str. 1 · D-86899 Landsberg am Lech · Tel 0 81 91 - 91 77-0 · Fax 0 81 91 - 3 29 03 7

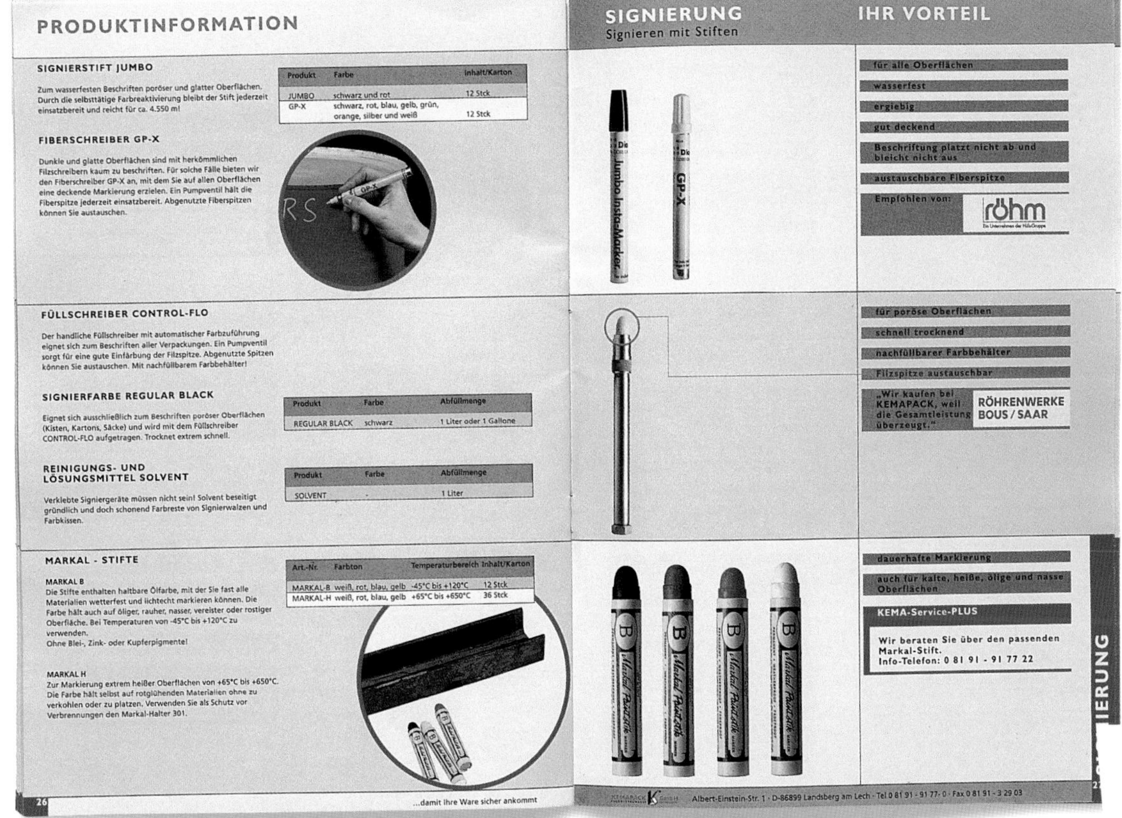

## PRODUKTINFORMATION

### SIGNIERSTIFT JUMBO

Zum wasserfesten Beschriften poröser und glatter Oberflächen. Durch die selbsttätige Farbreaktivierung bleibt der Stift jederzeit einsatzbereit und reicht für ca. 4.550 m!

| Produkt | Farbe | Inhalt/Karton |
|---|---|---|
| JUMBO | schwarz und rot | 12 Stck |
| GP-X | schwarz, rot, blau, gelb, grün, orange, silber und weiß | 12 Stck |

### FIBERSCHREIBER GP-X

Dunkle und glatte Oberflächen sind mit herkömmlichen Filzschreibern kaum zu beschriften. Für solche Fälle bieten wir den Fiberschreiber GP-X an, mit dem Sie auf allen Oberflächen eine deckende Markierung erzielen. Ein Pumpventil hält die Fiberspitze jederzeit einsatzbereit. Abgenutzte Fiberspitzen können Sie austauschen.

### FÜLLSCHREIBER CONTROL-FLO

Der handliche Füllschreiber mit automatischer Farbzuführung eignet sich zum Beschriften aller Verpackungen. Ein Pumpventil sorgt für eine gute Einfärbung der Filzspitze. Abgenutzte Spitzen können Sie austauschen. Mit nachfüllbarem Farbbehälter!

### SIGNIERFARBE REGULAR BLACK

Eignet sich ausschließlich zum Beschriften poröser Oberflächen (Kisten, Kartons, Säcke) und wird mit dem Füllschreiber CONTROL-FLO aufgetragen. Trocknet extrem schnell.

| Produkt | Farbe | Abfüllmenge |
|---|---|---|
| REGULAR BLACK | schwarz | 1 Liter oder 1 Gallone |

### REINIGUNGS- UND LÖSUNGSMITTEL SOLVENT

Verklebte Signiergeräte müssen nicht sein! Solvent beseitigt gründlich und doch schonend Farbreste von Signierwalzen und Farbkissen.

| Produkt | Farbe | Abfüllmenge |
|---|---|---|
| SOLVENT | - | 1 Liter |

### MARKAL - STIFTE

**MARKAL B**

Die Stifte enthalten haltbare Ölfarbe, mit der Sie fast alle Materialien wetterfest und lichtecht markieren können. Die Farbe hält auch auf öliger, rauher, nasser, vereister oder rostiger Oberfläche. Bei Temperaturen von -45°C bis +120°C zu verwenden.

Ohne Blei-, Zink- oder Kupferpigmente!

**MARKAL H**

Zur Markierung extrem heißer Oberflächen von +65°C bis +650°C. Die Farbe hält selbst auf rotglühenden Materialien ohne zu verkohlen oder zu platzen. Verwenden Sie als Schutz vor Verbrennungen den Markal-Halter 301.

| Art.-Nr. | Farbton | Temperaturbereich | Inhalt/Karton |
|---|---|---|---|
| MARKAL-B | weiß, rot, blau, gelb | -45°C bis +120°C | 12 Stck |
| MARKAL-H | weiß, rot, blau, gelb | +65°C bis +650°C | 36 Stck |

26 ...damit Ihre Ware sicher ankommt

## SIGNIERUNG — IHR VORTEIL

Signieren mit Stiften



- für alle Oberflächen
- wasserfest
- ergiebig
- gut deckend
- Beschriftung platzt nicht ab und bleicht nicht aus
- austauschbare Fiberspitze

Empfohlen von: röhm

- für poröse Oberflächen
- schnell trocknend
- nachfüllbarer Farbbehälter
- Filzspitze austauschbar

„Wir kaufen bei KEMAPACK, weil die Gesamtleistung überzeugt." RÖHRENWERKE BOUS / SAAR

- dauerhafte Markierung
- auch für kalte, heiße, ölige und nasse Oberflächen

KEMA-Service-PLUS

Wir beraten Sie über den passenden Markal-Stift. Info-Telefon: 0 81 91 - 91 77 22

SIGNIERUNG

KEMAPACK GmbH Albert-Einstein-Str. 1 · D-86899 Landsberg am Lech · Tel 0 81 91 - 91 77-0 · Fax 0 81 91 - 3 29 03 27

**Packaging Products**

KEMAPACK CL: Kemapack CD, AD, D: Carina Orschulko P: Christian Döge CW: Petra Von Glyscinski Germany 1997 *SIZE: 299×210*

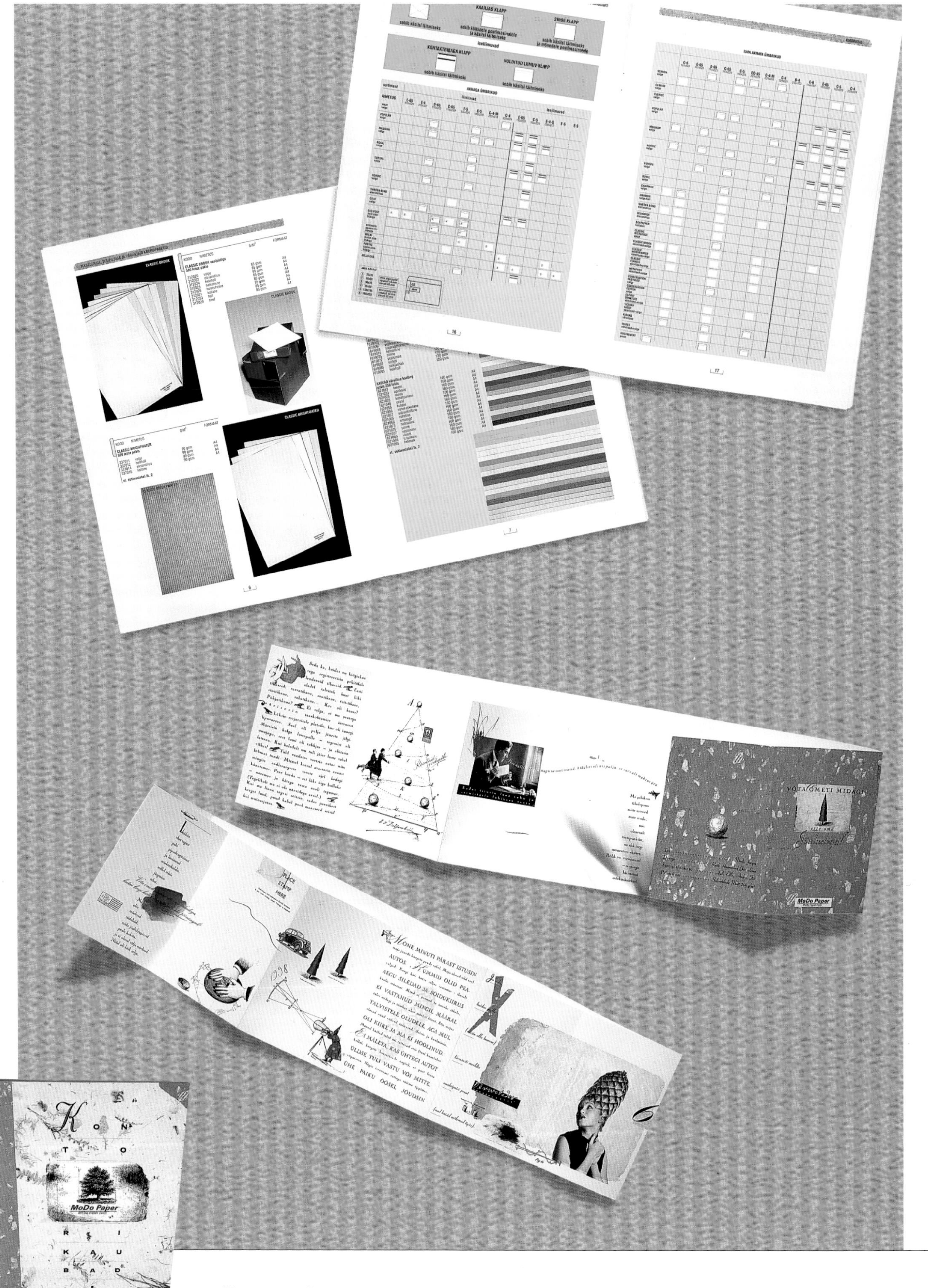

## Office Supplies & Paper

MODO PAPER CL: MoDo Paper Eesti CD, AD, P: Ruth Huimerind D: Jüri Lõun CW: Madis Jürgen Estonia 1997 *SIZE: 125×85, 300×214*

Pourquoi maman s'est-elle enrhumée ? Pourquoi le bébé hurle-t-il ? Pourquoi papa va-t-il travailler à pied ? Le livre-rébus d'un kleptomane en herbe.

ISBN : 2 84156 080 5
32 pages
17 x 17 - **68 F** - 10,50 €

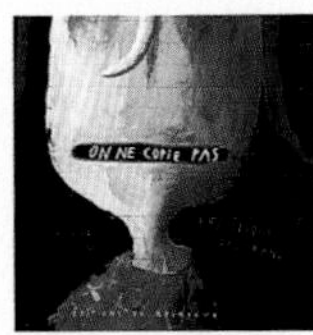

Un ouvrage qui fait définitivement le point sur les techniques pour bien copier : espérons que les écoliers sauront en prendre de la graine.

ISBN : 2 84156 083 X
50 pages couleur buvard compris
17 x 17 - **68 F** - 10,50 €

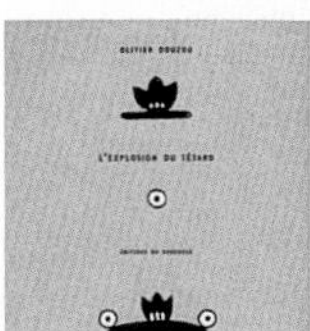

Ce livre donne une explication inédite sur la mutation des têtards…
Un clin d'œil à la fable de la Fontaine, un livre sur l'éclosion et l'explosion.

ISBN : 2 84156 088 0
40 pages
17 x 17 - **68 F** - 10,50 €

L'indifférence d'une brochette de gamins que rien, pas même une inondation géante, ne semble pouvoir faire bouger… Seule la gourmandise les sortira de leur torpeur.

ISBN : 2 84156 081 3
48 pages
17 x 17 - **68 F** - 10,50 €

Les déboires d'un Martien arrivé sur Terre sans chapeau… Un livre sous forme de questions-réponses qui nous emmène dans le monde secret de José Parrondo.

ISBN : 2 84156 092 9
48 pages
17 x 17 - **68 F** - 10,50 €

Chaque nuit, Ange, le gardien de nuit malicieux de notre fabrique à rêves, fait sa ronde… Un bric-à-brac de souvenirs sort de l'ombre…

ISBN : 2 84156 087 2
48 pages
20 x 20 - **72 F** - 11,10 €

Ça va pas. Pourtant, à l'intérieur de soi, il y a plein de choses qu'on voudrait exprimer, mais on ne sait pas par quel bout les attraper. On se fait un sang d'encre et avec une tache d'encre, on s'amuse… Et ça va.

ISBN : 2 84156 024 4
48 pages
17 x 17 - **68 F** - 10,50 €

Madame Ida est dans tous ses états : Luchien - son chien - il n'est plus là. Pour un os peut-être il a rongé son frein… Alors Madame Ida cherche très loin, dans tous les endroits… Mais c'est à l'envers qu'elle le retrouvera.

ISBN : 2 84156 030 9
40 pages
17 x 17 - **68 F** - 10,50 €

Une ronde avec "une amie très globe-trotter", "une amie très hospitalière", "un ami très bricoleur"… Des individus vivant chacun leur vie, un peu partout sur Terre, si lointains et si proches.

ISBN : 2 84156 029 5
48 pages
20 x 20 - **72 F** - 11,10 €

Il était une fois une archiduchesse qui faisait sécher ses drôles de chaussettes : des chaussettes avec des bosses, des maisons sur le dos, et même des cornes… des chaussettes qui ressemblent à des animaux…

ISBN : 2 84156 039 2
32 pages
17 x 17 - **60 F** - 9,20 €

La grenouille fait coa, l'éléphant wruuuuuuuuunnnfff, le canard coin-coin et tonton tousse. La vache fait meuh et tonton tousse, la souris fait couic couic, et tonton fait kuf fuf et puis plouf.

ISBN : 2 84156 045 7
32 pages
17 x 17 - **60 F** - 9,20 €

Qui est ce bonhomme habillé en noir qui fait danser Lili, pend le cochon et met en colère mère-grand ?… Qui est ce monsieur qui tire les ficelles du petit théâtre de marionnettes tous les soirs et fait relâche tous les dimanches ? Qui est au bout du fil ?

ISBN : 2 84156 046 5
48 pages
20 x 20 - **72 F** - 11,10 €

Pourquoi tombent-elles, ces dents qu'on dit de lait ? Et où vont-elles ces souris qui ne font que passer ? Vers un palais. Un palais d'OGRE, un palais de géant : tremblez, petits enfants !
Ce livre va vous donner les chocottes.

ISBN : 2 84156 033 3
48 pages
20 x 20 - **72 F** - 11,10 €

Il s'appelle Michel Navratil, il a 90 ans. Il est l'un des derniers rescapés du naufrage du *Titanic*. Ce livre raconte son histoire à bord du géant mythique qui, un soir de 1912, est entré dans la légende.

ISBN : 2 84156 038 4
48 pages
20 x 20 - **72 F** - 11,10 €

Parce qu'il y a des jours où tout part de travers, des jours sans, des jours où tout va mal, on va *Au Petit Bonheur la Chance* - magasin du hasard, des croyances et superstitions - s'acheter tous les grigris et porte-bonheur pour voir la vie sous un jour meilleur.

ISBN : 2 84156 044 9
48 pages
17 x 17 - **68 F** - 10,50 €

*Esquimau* est destiné à tous les enfants qui, avant de naître, se trouvaient dans un lieu sûr en forme d'igloo. Juste avant la séparation d'une mère banquise qui les fait dériver vers un monde nouveau.

ISBN : 2 84156 047 3
48 pages
17 x 17 - **68 F** - 10,50 €

Zélie a fait son choix dans la vitrine : deux belles chaussures avec talons qui la feront ressembler (presque) à une dame. Mais, il y a l'avis de la vendeuse, l'avis de sa maman, la mode…

ISBN : 2 84156 058 9
48 pages
20 x 20 - **72 F** - 11,10 €

Cet ouvrage rend hommage à deux drôles d'oiseaux partis tout là-haut sous d'autres cieux : Prévert et Doisneau. "Monsieur Pivert a une plume si légère qu'elle piège tous les mots, et Monsieur Moineau prend des photos au piège de sa cage."

ISBN : 2 84156 056 2
48 pages
17 x 17 - **68 F** - 10,50 €

## Children's Books

EDITIONS DU ROUERGUE CL: Editions Du Rouergue CD, I: Frederique Bertrand
AD: Olivier Douzou France 1998 *SIZE: 194×195*

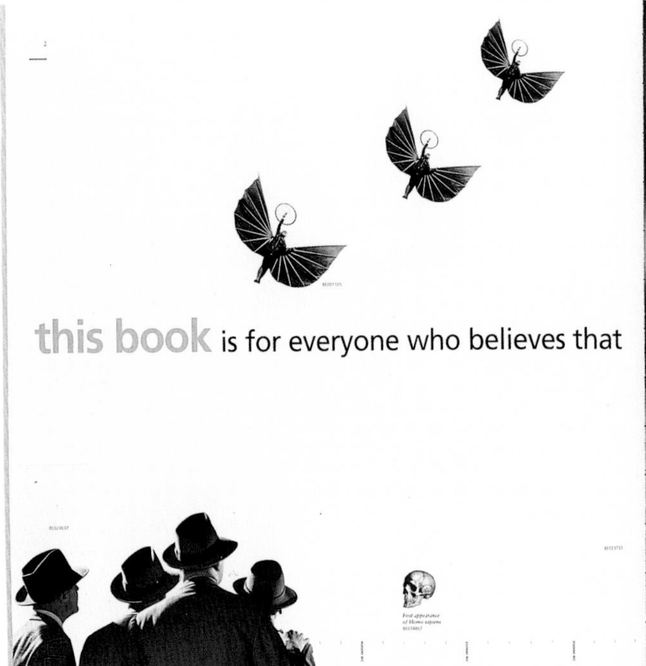
this book is for everyone who believes that

imagination is as important as experience

and time is a river

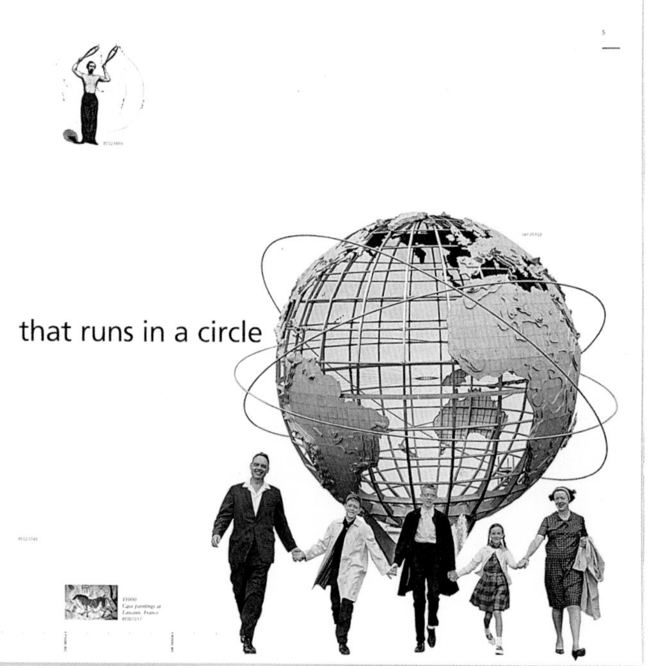
that runs in a circle

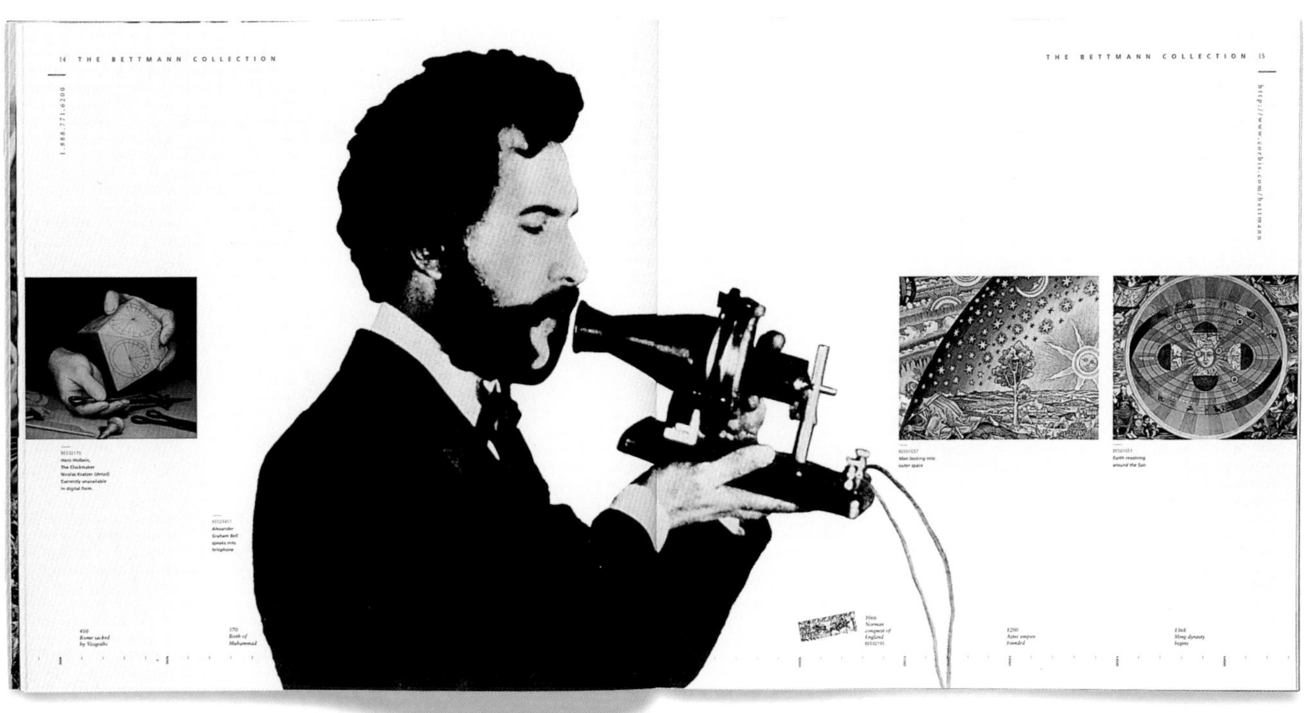

## Digital Archive Imagery

CORBIS CL, CW: Corbis Corporation AD, D: Jack Anderson D: John Anicker / Margaret Long / Mary Hermes P: Corbis Archive CW: Matthaeus Halverson Ayriss Advertising DF: Hornall Anderson Design Works, Inc. USA 1997 *SIZE: 267×267*

http://www.corbis.com/bettmann

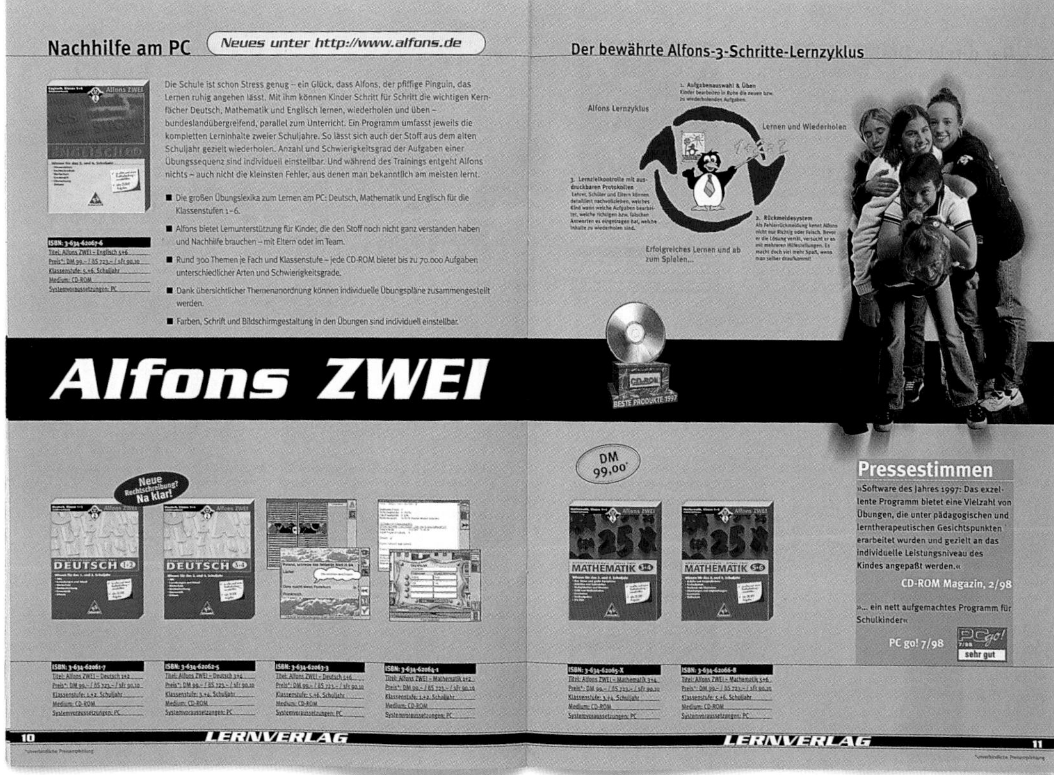

## Books

LERNVERLAG CL: Lernverlag CD: Liane Lahl P: Carsten Rottenbach I: Walter Werner
CW: Systhema Verlag GmbH DF: Pro Design Germany 1998 *SIZE: 297×210*

## Books

SMART BOOKS CL: Smart Books Publishing AG CD: Christof Täschler DF: Kabeljau Design Switzerland 1997 *SIZE: 210×148*

Willkommen zu Macintosh!

Max Schlapfer
**Willkommen zu Macintosh!**
448 Seiten mit CD-ROM
ISBN: 3-908488-09-5
sFr. 65.–/DM 69.–/öS 504.–

Dieses SmartBook ist der perfekte Einstieg in die Welt des Macintosh und zugleich ein Muss für alle, die mehr über ihren Lieblingscomputer wissen möchten.
Es ist ein leichtverständlicher, lockerer und unterhaltsamer Begleiter für die erste Zeit. Auch wenn Sie sich bereits ein wenig auskennen, wird «Willkommen zu Macintosh!» Ihr Wissen erweitern, offene Fragen beantworten und Sie auf neue Ideen und Arbeitstechniken bringen.
Erfahren Sie, wie Sie sich die verschiedenen Hilfesysteme zunutze machen, wie Sie Ihre Festplatte geschickt organisieren und was es mit Fachbegriffen wie «Byte», «Font» oder «CD-ROM» auf sich hat. Jede Seite enthält wertvolle Informationen. Die erklärenden Illustrationen lockern nicht nur den Stoff auf, sondern machen das Fachbuch zu einer angenehmen und kurzweiligen Lektüre. Komplexe Zusammenhänge werden verständlich. Was Sie lesen, können Sie sofort in die Praxis umsetzen.
Auf der beiliegenden CD-ROM finden Sie ausgesuchte Programme, Bilder, Schreibtischhintergründe, Töne, Schriften und Icons, mit denen Sie Ihren neuen Computer erkunden und nach Ihrem Geschmack einrichten können.

1500 Tips und Tricks für den Macintosh

**Beeindrucken Sie Ihre Freunde!**
Das SmartBook «1500 Tips und Tricks für den Macintosh» ist die geballteste Ladung an Tips, die je für den Macintosh erschienen ist!
**Die Standardlektüre für jeden Mac-User!**

Thomas Maschke
**1500 Tips und Tricks für den Macintosh**
688 Seiten mit CD-ROM
ISBN: 3-908488-32-X
sFr. 78.–/DM 89.–/öS 650.–

8 Bücher für Macintosh

**Dieses Buch setzt einen Standard in Sachen Hilfe zur Selbsthilfe, Support und Wissen um Ihren Lieblingscomputer.**

Thomas Maschke
**Erste Hilfe für den Macintosh**
736 Seiten mit CD-ROM
ISBN: 3-908488-31-1
sFr. 78.–/DM 89.–/öS 650.–

Fast alle möglichen und unmöglichen Probleme, die mit der Nutzung eines Macintosh auftreten können, werden hier behandelt.
Zeigen Sie Ihrem Macintosh, wo's langgeht, treiben Sie ihm immer wiederkehrende Systemfehler und andere Marotten aus.
Wie macht man einen Power Macintosh schneller, wie behebt man SCSI-Probleme, was ist zu tun, wenn lästige Viren einem das Leben schwer machen? Dieses Werk weiss Rat!
Ob es sich um Datenrettung, Systemabstürze, PostScript-Fehler oder eben Virenattacken handelt – mit «Erste Hilfe für den Macintosh» haben Sie einen kompetenten Berater und verschiedene Werkzeuge (auf der CD-ROM) zur Hand, die Sie von Hilfe unabhängig machen, die von aussen kommen sollte, doch nie kommen wird.

Erste Hilfe für den Macintosh

**Auf der CD-ROM**
befinden sich über 200 wertvolle Programme und Werkzeuge, die Ihnen in praktisch jeder Situation aus der Patsche helfen. Nicht länger zögern: Kaufen! Dieses Buch amortisiert sich sofort und gehört neben jeden Computer! Es ist ein Muss für wissbegierige Einsteiger, Fortgeschrittene und selbst für Profis.

Das Buch zu Mac OS 8
Produktiver mit System 8 - so wird's gemacht

**«Das Buch zu MacOS8 – mehr Spass und Effizienz mit System 8!»**
Aus der Feder von Bestseller-Autor Thomas Maschke: Das grosse Buch zum grossen Wurf von Apple. Der Autor zeigt Ihnen, wie Sie das System von der ersten Minute an perfekt nutzen. Schritt für Schritt führt er Sie durch Installation und Anpassung zum perfekten Einsatz, so dass Sie sofort produktiv sind. Was ist neu, was ist besser? Er verrät haufenweise Tips und Tricks (vor allem solche, die nicht im Handbuch stehen), erklärt den Umgang mit den Schlüsseltechnologien und zeigt Modifikationsmöglichkeiten auf.

Thomas Maschke NEU
**Das Buch zu MacOS8**
Produktiver mit System 8
– so wird's gemacht
224 Seiten • ISBN: 3-908488-41-9
sFr. 45.–/DM 49.–/öS 358.–

- Sparen Sie Geld und Zeit!
- Arbeiten Sie noch besser und schneller!
- Wir wünschen Ihnen viel Spass mit Ihrem System 8!

Bücher für Macintosh 9

## Computer Software

MAXIS CL, CW: Maxis AD, D: Jack Anderson D: David Bates / John Anicker P: Dave Crozier DF: Hornall Anderson Design Works USA 1994 *SIZE: 213×137*

## Multimedia

ŒIL POUR ŒIL CL: œil Pour œil CD, AD, D: Jean-Jacques Tachdjian DF: i comme image 1996 *SIZE: 210×101, 200×200, 210×210*

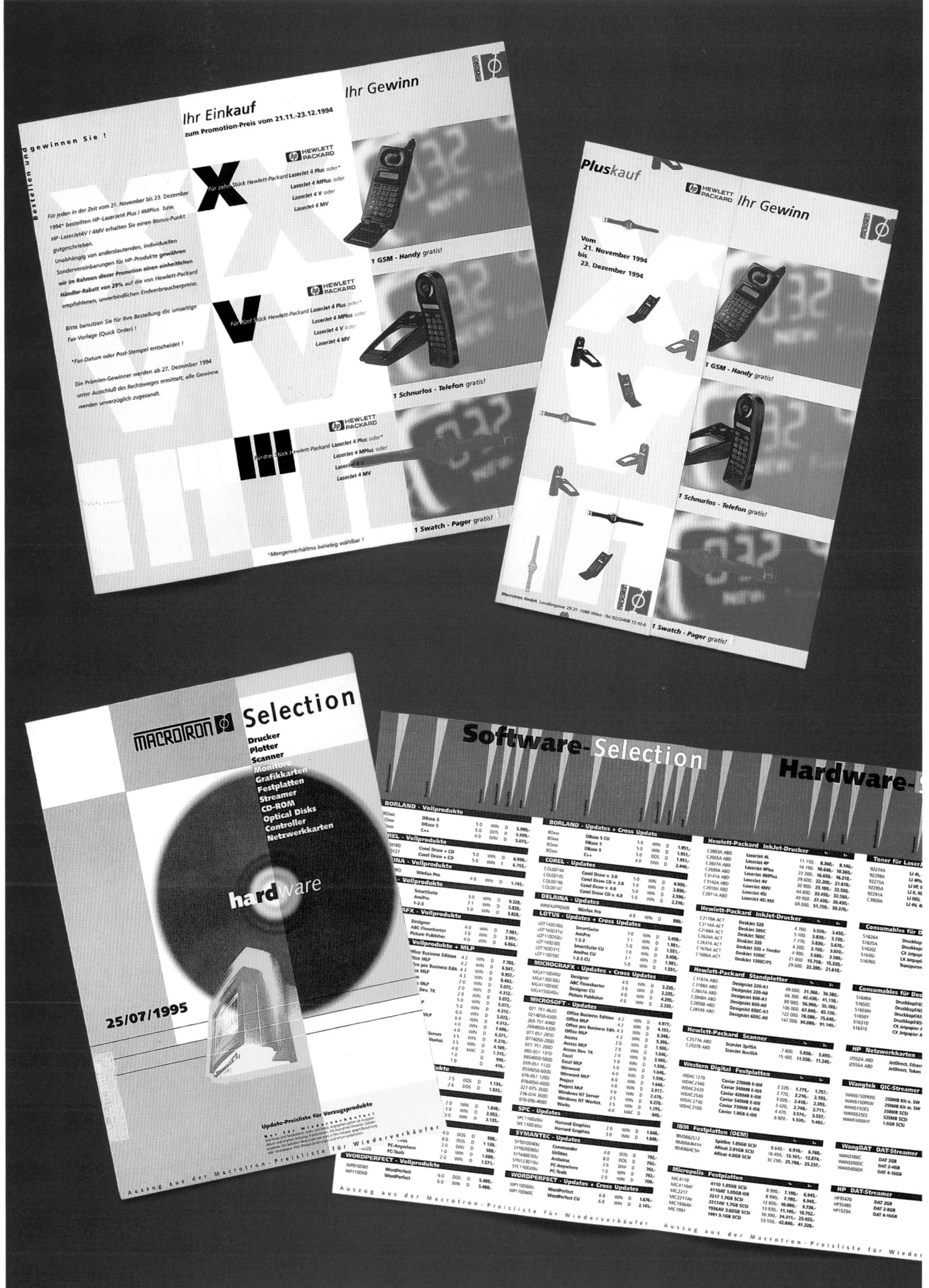


## Computers

MACROTRON CL: Macrotron Austria CD, AD, D: Lothar Ämilian Heinzle DF: Atelier Heinzle Austria 1995 *SIZE: 296×209, 296×140*

ACCESS THE FULL POWER OF YOUR TOOLS SO YOU CAN GET YOUR JOB DONE

▸ The New Microsoft Office Suite ◂

Send The Office Catalog to an Associate or Friend–

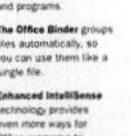

See your retailer today or call: (800) OFFICE95

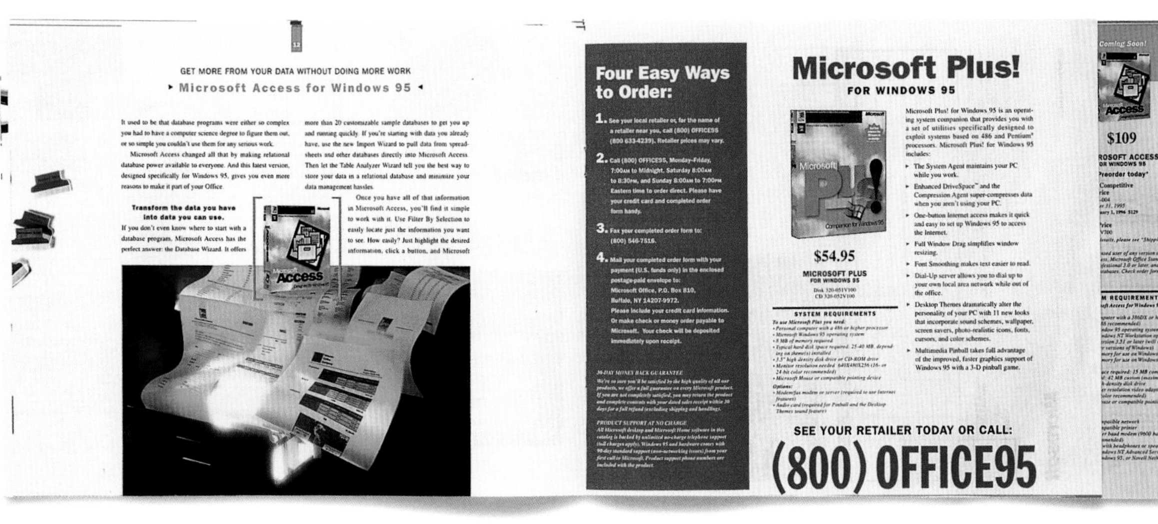


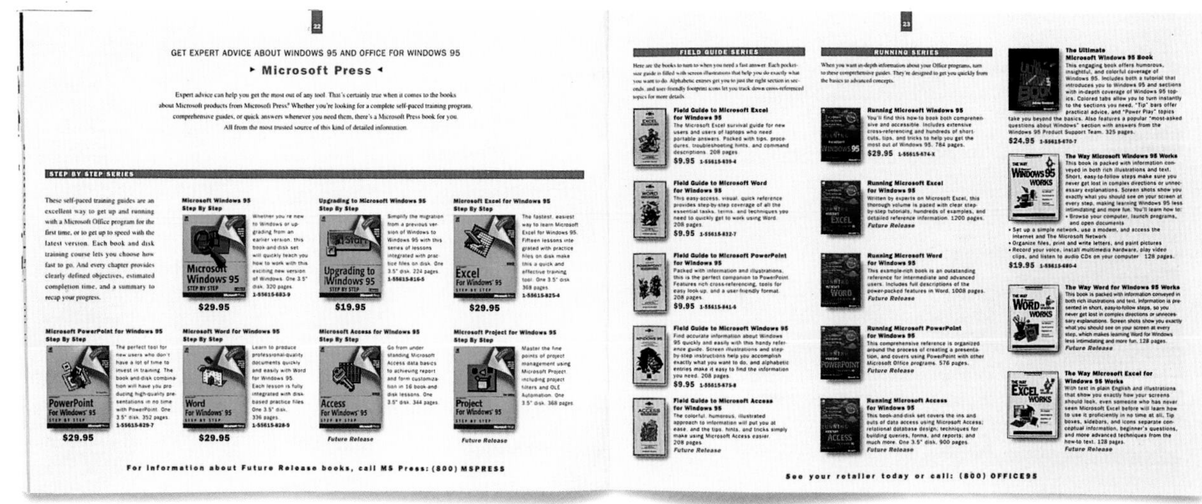

## Computer Software

MICROSOFT WINDOWS CL: Microsoft Corporation AD, D: John Hornall D: Larry Anderson / Debra Hampton / Eulah Sheffield P: Darrell Peterson CW: Jeff Fraga DF: Hornall Anderson Design Works USA 1995 *SIZE: 217×278*

# business

fonts

paper samples

medical

business services

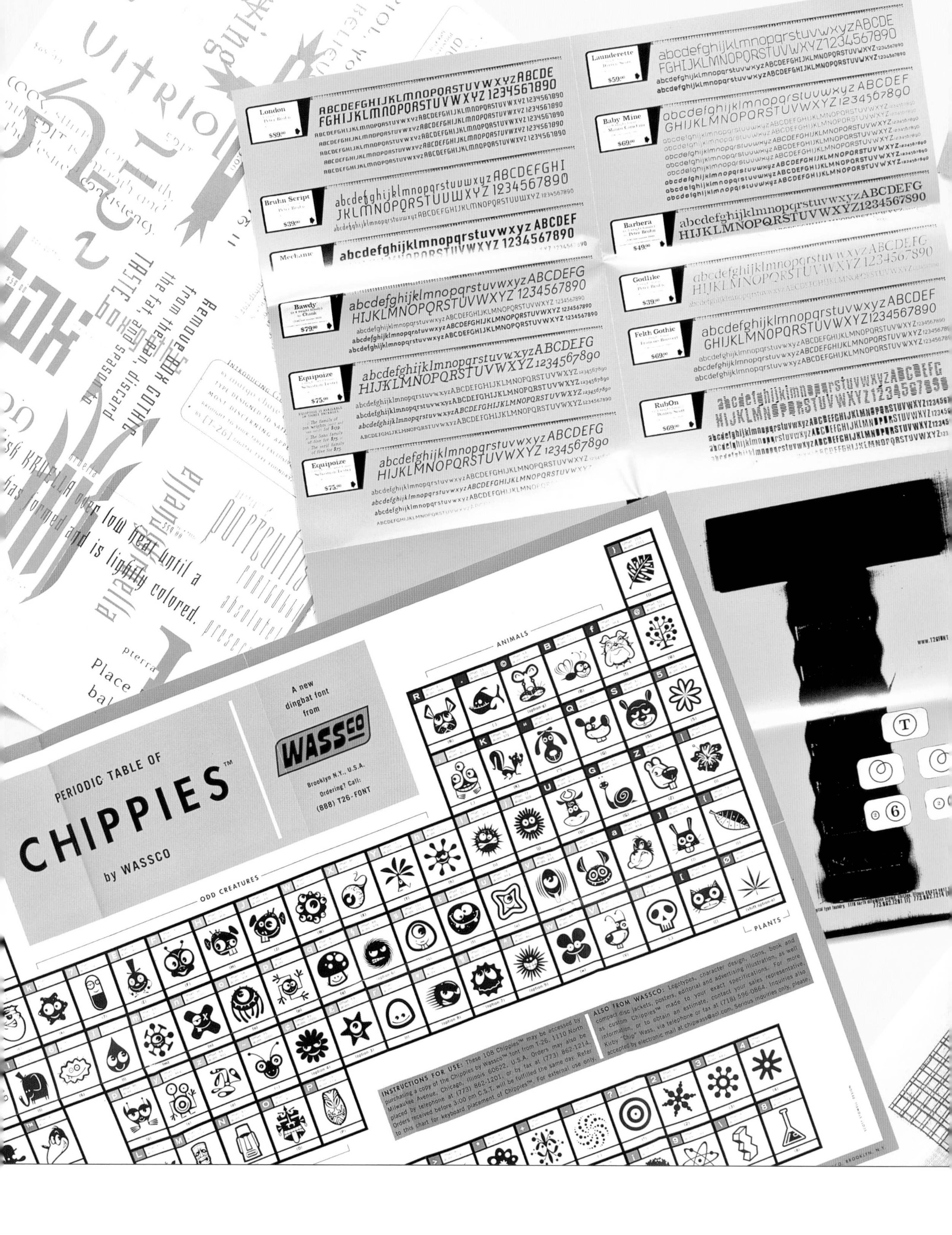

PERIODIC TABLE OF
CHIPPIES™
by WASSCO
A new dingbat font from
WASSCO
Brooklyn N.Y., U.S.A.
Ordering? Call:
(888) T26-FONT
ANIMALS
ODD CREATURES
PLANTS
London
Bruhn Script
Mechanic
Bawdy
Equipoize
Launderette
Baby Mine
Barbera
Godlike
Felth Gothic
RubOn

**Fonts**

[T-26] CL: [T-26] Digital Type Foundry CD, AD, D, CW: Carlos Segura DF: Segura Inc. USA 1998 *SIZE: 266×176, 203×130*

## Fonts

2REBELS CL: 2Rebels / Font Shop CD, D, P: Denis Dulude CD, D: Fabrizio Gilardino P: Pol Baril
CW: Michel Loslier DF: 2Rebels Canada 1997 *SIZE: 297×140*

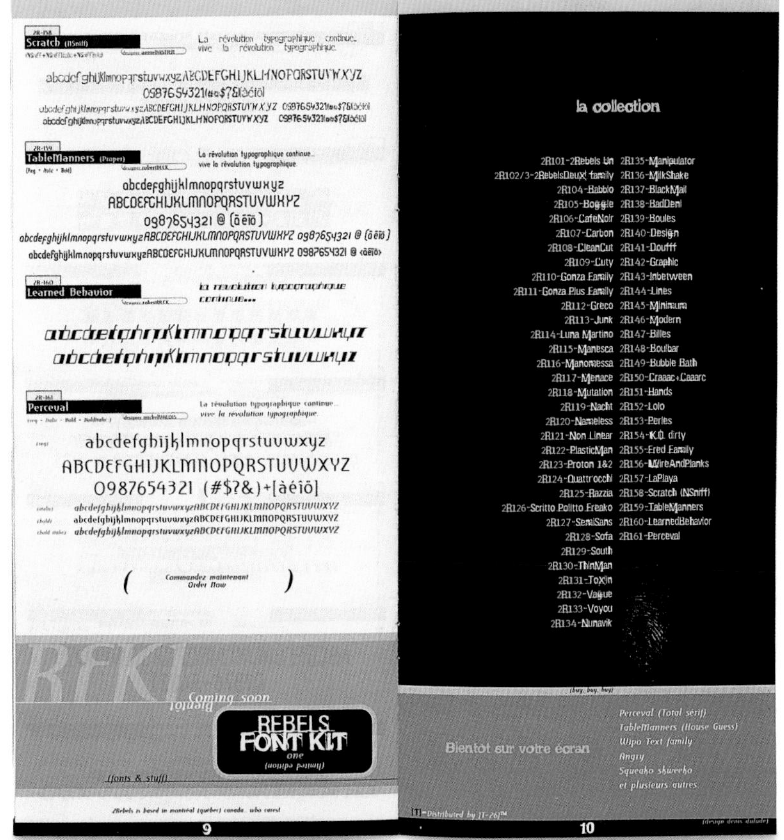


## Fonts

2REBELS @ FONTSHOP CL: FontShop AD, DF: 2Rebels Canada 1996 *SIZE: 297×140*

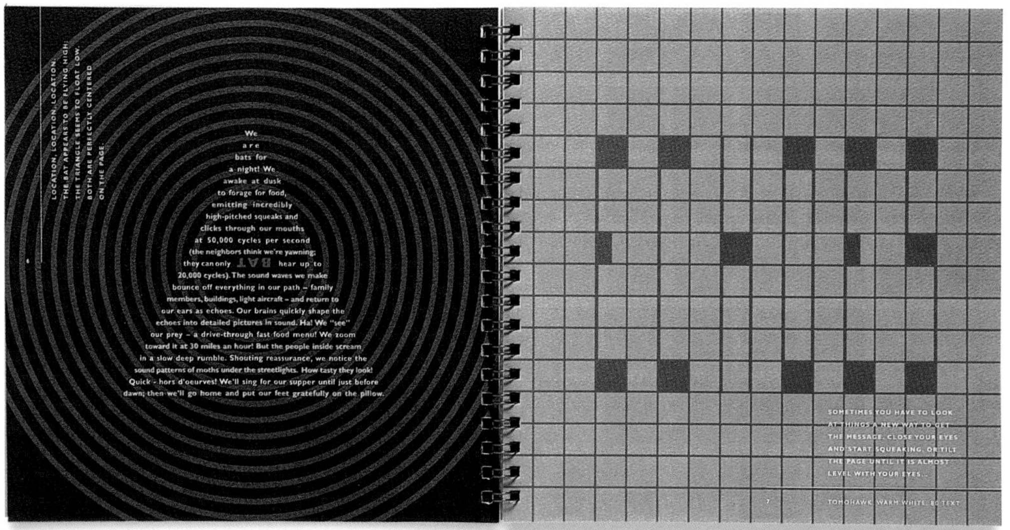
LOCATION, LOCATION, LOCATION.
THE BAT APPEARS TO BE FLYING HIGH;
THE TRIANGLE SEEMS TO FLOAT LOW.
BOTH ARE PERFECTLY CENTERED
ON THE PAGE.
We are bats for a night! We awake at dusk to forage for food, emitting incredibly high-pitched squeaks and clicks through our mouths at 50,000 cycles per second (the neighbors think we're yawning; they can only BAT hear up to 20,000 cycles). The sound waves we make bounce off everything in our path – family members, buildings, light aircraft – and return to our ears as echoes. Our brains quickly shape the echoes into detailed pictures in sound. Ha! We "see" our prey – a drive-through fast food menu! We zoom toward it at 30 miles an hour! But the people inside scream in a slow deep rumble. Shouting reassurance, we notice the sound patterns of moths under the streetlights. How tasty they look! Quick - hors d'oeurves! We'll sing for our supper until just before dawn; then we'll go home and put our feet gratefully on the pillow.
SOMETIMES YOU HAVE TO LOOK AT THINGS A NEW WAY TO GET THE MESSAGE. CLOSE YOUR EYES AND START SQUEAKING, OR TILT THE PAGE UNTIL IT IS ALMOST LEVEL WITH YOUR EYES...
TOMOHAWK WARM WHITE, 80 TEXT

12
BITTER'S BEST EXPERIENCED IN TINY HELPINGS. PILLS. SHREDS OF ZEST. THE MEMORY OF THE ONE WHO SAID, "YOUR TASTE IS IN YOUR MOUTH."
13
MOHAWK SATIN, COOL WHITE, 80 TEXT
SWEET
"HEY COOKIE!" "GIMME SOME SUGAR!" "THAT'S MY NEW DO YOU'RE FLUFFIN', YOU SLY LITTLE MUFFIN!"
"GOTTA RUN, HONEYBUN!"
"BYE, BYE, SWEETIE PIE!"

Our skin feels hot, cold, pressure and pain.
Why do we say we are touched by our emotions?

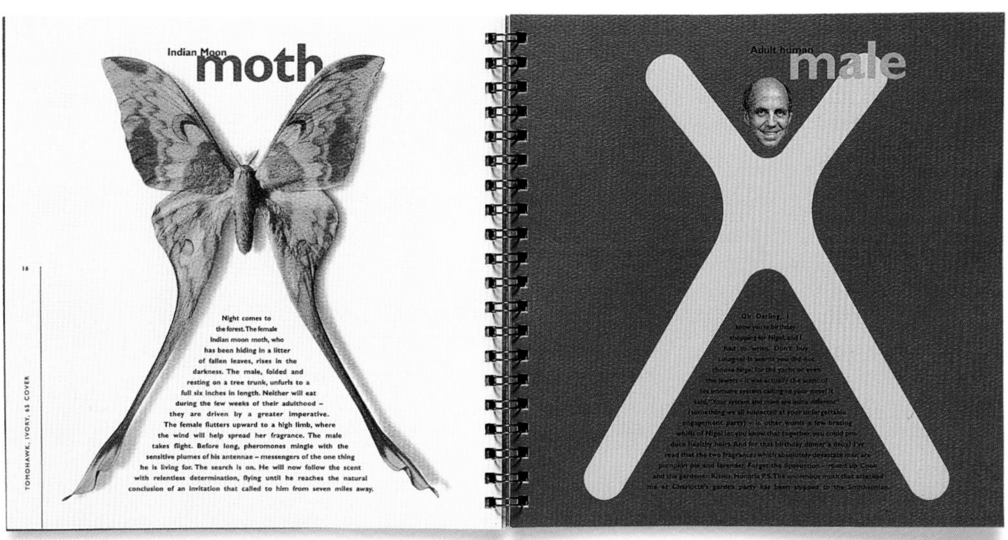


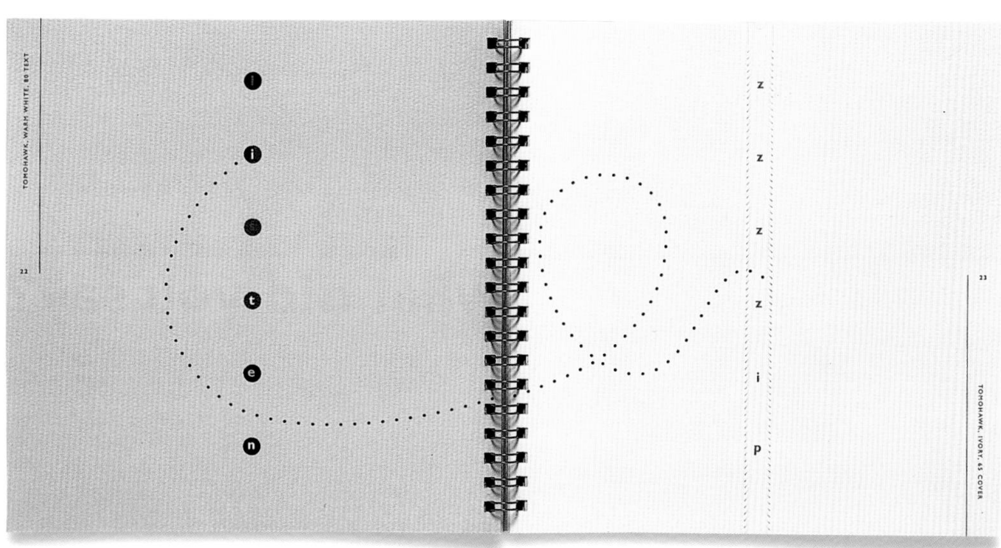


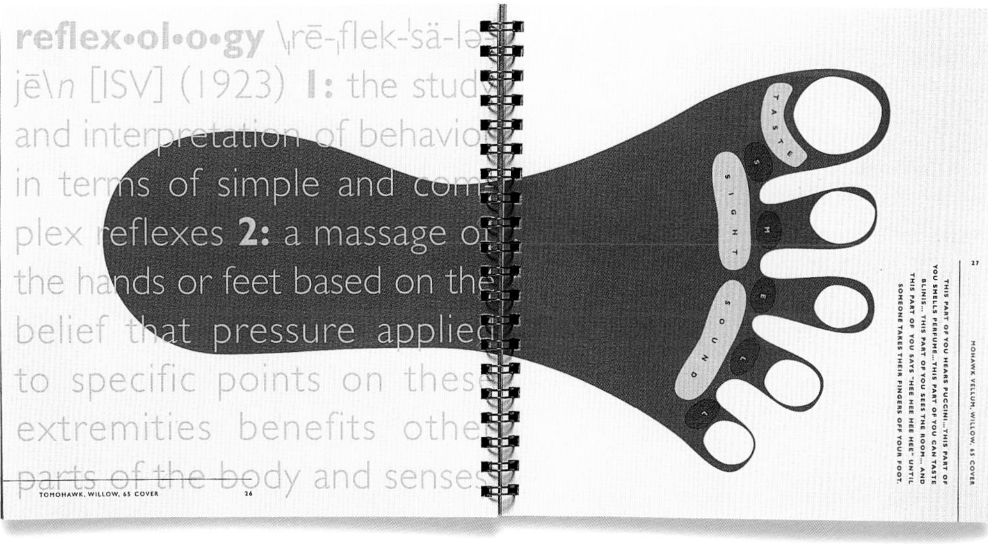


**Specialty Papers**

MOHAWK PAPER MILLS CL: Mohawk Paper Mills AD, D: Jack Anderson / Lisa Cerveny D: Mary Hermes / Jana Nishi / Jana Wilson P: Tom Collicott I: Dave Julian CW: Suky Hutton DF: Hornall Anderson Design Works, Inc. USA 1998 *SIZE: 178×178*

What makes
sense

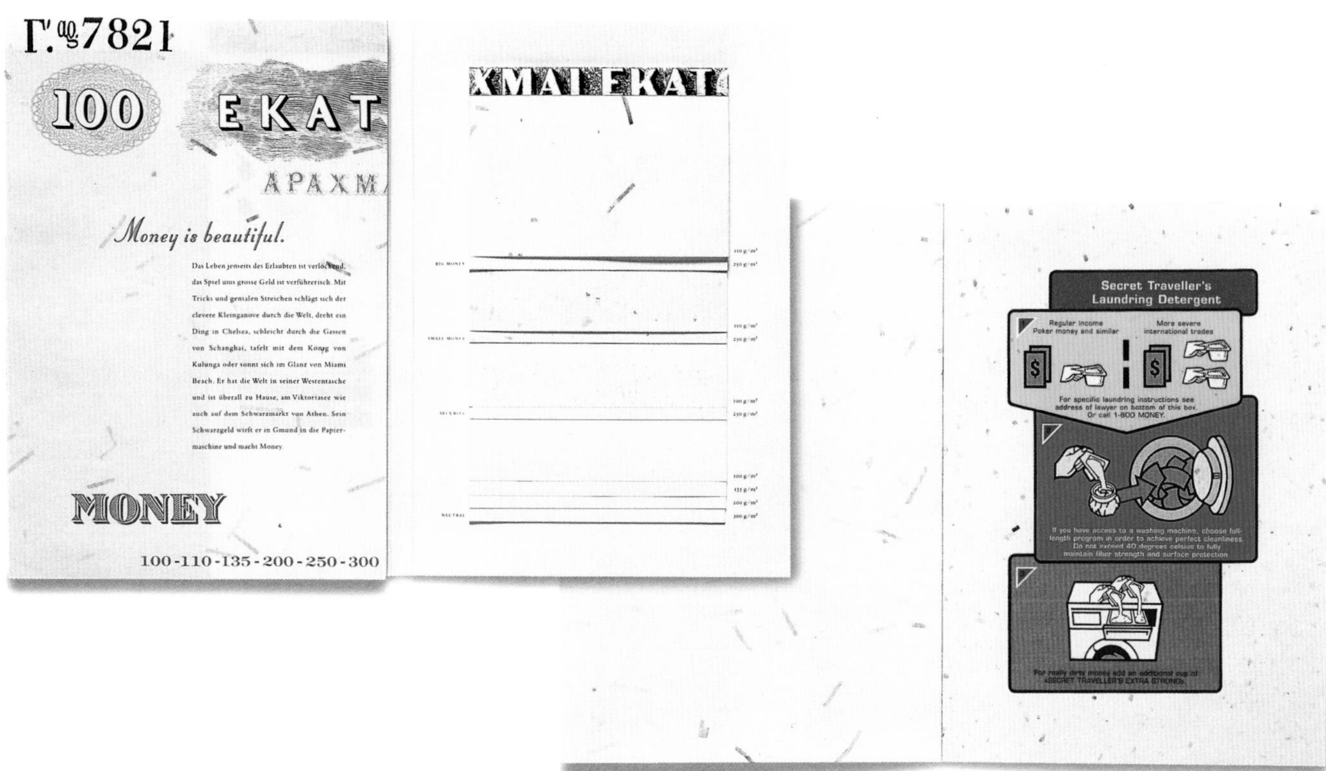


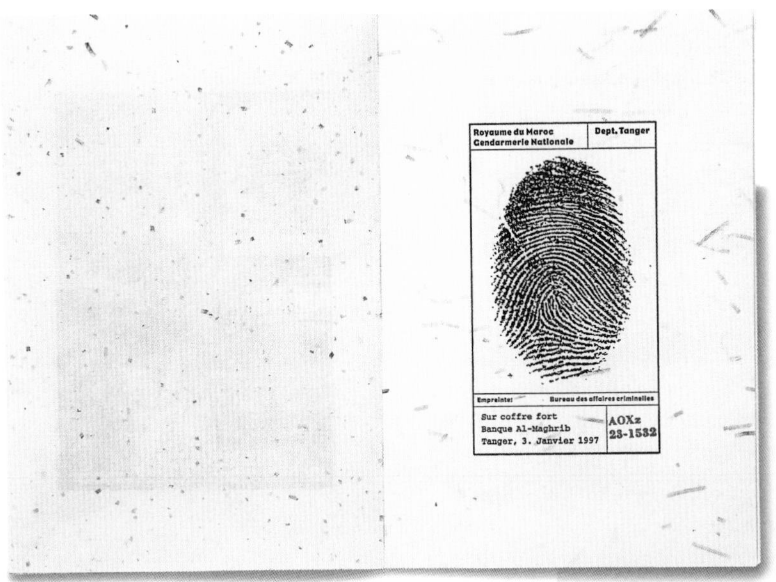

## Paper

GMUND CL: Büttenpapierfabrik Gmund CD, AD, D: Lucia Frey / Heinz Wild P: Henny Garfunkel / Michael Martin / Pascal Wüest
DF: Wild & Frey Switzerland 1997 *SIZE: 210×150*

## Giftwrapping Paper

STEWO CL: Stewo AG CD, AD, D: Lucia Frey / Heinz Wild P: Frank Tomio CW: Daniel Müller
DF: Wild & Frey Switzerland 1995 *SIZE: 304×219*

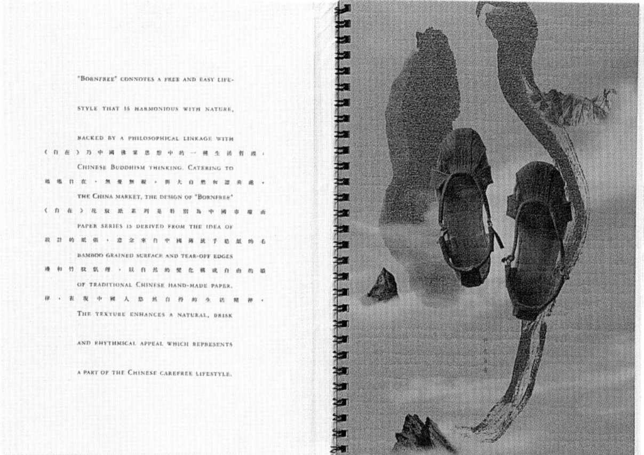

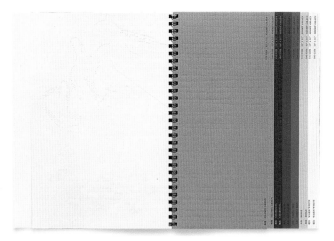

## Paper

BORNFREE RECYCLED PAPER CL: Tokushu Paper Mfg Co Ltd. CD, AD, D, Chinese Ink Illustration: Kan Tai-keung AD, D: Eddy Yu Chi Kong D, I: Benson Kwun / Leung Wai Yin P: C K Wong I: John Tam Seal Engraving: Yip Man Yam Chinese Calligraphy: Yip Man-Yam / Chui Tze-Hung / Yung Ho-Yin DF: Kan & Lau Design Consultants Hong Kong 1997 *SIZE: 247×177*

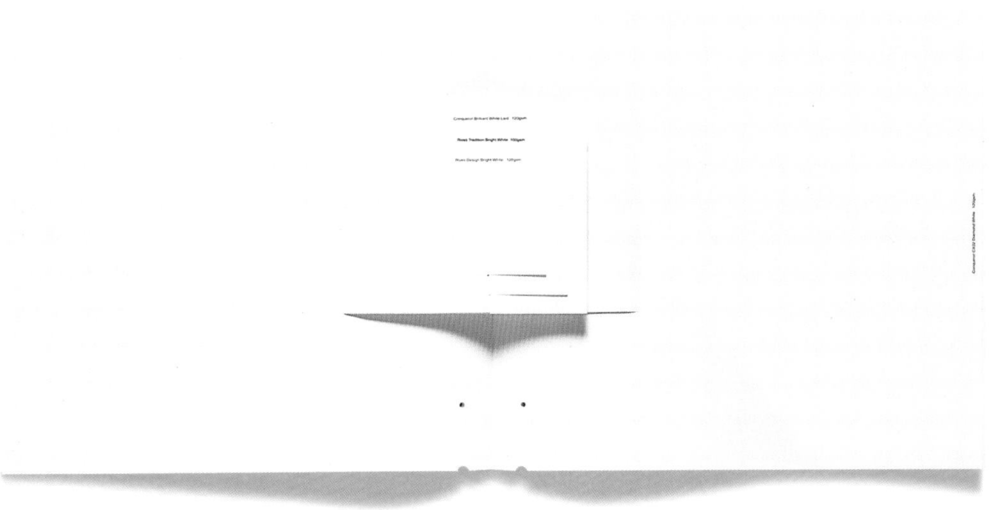

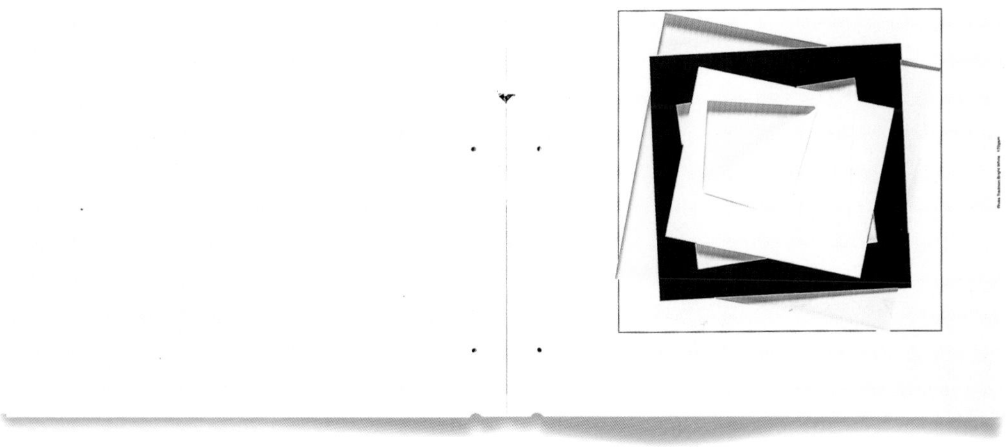

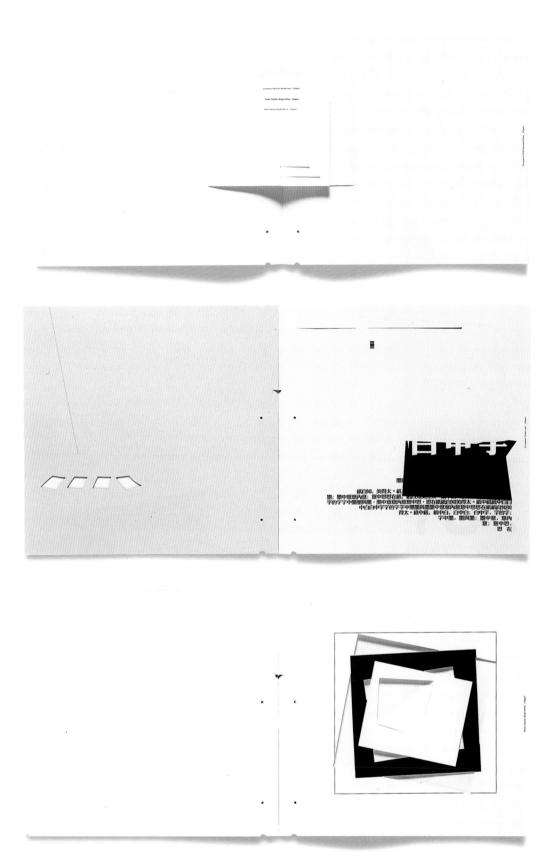

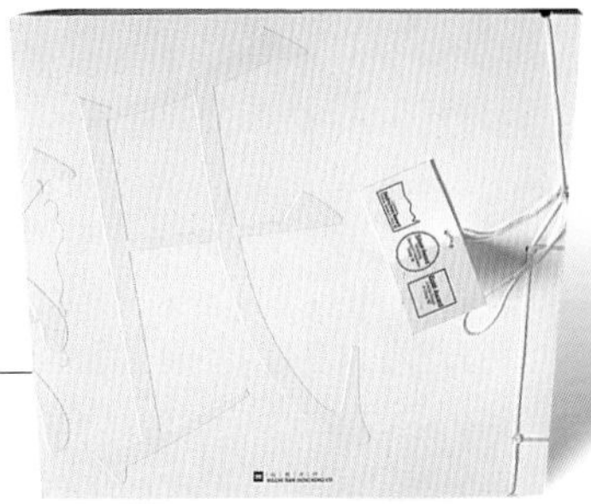

**Paper**

WIGGINS TEAPE CL: Wiggins Teape Ltd. D, CW: Esther Kit-Lin Liu Hong Kong 1996 *SIZE: 244×260*

Dear Diary,
On my first day here I was blinded by Artica's pristine beauty. But after a couple more days, I'm starting to notice the details that make the country unique, like the Artica seal I photographed, and realize now that Artica is much more varied than my first impression suggested.
As I write this I'm starting to notice the incredible variety in the white landscape. Good thing too. There's a lot of white in Artica!
Artica is available in both, 84 bright Artica Copy and 90 bright Artica Laser.
Notes
Dear Diary,
Summer was too brief. I saw this iceberg on the horizon today. Even though it means winter will be here soon, it is majestic.
Artica is vast. I focus on the monumental views and often forget to look at what's right in front of my nose, like these ice crystals. Each one is perfect. Billions of crystals, each one different, each one perfect.
Careful attention to detail ensures Artica's consistent high quality.
Notes

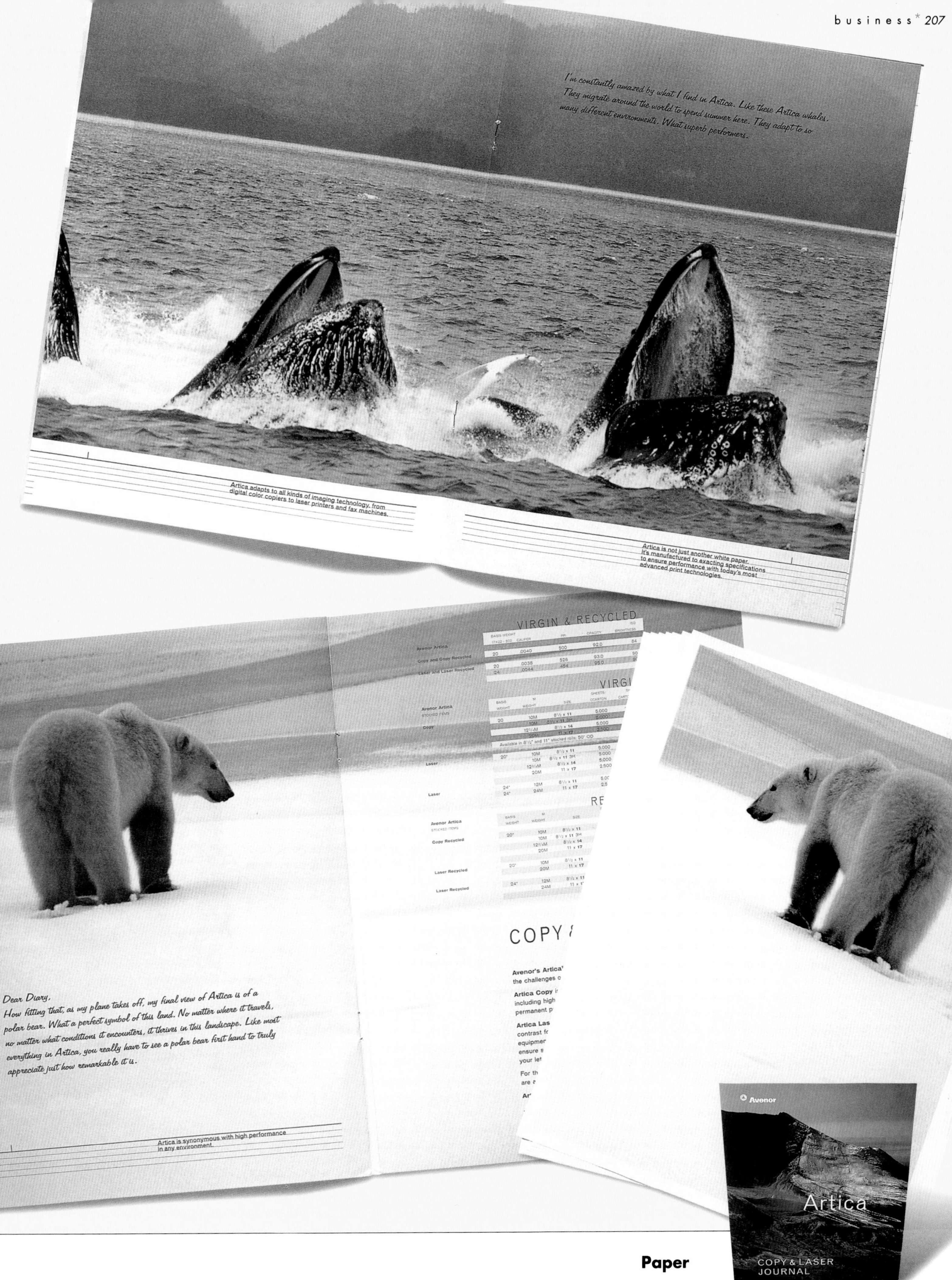
I'm constantly amazed by what I find in Artica. Like these Artica whales. They migrate around the world to spend summer here. They adapt to so many different environments. What superb performers.
Artica adapts to all kinds of imaging technology, from digital color copiers to laser printers and fax machines.
Artica is not just another white paper. It's manufactured to exacting specifications to ensure performance with today's most advanced print technologies.
VIRGIN & RECYCLED
COPY
Dear Diary,
How fitting that, as my plane takes off, my final view of Artica is of a polar bear. What a perfect symbol of this land. No matter where it travels, no matter what conditions it encounters, it thrives in this landscape. Like most everything in Artica, you really have to see a polar bear first hand to truly appreciate just how remarkable it is.
Artica is synonymous with high performance in any environment.
Avenor
Artica
COPY & LASER
JOURNAL

## Paper

**AVENOR ARTICA** CL: Avenor Inc. CD, AD, D: Roslyn Eskind D: Gary Mansbridge / Heike Sillaste P: Malcom Waddell / Stock Photography CW: Kelvin Browne DF: Roslyn Eskind Associates Ltd. Canada 1998 *SIZE: 292×224*

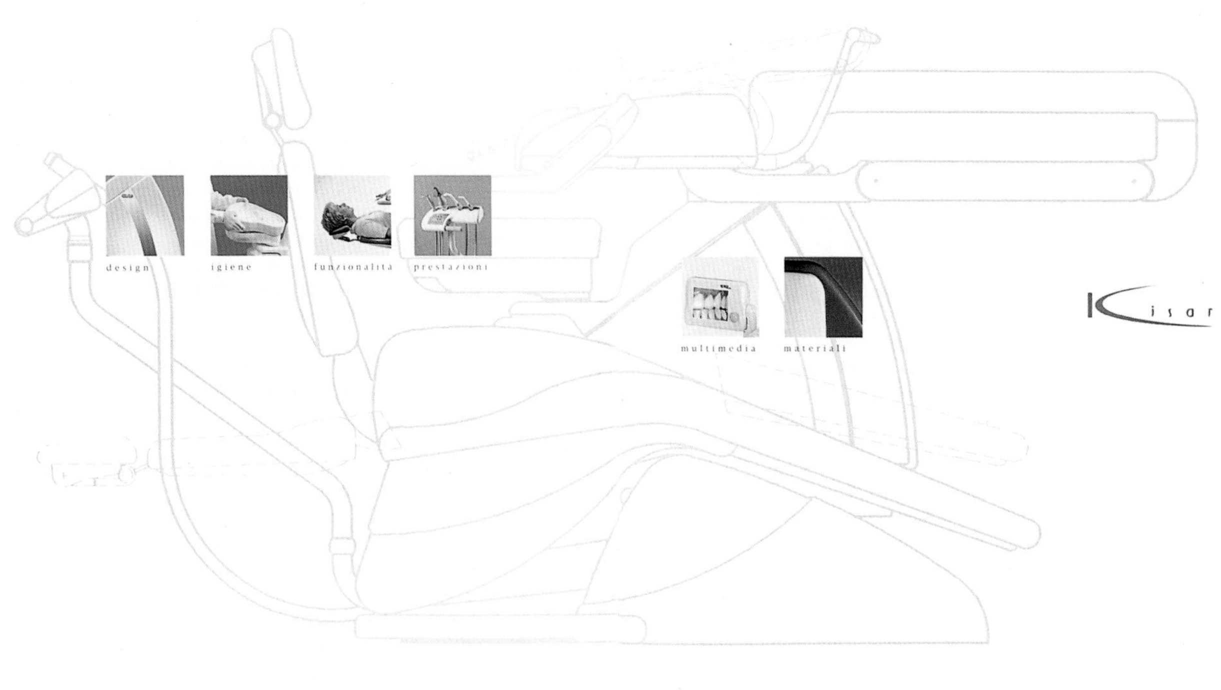


1

d e s i g n

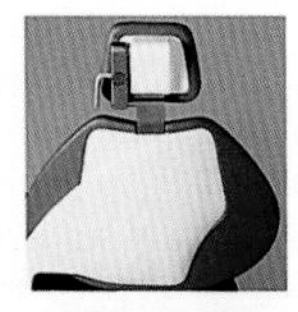

Da tempo ormai tutti consideriamo il design un valore. Abbiamo scoperto che anche prodotti impensabili potevano essere belli e che vivere e lavorare vicino a cose belle migliora la qualità della vita. Il riunito è forse il compagno di lavoro più importante nella vita professionale di un odontoiatra. Oltre ad essere necessario per lo svolgimento della pratica clinica quotidiana, è l'oggetto al fianco del quale si passa la maggior parte del tempo, è lo strumento che qualifica ed identifica il prestigio dello studio, è il bene strumentale che accompagna il vostro lavoro e quello dei vostri collaboratori per molti anni. A tutto questo abbiamo pensato progettando KISAR, e per essere sicuri che il risultato fosse ottimale, gli spunti creativi li abbiamo colti dalla natura. Per la sua affidabilità ed il livello tecnologico ormai raggiunto, la vita media dei riunito continua ad allungarsi ed è per questo che abbiamo voluto darvi oltre alle prestazioni, funzionalità e caratteristiche che potevate desiderare, anche un riunito che fosse bello!

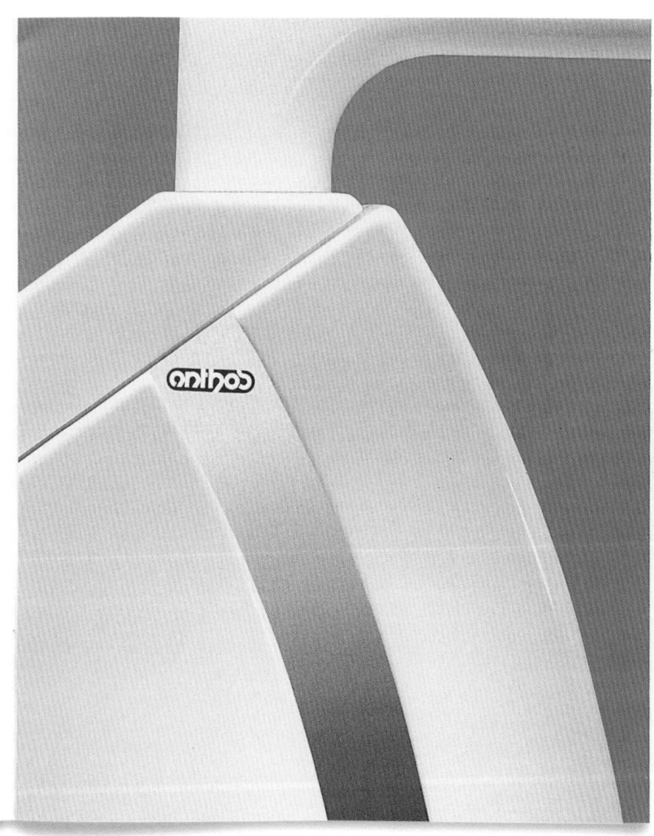

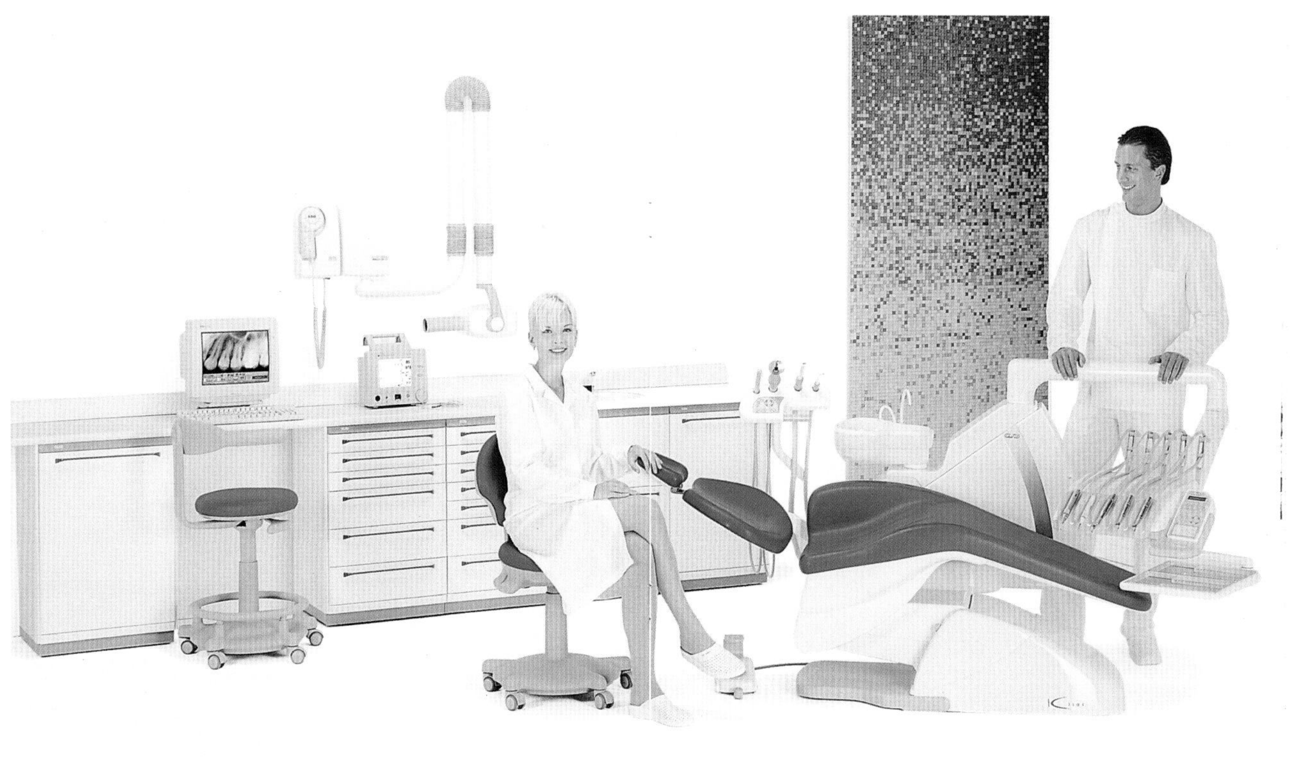

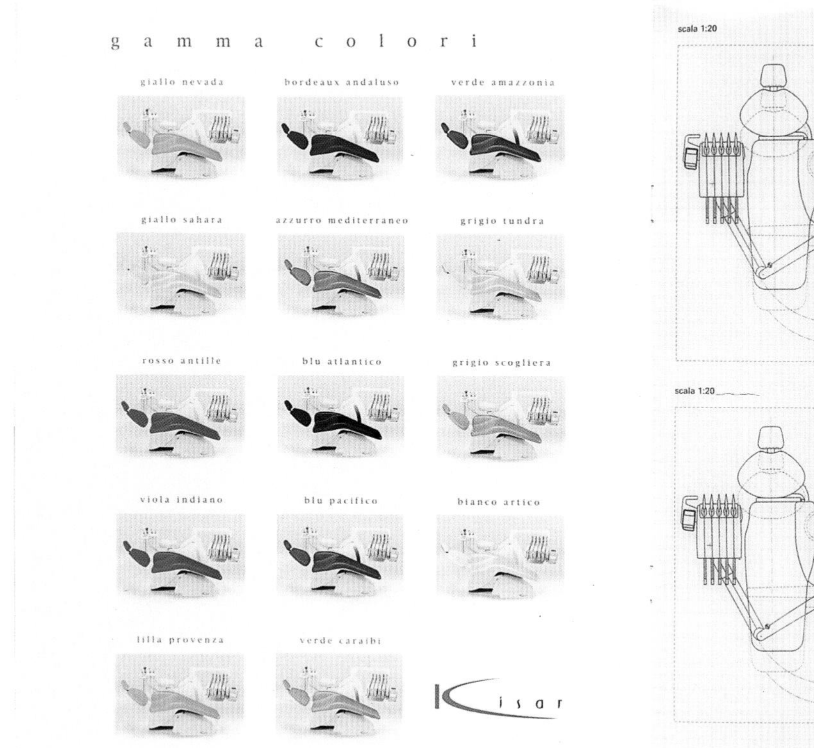


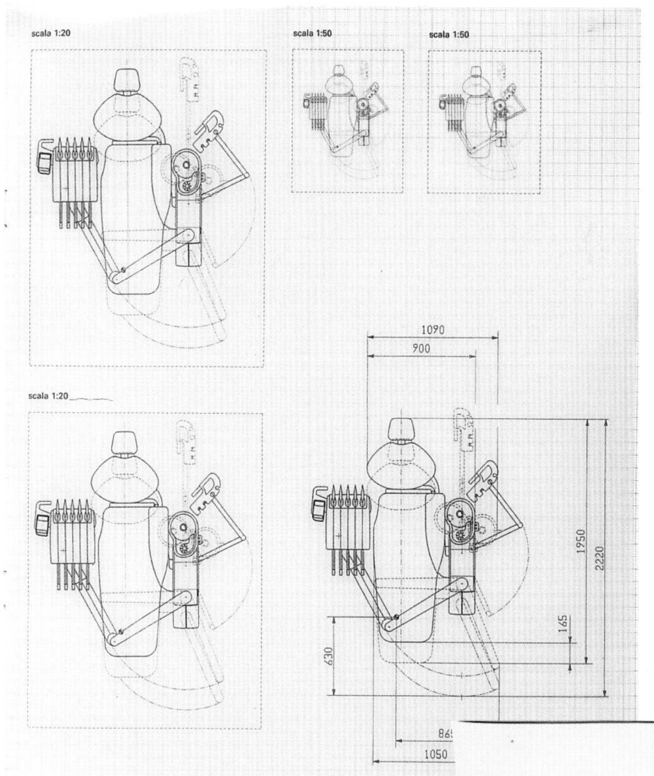


## Dental Tools & Equipment

KISAR CL: Cir Anthos CD, AD, D, DF: Kuni-Graphic Design Company Italy 1997 *SIZE: 310×260*

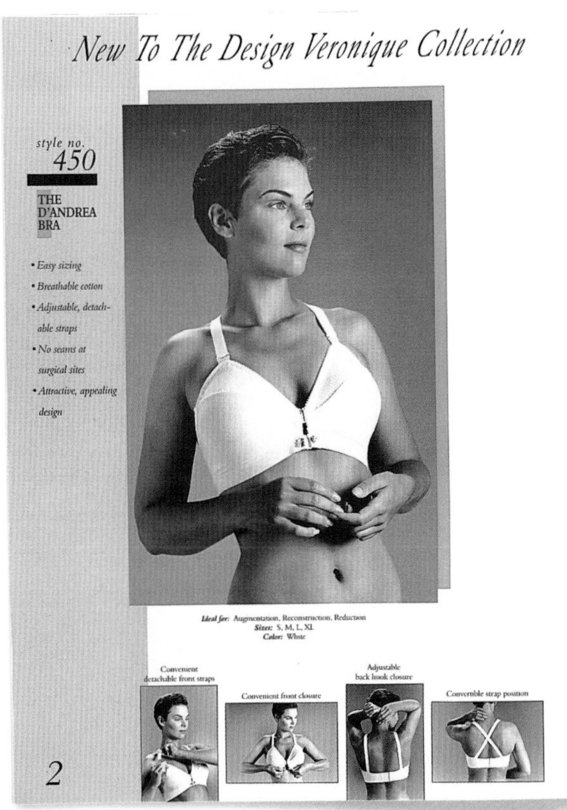

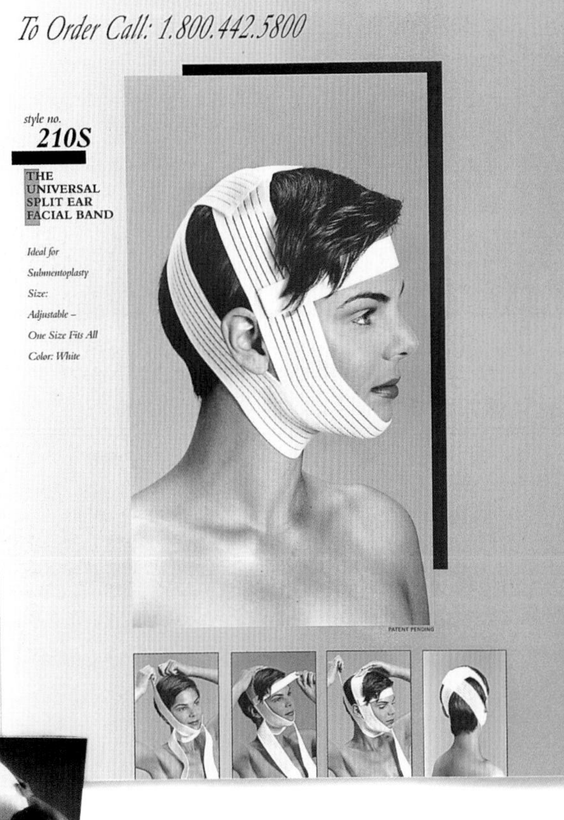


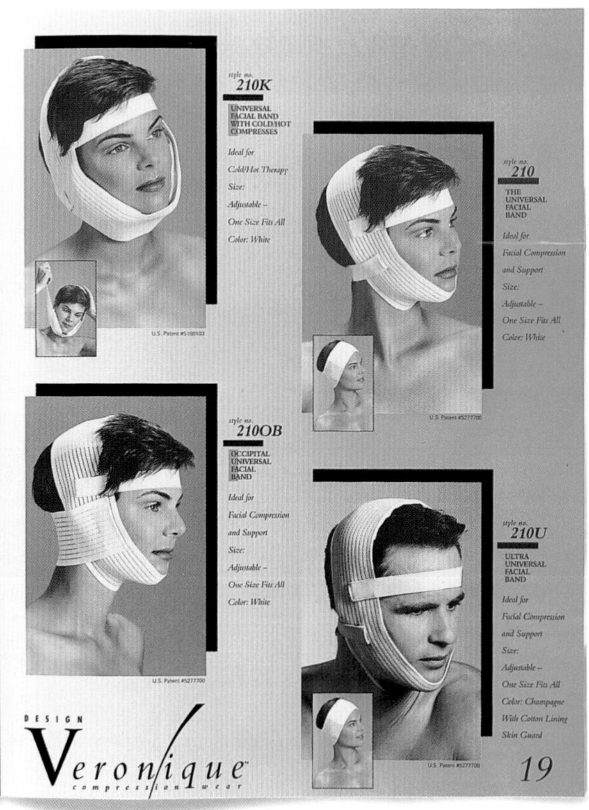

## Surgical Garments

DESIGN VERONIQUE CL: Design Veronique CD, AD, D: Jaime Aguinaldo / Steven Isakson
DF: Image Nation Design Group USA 1997 *SIZE: 280×216*

## International Courier Service

FEDEX CANADA CL: Federal Express Canada CD: Claude Dumoulin D: Dan Wheaton I: Michael Martchenko CW: Bob Snow / Wayne Tindall DF: The Riordon Design Group Inc. Canada 1997 *SIZE: 280×215*

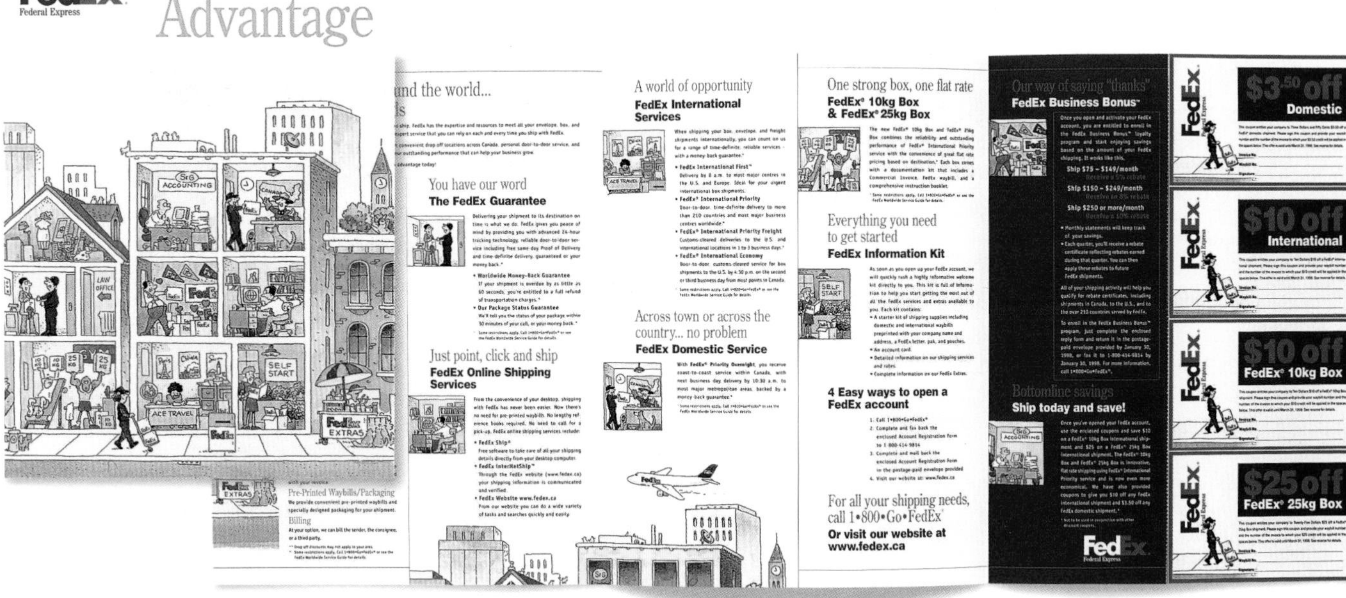


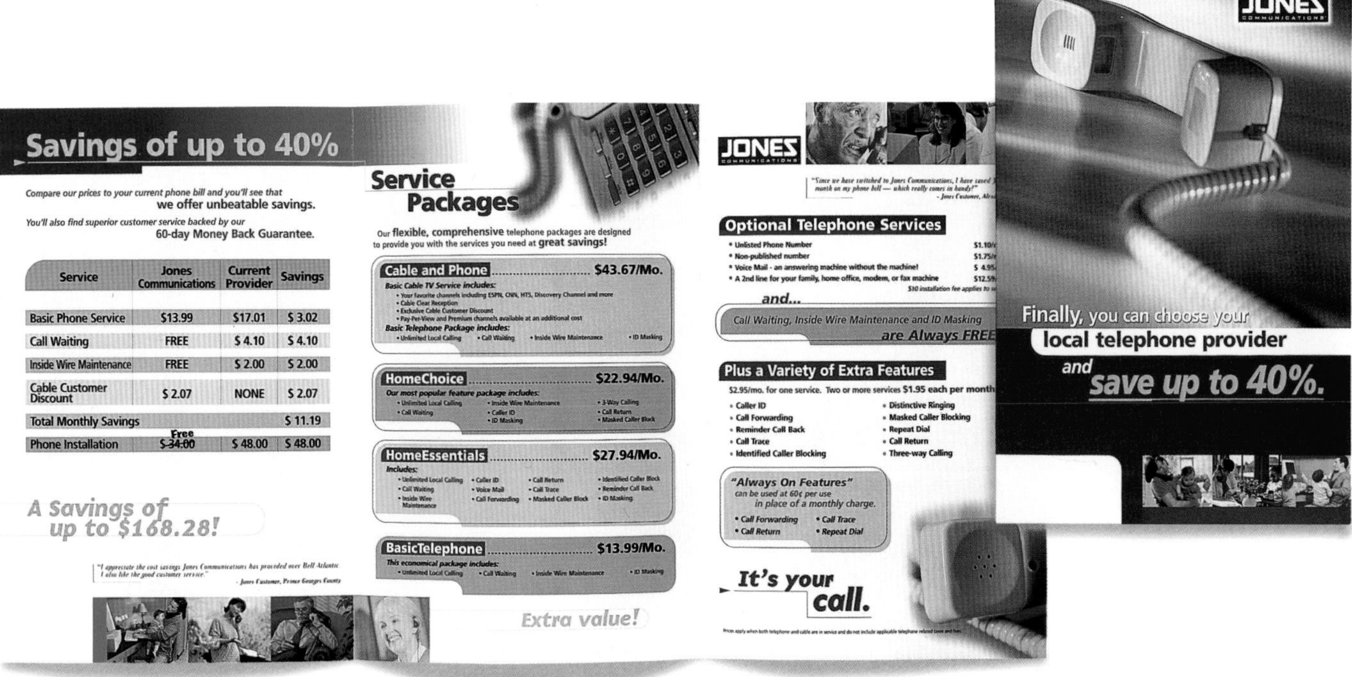


## Telecommunications Services

JONES CL: Jones Communications AD, D: Wicky W. Lee D: Katrina Mansfield DF: D4 Creative Group USA 1998 *SIZE: 229×152*

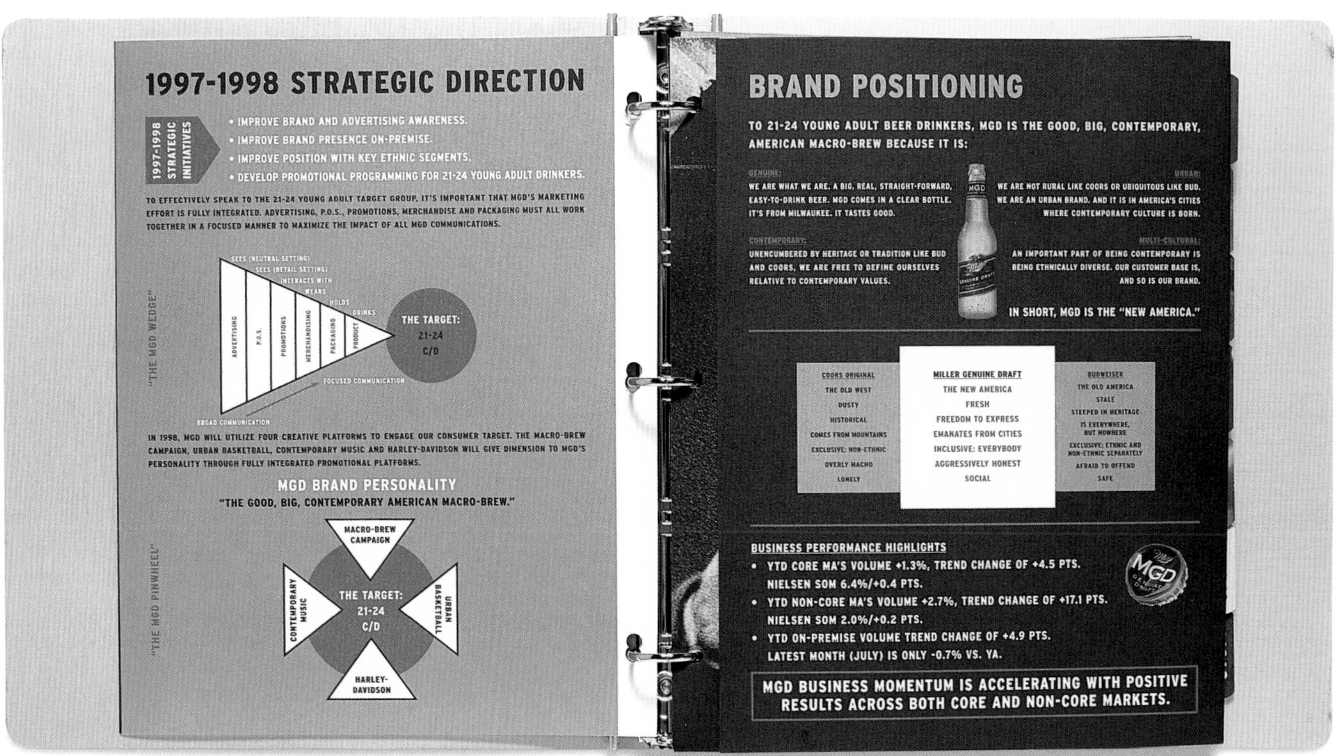
1997-1998 STRATEGIC DIRECTION
1997-1998 STRATEGIC INITIATIVES
• IMPROVE BRAND AND ADVERTISING AWARENESS.
• IMPROVE BRAND PRESENCE ON-PREMISE.
• IMPROVE POSITION WITH KEY ETHNIC SEGMENTS.
• DEVELOP PROMOTIONAL PROGRAMMING FOR 21-24 YOUNG ADULT DRINKERS.
TO EFFECTIVELY SPEAK TO THE 21-24 YOUNG ADULT TARGET GROUP, IT'S IMPORTANT THAT MGD'S MARKETING EFFORT IS FULLY INTEGRATED. ADVERTISING, P.O.S., PROMOTIONS, MERCHANDISE AND PACKAGING MUST ALL WORK TOGETHER IN A FOCUSED MANNER TO MAXIMIZE THE IMPACT OF ALL MGD COMMUNICATIONS.
"THE MGD WEDGE"
SEES (NEUTRAL SETTING)
SEES (RETAIL SETTING)
INTERACTS WITH
WEARS
HOLDS
DRINKS
ADVERTISING
P.O.S.
PROMOTIONS
MERCHANDISING
PACKAGING
PRODUCT
THE TARGET: 21-24 C/D
FOCUSED COMMUNICATION
BROAD COMMUNICATION
IN 1998, MGD WILL UTILIZE FOUR CREATIVE PLATFORMS TO ENGAGE OUR CONSUMER TARGET. THE MACRO-BREW CAMPAIGN, URBAN BASKETBALL, CONTEMPORARY MUSIC AND HARLEY-DAVIDSON WILL GIVE DIMENSION TO MGD'S PERSONALITY THROUGH FULLY INTEGRATED PROMOTIONAL PLATFORMS.
MGD BRAND PERSONALITY
"THE GOOD, BIG, CONTEMPORARY AMERICAN MACRO-BREW."
"THE MGD PINWHEEL"
MACRO-BREW CAMPAIGN
CONTEMPORARY MUSIC
THE TARGET: 21-24 C/D
URBAN BASKETBALL
HARLEY-DAVIDSON
BRAND POSITIONING
TO 21-24 YOUNG ADULT BEER DRINKERS, MGD IS THE GOOD, BIG, CONTEMPORARY, AMERICAN MACRO-BREW BECAUSE IT IS:
GENUINE:
WE ARE WHAT WE ARE. A BIG, REAL, STRAIGHT-FORWARD, EASY-TO-DRINK BEER. MGD COMES IN A CLEAR BOTTLE. IT'S FROM MILWAUKEE. IT TASTES GOOD.
URBAN:
WE ARE NOT RURAL LIKE COORS OR UBIQUITOUS LIKE BUD. WE ARE AN URBAN BRAND. AND IT IS IN AMERICA'S CITIES WHERE CONTEMPORARY CULTURE IS BORN.
CONTEMPORARY:
UNENCUMBERED BY HERITAGE OR TRADITION LIKE BUD AND COORS, WE ARE FREE TO DEFINE OURSELVES RELATIVE TO CONTEMPORARY VALUES.
MULTI-CULTURAL:
AN IMPORTANT PART OF BEING CONTEMPORARY IS BEING ETHNICALLY DIVERSE. OUR CUSTOMER BASE IS, AND SO IS OUR BRAND.
IN SHORT, MGD IS THE "NEW AMERICA."
COORS ORIGINAL
THE OLD WEST
DUSTY
HISTORICAL
COMES FROM MOUNTAINS
EXCLUSIVE: NON-ETHNIC
OVERLY MACHO
LONELY
MILLER GENUINE DRAFT
THE NEW AMERICA
FRESH
FREEDOM TO EXPRESS
EMANATES FROM CITIES
INCLUSIVE: EVERYBODY
AGGRESSIVELY HONEST
SOCIAL
BUDWEISER
THE OLD AMERICA
STALE
STEEPED IN HERITAGE
IS EVERYWHERE, BUT NOWHERE
EXCLUSIVE: ETHNIC AND NON-ETHNIC SEPARATELY
AFRAID TO OFFEND
SAFE
BUSINESS PERFORMANCE HIGHLIGHTS
• YTD CORE MA'S VOLUME +1.3%, TREND CHANGE OF +4.5 PTS. NIELSEN SOM 6.4%/+0.4 PTS.
• YTD NON-CORE MA'S VOLUME +2.7%, TREND CHANGE OF +17.1 PTS. NIELSEN SOM 2.0%/+0.2 PTS.
• YTD ON-PREMISE VOLUME TREND CHANGE OF +4.9 PTS. LATEST MONTH (JULY) IS ONLY -0.7% VS. YA.
MGD BUSINESS MOMENTUM IS ACCELERATING WITH POSITIVE RESULTS ACROSS BOTH CORE AND NON-CORE MARKETS.

PROMO MATRIX
TAVERN
DANCE
URBAN
GAY
SPORTS
IT'S TIME TO KICK A KEG.
IT'S TIME FOR A GOOD OLD MACRO-BREW.
IT'S TIME TO KICK YOUR FRIEND'S ASS ...AGAIN.
IT'S TIME MILWAUKEE VISITS YOU.
IT'S TIME FOR BEER AND A HAIRCUT.
IT'S TIME TO GET PAINTED.
IT'S TIME TO HAVE ONE WITH THE NEIGHBORS.
IT'S TIME FOR A BEER YOU DON'T HAVE TO GET DRESSED UP FOR.
IT'S TIME FOR MAN'S BEST FRIEND ...AND DOGS.
IT'S TIME TO GROOVE.
ES HORA PARA LA MAS FRIA.
THESE PROMOTIONS ARE TOTALLY FLEXIBLE. TOTALLY CUSTOMIZABLE. TOTALLY YOUR CALL. JUST CONSIDER THEM A RESOURCE FOR YOUR OWN MGD IMAGINATION...
WHAT'S MORE, EVERYTHING YOU NEED – FROM P.O.S. TO MERCH & WEARABLES, FROM RECIPES TO SELL SHEETS & TRIVIA – CAN BE FOUND IN THIS MGD ON-PREMISE PROMOTIONS SALES TOOL.
IT'S TIME TO SELL
MORE BEER.
TIME TO SELL
SOME
BEER.
IT'S MILLER TIME.
THE GIG
TAVERN
DANCE
URBAN
GAY
SPORTS
STUFF

**Premium Goods**

MILLER CL: Miller Brewing Company CD, CW: Lori O' Projects AD, D: Kevin Wade D: Martha Graettinger
CW, DF : Planet Design Company USA 1997 *SIZE: 295×257*

**Telephone Cards**

TELEKOM SLOVENIJA CL: Telekom Slovenija CD: Jadranka Jezeršek AD, D: Sajo Vrukalo CW: Barbara Simoniti DF: Agencija Imelda 8000 Slovenia 1997 *SIZE: 310×219*

GoCARDs are postcards which are distributed free in over 1,500 of America's most popular restaurants, bars, cafés, health clubs and record stores. They are taken and enjoyed by one of the most sought after consumer groups: Generation X-ers and thirty-somethings with high discretionary income.
They inform people about museum exhibitions, theater performances, concerts and events. They provide an intelligent and upscale environment in which brand advertisers can extend a campaign to its creative limits and reliably measure the results of their advertising.
GO CARD
POSTCARD ADVERTISING
1997/1998
Fame
One interesting aspect of Postcard Advertising is the exactness with which the popularity of particular ads may be measured. At the end of each ad period a tally is made of the quantity of each card remaining. The fastest moving cards qualify for admission into the GoCARD Hall of Fame. Here are the 1996 inductees:
Top 5 Individual GoCARDs
Top GoCARD Campaign of 1996

## Postcard Advertising

GO CARD CL: Go Card CD, AD, D: John Ball D: Eric Freedman CW: Alan Woolan / John Kuraoka DF: Mires Design Inc. USA 1997 *SIZE: 220×146*

## Premium Goods

GODZILLA CL: Portal Publications CD, AD, D: Jaime Aguinaldo / Steven Isakson DF: Image Nation Design Group USA 1998 *SIZE: 280×215*

# index

# index of submittors

# index of clients

*

Art Director
···**Yutaka Ichimura**···

Designer
···**Yuka Tamaki**···

Editor
···**Maya Kishida**···

Photographer
···**Kuniharu Fujimoto**···

Translator
···**Douglas Allsopp**···

Typesetter
···**Kenichi Hayakawa**···

Publisher
···**Shingo Miyoshi**···

*

# Effective Sales Catalog Design

An International Catalog and Brochure Collection

First edition
published in 1999
by P·I·E Books

Publisher **P·I·E BOOKS**

#301, 4-14-6, komagome, Toshima-ku,
Tokyo, 170-0003 JAPAN

Editorial Tel: 03-3949-5010 Fax: 03-3949-5650
Sales Tel: 03-3940-8302 Fax: 03-3576-7361
e-mail: piebooks@bekkoame.ne.jp



ISBN4-89444-098-9

Printed in Hong Kong

### POSTER GRAPHICS Vol.2

Pages: 256 (192 in Color)

700 posters from the top creators in Japan and abroad are showcased in this book - classified by business. This invaluable reference makes it easy to compare design trends among various industries and corporations.

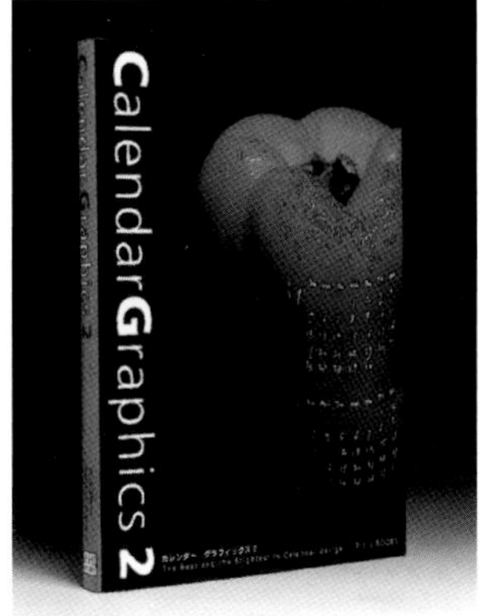

### CALENDAR GRAPHICS Vol.2

Pages: 224 (192 in Color)

The second volume of our popular "Calendar Graphics" series features designs from hundreds of 1994 and 1995 calendars from around the world. A rare collection including those on the market as well as exclusive corporate PR calendars.

### BROCHURE & PAMPHLET COLLECTION Vol.4

Pages: 224 (Full Color)

The fourth volume in our popular "Brochure & Pamphlet" series. Twelve types of businesses are represented through artworks that really sells. This book conveys a sense of what's happening right now in the catalog design scene. A must for all creators.

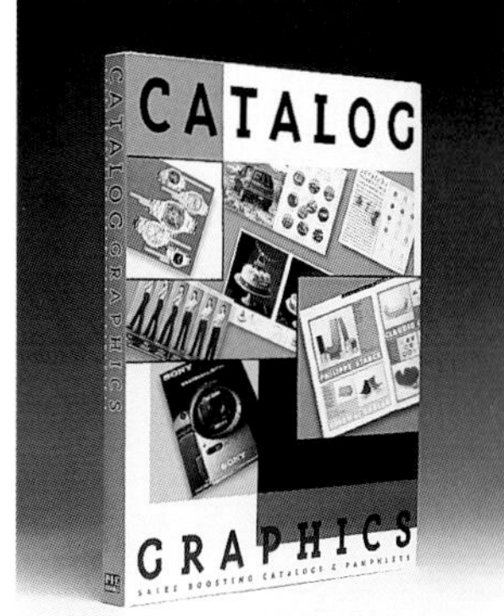

### CATALOG GRAPHICS

Pages: 224 (Full Color)

Here you will find hundreds of practical catalogs and pamphlets, all designed to SELL. Including product descriptions and pictures, prices and options, even order forms, this is an essential collection for anyone seeking ways to stimulate the consumers' desire to buy.

### COMPANY BROCHURE COLLECTION Vol.3

Pages: 224 (Full Color)

Company guides and employment manuals from manufacturers, service industries, retailers and distributors; admissions handbooks from universities and professional schools; facilities guides from hotels and sports clubs... Features seldom-seen informational catalogs, categorized by industry.

### CORPORATE PROFILE GRAPHICS Vol.3

Pages: 224 (Full Color)

The latest catalogs from companies, schools, and facilities around the world. Covers as well as selected inside pages of 200 high-quality catalogs are included, allowing full enjoyment of concepts and layout. Arranged by industry.

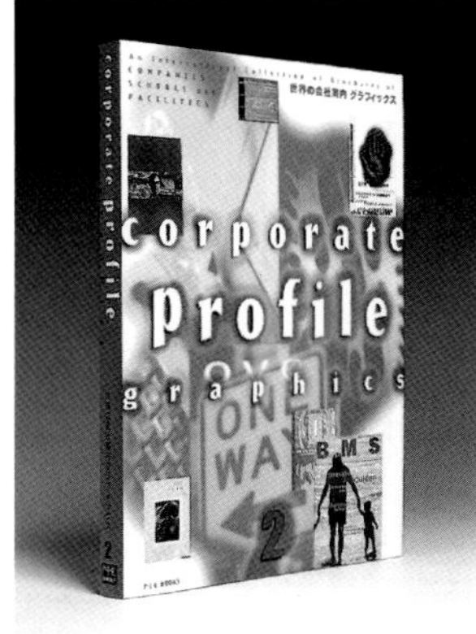

### CORPORATE PROFILE GRAPHICS Vol.2

Pages: 224 (Full Color)

The latest volume in our popular "Brochure and Pamphlet Collection" series, featuring 200 carefully selected catalogs from companies around the world. A wide variety, including school brochures, company profiles, and facility guides, is presented.

### NEW TYPOGRAPHICS Vol.2

Pages: 224 (Full Color)

The latest in international typographic design! Simple, modern design; stimulating visuals; experimental typography; creative yet readable styles... We bring you 400 exhilarating new works from countries that include Germany, Switzerland, the Netherlands, England, America, and Japan.

### EVENT FLYER GRAPHICS

Pages: 224 (Full Color)

Here's a special selection zooming in on flyers promoting events. This upbeat selection covers wide-ranging music events, as well as movies, exhibitions and the performing arts.

### ADVERTISING FLYER GRAPHICS

Pages: 224 (Full Color)

The eye-catching flyers selected for this new collection represent a broad spectrum of businesses, and are presented in a loose classification covering four essential areas of modern life styles: fashion, dining, home and leisure.

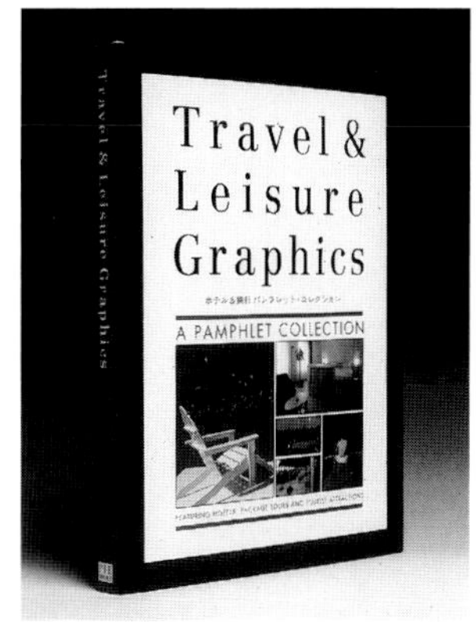

### TRAVEL & LEISURE GRAPHICS

Pages: 224 (Full Color)

A giant collection of some 400 pamphlets, posters and direct mailings exclusively created for hotels, inns, resort tours and amusement facilities.

### NEW LOGO AND TRADEMARK DESIGN

Pages: 272 (Full Color)

The definitive collection of the latest logomarks from all over the world. With designs ranging from the orthodox to those of audacious young designers, this essential book presents CIs from all types of business, product and event logos, and more. Conveniently arranged by industry.

### ONE & TWO COLOR GRAPHICS

Pages: 224 (Full Color)

A giant collection of effective 1 and 2 color designs! Using a minimum number of colors, these designs use eye-catching color combinations, or purposefully subdued colors, to make an impression. These pieces from all corners of the world provide the viewer with strong images and ideas.

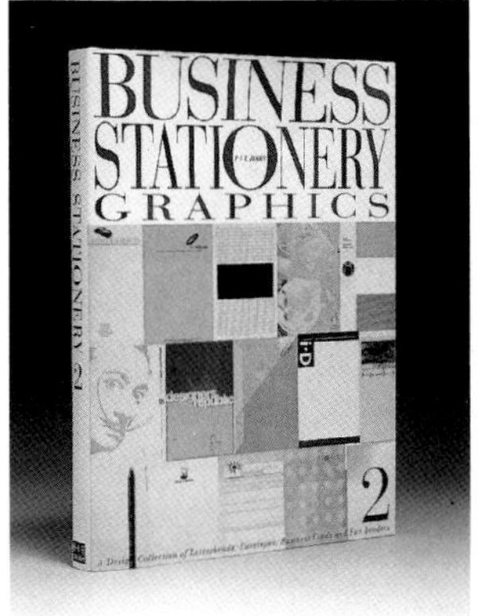

### BUSINESS STATIONERY GRAPHICS Vol.2

Pages: 224 (176 in Color)

The second volume in our popular "Business Stationery Graphics" series. This time the focus is on letterheads, envelopes and business cards, all classified by business. This collection will serve artists and business people well.

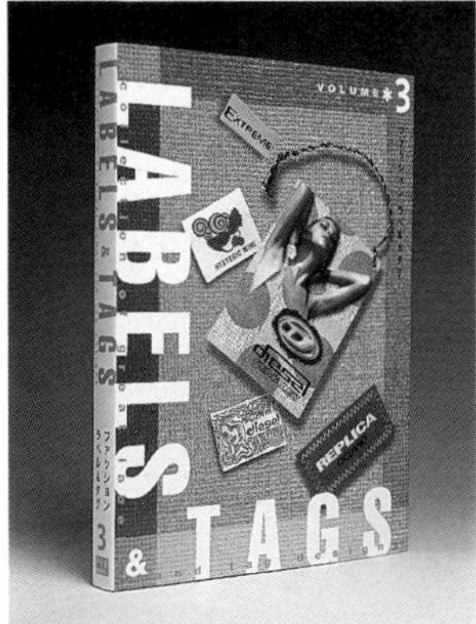

### LABELS & TAGS Vol.3

Pages: 216 (Full Color)

From ladies', men's, and unisex fashions, to kids' clothing, jeans, and sports brands, here are more than 1,000 unique labels and tags, classified by item. Expanding the possibilities of fashion graphics, this is the must-have book that designers have been waiting for!

### PRIVATE GREETING CARDS

Pages: 224 (Full Color)

A big, new collection of greetings, announcements, and invitations! Christmas, New Year's, and other seasonal cards; birth and moving announcements; invitations to weddings and exhibitions... 450 cards by designers around the world, even more fun just because they're private!

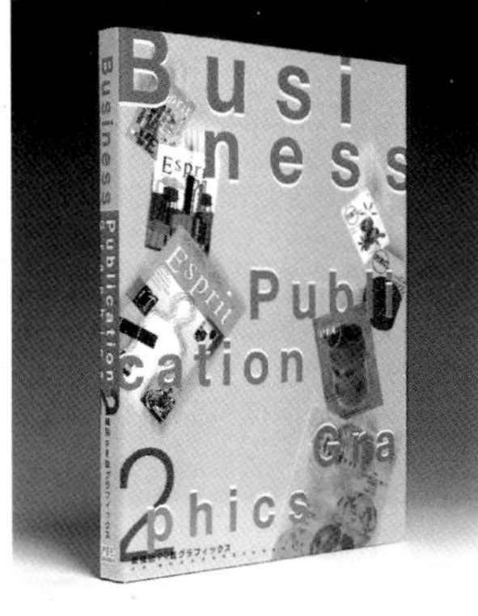

### BUSINESS PUBLICATION GRAPHICS Vol.2

Pages: 224 (Full Color)

One volume offering more than 150 samples of regularly published PR and other informative magazines, covering different business sectors from fashion labels to non-profit organizations. This overviews the current trends in PR magazine design purposing to attract the attention of a specific readership in commercial activities.

### POSTCARD GRAPHICS Vol.4

Pages: 224 (192 in Color)

Our popular "Postcard Graphics" series has been revamped for "Postcard Graphics Vol.4". This first volume of the new version showcases approximately 1000 pieces ranging from direct mailers to private greeting cards, selected from the best from around the world.

### SEASONAL CAMPAIGN GRAPHICS

Pages: 224 (Full Color)

A spirited collection of quality graphics for sales campaigns planned around the four seasons and Christmas, St. Valentine's Day and the Japanese gift-giving seasons, as well as for store openings, anniversaries, and similar events.

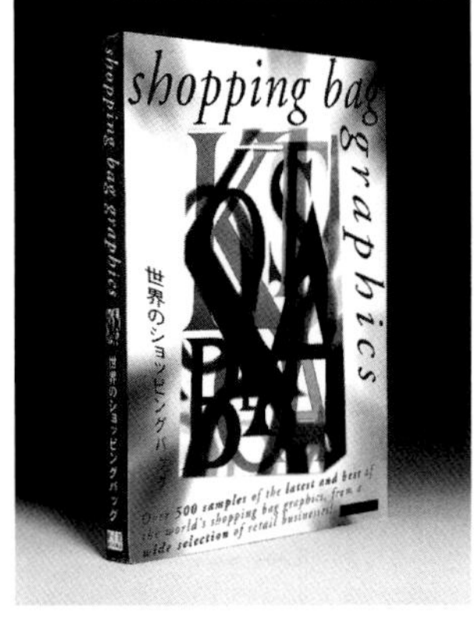

### SHOPPING BAG GRAPHICS

Pages: 224 (Full Color)

Over 500 samples of the latest and best of the world's shopping bag graphics, from a wide selection of retail businesses! This volume features a selection of the best in shopping bag graphics originating in Tokyo, New York, Los Angeles, London, Paris, Milan and other major cities worldwide, presented here in a useful business classification.

### MAGAZINE ADVERTISING GRAPHICS

Pages: 224 (Full Color)

Conceptual, distinctively original magazine ads, selected from 19 countries for their novel, high-impact visuals and attention-grabbing copy (Japanese and English translations provided where copy is essential to the ad's effectiveness). All are model examples of successful promotion production.

### PRESENTATION GRAPHICS

Pages: 192 (Full Color)

31 creators from 8 countries illustrate the complete presentation process, from the first idea sketches and color comps, to presentations and the final result. We show you aspects of the design world that you've never seen before in this unique, invaluable book.

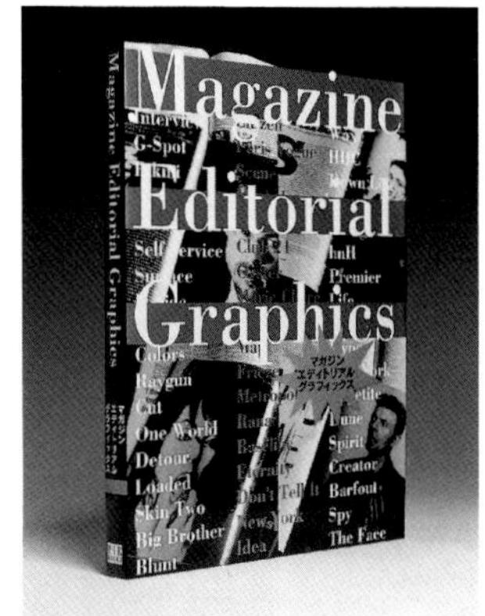

### MAGAZINE EDITORIAL GRAPHICS

Pages: 224 (Full Color)

The stylish world of editorial and cover design in a new collection! English avant-garde, French new wave, American energy... 79 hot publications from 9 countries have been selected, all featuring the graphic works of top designers. A veritable New Age design bible.

### PROMOTIONAL GREETING CARDS

Pages: 224 (Full Color)

A total of 500 examples of cards from designers around the world. A whole spectrum of stylish and inspirational cards, ranging from corporate invitations to private wedding announcements, classified by function for easy reference.

**DIRECT MAIL GRAPHICS Vol.1**

Pages: 224 (176 in Color)

The long-awaited design collection featuring direct mailers with outstanding sales impact and quality design. 350 of the best pieces, classified into 100 business categories. A veritable textbook of current direct marketing design.

**The Paris Collections / INVITATION CARDS**

Pages: 176 (Full Color)

This book features 400 announcements for and invitations to the Paris Collections, produced by the world's top fashion brands over the past 10 years. A treasure trove of ideas and pure fun to browse through.

**FASHION & COSMETICS GRAPHICS**

Pages: 208 (192 in Color)

We have published a collection of graphics from around the world produced for apparel, accessory and cosmetic brands at the vanguard of the fashion industry. A total of about 800 labels, tags, direct mailers, etc., from some 40 brands featured in this book point the way toward future trends in advertising.

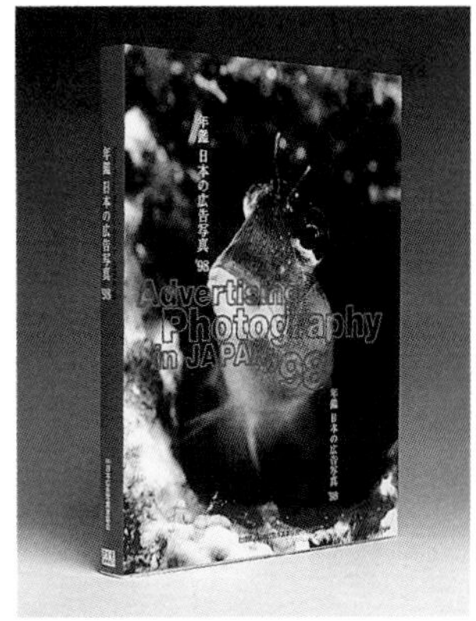

**ADVERTISING PHOTOGRAPHY IN JAPAN '98**

Pages: 224 (Full Color)

Japan's only advertising photography annual! 425 photos selected from talked-about ads of the last four years, these high quality photos stand on their own outside the framework of advertising. The 7th in a series, it was compiled under the supervision of the Japan Advertising Photographers' Association.

**CATALOGS and INFORMATION ON NEW PUBLICATIONS**

If you would like to receive a free copy of our general catalog or details of our new publications, please fill out the enclosed postcard and return it to us by mail or fax.

**CATALOGE und INFORMATIONEN ÜBER NEUE TITLE**

Wenn Sie unseren Gesamtkatalog oder Detailinformationen über unsere neuen Titel wünschen.fullen Sie bitte die beigefügte Postkarte aus und schicken Sie sie uns per Post oder Fax.

**CATALOGUES ET INFORMATIONS SUR LES NOUVELLES PUBLICATIONS**

Si vous désirez recevoir un exemplaire qratuit de notre catalogue généralou des détails sur nos nouvelles publication. veuillez compléter la carte réponse incluse et nous la retourner par courrierou par fax.

**P·I·E BOOKS**

#301, 4-14-6,komagome, Toshima-ku, Tokyo 170-0003 JAPAN
TEL : 03-3940-8302 FAX : 03-3576-7361